Balanced Reading Strategies and Practices

Assessing and Assisting Readers with Special Needs

D. Ray Reutzel
Brigham Young University

Robert B. Cooter, Jr.
Dallas Public Schools

Merrill,
an imprint of Prentice Hall
Upper Saddle River, New Jersey   Columbus, Ohio

Library of Congress Cataloging-in-Publication Data

Reutzel, D. Ray (Douglas Ray), 1953–
    Balanced reading strategies and practices : assessing and assisting readers with special
needs / D. Ray Reutzel, Robert B. Cooter, Jr.
        p.   cm.
    Includes bibliographical references and index.
    ISBN 0-02-324715-0
    1. Reading.   2. Reading—Remedial teaching.   3. Child development.
I. Cooter, Robert B.   II. Title.
LB1050.R477   1999
372.43—dc21   98-8778
                                                                                  CIP

Cover Art: © Melissa Taylor
Editor: Bradley J. Potthoff
Production Editor: Mary M. Irvin
Design Coordinator: Diane C. Lorenzo
Cover Designer: Diane C. Lorenzo
Production Coordination and Text Design: Elm Street Publishing Services, Inc.
Production Manager: Pamela D. Bennett
Director of Marketing: Kevin Flanagan
Marketing Manager: Suzanne Stanton
Advertising/Marketing Coordinator: Krista Groshong

This book was set in Souvenir by The Clarinda Company and was printed and bound by
R. R. Donnelley & Sons Company. The cover was printed by Phoenix Color Corp.
© 1999 by Prentice Hall, Inc.
Upper Saddle River, NJ 07458

Printed in the United States of America

10 9 8 7 6 5 4

ISBN 0-02-324715-0

Prentice-Hall International (UK) Limited, *London*
Prentice-Hall of Australia Pty. Limited, *Sydney*
Prentice-Hall of Canada, Inc., *Toronto*
Prentice-Hall Hispanoamericana, S. A., *Mexico*
Prentice-Hall of India Private Limited, *New Delhi*
Prentice-Hall of Japan, Inc., *Tokyo*
Pearson Education Asia Pte. Ltd., *Singapore*
Editora Prentice-Hall do Brasil, Ltda., *Rio de Janeiro*

For my wife, children, and the many wonderful students who have helped me learn and grow.
—DRR

For Kathy . . . Sweetheart, this one's for you.
—RBC

About the Authors

D. Ray Reutzel

D. Ray Reutzel is Karl G. Maeser Research Professor and Associate Dean of the School of Education at Brigham Young University. He earned his doctorate in Curriculum and Instruction with an emphasis in reading and language arts from the University of Wyoming, Laramie, in 1982. He teaches courses in research design, reading, and language arts for preservice and in-service teachers at BYU. He has taught in kindergarten and grades 1, 3, 5, and 6 as an elementary school teacher.

Dr. Reutzel took a leave from his university faculty position to return to full-time, first-grade classroom teaching in Sage Creek Elementary School in 1987–1988. While in the elementary classroom, he established a model first-grade balanced literacy classroom that has been visited by observers from throughout the country. In 1987, Dr. Reutzel received BYU's College of Education Excellence in Research Award. In the same year, his work was recognized by the American Educational Research Association (AERA) as one of the Distinguished Research Papers at the 1988 Annual Meeting.

Dr. Reutzel is the author of more than 100 articles, books, book chapters, and monographs. He has published in *Reading Research Quarterly, Journal of Reading Behavior, Journal of Literacy Research, Journal of Educational Research, Reading Psychology, Reading Research and Instruction, Language Arts,* and *The Reading Teacher,* among others. He has served as an editorial review board member or guest reviewer for *The Elementary School Journal, The Reading Teacher, Reading Research Quarterly, The Journal of Reading Behavior, The NRC Yearbook, American Reading Forum Yearbook, Reading Psychology,* and *Reading Research and Instruction.* Dr. Reutzel is an author of the *Literacy Place* program published by Scholastic, Inc. of New York.

Dr. Reutzel lives in Springville, Utah, with his wife, Pam, and his five children and grandchild. His hobbies include reading, skiing, fishing, singing, playing the piano, and trying to keep up with his wife and children.

Robert B. Cooter, Jr.

Dr. Robert B. Cooter, Jr., is currently Assistant Superintendent for Reading for Dallas Public Schools. He was appointed to serve as Dallas' first "Reading Czar" and direct the innovative *Dallas Reading Plan* as well as a large cadre of "Lead Reading Teachers."

Dr. Cooter has worked with teachers and school districts around the nation seeking to construct what he terms "balanced literacy programs." He has taught grades 1, 3, 4, 7, 11, and 12 in the public schools, and also served as a Title I reading teacher. His best-selling textbook, *Teaching Children to Read: From Basals to Books* (Merrill/Prentice Hall, 1996), which was co-authored by D. Ray Reutzel, is used at more than 200 universities and colleges to train elementary teachers. Robert Cooter has authored or co-authored several other books, including *The Flynt-Cooter Reading Inventory for the Classroom, Teaching Reading in the Content Areas,* and *The Flynt/Cooter English–Español Reading Inventory for the Classroom,* all published by Merrill/Prentice Hall.

Dr. Cooter was formerly dean of the College of Education and professor of Reading and Literacy Education at Austin Peay State University, where he taught courses for preservice and practicing teachers. Robert Cooter previously served as chair of the Department of Curriculum and Instruction at Texas Christian University and, prior to that time, directed the Reading Center at Bowling Green State University in Ohio. He has earned degrees in Reading/Literacy Education at George Peabody College for Teachers at Vanderbilt University and The University of Tennessee.

Dr. Cooter has published approximately 50 articles on balanced literacy programs and related topics in such journals as *The Reading Teacher, Journal of Reading, Reading Psychology, Reading Research and Instruction, Journal of Educational Research,* and *Language Arts.* He previously served as editor of the professional journal for the College Reading Association—*Reading Research and Instruction.*

A native of Nashville, Tennessee, Bob Cooter enjoys performing Southern folktales for children of all ages, fly fishing, sailing, listening to good blues, donning leather and riding his Harley-Davidson ("Hawg"), and dining on catfish and cheese grits. He lives in downtown Dallas with his wife and best friend, Dr. Kathleen Spencer Cooter, a Texas Christian University professor and lab school principal. Bob is the proud father of five children and three stepchildren, has four beautiful grandchildren, and is owned by a hound dog of unknown breed or utility.

Preface

After several years of significant change in reading instruction, the field seems to be settling somewhere between the extremes—phonics versus whole language. Today many teachers and reading scholars regard balanced reading instruction as the only viable approach to take in reading instruction, given the current philosophy and classroom practice (Baumann, Hoffman, Moon, & Duffy-Hester, 1998). As we have worked in classrooms and clinics, it has become increasingly apparent that both students and the profession as a whole will benefit from a *balanced* reading position.

Balanced Reading Strategies and Practices offers preservice teacher candidates a practical resource for understanding issues related to reading instruction and assessment. In addition, it provides ready-to-use assessment tools and related instructional strategies for reading practica in school classrooms and clinics. As the philosophy of inclusion becomes accepted in increasing numbers of schools, there is a recognized need to help students with special learning needs. The broader fundamental concept of this book, however, is that all learners are special and have special needs.

For the practicing educator, this book provides research-validated strategies and assessment tools to inform instruction, meet the needs of individual learners, and develop an understanding of the issues related to effective reading instruction. For those practitioners in special education "resource" rooms, Title I reading programs, and university reading clinics, this volume provides a balanced or comprehensive approach to helping students with special needs, rather than representing a singular point of view. Previously published books used in corrective reading settings have generally taken a behaviorist view of the child, his learning, and the solutions to his learning challenges. We assert in this text that a balanced view incorporates and combines various approaches, understandings, assessment tools, and instructional strategies from behaviorist, cognitive, and constructivist views of learning and teaching reading. In other words, this text offers a comprehensive approach rather than a singular view or philosophy.

Our intent was to create a book that serves as a ready reference for classroom teachers as their students advance along the path to becoming fluent readers and writers. This text is not, by the way, intended as a college course textbook for diagnosis and correction, nor is it to be read from beginning to end, page by page. Rather, it is to be used as a *reference tool* for specific questions and specific solutions related to the instructional challenges faced by special needs learners and their teachers. Each chapter includes a teacher's background knowledge briefing, assessment ideas and tools, and highly effective research-proven instructional strategies. This book is also ideal for use in reading practica courses—both developmental and corrective. We trust it will provide teachers with the tools and strategies they need to develop individual educational plans to help all students become literate.

ACKNOWLEDGMENTS

Our thanks to the reviewers of our manuscript for their insightful comments: Carole L. Bond, University of Memphis; James D. Bowman, East Tennessee State University; Gerald J. Calais, McNeese State University; Eugene H. Cramer, University of Illinois at Chicago; Lane Roy Gauthier, University of Houston; Maribeth Henney, Iowa State University; Michael W. Kibby, SUNY at Buffalo; Cynthia R. Lumpkin, Troy State University—Dothan; Grace G. Nunn, Eastern Illinois University; Janet Richards, University of Southern Mississippi; Leonie M. Rose, Central Michigan University; Robert T. Rude, Rhode Island College; and Sam L. Sebesta, University of Washington.

Through your comments and observations, please let us know whether we have achieved our aim. Best wishes as you work to help every child become a successful reader and a personally fulfilled individual.

D. Ray Reutzel
Robert B. Cooter, Jr.

Contents

Chapter 5

Chapter 6

Chapter 7

Chapter 8

Chapter 9

Chapter 10

Chapter 11

Chapter 12

Chapter 13

Chapter 14

Chapter 15

Chapter 16

Assessing and Assisting Special Needs Readers: English as a Second Language   371

Chapter 1

Balanced Reading Programs:
A Context for Assessment and Instruction

A teacher sits across a table from one of his students in mid-October. Like students in schools everywhere, this child is struggling in reading development and looks to the teacher for encouragement and help. The basic reading program adopted by the school system, while effective with many of the other students, is simply not working very well for this child. The teacher considers the classroom evidence he has assembled from teaching-learning activities thus far in the year and begins to see a pattern. Yes, this child does have some rather consistent problems with her reading comprehension. The question is, how can the teacher determine the cause or causes? One thing the teacher notes is that the student has some noticeable language differences, and also has trouble with word identification from time to time. Could it be that these factors are the reason for the child's comprehension problems, or are the problems due to something else altogether? How can this teacher accurately and quickly assess the problems facing students in his classroom—those who seem to be having minor or even major difficulties in their reading development?

The scenario above is certainly familiar to anyone who has taught reading to another for more than a few minutes. *Balanced Reading Strategies and Practices: Assessing and Assisting Readers with Special Needs* has been developed as a classroom tool for teachers who are in need of practical teaching and assessment ideas. It is also for teachers seeking to teach in a balanced way, creating a harmonious and productive classroom. It occurs to us that it may be as useful to know what this book is *not* as what it *is*. For instance, this book is not really intended to serve as a basic introductory text on reading instruction and assessment. Rather, it is a supplemental book for new or experienced teachers who need an exhaustive collection of classroom-proven strategies, especially for those times when a student exhibits specific reading problems. [Note: For those who are just beginning the study of reading/literacy education and require a more complete orientation to the field, we suggest our companion text *Teaching Children to Read: From Basals to Books,* 2nd edition (Reutzel & Cooter, 1996) as a starting point, or one of the other major textbooks used in reading methods courses.] In this book one can quickly turn to a chapter that presents current thinking on ways to assess and teach specific reading skills and processes, such as *reading vocabulary, alphabetic principle, phonemic awareness, reading fluency,* and so on. It can also serve as a valuable supplemental text for reading methodology courses at the undergraduate or graduate level.

In this first chapter we discuss the practical orientation of *Balanced Reading Strategies and Practices: Assessing and Assisting Readers with Special Needs* and what we mean by "balanced reading programs." We also describe the stages of learning that students pass through on their way to becoming independent readers. Finally, we compare traditional reading methods with balanced reading programs through specific lesson plans. As you read this first chapter, you will become acquainted with the essential elements of balanced reading programs in order to help you plan successful reading lessons for all learners.

Balanced Reading Programs: New Ways of Viewing Assessment and Instruction

In recent years there has been much controversy among reading educators—some favoring more traditional reading programs (i.e., basal textbooks used to teach reading) and others advocating "whole language" teaching. We define traditional approaches to reading instruction as those relying heavily on teacher-directed skill instruction, usually in conjunction with basal reader textbooks. Traditional approaches to reading instruction use what is sometimes called a "parts to whole" perspective, or "skills-first, real reading later." For example, in traditional kindergarten and first-grade reading programs, students often receive a great deal of instruction on alphabet letters/sounds and phonic analysis through activities that are very much isolated from the reading of popular stories (i.e., using skill pages and workbook activities only). This sometimes creates the impression for students that reading *instruction* is something far removed from reading interesting books. One time, while working in one of our classrooms with a third grader having reading problems, the student was asked, "Would you like to read for awhile?" The child seemed almost astonished and said emphatically, "No, not really!" But when the next statement from his teacher's lips was "Oh, okay, . . . I just thought you might enjoy sharing this book with me about a dog who starts talking after eating some alphabet soup," the child brightened up immediately and said, "Oh! Sure, I want to do *that!*" The clear message from this exchange was that the child loved great books, but that he did not think of reading instruction and the enjoyment of books as activities that are in any way related!

Another way of viewing the teaching of reading is through *whole language* teaching. Whole language is not actually an approach or practice, but rather a perspective or philosophical stance (Altwerger, Edelsky, & Flores, 1987). Whole language teachers attempt to integrate the four language modes of listening, speaking, reading, and writing across all curriculum areas. Reading in authentic literature (such as children's or adolescent books) and writing/authoring experiences (e.g., letters, poems, songs, stories, etc.) are two of the hallmarks of whole language teaching. Whole language advocates (as well as many others not calling themselves whole language teachers) feel that students should be *immersed* daily in high-quality and "natural" reading and writing experiences. While this perspective is quite attractive, the way it has been implemented in recent years is problematic, indeed.

For some reason, many so-called whole language proponents during the past decade or so in the United States deviated markedly from the original *balanced reading programs* of such New Zealand teachers as Silvia Ashton-Warner, Don Holdaway, Margaret Mooney, and Marie Clay. Balanced reading programs, as practiced in many New Zealand and Australian classrooms, are the roots from which American whole language perspectives have sprung. A particularly alarming aspect of American whole language publications has been the omission of guided, teacher-led instruction within the context of appropriately leveled books or texts matched to students' development and interests. Further, the word *skill* seems to have become almost a four-letter word in the metaphorical sense for these writers. It seemed that all one would need to do to teach reading is to simply surround students with quality books (perhaps a kind of learning osmosis?!).

Unfortunately for many students, this sort of incomplete teaching contributed to the virtual collapse of quality reading instruction in California and other states during the late 1980s and 1990s. As a result of an unprecedented falling of reading test scores in California, a state-level reading task force comprised of talented reading teachers and others concluded that what was needed was a more "balanced" approach to the teaching of reading. In their report titled *Every Child a Reader* (1995), the California Reading Task Force concluded the following:

> *Recommendation 1:*
> Every school and district must organize and implement a comprehensive and *balanced reading program* that is research-based and combines skills development with literature and language-rich activities. (p. iii)

The California Reading Task Force report also spoke to the assessment and intervention aspects of balanced reading programs:

> *Recommendation 2:*
> Schools and districts must provide every teacher with a repertoire of diagnostic tools to continuously monitor and modify instruction, to ensure every child's optimal development, and to identify students who need help in reading.

> *Recommendation 3:*
> Schools must have an effective, rigorous, and proven intervention program as part of their comprehensive literacy plan for instruction with an emphasis on early intervention . . . . (p. iii)

In the next section we describe balanced reading programs in more detail.

WHAT ARE BALANCED READING PROGRAMS?

Balanced reading programs teach students developmentally relevant literacy skills within the context of appropriately leveled reading materials of interest to the learner. Just which skills will be taught depends upon where students are in their reading development. Balanced reading programs, as described in *Reading in Junior Classes* (a handbook for new teachers in New Zealand, 1985), have several hallmarks:

- *Balanced reading programs rely heavily on a teacher's understanding of what we sometimes refer to as the "milestones of reading development."* The teachers' ability to conduct careful assessment of what students are able to do in reading and writing based on the milestones of reading development, and their ability to plan appropriate instruction based on their ongoing assessment program, is directly related to success of balanced reading programs.

- *Balanced reading programs use a model for teaching known as* Reading To, With, and By. This is a flexible model for instruction described by Mooney (1990) that can be interpreted by teachers in many different ways according to their own style and preferences. However, the key practices that should occur daily are the following:

  Reading *to* Children. Every student should be read to each day. It might take the form of teacher read alouds, one-to-one reading by a peer or adult, or what is sometimes called "lap reading" (most often with a family member).

  Reading *with* Children. The teacher should read with each student daily. This commonly occurs in small reading groups during a guided reading session, in a language experience activity (LEA), or during shared reading experiences.

  Reading *by* Children. There should be independent reading opportunities for children daily. It may simply be a time set aside during the day for twenty minutes or so of pleasure reading (i.e., Drop Everything and Read, or "DEAR" time; Sustained Silent Reading, or "SSR" time), or it could be in the form of performance reading, as with a Readers' Theater. Sometimes students will read to each other in a buddy or assisted reading period, as when second graders read to fifth-grade partners once a week.

  Teachers making transitions from teaching exclusively with basal readers to using quality literature for instruction will often use Reading To, With, and By with their basals as a starting point. (Note: As we continue in this chapter and compare traditional instruction with balanced reading programs, keep this idea of Reading To, With, and By in mind for your own evaluation purposes.)

- *The "balance" in balanced reading instruction has to do with creating an appropriate kind of harmony in the learning environment.* While some may speak of the "balance" in balanced reading programs as a kind of teeter-totter relationship or "equity" between the rote teaching of skills and the reading of quality literature, we see it quite differently. Indeed, it is not a kind of politically correct equity that we seek at all. Learning to read the English language should essentially be a naturally developing act somewhat akin to what goes on in our Earth's ecosystem. Imagine, if you will, an Earth where there was suddenly absolute equity among all things—spores, insects, bacteria, humans, trees, animals, and atmospheric elements such as oxygen and carbon dioxide. What would happen? For starters, all humans would probably die quickly from the ensuing atmospheric changes and a lack of food. In short, it would not work!

What is needed in balanced reading instruction, at least from our perspective, is a more harmonious balance akin to what is found in our present ecosystem. Consider another metaphor to see what we mean. What do you see when white light passes through a prism? (Answer: the full spectrum of colors) What we see in white light is actually the perfect melding of all colors of the rainbow, and not necessarily in the same amounts. In balanced reading instruction you will find skill instruction in decoding, comprehension, language/vocabulary, and reading/study strategies; quality and appropriately leveled reading materials according to where the student is in his reading development; and sundry methods of teaching and learning, from teacher-led instruction to cooperative groups. All of this is taught using the myriad methods and materials teachers like to employ that make Reading To, With, and By possible. In sum, balanced reading programs are a kind of seamless symmetry and equilibrium—not equity.

Like our ecosystem and the changing seasons, balanced reading programs can be quite different from child to child, and from teacher to teacher. Needs of the students dictate the kinds of learning activities selected by the teacher. For example, some students may require a great deal of phonics instruction in the early years, whereas other students can require virtually no phonics instruction. Similarly, some teachers enjoy great success using a Reading Workshop format (see Reutzel & Cooter, 1996) with some learners, while other teachers find greater success using the more teacher-directed Reconciled Reading Lesson format (Reutzel, 1985). Different needs, different students, and different teaching styles make it necessary for varied organizational approaches to be used in teaching reading.

• *The teaching of skills in balanced reading programs proceeds from* whole to parts to whole. Any reading skill or strategy to be learned should be taught within the context of an interesting story or text. Skill instruction begins with the sharing or reading of *whole* text, then focuses next on the learning and application of the new reading skill/strategy (the *part* of reading to be learned). In the final stages of the learning experience, the reading skill/strategy should be taken back into *whole* text reading, and applied still later in other whole text contexts (Department of Education, 1985). This process helps students understand the usefulness of what they have learned. Later in the chapter we take a much closer look at this important principle.

Because balanced reading instruction begins with a knowledge of learning milestones, we proceed next to a more complete description of what that means in the classroom. Later, we compare traditional methods for teaching reading with balanced reading programs.

THE MILESTONES OF READING DEVELOPMENT: KNOWING WHICH SKILLS TO TEACH AND WHEN

In some areas of study, particularly mathematics, it is possible to say with some assurance which skills must be taught before others can be learned. For example, in order to perform division functions, one must know multiplication and subtraction skills. In reading, like mathematics, there are some skills that must be learned before others can be acquired (e.g., alphabetical order before dictionary skills, etc.). However, some reading/literacy skills may be learned within a wide span of time in the student's literacy development. Thus, knowing which reading skills are prerequisite and sequential, and which are more flexible in terms of instructional timing, can be very important indeed. In this section, we briefly summarize research pertaining to the *general* stages of reading development to assist you in accurately assessing students in the classroom. In later chapters, we describe more precisely the development of reading skills in specific areas (such as phonics, comprehension, phonemic awareness, fluency, and so on).

Some years ago, two teachers had a discussion about what is meant by a "beginning reader." They began to gather classroom data to create a reading development continuum (Cochrane, Cochrane, Scalena, & Buchanan, 1984). Such a continuum would, of course, be extremely helpful to them and their fellow teachers in more accurately assessing student reading development and planning future instruction. [Note: For more research on reading development that is quite compatible with Cochrane et al. (1984), see also Sulzby (1985).] Cochrane and his colleagues divided the development of reading into two overarching categories: (a) preindependent reading and (b) independent reading. Within each of these super-categories, these teachers described three more subdivisions. Within the preindependent reading category, for example, the three subordinate divisions or stages include: (a) the magical stage, (b) the self-concepting stage, and (c) the bridging stage. Within the independent reading category, the three subordinate divisions or stages are: (a) the take-off stage, (b) the independent reading stage, and (c) the skilled reading stage. Their continuum is shown in Figure 1.1 in checklist form, just as we have adapted it for our own classrooms.

THE MYSTERY OF READING: THE MAGICAL STAGE

Long before children enter school, they begin noticing print in their environment and learn that printed language stands for words they have heard others use, or that they have used themselves. Preschool children spontaneously learn to recognize billboards displaying their favorite TV channel logo. They can recognize a popular soda brand logo or pick out their favorite cereal at the local supermarket. While they may not be able to read the print exactly on each of these objects, when asked to tell someone what the soda can says, they may respond with "soda" or "pop."

Children at this stage of reading development love to have books read to them. In quiet moments, these children may crawl up into a large comfortable chair to hold, look at, and tell a story from the pictures in their favorite books. When he

Figure 1.1   Reading Development Continuum

Observation Checklist for Reading Development

Student: _____   Year: _____

Teacher: _____   School: _____

Directions: Write in the date(s) as the child exhibits the behaviors listed below.

A. PRE-INDEPENDENT READING STAGES

1. *Magical Stage* [Sulzby's (1985) "Story Not Formed" level occurs about here]
   - _____ Displays an interest in handling books
   - _____ Sees the construction of meaning as magical or exterior to the print and imposed by others
   - _____ Listens to print read to him for extended periods of time
   - _____ Will play with letters or words
   - _____ Begins to notice print in environmental context (signs, labels)
   - _____ Letters may appear in his drawings
   - _____ May mishandle books—observe them upside down; may damage them due to misunderstanding the purpose of books
   - _____ Likes to "name" the pictures in a book, e.g., "lion," "rabbit"

2. *Self-Concepting Stage* [Sulzby's (1985) "Story Formed" level begins here]
   - _____ Self-concepts himself as a reader, i.e., engages in readinglike activities
   - _____ Tries to magically impose meaning on new print
   - _____ "Reads" or reconstructs content of familiar storybooks
   - _____ Recognizes his name and some other words in high environmental contexts (signs, labels)
   - _____ His writing may display phonetic influence, i.e., wtbo = Wally, hr = her
   - _____ Can construct story meaning from pictorial clues
   - _____ Cannot pick words out of print consistently
   - _____ Orally fills in many correct responses in oral cloze reading
   - _____ Rhymes words
   - _____ Has increasing control over nonvisual cueing systems
   - _____ Gives words orally that begin similarly
   - _____ Displays increasing degree of book handling knowledge
   - _____ Is able to recall key words
   - _____ Begins to internalize story grammar, i.e., knows how stories go together: "Once upon a time," "They lived happily ever after"

3. *Bridging Stage* [Sulzby's (1985) "Story Formed" to "Written Language-Like" level]
   - _____ Can write and read back his own writing
   - _____ Can pick out individual words and letters

continued

_____ Can read familiar books or poems that could not be totally repeated without the print
_____ Uses picture clues to supplement the print
_____ Words read in one context may not be read in another
_____ Has increasing control over visual cueing system
_____ Enjoys chants and poems chorally read
_____ Can match or pick out words of poems or chants that have been internalized

B. INDEPENDENT READING STAGES

1. *Take-off Stage* [Sulzby's (1985) "Print Watched" to "Holistic" level]
_____ Excited about reading
_____ Wants to read to you often
_____ Realizes that print is the base for constructing meaning
_____ Can process (read) words in new (alternate) print situations
_____ Aware of and reads aloud much environmental print (signs, labels, etc.)
_____ Can conserve print from one contextual environment to another
_____ May exhibit temporary tunnel vision (concentrates on words and letters)
_____ Oral reading may be word-centered rather than meaning-centered
_____ Has increasing control over the Reading Process

2. *Independent Reading Stage* [Sulzby's (1985) "Holistic" level]
_____ Characterized by comprehension of the author's message by reader
_____ Reader's construction of meaning relies heavily on author's print or implied cues (schema)
_____ Desires to read books to himself for pleasure
_____ Brings his own experiences (schemata) to the print
_____ Reads orally with meaning and expression
_____ May see print as a literal truth—what the print says is right (legalized)
_____ Uses visual and nonvisual cueing systems simultaneously (cyclically)
_____ Has internalized several different print grammars, i.e., fairy tales, general problem-centered stories, simple exposition

3. *Skilled Reading Stage*
_____ Processes material further and further removed from his own experience
_____ Reading content and vocabulary become a part of his experience
_____ Can use a variety of print forms for pleasure

continued

_____ Can discuss several aspects of a story
_____ Can read at varying and appropriate rates
_____ Can make inferences from print
_____ Challenges the validity of print content
_____ Can focus on or utilize the appropriate grammar or structuring of varying forms of print, e.g., stories, science experiments, menus, diagrams, histories

Note: Adapted from Cochrane, Cochrane, Scalena, and Buchanan. (1984), *Reading, Writing, and Caring.* Richard C. Owen Publishers, Inc., New York, New York; and E. Sulzby's (1985) "Children's emergent reading of favorite storybooks: A developmental study." *Reading Research Quarterly 20(4),* 458–481.

was 2 years old, Jeremy enjoyed the naming of each animal in his favorite picture book. After naming each picture, he would enthusiastically make the sounds of each, such as the roaring of a lion or the crowing of a rooster. Parents and teachers of readers who find themselves journeying through the magical stage of reading development may see children who hold books upside down, turn the pages from the back to the front, and even tear out a page unintentionally. Although this may concern parents on one level, children who behave in these ways evidence a need for exposure to and understanding of the purpose of books. Withholding books from these children because they do not know how to handle them or read them at this stage would most certainly prove to be detrimental.

Children in the magical reading developmental stage develop a marked preference for a single or favorite book. Willing adults are often solicited to read this book again and again. Although parents and others may tire rapidly of this book, the affection and familiarity increases with each reading for the child. Favorite books are often repeatedly read to the point where the child memorizes them. Some parents even try to skip pages or sentences in these books, thinking their child will not notice; they soon learn, however, that their child has internalized these books, and the unsuspecting adult will be caught every time.

The reading of entire contexts such as those found on product logos and in books constitutes evidence to support the fact that young children prefer to process printed language from the whole to the parts. That is, reading the entire context of a sign or label and memorizing an entire book is preferred by young children much before they want or need to focus on the details and parts of printed language.

LOOK, MOM, I'M READING: THE SELF-CONCEPTING READING STAGE

The self-concepting reading developmental stage describes the child who has come to view himself as a reader. Although this child may not yet be able to read exactly what the print says, he is certainly aware of printed language and his own progress toward breaking the literacy barrier. Children in this stage will try to read unfamiliar books by telling the story from the pictures and from their own imaginations. Selected words are readily recognized, such as their own name, favorite food labels, and signs on bathroom doors. These readers will try to reconstruct the text of a favorite story from memory and picture clues. These children evidence an increasing awareness of words and sounds. They often ask questions about how words begin and about rhyming words. If given a chance, these children can also complete a sentence when asked to do so. For example, while reading "The Three Little Pigs," a teacher may say, "And the Big Bad Wolf knocked at the door and said, 'Little Pig, Little Pig . . . .'" Children at this stage will immediately fill in the hanging sentence with "Let me come in."

SPANNING THE GAP: THE BRIDGING STAGE

Children at the bridging stage of reading development can pick out familiar words and letters in familiar contexts and books. They often cannot, however, pick these same words out of an unfamiliar book or context when asked to do so. Children in the bridging stage can reconstruct stories from books with greater precision than can children in the previous stage. In fact, children in the bridging stage can no longer reconstruct the story completely without using the print, although they will continue to use picture clues to augment their growing control over the print system.

Children in the bridging stage can also read back what they have written. It has long been a disappointment for us when teachers and parents fail to count these early behaviors as real reading by brushing them aside as cute. Parents or teachers will often remark, "She's not reading. She's got that book memorized." Only by understanding that reading is a developmental process and that memorizing favorite print and books is universal among children will parents and teachers be able to enjoy, recognize, and support the progress their children make toward conventional reading behaviors and skills.

BLAST OFF! THE TAKE-OFF STAGE

If you are an unoccupied adult, look out for kids in the take-off stage! They are excited about reading and will perform for any reluctantly willing audience. In fact, they want to demonstrate their emerging ability as frequently as others will allow. Children at this stage of reading development have a clear understanding that print forms the basis for reading the story and constructing meaning. Words read in one book or context are now recognized in new or unfamiliar contexts. Signs and environmental print are subjects of intense interest among take-off readers. It seems as if print has a magnetic appeal for these children.

One autumn evening in a parent-teacher conference while one of the authors was teaching first grade, a parent said that her son, Curt, had requested new breakfast cereals. When his mother asked why, Curt responded, "There's not enough to read on these boxes." His mother then bought him cereal in a box that seemed to display enough print to satisfy his appetite.

Oral reading during the take-off stage may become word- or letter-centered. Although oral reading before this time may have failed to perfectly represent the print on the page, it was smooth, fluent, and filled with inflection. The fact that words and letters have been discovered at this stage of development may lead to a situation in which children appear to temporarily regress in their reading development. Children in this stage need to focus on print details, which leads to less fluent and inflected oral reading for a time. With sustained opportunities to read and gain control over the reading process and print system, however, fluency and inflection will soon return.

I Can Do It By Myself! The Independent Stage

The take-off reader wants an audience, but the independent reader takes great pride in reading books to himself for pleasure. The independent reader has developed control over the entire reading process and cueing systems. Reading is now carried on with simultaneous use of the author's printed clues and the reader's own store of background experiences and knowledge, called *schemata*. Fluency and inflection have returned to oral reading. In fact, chunks or phrases are now read fluently, with no laboring over single words. The independent reader is predicting ahead of the print and using context not just as an aid to decoding, but also to construct meaning (Stanovich, 1980). The ability to critically analyze print, however, has not yet been achieved. Thus, these readers may believe everything they read or may exhibit a tendency toward seeing anything in print as literal, truthful, and absolute.

Reaching the Summit: The Skilled Reader

The skilled reader not only understands print, but uses print to support and extend thinking. Although this stage is the final stage of reading development, it is not a destiny. The process of becoming skilled in reading is a lifelong journey. The journey to skilled reading involves processing print that is further and further removed from one's own experiences and knowledge. In other words, print is now used increasingly as a means to acquire new and unfamiliar information. The variety of printed media that skilled readers process increases from narratives and textbooks to magazines, newspapers, TV guides, tax forms, and so on. The skilled reader can talk about different types of text organizations, make inferences from print, use print to substantiate opinions, challenge the surface validity of printed materials, and vary his reading rate according to the personal purposes for reading, such as by skimming and scanning. Although more research is needed to corroborate the descriptions offered by Cochrane et al. (1984) in the reading development continuum, this model provides a useful framework for parents, teachers, and scholars through which they can view the development of a reader with increased understanding and a good deal less anxiety.

The Next Step

Once teachers understand which skills should be taught, the issue of *how* to teach them is of interest. In the next section we present a way of teaching skills in balanced reading programs that has proven to be most successful.

TEACHING SKILLS IN BALANCED READING PROGRAMS

"THE WAY WE WERE": TRADITIONAL METHODS OF TEACHING READING SKILLS

An especially crucial aspect of balanced reading programs is how skills are taught. Traditional reading programs teach skills from a "parts to whole" perspective, whereas balanced reading programs teach skills from "whole to parts to whole." "Parts to whole" teaching usually includes the following steps:

The teacher . . .

1. names and defines the skill or part of language to be learned.
2. models using the skill.
3. leads students through a guided practice session using the skill.
4. asks students to participate in an independent demonstration of their knowledge of the skill.
5. checks for understanding and reteaches as necessary.
6. concludes with a literature application activity.

Following is a sample lesson plan sequence from a traditional "parts to whole" perspective. The reading skill presented is *beginning sounds in words*. It is assumed that students have already been taught to think about what an unknown word in print might be based on—*What word would make sense?* (called *context clues* by teachers). Beginning sounds is the first phonics skill students should learn for decoding unknown words in print and should be used in conjunction with context clues. Note that the sample lesson begins by naming the "part" of language or skill to be learned (beginning sounds) and works toward using the skill in a story or "whole" text.

BEGINNING SOUNDS IN WORDS: A TRADITIONAL "PARTS TO WHOLE" SCHEME

Objective:

As a result of this lesson, students will be able to identify unknown words found in reading selections using the strategy of context clues and beginning sounds in words.

1. *Name and define the "part" of language or the skill to be learned.*
   Begin by explaining to students what it is that they will about learn today. For example, the teacher might say "Girls and boys, we all sometimes come to a word in a story that we don't know. We learned earlier that good readers ask themselves, 'What word would make sense in this sentence?' Then they make the best guess they can and continue reading. However, sometimes there is more than one word that would make sense, so we need to have another way to figure out what the word might be. Good readers usually figure out which word that starts with that particular beginning sound would make sense. Then, they continue reading."

2. *Model using the skill.*

Project an overhead transparency having three sentences on it, each having a word with all but the first letter covered. Explain that you are pretending that the partly covered word is a word you do not recognize. Based on context, guess what the word might be. Next, through "thinking aloud," tell the class how you decided the identity of each word. *Use only nouns with single consonant sounds for easy understanding.*

> *Materials needed:* Overhead transparency of sentences, each with a word covered (all but first letter) with a stick-on note. Note: This is called a "modified cloze" activity. Example: Jason pulled his r___ wagon down the street. (unknown word is, of course, *red*)

> *Assessment:* Watch to be sure that students are attending. After demonstrating, ask if a volunteer would like to tell you in his own words how the strategy works.

3. *Lead students through guided practice(s) using the new language skill/ knowledge.*

Say, "Now that we have a little better idea what to do when you come to an unknown word, I want to see if you can do what I just did with sentences found on page 36 of your reading workbook. Let's do the first two together." After reading the first sentence aloud, ask for a volunteer to say what he thinks the unknown word might be, then discuss why it could not have been other words that start with the same sound (they don't make sense).

> *Materials needed:* Page 36 of the reading workbook (having ten sentences, each with one word that shows only the first consonant sound followed by a blank)

4. *Have students participate in an independent demonstration and assessment.*

Now ask students to complete the remainder of the workbook page on their own by supplying the missing word in each sentence.

> *Materials needed:* Page 36 of the workbook

5. *Check for understanding.*

As students complete this assignment, move about the room making "house calls" to check for understanding. If the students seem to be able to do this activity well, then move on to the next step. If some or many do not seem to understand, reteach as necessary using other examples.

> *Materials needed:* N.A.

> *Assessment:* Collect the workbook page and check for understanding. An 80% correct criterion will be used to determine whether students sufficiently understand.

6. *Provide a literature application activity.*

Share an excerpt from the book *Mufaro's Beautiful Daughters: An African Tale* by John Steptoe. Then, have students work in pairs to fill in missing words on photocopies of pages 2–5 from the book. When finished, discuss each response as a group and emphasize how each correct guess made sense with the story.

Materials needed:

1. Book: Steptoe, J. (1987). *Mufaro's Beautiful Daughters: An African Tale.* New York: William Morrow.

2. Photocopies of pp. 2–5, with selected words blanked out (all but the beginning consonant sound)

3. Pencils for each group of two students

There are several things going on in the traditional lesson plan above that are worth noting for our comparison with balanced reading lessons. First, this lesson *began* by naming and defining the skill or part of language to be studied. The trouble with beginning a skill lesson in this way, however, is that the teacher is leading with abstract information. This practice makes it more difficult for students to comprehend, mainly because there is a lack of language context. Second, and similarly, these first tasks lack interesting language samples drawn from popular children's books—students are asked to read contrived and rather boring sentences, instead. This makes it harder for students to see a natural connection between what they are learning and authentic reading and writing activities. Finally, students do not have the opportunity to try out their new knowledge on a real book or other written texts until the very end of the lesson. This can be devastating to student interest in reading. As an important aside, we want to mention that lessons such as the one above are often done in one session that can last up to 45 minutes—an ocean of time for many youngsters!

In contrast, the next section examines the way reading skills and language elements are taught in balanced reading programs.

TEACHING READING SKILLS IN BALANCED READING PROGRAMS: MINILESSONS

The method used to teach skills and language elements in balanced reading classrooms has much in common with that used in traditional approaches, but includes some very different techniques, as well. These differences are significant. The two most prominent differences in balanced reading skill instruction are 1) skills are most often taught via *minilessons* (5–10 minutes per session), rather than lengthy lessons of 30–45 minutes, and 2) skills are taught from *whole to parts to whole,* rather than from only parts to whole. Let us explain what we mean.

Minilessons are typically whole-class or group lessons that last approximately 5–10 minutes each and may be used to teach reading strategies and skills, promote student responses to what they have read, or to teach a necessary procedure (Hagerty, 1992). Since they are so brief, it usually takes several of these five- to ten-minute sessions for many skills to be fully taught and learned. Minilessons allow teachers to quickly get to the point and end a lesson before student attention fades. They are not, by the way, always meant to be lessons in which "outcomes" are required. Sometimes minilessons are simply opportunities for students to take part in a literate behavior (i.e., enjoy reading a book, poem, or song, or participate in writing).

Hagerty (1992) describes three types of minilessons: 1) procedural, 2) literary, and 3) strategy/skill. A listing of possible minilesson topics is found in Table 1.1.

A *procedural reading minilesson,* for example, might involve the teacher and students in learning how to handle new books received for the classroom library, as well as how to repair worn books. The teacher may demonstrate how to break in a new book's binding by standing the book on its spine and opening a few pages on either side of the center of the book and carefully pressing them down. Cellophane tape and staplers may be used to demonstrate how to repair tears in a book's pages or cover. A *literary reading minilesson* for early readers might involve a child presenting the teacher with a small booklet written at home in the shape of a puppy that retells favorite parts from the book *Taxi Dog* (Barraca, ____). An upper elementary level student may be shown how to assemble a poster resembling the front page of a newspaper in order to depict major events from a novel just read, such as Betsy Byars's *The Summer of the Swans* (1970).

An example of a *strategy/skill reading minilesson* for early readers might occur during the reading of a big book entitled *Cats and Mice* (Gelman, 1985), in which the teacher makes note of the fact that many of the words in the book end with the participle form of *-ing.* Noticing this regularity in the text, the teacher draws children's attention to the function of *-ing.* For example, while rereading *Cats and Mice* the next day, the teacher may cover each *-ing* ending with a small self-adhesive note, then peel it away while reading to emphasize the word ending. A minilesson for more advanced readers might pertain to patterns used by nonfiction writers to make information easier to understand (i.e., cause/effect, description, problem-solution, comparisons, etc.). This could involve 1) describing the patterns used, 2) searching for examples in science, mathematics, and social studies materials, then 3) writing/creating examples of these patterns pertaining to a topic of the student's choice.

As previously mentioned, balanced reading programs follow a "whole to parts to whole" pattern for teaching minilessons. This is the subject of the next section.

"WHOLE TO PARTS TO WHOLE" TEACHING

We saw earlier how traditional reading lessons follow a "parts to whole" pattern for teaching. That is, they begin with the utterly abstract task of naming/defining the skill to be learned without the benefit of meaningful context. Balanced reading programs, on the other hand, proceed from "whole to parts to whole." Thus, reading lessons usually include these steps:

1. Reading "whole" text that makes sense and is interesting to the student (i.e., a story, song, poem, nonfiction passage, etc.).

2. Introduce and model how to use the "part" of language or skill to be learned. The skill or part of language should be explained and demonstrated using the whole text just read in Step 1.

3. Have students practice using the skill in different excerpts from that same passage (or a similar text in the very same format, as demonstrated by the teacher in Step 2). First attempts to "try out" the skill are done through *whole group guided practice* by student volunteers (it is very important to call on

Table 1.1   Possible Minilesson Topics

Procedural Minilessons	Literary Minilessons	Strategy/Skills Minilessons
Where to sit during reading time	Differences between fiction and nonfiction books	How to choose a book
Giving a book talk	Learning from dedications	Selecting literature log topics
How to be a good listener in a share session	Books that show emotion	Connecting reading material to your own life
What is an appropriate noise level during reading time	Books written in the first, second, or third person	Tips for reading aloud
What to do when you finish a book	Author studies	Figuring out unknown words
What kinds of questions to ask during a share session	How authors use quotations	Using context
Running a small group discussion	How the story setting fits the story	Substituting
Self-evaluation	Characteristics of different genres	Using picture clues
Getting ready for a conference	Development of characters, plot, theme, mood	Using the sounds of blends, vowels, contractions, etc.
How to have a peer conference	How leads hook us	Using Post-its to mark interesting parts
Where to sit during minilessons	How authors use the problem/event/solution pattern	Monitoring comprehension (Does this make sense and sound right?)
Taking care of books	Differences between a picture book and a novel	Asking questions while reading
Keeping track of books to read	Titles and their meanings	Making predictions
Rules of the workshop	Characters' points of view	Emergent strategies
	Examples of similes and metaphors	Concept of story
	Examples of foreshadowing	Concept that print carries meaning
	How authors use dialogue	Making sense
	Predictable and surprise endings	Mapping a story
	Use of descriptive words and phrases	How to retell a story orally
	How illustrations enhance the story	Looking for relationships
	Secrets in books	Looking for important ideas
		Making inferences
		Drawing conclusions
		Summarizing a story
		Distinguishing fact from opinion
		Emergent reader skills: directionality, concept of "word," sound/symbol relationships

Note: From *Readers workshop: Real reading* (pp. 113–115), by P. Hagerty, 1992, Ontario, Canada: Scholastic Canada. Copyright 1992 by Scholastic Canada. Reprinted by permission.

volunteers only at this point), followed by *independent practice* exercises to demonstrate students' understanding.

4. Check for understanding and reteach as necessary.

5. Before ending the minilesson series, lead a "whole" text reapplication activity in which the new skill learned is applied in other interesting readings. This vividly shows students how this skill can be used in many reading situations.

6. If the skill is one that will be tested on state- or district-mandated instruments, offer a test-wiseness practice lesson so that students understand the format of the test and can thus best demonstrate their reading ability.

To illustrate the "whole to parts to whole" nature of balanced reading lessons, we offer below a minilesson series (a plan that requires several minilessons spread over perhaps a week) that we have used in our first grade classrooms. Like the traditional plan offered earlier in the chapter, this lesson pertains to the skill "beginning sounds in words." Look carefully for similarities and differences between traditional and balanced reading lessons.

BEGINNING SOUNDS IN WORDS: A BALANCED READING "WHOLE TO PARTS TO WHOLE" SCHEME

Objective:

As a result of this lesson, students will be able to identify unknown words found in reading selections using the strategy of context clues and beginning sounds in words.

Materials needed: Enlarged version of *Elmer* (McKee, 1968), overhead transparencies adapted from page 7 of the book, and teacher-made practice sheets (from pages 9, 11, and 13) in a modified cloze format.

Day 1 Activity: Shared Book Experience (Whole)

Using a big book version of *Elmer,* read the book aloud with the class and discuss the students' favorite parts. This provides children with "whole" text as a context for learning.

Day 2 Activity: Teacher Input and Modeling (Parts)

Begin the minilesson by rereading portions of *Elmer* to remind the children of the story line. Next, explain that, when reading, sometimes we come to words we do not know. Good readers usually look at the beginning sound of the word and try to think of a word they know that begins with that same sound *and* that would make sense in the sentence. Then, after making a logical guess, they continue reading. As they continue to read, the meaning of the story helps them to know whether their guess was correct. (Note: When introducing beginning sounds, teachers choose examples that are nouns or verbs and that have a *single* consonant as the beginning sound. These examples are easiest for children to understand.)

The essence of modeling is the teacher, in effect, thinking aloud for students so they can understand thought processes used to solve literacy problems. To illustrate beginning sounds in words, the teacher may begin by showing on the overhead

Figure 1.2   Whole Text Example from *Elmer* (McKee, 1968, p. 7)

Note: This should be shown/demonstrated on an overhead projector or other enlarged print format.

> But Elmer himself wasn't happy. "Whoever heard of a patchwork elephant?"
>
> he thought. "No wonder they laugh at me!" One morning, just as the others
>
> were waking up, Elmer slipped away.

projector a transparency adapted from page 7 of the book (see Figure 1.2). The teacher and class should reread the page chorally.

Next, the teacher puts another copy of page 7 on the overhead projector, this time with a selected word deleted (all but the beginning sound) and replaced with a blank in a kind of modified cloze format (see Figure 1.3). Note that only one word has been deleted in this first example, so that, while the teacher is modeling the thought process, the students will have a maximum amount of context to help them realize that the missing word is "morning." You may well want to model several such examples from the book to make sure that students 1) understand the strategy, and 2) think that reading is "easy" for them to do. Convincing children that reading is a skill they can do easily is half the battle!

Speaking aloud, the teacher then reads the passage and "thinks" or "guesses" what the missing word might be for each of the blanks. The emphasis should always be on what makes sense within the context of the passage. When beginning sounds are used in conjunction with *context clues* (the meaning of the sentence), a child can easily determine the unknown word for the reason that "it begins with the right sound." As mentioned above, it is essential that you choose words for

Figure 1.3   Modified text example from *Elmer* (McKee, 1968, p. 7)

Note: This should be shown/demonstrated on an overhead projector or other enlarged print format. When preparing your transparency, try using a font on your computer that closely resembles that found in the book, such as "Century Schoolbook" or "Geneva."

> But Elmer himself wasn't happy. "Whoever heard of a patchwork elephant?"
>
> he thought. "No wonder they laugh at me!" One m_____, just as the oth-
>
> ers were waking up, Elmer slipped away.

Figure 1.4   Teacher-Made Practice Sheet from *Elmer* (McKee, 1968, p. 11)

> After a long walk Elmer f_____ what he was looking for—a large b_____ cov-
>
> ered with elephant-colored berries. Elmer caught hold of the bush and shook
>
> it until the b_____ fell on the ground.

teaching this skill that make the identification process effortless and certain. After this demonstration, ask the children if they have any questions. They are then ready for the next minilesson.

Day 3 Activity: Guided and Independent Practice

Children at this point have some understanding of beginning sounds in words demonstrated as a combination strategy with context clues. To make this strategy their own, however, they must practice it themselves. Another familiar page of text, for example page 11, is selected from *Elmer* (McKee, 1968), and a practice sheet is produced *in the same format as was demonstrated by the teacher* (see Figure 1.4). Children complete the practice exercise with assistance from the teacher, or in collaboration with other students, if desired. The teacher or parent volunteer then reviews the practice sheet for accuracy. Remember, as long as the student response 1) begins with the correct sound, and 2) makes sense, it should be accepted.

The last step at this stage is a final practice sheet from the book, such as page 13, that the child completes without any assistance from others. This practice sheet is in the exact format as was modeled by the teacher and practiced using the sheet shown in Figure 1.4. If this exercise is completed without difficulty, the minilesson moves on to the last stage. If there are problems, however, then reteaching should be done.

Day 4 Activity: Whole Text Reapplication (Whole)

The goal here is to help students understand that this new word identification strategy they have learned can be used with almost any text. In other words, it's practical and worth knowing! Gather students around to enjoy a new book, poem, or song shown in enlarged print so everyone can read the text. After a first reading, reread the text with students (after having strategically placed stick-on note sheets over all but the first letter of some preselected words in the passage). Students then volunteer during this rereading of the new selection to try to guess what the covered word could be, based on the beginning sound and the context of the passage. Praise the students for their successful guesses and explain that they are able to do this because of the new skill they have learned—beginning sounds in words.

Figure 1.5   Basal Reader Skillsheet

Phonics Skill: Beginning Sounds

Name _____

Example: Sam will be in the football g _____ on Saturday.

1. We rode to Sam's football game in the c_____.
2. Jim s_____ next to Mary on the grass.
3. Sam threw the f_____ to Max and won the game.
4. We plan to go see Sam's next g_____ on Saturday.
5. Next time, I will bring a ch_____ to sit on instead of the grass.

Day 5 Activity: Test-Wiseness Lesson (Optional)

To satisfy state and local school district testing/accountability requirements, most teachers are required to give some sort of test to children on various reading skills and strategies. This may take the form of end-of-basal tests, standardized achievement tests, or district-constructed tests. In the preceding example, one can be reasonably sure that all children have acquired the ability to use beginning sounds in words with context clues, at least on a novice level. But one more step may be needed to help students apply the strategy on a test. Recognizing that most districts rely on end-of-basal tests because of their easy access (they already own basal series), one or two of the basal reader skill sheets dealing with beginning sounds in words (in this case) may be duplicated for each student (see Figure 1.5 for an example). By working through an example or two with the teacher and then completing the remainder of the practice sheet themselves, students will become acquainted with the format of the test (but not the actual test itself). This final step in the teaching process to prepare children for mandated testing is known as a *test-wiseness lesson.*

OUR RESEARCH ON "WHOLE TO PARTS TO WHOLE" INSTRUCTION

How do students perform in balanced reading programs compared to students in more traditional classrooms (especially those exposed to basal readers exclusively)? Our research (Reutzel & Cooter, 1990) suggests that students taught using "whole to parts to whole" strategies perform at least as well as students taught using traditional teaching methods, and usually much better. Furthermore, "whole to parts to whole" strategies help students understand why skills are being taught, how the skills being learned make the task of reading easier and more enjoyable, and how reading can be a beneficial and enjoyable recreational activity.

An Invitation

In this first chapter we introduced you to the notion of balanced reading programs and partially demonstrated how they differ from traditional classroom methods—but this is only the beginning! In the remainder of this book, we offer you the most current information regarding effective classroom assessment and teaching strategies for reading instruction. We urge you to read chapters 2 and 3 next to give yourself a deeper understanding of portfolio assessment strategies for the classroom, so that your teaching choices are as well-informed as possible and include time-saving and classroom-proven ideas.

The remainder of the book (chapters 4 through 16), once read, may be used as a handy reference tool in your professional library for the teaching of reading. For instance, if you have a small group of children who seem to struggle with nonfiction (expository) readings, then chapter 10 will help you to assess their *specific* need areas and to select teaching/learning strategies to overcome their problems. On the other hand, students who seem to lack the ability to read smoothly and in a way that sounds like normal oral speech can be helped with ideas found in chapter 12.

We know that your time is precious and that it is difficult to pore through all the books and journals on reading instruction to find the "just right" idea for your students. We, too, have experienced this time crunch dilemma and know how frustrating it can sometimes be when a teacher looks into the eyes of a child who has a special learning need. When we began this project several years ago, our goal was to fill the pages of this book with practical classroom assessment and teaching strategies for the experienced (and novice) teacher to satisfy these special needs—to serve, in effect, as a teacher's assistant. Along the way we have tested out most of these ideas ourselves, or have asked practicing teachers to do so. As you use this book with your students in coming years, we trust that you will find our goal was largely met and, if time permits, you'll take time to write us and suggest ways that the next edition can be even better. Happy teaching!

References

Altwerger, B., Edelsky, C., & Flores, B. M. (1987). Whole language: What's new? *The Reading Teacher, 41*(2), 144–154.

Baumann, J. F., Hoffman, J. V. Moon, J., & Duffy-Hester, A. M. (1998). Where are teachers' voices in the phonics/whole language debate? Results from a survey of U. S. elementary classroom teachers. *The Reading Teacher, 51*(8), p. 636–650.

Byars, B. (1970). *The summer of the swans.* New York: Viking.

California Reading Task Force. (1995). *Every child a reader.*

Cochrane, O., Cochrane, D., Scalena, D., & Buchanan, E. (1984). *Reading, writing and caring.* New York: Richard C. Owen Publishers, Inc.

Department of Education. (1985). *Reading in Junior classes.* Wellington, New Zealand. New York: Richard C. Owen Publishers, Inc.

Gelman (1985). *Cats and Mice.* New York: Scholastic.

Hagerty, P. (1992). *Reader's workshop: Real reading.* New York: Scholastic.

McKee, D. (1968). *Elmer.* New York: McGraw-Hill.

Mooney, M. E. (1990). *Reading to, with, and by children.* Katonah, NY: Richard C. Owen Publishers, Inc.

Reutzel, D. R. (1985). Reconciling schema theory and the basal reader lesson. *The Reading Teacher, 39,* 194–197.

Reutzel, D. R., & Cooter, R. B., Jr. (1990). Whole language: Comparative effects on first grade reading achievement. *Journal of Educational Research, 83,* 252–257.

Reutzel, D. R., & Cooter, R. B., Jr. (1996). *Teaching children to read: From basals to books.* New York: Merrill, an imprint of Prentice-Hall.

Stanovich, K. (1980). Toward an interactive-compensatory model of individual differences in the development of reading fluency. *Reading Research Quarterly, 16*(1), 37–71.

Steptoe, J. (1987). *Mufaro's Beautiful Daughters: An African Tale.* New York: William Morrow.

Sulzby, E. (1985). Children's emergent reading of favorite storybooks: A developmental study. *Reading Research Quarterly, 20*(4), 458–481.

Chapter 2

Portfolio Assessment in a Balanced Reading Program: Part I

Many people in today's world collect and share samples of their work and accomplishments to demonstrate their competence. In the financial world, investors have spoken for many years of their *portfolios,* a term suggesting a collection of stocks in which they have chosen to invest time and energy. Photographers, artists, and newly graduated teachers often collect samples of their work in the form of portfolios to share with prospective employers.

In public schools, teachers and researchers have adopted the portfolio concept for use in the classroom as a way of reflecting a student's growth in literacy over time. Why has this trend come about? Wiener and Cohen (1997) explain that the interest in portfolios as an assessment tool is "a natural outgrowth of changing methodologies for teaching reading and writing" (p. 3). As politicians, interested family members, and the business community insist on greater accountability and proof that instructional goals are being met in our schools, teachers and administrators are likewise seeking more effective ways to assess student learning. **Portfolio assessment,** as defined by Arter and Spandel (1992), is

> a purposeful collection of student work that tells the story of the student's efforts, progress, or achievement in given areas. This collection must include student participation in selection of portfolio content; the guidelines for selection; the criteria for judging merit; and evidence of student reflection. (p. 36)

Portfolio assessment represents a very substantial shift in the measurement of reading growth from more product-oriented quantitative methods (e.g., standardized tests, checklists, worksheets) to more process-oriented qualitative methods (e.g., running records, story retellings, parent surveys/conference information, writing samples, etc.). Although portfolios may well include standardized test information as part of the "data net," depending on the goals and needs of reporting to families and school districts, portfolios contain much greater detail. As Spencer (1998) explains, "if done well, portfolios capture the richness of reading . . . standardized tests can't capture the richness and complexities of reading—they are only one-dimensional, whereas portfolios are *multidimensional.*" (p. 2). Thus, comparing traditional reading tests to portfolios is much like comparing a black-and-white photo to a color movie (Reutzel & Cooter, 1996). In this chapter, we go into some detail regarding the purpose, audience, and contents of portfolios.

BACKGROUND BRIEFING FOR TEACHERS: WHAT ARE PORTFOLIOS IN BALANCED READING CLASSROOMS?

A portfolio, literally speaking, is a folder or other storage place for collecting student exhibits that reflect the "whole picture" of her reading development (Jongsma, 1989). Further, a portfolio is a *philosophy* of viewing assessment as well as a *place* for gathering evidence of student growth and development in reading (Valencia, 1990). Cooter and Flynt (1996) explain that

> the *philosophy* of portfolios suggests that we should consider all factors related to reading when assessing students. . . . Portfolios are consistent with newer curriculum designs (Farr, 1991, p. 2) that emphasize the integration of the language arts (listening, speaking, reading and writing). They focus on the processes of constructing meaning, use of quality literature and other information aids, problem solving and application skills, and student collaborations. Therefore, portfolios are a means for dynamic and ongoing assessment (Tierney, 1992).
>
> Portfolios also represent a *place* for collecting student work samples that provide "windows" on the strategies used by students when reading and writing (Farr, 1991; Tierney, 1992; Farr & Tone, 1994). File folders, storage boxes, hanging files, and notebooks are a few of the common portfolio containers used to hold daily samples or "evidence" of student learning. This puts the responsibility and control for [reading] assessment back into the hands of those most affected by it—teachers and students (Valencia, 1990, p. 5), and provides the foundation for teacher/student conferences (Farr, 1991, p. 42).

There are several different types of portfolios commonly used in balanced reading classrooms (Barr & Johnson, 1997). We choose to maintain three rather distinct sets: *student portfolios, teacher portfolios,* and *family portfolios.* A *student portfolio* is kept by the student. Work samples may be placed into the portfolio by the student *or* her teacher. In contrast, *teacher portfolios* are kept by the teacher through the academic year and include representative samples of the student's development selected over time from the student portfolio. The third type of portfolio commonly used—*family portfolio*—is constructed prior to family conferences using contents from the teacher portfolio. The family portfolio helps the teacher explain and demonstrate to parents or guardians the child's reading/literacy development, key activities used in the classroom to facilitate that development, and ways in which they can help their child at home. Family portfolios are a splendid accountability tool for parent-teacher conferences and can inspire greater confidence and support for the teacher and curriculum.

So, what should be included in a portfolio in a balanced reading program? In the next section we describe some of the most fundamental elements that teachers around the world have chosen to include.

BASIC ELEMENTS OF BALANCED READING PROGRAM PORTFOLIOS

As discussed in Chapter 1, assessment should be directly related to developmental milestones in reading and should help teachers make instructional decisions. Chapters 4 through 15 of this book include detailed suggestions for reading assessment and instruction. Certainly, any of these activities that offer insights into a child's reading development are appropriate choices for inclusion in portfolios. Our purpose in this chapter is simply to introduce the notion of portfolios and to describe some of the first items teachers choose to include.

Basic elements commonly included in reading portfolios are shown in Figure 2.1 and described briefly below. Of course, the form these elements may take depends greatly on where the student is in her development. Indeed, there may be students for whom some of these elements may not be appropriate. Still, Figure 2.1 is a

Figure 2.1 Beginning Choices for Balanced Reading Portfolios

helpful way to look "over the shoulder" of many practicing teachers as they make choices concerning portfolio contents.

Note that, of the sixteen elements we have listed, seven are highlighted. These seven are primary elements that most reading portfolios usually include. We describe these seven elements first, followed by descriptions of nine other options for inclusion. Of course, many possibilities exist beyond those listed here.

Running Records—An assessment procedure for analyzing oral reading errors (miscues) that may be used with any book at or near the student's developmental reading level. Running records are primarily used with readers in their early years of development. In chapter 3 we describe running records in detail.

Anecdotal Notes—Observations the teacher writes while observing a student reading. They focus on major milestones in the student's reading development, as discussed in chapter 1, and/or other reading skills that the teacher may be emphasizing or about to emphasize in class. Many teachers like to make their notes on self-adhesive labels such as those used on a computer printer to print addresses. These notes can then be dated and easily attached to the inside of students' portfolio folders at the end of the day.

Reading Milestone Checklist—Based on the research of Cochrane and others (1984) and Sulzby (1985) discussed in chapter 1, this Reading Milestones Checklist (see Figure 2.2) can be duplicated and placed in each student's reading

Figure 2.2   Reading Milestones Checklist

> ## Reading Milestones Checklist for Emergent Reading (Abbreviated Version)
>
> Student: _____   Year: _____
> Teacher: _____   School: _____
>
> **Directions:** *Write the date(s) on the appropriate blank as the child exhibits the behaviors listed below.*
>
> ### A. PRE-INDEPENDENT READING STAGES
>
> 1. MAGICAL STAGE (Sulzby's "Story Not Formed" occur here and before)
>   _____ Displays an interest in handling books.
>   _____ Listens to print read to him for extended periods of time.
>   _____ Begins to notice print in environmental context (signs, labels).
>   _____ Letters may appear in his drawings.
>   _____ Likes to "name" the pictures in a book, e.g., "lion," "rabbit."
>
> 2. SELF-CONCEPTING STAGE (Sulzby's "Story Formed" level begins here)
>   _____ "Reads" or reconstructs content of familiar storybooks.
>   _____ Recognizes his name and some other words in high environmental contexts (signs, labels).
>   _____ Writing displays phonetic influence, e.g., wtbo = Wally, hr = her.
>   _____ Constructs story meaning from pictorial clues.   **continued**

_____ Cannot pick words out of print consistently.

_____ Rhymes words.

3. _____ BRIDGING STAGE (Sulzby's "Story Formed" to "Written Language-Like")

    _____ Can write and read back his own writing.

    _____ Can pick out individual words and letters.

    _____ Can read familiar books or poems which could not be totally repeated without the print.

    _____ Words read in one context may not be read in another.

    _____ Increasing control over visual cueing system.

    _____ Can match or pick out words of poems or chants that have been internalized.

B. INDEPENDENT READING STAGES

I. TAKE-OFF STAGE (Sulzby's "Print Watched" to "Holistic")

    _____ Wants to read to you often.

    _____ Realizes that print is the base for constructing meaning.

    _____ Aware of and reads aloud much environmental print (signs, labels, etc.).

    _____ Exhibits temporary tunnel vision (concentrates on words and letters).

    _____ Oral reading is word-centered rather than meaning-centered.

2. INDEPENDENT READING (Sulzby's "Holistic" level)

    _____ Comprehends the author's message.

    _____ Desires to read books to himself for pleasure.

    _____ Reads orally with meaning and expression.

    _____ Sees print as a literal truth. What the print says is right (legalized).

    _____ Has internalized several different print grammars, e.g., fairy tales, general problem-centered stories, simple exposition.

3. SKILLED READER

    _____ Processes material further and further removed from his own experience.

    _____ Reading content and vocabulary become a part of his experience.

    _____ Can use a variety of print forms for pleasure.

    _____ Can discuss several aspects of a story.

    _____ Can read at varying and appropriate rates.

    _____ Can make inferences from print.

    _____ Challenges the validity of print content.

    _____ Can focus on or utilize the appropriate grammar or structuring of varying forms of print, e.g., stories, science experiments, menus, diagrams, histories.

Note: Adapted from Cochrane, Cochrane, Scalena, and Buchanan. (1988), *Reading, Writing, and Caring.* Richard C. Owen Publishers, Inc., New York, New York; and E. Sulzby's (1991) "Classification scheme for emergent reading of favorite storybooks."

portfolio. As observations are recorded (see Anecdotal Notes above), the teacher writes the date in the blank to the left of each milestone indicating when the student was observed exhibiting that skill or behavior. As dates begin to cluster in each category, it becomes possible to accurately identify the student's stage of development. This then helps the teacher to anticipate the student's next developmental milestone. This kind of knowledge is key for strategic planning of instruction.

Reading Logs—Daily records of student reading habits and interests, usually kept during self-selected reading (SSR) periods (Cambourne & Turbill, 1990). Students keep these records by completing simple forms held in a reading log folder at students' desks or in other appropriate locations.

Interest Inventories—One of the most important and elusive aspects of reading assessment is *affect,* which deals with a student's feelings about the reading act (Mathewson, 1985). Attitude, motivation, interest, beliefs, and values are all aspects of affect that have profound effects on reading development. Teachers building balanced literacy programs require information in student portfolios that not only provides insights into reading materials and teaching strategies that may be employed, but also into positive affective aspects that drive the reading process. Ultimately, selection of materials and strategies should be based at least in part on affective considerations. A starting point for many teachers is the interest inventory. Students are asked to complete or verbally respond to items on a questionnaire such as that shown in Figure 2.3. Responses give teachers a starting point for choosing reading materials that may interest the student and elicit the best reading possible, according to her abilities.

Retellings—An ideal way to find out if a child understands a story she has read is through retellings (Gambrell, Pfeiffer, & Wilson, 1985; Morrow, 1985). This is accomplished not by simply asking "Do you understand the story?" but by asking her to retell the story in her own words. In chapter 3 we describe in more detail how retellings may be used as part of a portfolio assessment program.

Family Surveys—When one is attempting to develop a clear understanding of a student's reading development, her reading behavior at home is obviously of great importance. Family surveys are brief questionnaires (too long, and they'll never be answered!) sent to the student's parents or primary care-givers periodically to provide the teacher with insights into her home reading behaviors. Teachers can then combine the family survey response with other assessment evidence from the classroom to develop a reliable profile of the student's reading ability. An example of a family survey is provided in Figure 2.4.

Story Maps—Story maps (Beck, Omanson, & McKeown, 1982; Routman, 1988) may be used to determine whether a student understands the basic elements of a narrative text or passage: setting, characters, challenge, events, solution, and theme. After reading the story, a student completes a story map. A generic format for the story map, such as the one shown in Figure 2.5, may be applied to almost any narrative text. Reading comprehension assessment and teaching procedures are discussed in detail in chapters 8 and 9 of this book.

Audio-Videotapes—Using audiotapes to record oral reading and retelling and videotapes to record students performing a variety of reading activities is a great way to periodically map reading growth. Recordings made at regular intervals, such

𝒲 Figure 2.3   Interest Inventory

Interest Inventory

Student's Name: _____

Date: _____

Instructions: Please answer the following questions on a separate sheet of paper.

 1. If you could have three wishes, what would they be?
 2. What would you do with $50,000?
 3. What things in life bother you most?
 4. What kind of person would you like to be when you are older?
 5. What are your favorite classes at school, and why?
 6. Who do you think is the greatest person? Why do you think so?
 7. Who is your favorite person? Why?
 8. What do you like to do in your free time?
 9. Do you read any parts of the newspaper? Which parts?
10. How much TV do you watch each day? What are your favorite shows, and why?
11. What magazines do you like to read?
12. Name three of your favorite movies.
13. What do you like best about your home?
14. What books have you enjoyed reading?
15. What kind of books would you like to read in the future?

as monthly, can be played back for careful analysis by the teacher and during parent–teacher conferences to demonstrate growth over time.

Self-Rating Scales—It is often true that no one knows better how she is doing at reading than the reader herself. In the process of assessment, a teacher should never fail to ask the student how she feels about her reading ability. Although this may be best achieved in a one-on-one reading conference, large public school class sizes frequently make this impractical. A good alternative to one-on-one interviews for older elementary children, however, is a student self-rating scale. Students complete a questionnaire that is tailored to obtain specific information about the reader—from the reader's point of view.

Rubrics (teacher- or school district-made)—As scoring guides or rating systems used in performance-based assessment (Webb & Willoughby, 1993; Farr & Tone, 1994; Reutzel & Cooter, 1996, p. 559), rubrics assist teachers in two ways. First, rubrics make the analysis of student exhibits in the portfolio simpler. Second, rubrics make the rating process more consistent and objective. Since any assess-

Figure 2.4   Family Survey

September 6, 199_

Dear Adult Family Member:

   As we begin the new school year, I would like to know a little more about your child's reading habits at home. This information will help me provide the best possible learning plan for your child this year. Please take a few minutes to answer the questions below and return this survey in the self-addressed stamped envelope provided. Should you have any questions, feel free to phone me at the school between 3:00 and 5:00 P.M. at 648-7696.

Cordially,

Mrs. Spencer
_____

I. **My child likes to read the following at least once a week (check all that apply):**

   comic books ____   sports page ____

   magazines (example: *Highlights*) ____   library books ____

   cereal boxes ____   cooking recipes ____

   TV Guide ____   comics page ____

   others (please name): ____

2. **Have you noticed your child having any reading problems? If so, please explain briefly.**

3. **What are some of your child's favorite books?**

4. **If you would like a conference to discuss your child's reading ability, please indicate which days and times (after school) would be most convenient.**

Figure 2.5   Story Map

Story Map

Name: _____   Date: _____

Title: _____   Author: _____

SETTING (Where and when did this story take place?)

CHARACTERS (Who were the main characters in this story?)

CHALLENGE (What is the main challenge or problem in the story?)

EVENTS (What were the events that happened in the story to solve the problem/challenge?)
      Event 1:
      Event 2:
      Event 3:
(List all the important events that happened.)

SOLUTION (How was the challenge/problem solved or not solved?)

THEME (What was this author trying to tell the reader?)

Note: Adapted from Routman, 1988.

ment process is rarely objective, value-free, or theoretically neutral (Bintz, 1991), rubrics clearly have an important role. Webb and Willoughby (1993, p. 14) explain that "the same rubric may be used for many tasks [once established] as long as the tasks require the same skills."

While there may be any number of ways to establish a rubric, Farr and Tone (1994) suggested a seven-step process of developing rubrics that may be adapted to reading assessment. Reutzel and Cooter (1996) modified the method slightly to conform to reading assessment needs and shortened the process to five relatively easy steps.

    Step 1:   Identify "anchor papers." Begin by collecting and sorting into several stacks reading exhibits from the portfolio (e.g., reading response activities, student self-analysis papers, content reading responses, etc.) according to *quality.* These are known as **anchor papers.** Try to analyze objectively why you feel that certain exhibits represent more advanced development in reading than others, and also why some exhibits cannot be characterized as belonging in the more "advanced" categories.

Step 2:   Choose a scoring scale for the rubric. Usually a three-, four-, or five-point scoring system is used. A three-point scale may be more reliable, meaning that if other teachers were to examine the same reading exhibits, they would be likely to arrive at the same rubric score (1, 2, or 3). However, when multiple criteria are being considered, a five-point scale or greater may be easier to apply. Yet a major problem with reading rubrics is that they imply a hierarchy of skills that does not really seem to exist in many cases. For example, in the upper grades, is the ability to *skim* text for information a higher- or lower-level skill than *scanning* text for information? Probably neither label applies in this instance. This brings us to Farr and Tone's (1994) third step.

Step 3:   Choose scoring criteria that reflect what you believe about reading development. Two points relative to reading rubrics need to be considered in Step 3: *scoring* and *learning milestones.* A rubric is usually scored in a hierarchical fashion. That is, using a five-point scale, if a student fulfills requirements for a 1, 2, and 3 score, but not the criteria for a 4, even if she may fulfill the criteria for a 5 she would be ranked as a 3. In disciplines such as mathematics, certain skills can be ranked hierarchically in a developmental sense. However, many reading skills cannot be ranked so clearly, and thus we recommend a procedure slightly different from that typically used to rank reading skills: *If a five-point rubric is being used, survey all five reading skills or strategies identified in the rubric when reviewing exhibits found in the portfolio. If the student has the ability to do four of them, for example, then rank the student as a 4 regardless of where those skills are situated in the rubric.* We hasten to add that this modification may not always be appropriate, however, especially with emergent readers for whom clearer developmental milestones are evident.

Step 4:   Select sample reading development exhibits for each level of the rubric as exemplars and write descriptive annotations. It is important for teachers to have samples of each performance criterion in mind when attempting to use a rubric. From the Step 1 process in which anchor papers or other kinds of exhibits (e.g., running records, literature response activities, story grammar maps, etc.) were identified, the teacher will have in her possession good examples, or *exemplars,* of each reading skill or strategy being surveyed. After a careful review of these anchor papers it will be possible to write short descriptive state-

Figure 2.6   Sample Rubric for a Fifth-Grade Reading Class

Cause-Effect Relationships: Scale for Oral and Written Response

Level 4: **Student clearly describes a cause and effect of water pollution and provides concrete examples of each.**
Student can provide an example not found in the readings.
"We read about how sometimes toxic wastes are dumped into rivers by factories and most of the fish die. I remember hearing about how there was an oil spill in Alaska that did the same thing to fish and birds living in the area."

Level 3: **Student describes a cause and effect of water pollution found in the readings.**
Student can define _pollution_.
"I remember reading about how factories sometimes dump poisonous chemicals into rivers and all the fish die. _Pollution_ means that someone makes a place so dirty that animals can't live there anymore."

Level 2: **Student can provide examples found in the readings of water pollution or effects that pollution had on the environment.**
"I remember reading that having enough clean water to drink is a problem in some places because of garbage being dumped into the rivers."

Level 1: **Student is not able to voluntarily offer information found in the readings about the cause and effects of pollution.**

ments, or annotations, that summarize what the teacher is searching for in the assessment for each level of the rubric.

Figure 2.6 is a sample rubric developed for a fifth-grade class wherein students were to describe (orally and through written response) cause-effect relationships based on in-class readings about water pollution.

Step 5: Modify the rubric criteria as necessary. In any assessment, the teacher should feel free to modify the rubric's criteria as new information emerges.

Standardized Test Data—Standardized test data are usually included in teacher portfolios and are sometimes discussed in parent-teacher conferences. These data do not really inform instruction—a prime motive for classroom assessment—but they do present a limited view of how the student compares to other students nationally who have also taken that particular test. Many times parents or guardians want to know how their child compares to others. Standardized tests are somewhat useful for that purpose. They may also help teachers who work mainly with students with learning problems to maintain perspective. It is sometimes easy to lose sight of what "normal reading development" is when you work only with students having learning problems. While we feel that standardized tests are not useful for making instructional decisions, they may be helpful in the situations mentioned above.

Observation Checklist—Teachers often find it helpful to use checklists as a quick reference classroom tool that incorporates what we know about reading development. The Reading Milestones Checklist presented earlier is one example. Some teachers find that checklists that include a kind of Likert scale can be useful in student portfolios, since many reading behaviors become more fluent over time. Diffily (1994), while teaching kindergarten and first grade, developed the checklist shown in Figure 2.7 for use with her students. While the reading behaviors listed in any scale or checklist naturally vary according to the grade level, these formats have proven to be quite helpful.

Literature Response Projects—There are many ways students can demonstrate their reading comprehension. In the past and in many classrooms today, workbook pages and skill sheets have been used in great numbers as a postreading assessment activity. Unfortunately, these kinds of activities are a poor substitute for actual demonstrations of competence (Sizer, 1994). As an alternative, a growing number of classroom teachers are having students complete literature response projects to demonstrate their understanding of what they have read.

Literature response projects can take many forms and may be completed by individual students or in literature response groups. The idea is for the student(s) to choose a creative way to demonstrate their competence. As we explore many aspects of reading comprehension, you will find numerous literature response ideas described in this book. For example, one group of sixth graders (Cooter & Griffith, 1989), decided to develop a board game in the form of Trivial Pursuit based on their reading of *The Lion, The Witch, and the Wardrobe* (Lewis, 1961). In an Ohio classroom, a student working independently decided to create a kind of comic strip that retold the book he had just completed. And a second-grade teacher in south Texas had her class make a "character report card" in which students graded a villain in a book on such character traits as honesty, trustworthiness, and so forth using inference skills and examples from the story to justify their opinions.

Teacher-Made Tests—Though often overused in many classrooms, paper and pencil tests do sometimes serve a purpose. However, we favor teacher-made tests that are taken from the books, songs, poetry, and other text forms used in the classroom. Note that the tests should always follow the same format as any teacher modeling examples presented to the student(s) to ensure transfer of learning. For instance, suppose that a teacher has chosen to use a cloze passage drawn from an old favorite classroom book such as *The Napping House* (Wood, 1984) to teach how context clues may be used to choose appropriate rhyming words. The teacher-made test developed to assess an individual student's understanding of this skill should then be in the form of a cloze passage (as opposed to a multiple-choice test).

Writing Samples—Reading and writing are reciprocal processes (Reutzel & Cooter, 1996), that is, as one skill is developed it tends to help the student to

Figure 2.7   Diffily's Literacy Development Checklist

Literacy Development Checklist

Student's Name: _____   Date: _____

	Seldom				Often
Chooses books for personal enjoyment	1	2	3	4	5
Knows print/picture difference	1	2	3	4	5
Knows print is read from left to right	1	2	3	4	5
Asks to be read to	1	2	3	4	5
Asks that story be read again	1	2	3	4	5
Listens attentively during story time	1	2	3	4	5
Knows what a title is	1	2	3	4	5
Knows what an author is	1	2	3	4	5
Knows what an illustrator is	1	2	3	4	5
In retellings, repeats 2+ details	1	2	3	4	5
Tells beginning, middle, end	1	2	3	4	5
Can read logos	1	2	3	4	5
Uses text in functional ways	1	2	3	4	5
"Reads" familiar books to self/others	1	2	3	4	5
Can read personal words	1	2	3	4	5
Can read sight words from books	1	2	3	4	5
Willing to "write"	1	2	3	4	5
Willing to "read" personal story	1	2	3	4	5
Willing to dictate story to adult	1	2	3	4	5

Note: Gratefully used by the authors with the permission of Deborah Diffily, Ph.D., Texas Wesleyan University.

develop the other. Writing is often a marvelous window for viewing students' understanding of phonics elements, use of context clues, and story elements, for example. Later in this book we directly address reading and writing connections and ways that writing samples can be used to assess reading development.

CHAPTER SUMMARY

In this chapter we surveyed what we consider to be the basic elements of reading portfolios. Certainly, much can be learned about students' reading development through collecting and studying classroom evidence such as students' literature response activities, writing products, phonemic awareness activities (in the early grades), and much more. And, although reading skills related to decoding and comprehension are key, we also wish to know about student reading interests, reading behaviors at home, and standardized data that help us understand how the child's reading skill compares to others. In chapter 3, running records and retellings—typical components of many portfolio systems—are discussed in detail. Indeed, building comprehensive reading portfolios and planning for instruction are examined throughout our book. So, having begun by considering the value and content of the portfolio in a balanced reading program, continue reading to discover more helpful strategies that you can use in your own classroom setting.

REFERENCES

Arter, J., & Spandel, V. (1992, Spring). Using portfolios of student work in instruction and assessment. *Educational Measurement: Issues and Practice, 34*–44.

Barr, R., & Johnson, B. (1997). *Teaching reading and writing in elementary classrooms* (2nd ed.). New York: Longman.

Beck, I. L., Omanson, R. C., & McKeown, M. G. (1982). An instructional redesign of reading lessons: Effects on comprehension. *Reading Research Quarterly, 17,* 462–481.

Bintz, W. P. (1991). Staying connected—Exploring new functions for assessment. *Contemporary Education, 62*(4), 307–312.

Cambourne, B., & Turbill, J. (1990). Assessment in whole language classrooms: Theory into practice. *Elementary School Journal, 90,* 337–349.

Cochrane, O., Cochrane, D., Scalena, D., & Buchanan, E. (1984). *Reading, writing and caring.* New York: Richard C. Owen Publishers, Inc.

Cooter, R. B., Jr., & Griffith, R. (1989). Thematic units for middle school: An honorable seduction. *Journal of Reading, 32*(8), 676–681.

Cooter, R. B., Jr., & Flynt, E. S. (1996). *Teaching reading in the content areas: Developing content literacy for all students.* Columbus, OH: Merrill, an imprint of Prentice Hall.

Diffily, D. (1994, April). *Portfolio assessment in early literacy settings.* Paper presented in a Professional Development Schools workshop at Texas Christian University, Fort Worth, TX.

Farr, R. (1991). *Portfolios: Assessment in the language arts.* ED334603.

Farr, R., & Tone, B. (1994). *Portfolio and performance assessment.* Fort Worth, TX: Harcourt Brace College Publishers.

Gambrell, L. B., Pfeiffer, W., & Wilson, R. (1985). The effects of retelling upon reading comprehension and recall of text information. *Journal of Educational Research, 78,* 216–220.

Jongsma, K. S. (1989). Questions & answers: Portfolio assessment. *The Reading Teacher, 43*(3), 264–265.

Lewis, C. S. (1961). *The lion, the witch, and the wardrobe.* New York: Macmillan Publishing Company.

Mathewson, G. (1985). Toward a comprehensive model of affect in the reading process. In H. Singer & R. B. Ruddell (Eds.), *Theoretical models and processes of reading* (3rd ed.) (pp. 841–856). Newark, DE: International Reading Association.

Morrow, L. M. (1985). Retelling stories: A strategy for improving children's comprehension, concept of story structure and oral language complexity. *Elementary School Journal, 85,* 647–661.

Reutzel, D. R., & Cooter, R. B., Jr., (1996). *Teaching children to read: From basals to books.* Columbus, OH: Merrill, an imprint of Prentice Hall.

Routman, R. (1988). *Transitions: From literature to literacy.* Portsmouth, NH: Heinemann Educational Books, Inc.

Sizer, T. (1994). *Reinventing our schools.* Bloomington, IN: Phi Delta Kappa.

Spencer, K. M. (1998). *Portfolio assessment in the special education classroom.* Unpublished manuscript, Texas Christian University.

Sulzby, E. (1985). Children's emergent reading of favorite storybooks: A developmental study. *Reading Research Quarterly, 20*(4), 458–481.

Tierney, R. J. (1992). Setting a new agenda for assessment. *Learning, 21*(2), 61–64.

Valencia, S. (1990). A portfolio approach to classroom reading assessment: The whys, whats, and hows. *The Reading Teacher, 43*(4), 338–340.

Webb, K., & Willoughby, N. (1993). An analytic rubric for scoring graphs. *The Texas School Teacher, 22*(3), 14–15.

Wiener, R. B., & Cohen, J. H. (1997). *Literacy portfolios: Using assessment to guide instruction.* Columbus, OH: Merrill, an imprint of Prentice Hall.

Wood, A. (1984). *The napping house.*

Chapter 3

Portfolio Assessment in a Balanced Reading Program: Part II
Running Records and Retellings

The principal purpose of reading assessment is to inform the teacher as to the instructional needs of his students. Reading assessment usually focuses on several key areas: knowledge of print concepts, decoding and word recognition ability, comprehension strategies, affect (interest, attitude, motivation), metacognitive factors (self-monitoring of one's comprehension), and conative factors (perseverance, persistence). Just which of these reading skill areas a teacher will focus on in first assessments depends on where the student appears to be in his general reading development, a decision based on classroom observations. For instance, a typical child in first grade will likely show signs of developing an awareness of print concepts, decoding strategies, and basic comprehension strategies for understanding stories. Thus, first-grade assessment programs usually begin in one or more of these areas.

In the early development of readers, teachers often focus on two very basic areas in their assessments: *decoding,* or the translation of letters and words into language, and *comprehension* of what has been read. An assessment procedure frequently used to measure decoding skill is the **running record** (Clay, 1993; Wiener & Cohen, 1997). To assess comprehension of story elements, such as setting, characters, problem, and solution, many teachers now prefer to use **retellings** (Tompkins, 1997). In this chapter we present the most current methods and ideas regarding the use of running records and retellings as important components in a teacher's reading assessment arsenal.

BACKGROUND BRIEFING FOR TEACHERS: WHAT ARE RUNNING RECORDS?

From the earliest days of formal reading instruction and research, the ability to decode words in print has been viewed as essential. In 1915, for example, William S. Gray published the *Standardized Oral Reading Paragraphs* for grades 1 through 8 which focused on oral reading errors and reading speed exclusively. In the 1930s and 1940s, Durrell (1940) and Betts (1946) discussed at length the value of studying oral reading errors as a way to inform reading instruction. These and other writings began the development of what we now refer to as informal reading inventories (IRI), in which oral reading errors are analyzed.

Half a century after Gray's test was released, Marie Clay (1966) began publishing landmark research detailing a systematic analysis of oral reading errors of emergent readers. The examination and interpretation of the relative "value" of oral reading errors (i.e., semantic and syntactic "acceptability") by Clay helped usher in a new age of understanding of decoding processes. A year later, it appears that Y. Goodman (1967) and other researchers mirrored Clay's thinking by employing careful studies of oral reading errors, or "miscue analysis," to better understand decoding patterns of emergent readers.

In the 1970s, Y. Goodman and Burke (1972), in an assessment manual called the *Reading Miscue Inventory* (RMI), and Clay (1972), in her manual called *The Early Detection of Reading Difficulties,* sought to formalize methodology for teachers who wish to focus on decoding assessment. Because of its complexity and impractical nature for classroom use, the *RMI* never really gained much acceptance beyond university research settings, although its theoretical base was widely heralded among reading education scholars. Of the two methodologies, Clay's "running records" for analyzing oral reading errors proved to be the more functional for most classroom teachers because of time and other real-world constraints. In the next section we describe in detail how running records are constructed and used to inform classroom teaching.

ASSESSING DECODING ABILITIES USING RUNNING RECORDS

Marie Clay (1972, 1985, 1993), a New Zealand educator and a former president of the International Reading Association, described the running record as an informal assessment procedure with high reliability (.90 on error reliabilities) that can inform teachers regarding a student's decoding development. The procedure is not difficult, but it does requires practice. Clay estimates that it takes about two hours of practice for teachers to become relatively proficient at running records. In essence, the teacher notes everything the student says or does while reading, including *all* the correct words read orally and *all* miscues (Wiener & Cohen, 1997). Clay recommends that three running records be obtained for each child on various levels of difficulty for initial reading assessment. Her criteria for oral reading evaluation are based on words correctly read aloud:

an easy (independent) text	95–100% correct
an instructional text	90–94% correct
a hard (frustration) text	80–89% correct

Books that children are presently reading tend to fall at the instructional or easy/independent levels. Running records are taken without having to mark a prepared script and may be recorded on a sheet of paper, requiring about 10 minutes to transcribe. Guidelines for administration follow:

1. A sample from the book(s) to be used is needed that is 100-200 words in length. For early readers, the text may fall below 100 words.

2. Complete a record for each page of the books. Make "tick" marks on a sheet of blank paper for each word said correctly. Errors should be described fully.

Figure 3.1 shows an example of one running record taken from an early readers book called *Martha Speaks* (Meddaugh, 1992, pp. 1–4). Following Figure 3.1 is an explanation of the basic miscue patterns shown.

Examples of errors (or miscues) in the oral reading sample shown in Figure 3.1 and the codes for these errors follow (based on Clay, 1985):

1. *Word call errors.* The child says a word that is different from the text in the book. Write the incorrect response(s), with the correct text under it.
   Child: *understood*
   Text: unusual

2. *Attempted decoding.* The child tries several times to say a word. Record each attempt, with the correct text under the trials.
   Child: *l . . . let . . . letters*
   Text: letters

3. *Self-correction.* The child corrects an error himself. Self-corrections are noted by writing SC.
   SC
   Child: *brin . . . brain*
   Text: brain

Figure 3.1 Example of a Running Record Using *Martha Speaks* (Meddaugh, 1992)

The day Helen gave Martha dog her alphabet soup,

understood
something ~~unusual~~ happened.

l . . . let . . . letters   *brin . . . brain*
The ~~letters~~ in the soup went up to Martha's brain

in
instead of down^ to her stomach.

That evening, Martha spoke.

"<u>Isn't it</u> time for my dinner?"

TA
Martha's family had many questions to ask her.

Of course, she had a lot to tell them!

4. If no word is given, then the error is noted with a dash —.
5. *Insertions.* The child adds a word that is *not* in the text. An insertion symbol (^) is recorded between the two appropriate ticks (words) and the inserted word is written above the insertion symbol.
   Child: *in*
   Text: instead of down ^ to her stomach.
6. *Teacher-assistance.* The child is "stuck" on a word he cannot call and the teacher pronounces the word. Record as TA (teacher-assisted).
   Child: TA
   Text: questions
7. *Repetition.* Sometimes children will repeat words or phrases. These repetitions are not scored as an error, but may be noted by drawing a line under the word(s) repeated.
   Child: <u>Isn't it</u> . . . *Isn't it time for my dinner?*
   Text: "Isn't it time for my dinner?"

By noting the percentage of miscues and by looking for repeating patterns, teachers can deduce how reading development is progressing for each child and which minilessons should be offered. However, this deduction process can be somewhat complicated and time consuming.

THE "MISCUE GRID": A FURTHER REFINEMENT OF THE RUNNING RECORD PROCESS FOR MISCUE ANALYSIS

As useful as the running record can be for teachers in planning instruction, many feel that the time required for administering and analyzing running records can be prohibitive in public school classes of 25 or more students. To make the process go more quickly and reliably, Flynt and Cooter (1996, 1998) developed a simplified process for completing running records that makes them more practical for classroom use. In their assessment instrument, *The Flynt/Cooter Reading Inventory for the Classroom,* teachers learn how to follow along during oral reading, noting miscues on a specially prepared protocol form called the Miscue Grid. They then complete the process by noting in a type of table or grid the kind of miscues that were made. By totaling the number of oral reading errors in each miscue category (i.e., word call errors, attempted decoding, etc.), the teacher is able to quickly determine "miscue patterns" and to plan instruction accordingly. Field-tested with hundreds of Title I reading teachers, the Miscue Grid has proven to be an extremely effective classroom tool. Figure 3.2 is an example of a completed Flynt/Cooter (1998) Miscue Grid for a student named Grace, again using *Martha Speaks* (Meddaugh, 1992) as the text.

TRANSLATING RUNNING RECORD INFORMATION INTO CLASSROOM INTERVENTION: AN EXAMPLE

In the example shown in Figure 3.2, we note that Grace has some difficulty with the text sample from *Martha Speaks.* Note that for each miscue, a tick mark is recorded under the appropriate column heading, classifying each miscue as a word call error, repetition, or other mistake. After all miscues have been studied and their

Figure 3.2 Grace's Running Record Miscue Grid* Using *Martha Speaks* (Meddaugh, 1992)

	Word call error	Attempt decode	Self-correct	Insertions	No word given	Teacher assist	Repetition
The day Helen gave Martha dog her							
understood alphabet soup, something ~~unusual~~	I						
I . . . let . . . letters happened. The ~~letters~~ in the soup went		I					
brin . . . brain SC *in* up to Martha's ~~brain~~ instead of down^			I	I			
to her stomach. That evening, Martha							
spoke. "Isn't it time for my dinner?"							I
TA Martha's family had many questions to						I	
ask her. Of course, she had a lot to							
tell them. "Have you always understood							I
are what we were saying?" "You bet! Do	I						
Betty you want to know what Benjie is really	I						
saying?" "Why don't you come when we							
always call?" "You people are^ so bossy. Come!				I			
Sit! Stay! You never say please."							
"Do dogs dream?" "Day and night. (100 wrds)							
This morning I dreamed I was chasing							
a giant meatloaf!"							
TOTALS	3	1	1	2	0	1	2

*Based on Flynt, E. S., & Cooter, R. B. (1998). *The Flynt/Cooter Reading Inventory for the Classroom,* 3rd edition. Columbus, OH: Merrill/Prentice Hall. Used with permission of the authors.

category identified, the tick marks in each column are totaled. This process reveals that with this passage, most of Grace's miscues are word call errors (3), insertions (2), and repetitions (2). With a total of 10 miscues of 100 words read (note that we do not count any miscues after the 100th word), simple subtraction tells us that Grace read with 90% accuracy, placing her within the "instructional" reading level according to Clay's system mentioned earlier. However, *conclusions should not be drawn from only one running record.* As already noted, a minimum of three running records should be taken and comparisons made across all three to determine whether a pattern of reading behavior exists.

If, in Grace's case, there seem to be consistent patterns of miscues as seen in the *Martha Speaks* selection, then the teacher may reasonably conclude that some sort of classroom intervention may be needed (usually in the form of minilessons). For the sake of efficiency, most teachers form short-term groups for children having the same needs (to help with insertion miscues, for example). Running records, when applied using the Flynt-Cooter (1998) grid system, can be a most informative addition to one's reading assessment program.

ASSESSING STORY COMPREHENSION THROUGH RETELLINGS

Retellings, the second common element of elementary classroom reading portfolios, are one of the best and most efficient strategies for finding out whether a child understands what he has read (Gambrell, Pfeiffer, & Wilson, 1985; Morrow, 1985), especially when compared to the seemingly endless and tedious question/answer sessions that so often characterize basal readers and their workbook pages (what we like to call the "Reading Inquisition"). Teachers who routinely use retellings for comprehension assessment find that they can monitor student progress effectively and thoroughly, and can do so in a fraction of the time required by traditional methods.

There are usually two phases in conducting a retelling with elementary students: *unaided recall* and *aided recall.* In the first phase, **unaided recall**, students simply retell the story they have just completed without being questioned by the teacher concerning specific details. (Note: This is a story that the students have already self-selected and read independently. It is also a different selection than the one[s] chosen for the running record[s].) While each student retells the story, the teacher notes important information that has been retold, such as characters, setting, central problem or challenge, conclusion, and theme/moral. It is critical that the teacher keep careful notes in student retellings. Thus, a **story grammar retelling sheet** like the one shown in Figure 3.3 can be most helpful to teachers. Of course, a teacher is not limited to using a specific format for making notes, but it is essential that careful and thorough notes be made for each retelling.

We have found that after students conclude the unaided recall portion of the retelling, it is often helpful to ask "What else can you remember about the story?" Students will often eagerly offer more information. You can usually use this "What else . . ." strategy each time the student seems to be finished for as many as three times before exhausting the student's ability to recall information in the *unaided recall* segment.

Figure 3.3   Story Grammar Retelling Record Sheet

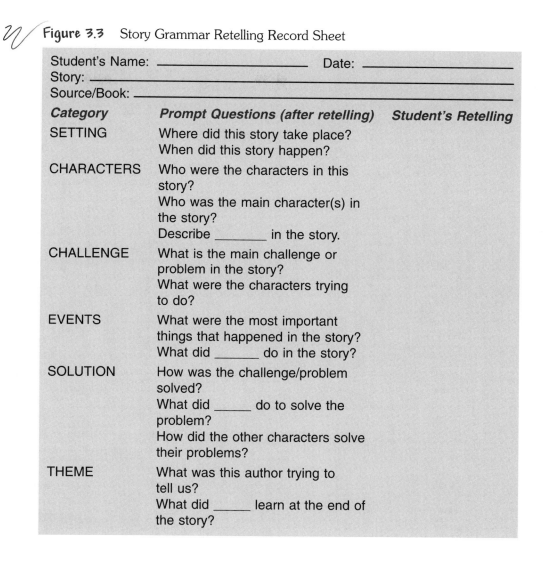

Category	Prompt Questions (after retelling)	Student's Retelling
SETTING	Where did this story take place? When did this story happen?	
CHARACTERS	Who were the characters in this story? Who was the main character(s) in the story? Describe _____ in the story.	
CHALLENGE	What is the main challenge or problem in the story? What were the characters trying to do?	
EVENTS	What were the most important things that happened in the story? What did _____ do in the story?	
SOLUTION	How was the challenge/problem solved? What did _____ do to solve the problem? How did the other characters solve their problems?	
THEME	What was this author trying to tell us? What did _____ learn at the end of the story?	

Student's Name: _____   Date: _____
Story: _____
Source/Book: _____

Once the student has seemingly recalled all the information he can without assistance, the assessment progresses to the second phase, **aided recall**. This is the act of questioning students about story grammar elements that were not recounted during the unaided recall portion of retellings. When using the story grammar retelling record sheet, it is relatively simple for the teacher to quickly survey the sheet for missing information, then use the generic questions provided to evoke further story memories by the student. For example, if a student retold most of the story during unaided recall, but neglected to describe the setting, the teacher might use the first question under SETTING (see Figure 3.3) on the Retelling Record Sheet, asking "Where did this story take place?" As in the first phase with unaided recall, the teacher records all memories the student has of the story and notes any story elements the student is unable to recall. If it appears that the student is consistently unable to remember certain story elements, then a minilesson should be offered to help him learn appropriate comprehension strategies.

ASSESSMENT OF NONFICTION EXPOSITORY TEXTS THROUGH RETELLINGS

Several years ago we began looking for new ways to assess students' understanding of nonfiction or **expository,** readings. Having experienced a great deal of success using story retellings, we wondered if it might be possible to use some form of retellings to assess students' understanding of specific content area information such as science, social studies, and mathematics; but there were several problems with attempting to make this sort of adaptation of retellings. First, there did not seem to exist a single "grammar" or basic structure for content texts (as there is for stories). For example, when students are retelling stories, or *narrative* texts, it is possible to listen for such elements as setting, characters, central problem of challenge, attempts to solve the problem, and a conclusion. In content texts, however, this sort of regular structure doesn't exist, or at least not to the same extent. The second problem was the related issue of whether students could actually retell expository information. This process seemed awkward to us, but probably not impossible. Finally, a rubric or system for questioning students, such as the Retelling Record Sheet mentioned above for story retellings, was not currently available. Despite these problems, our successful experiences with story retellings caused us to continue looking for possible ways to better assess students' comprehension of content selections.

We have concluded that a form of retelling *is* possible for assessing content texts, but it does require a bit more preparation than story retellings. Teachers must account for two things in the assessment: 1) the actual *content* of the passage, and 2) the student's ability to use *content reading strategies* to understand different organization patterns used by authors (such as cause/effect). To assess students in these two areas, teachers must analyze the text(s) carefully for the reading conference. A discussion of some specific suggestions for performing this analysis follows.

Analyzing Text Content

The purpose of a content analysis is to help teachers identify important facts, concepts, and generalizations presented in a given unit of study. This information can be used to monitor student comprehension during the retelling phase. *Facts,* of course, are individual bits of information, or details, presented in a unit under study. For example, in a science unit dealing with the solar system of which Earth is a part, some of the facts to be learned might include atmosphere, satellite, and planet. For a history unit pertaining to the Civil Rights movement, important facts might include the contribution of Rosa Parks, *Brown v. Board of Education,* and the march on Washington.

Concepts are categories or "bundles" of information into which we group facts (Martorella, 1985). In the previous example of a science unit about the solar system, the facts of satellite and planet could be grouped into a single concept called "objects orbiting the sun." Concepts usually are stated in a simply worded phrase that captures the main idea.

A *generalization,* on the other hand, is a principle or conclusion that applies to the entire class or sample being examined (Harris & Hodges, 1981). For our purposes, one or more generalization is teacher generated, written in the language of the students, and expressed in one or more complete sentences. Generalizations organize and summarize a large amount of information—often an entire unit. Two examples of generalizations follow:

The Civil Rights movement sought to gain equal rights for all Americans.
Our solar system is made up of many different bodies and phenomena.

Once facts, concepts, and generalizations have been identified, they can be used to organize a schema for recording retelling information and for asking questions to follow up on information not mentioned during the student's retelling.

Identifying Organizational Schemes Used in Expository Texts

In addition to the basic facts, concepts, and generalizations included in a selection, the student's understanding of the overall structure or organization that is used to present information in expository texts is an important comprehension factor. Narrative texts use a story grammar scheme of organization, which includes the elements of setting, theme, characterization, plot, and resolution. Expository texts, however, are quite different in their organization schemes. The structure of an expository text tends to be much more compact, detailed, and explanatory (Heilman, Blair, & Rupley, 1990).

Similar to the story grammar research for the narrative text, five common expository text structures have been described by Meyer and Freedle (1984): *description, collection, causation, problem/solution,* and *comparison.* These five expository text patterns of organization are described along with examples taken from content textbooks:

- *Description.* Explains something about a topic or presents a characteristic or setting for a topic.

  Decimals are another way to write fractions when the denominators are 10, 100, and so on. (From *Merrill Mathematics* [Grade 5], 1985, p. 247.)

- *Collection.* A number of descriptions (specifics, characteristics, or settings) presented together.

  ### Water Habitats

  Freshwater habitats are found in ponds, bogs, swamps, lakes, and rivers. Each freshwater habitat has special kinds of plants and animals that live there. Some plants and animals live in waters that are very cold. Others live in waters that are warm. Some plants and animals adapt to waters that flow fast. Others adapt to still water. (From *Merrill Science* [Grade 3], 1989, p. 226)

- **Causation.** Elements grouped according to time sequence with a cause-effect relationship specified.

America Enters the War

On Sunday, December 7, 1941, World War II came to the United States. At 7:55 A.M. Japanese warplanes swooped through the clouds above <u>Pearl Harbor</u>. Pearl Harbor was the American naval base in the Hawaiian Islands. A deadly load of bombs was dropped on the American ships and airfield. It was a day, Roosevelt said, that would "live in infamy." *Infamy* (IN_fuh_mee) means remembered for being evil.

The United States had been attacked. That meant war. (From *The United States: Its History and Neighbors* [Grade 5], Harcourt Brace Jovanovich, 1985, p. 493.)

- **Problem/Solution.** Includes a relationship (between a problem and its possible cause[s]) and a set of solution possibilities, one of which can break the link between the problem and its cause.

Agreement by Compromise (Events That Led to the Civil War)

For a while there was an equal number of Southern and Northern states. That meant that there were just as many Senators in Congress from slave states as from free states. Neither had more votes in the Senate, so they usually reached agreement on new laws by compromise. (From *The United States and the Other Americas* [Grade 5], Macmillan, 1980, p. 190.)

- **Comparison.** Organizes factors on the basis of differences and similarities. Comparison does not contain elements of sequence or causality.

Segregation

Segregation laws said that blacks had to live separate, or apart, from whites. Like whites, during segregation blacks had their own parks, hospitals, and swimming pools. Theaters, buses, and trains were segregated.

Many people said that the segregation laws were unfair. But in 1896, the Supreme Court ruled segregation legal if the separate facilities for blacks were equal to those for whites. "Separate but equal" became the law in many parts of the country.

But separate was not equal . . . . One of the most serious problems was education. Black parents felt that their children were not receiving an equal education in segregated schools. Sometimes the segregated schools had teachers who were not as well educated as teachers in the white schools. Textbooks were often very old and out-of-date, if they had any books at all. But in many of the white schools the books were the newest ones. Without a good education, the blacks argued, their children would not be able to get good jobs as adults.

Finally in 1954, the Supreme Court changed the law. (Adapted from *The American People* [Grade 6], American Book Company, 1982, p. 364.)

In Table 3.1, we contrast the common elements of narrative and expository texts.

Thus, in assessing students' understanding of expository texts, one task for teachers is to devise retelling procedures that assess the information—facts, concepts, and generalizations—found in the text to be read. In addition, the teacher must assess the student's ability to comprehend the different forms of writing—

Table 3.1   Elements of Narrative and Expository Texts In Contrast

Narrative Text Elements	Expository Text Elements
Setting	Description
Characters	Collection
Problem(s)	Causation
Attempts to Resolve Problem(s)	Problem/Solution
Resolution	Comparison
Theme/Moral	

description, collection, causation, problem/solution, and comparison—used by the textbook authors. In the next section we bring it all together with a classroom-proven format for expository retelling.

A Procedure for Conducting and Analyzing Expository Text Retellings

Cooter and Cooter (1998) have learned that the same basic process that teachers use to assess student comprehension in narrative texts using story retellings can be applied to assessing comprehension of expository texts. Building on the earlier work of Flynt and Cooter (1996), they have identified a six-step process for determining the following: how well students generally comprehend expository texts; types of expository writing techniques that may be confusing a student; and how this information can be used to plan instruction. Here is the process:

Step 1:   Conduct a content analysis of the text to be read as described earlier in this chapter. Outline the *facts, concepts,* and *generalizations* contained therein.

Step 2:   Identify the types of expository writing techniques used in presenting the information in Step 1 (i.e., *collection, description, causation, problem/solution, comparison).*

Step 3:   Integrate the information you learned in Steps 1 and 2 so that you can tell not only *what* is being presented in the text, but also *how* it is being presented. Table 3.2 is an example of this process using a passage about how microwave ovens work (Flynt & Cooter, 1998).

Step 4:   Create a "passage retelling form" based on the information you determined in the earlier steps. This will be used to mark off information recalled during the retelling phase, and will also serve as a prompt for comprehension checking after the retelling is complete. In Figure 3.4 we offer a passage retelling form example adapted from the Flynt and Cooter (1998) passage concerning how a microwave oven works.

Step 5:   Have the student silently read the expository passage you have selected. Then, ask him to retell everything that he can remember about

Table 3.2   Content Analysis/Expository Text Type Analysis (Microwave oven passage)

Content Analysis	Expository Text Type Used in the Passage
1. Magnetron tube invention made microwave ovens possible. (fact)	Causation
2. Magnetron tubes were first used for radar. (fact)	Description
3. Dr. Percy Spencer discovered that the magnetron tube could heat food from the inside out. (fact)	Description
4. "Radar range" was the name of the first microwave oven. (fact)	Description
5. Modern microwave ovens are less expensive, smaller, have more features and power. (facts)	Comparison
6. Some consider microwaves to be the most significant invention for cooking since fire was discovered. (generalization)	Causation
7. Microwave ovens use electromagnetic energy to function. (fact)	Description
8. Features found on most microwave ovens include defrost, reheat, and constant temperature cooking. (fact)	Description

the passage without any prompting from you (unaided recall). Record all his responses on the retelling form you created for this passage. When the student seems to have told you all that he can recall about the passage, then ask questions relating to any information that the student did not include from the passage during the unaided recall/retelling. Record these responses as well.

Step 6:   Analyze the retelling form for information not recalled. This will help you to understand the kinds of information the student did not recall (facts, concepts, and/or generalizations). Also, examine any types of expository writing patterns that he may have had trouble comprehending (comparison, problem/solution, causation, etc.). This process is what Cooter and Cooter (1998) refer to as *Miscomprehension Analysis*. Once the analysis is completed, instruction targeting these problems can be planned accordingly.

When conducting an assessment activity like the one presented above, it is important to remember that conclusions should not be drawn from retelling just one passage. Rather, the teacher must always be looking for a *pattern* of behavior over time before drawing any conclusions about a student's needs.

Figure 3.4   Expository Passage Retelling Form (Microwave oven passage)

James Bowie Middle School

Ms. K. Spencer's 5th Grade

Student's Name: _____   Date: _____

Passage: *Cooking Without Fire* (Level 6)

Prompt Questions (after retelling)   *Student's Retelling*

(Expository Text Structure Element)

_____   1. What invention led to the development of   (causation)
             the microwave oven?
             (magnetron tube)

_____   2. What was the magnetron tube first used   (description)
             for?
             (radar)

_____   3. What did Dr. Percy Spencer discover   (description)
             about the magnetron tube?
             (it could heat food from the inside out)

_____   4. What was the name given to the first   (description)
             microwave oven?
             (radar range)

_____   5. Name two ways that today's microwave   (comparison)
             ovens differ from the first ones.
             (not as bulky, more features, more power,
             less expensive)

_____   6. Explain why some people consider   (causation)
             microwave cooking the first new method
             of cooking since the discovery of fire.
             (it requires no fire or element of fire
             to cook food)

_____   7. What type of energy is used by the   (description)
             microwave to cook food?
             (electromagnetic)

_____   8. What are two features found on most   (description)
             microwave ovens, according to the
             passage?
             (defrost, reheat, constant temperature
             cooking)

CHAPTER SUMMARY

In this chapter we took a brief look at two basic elements of reading portfolios: running records and retellings. Running records help teachers to gain insights into decoding strategies used by readers when they come across an unfamiliar word in print. Decoding knowledge that may be assessed using the running record includes, but is limited to, context clues (both a decoding and a comprehension skill), beginning sounds in words, ending sounds, medial sounds, root words, affixes, onset and rime, consonant digraphs and blends, and various other phonics elements. Running records are often constructed using stories selected and preread by students themselves, thus capitalizing on student interests and background knowledge.

Retelling is another essential portfolio component that helps teachers monitor students' comprehension in narrative (story) texts. The retelling progresses from unaided recall, in which a student retells the story to the best of his ability without any prompting from the teacher, to aided recall, in which teachers ask specific questions about story grammar elements not already covered by the student in his initial retelling. A Retelling Record Sheet was offered in this chapter to help teachers monitor retellings. It also provides general questions that may be easily adapted to most stories during aided recall questioning.

Finally, we discussed how teachers can use a similar form of retelling to assess students' recall of nonfiction materials (expository texts). This process requires that teachers first conduct a content analysis of the materials to discover important facts, concepts, and generalizations that students may learn, and also the writing patterns (such as cause/effect) used by the author of the new material. A new process for assessing expository text comprehension, known as Miscomprehension Analysis (Cooter & Cooter, 1998), was demonstrated using a brief expository passage.

In summary, running records and retellings help teachers accomplish the main purposes of assessment: to learn where students are in their literacy development, and to help teachers tailor learning activities to each student's unique need.

REFERENCES

Betts, E. (1946). *Foundations of reading instruction.* New York: American Book.

Clay, M. (1966). *Emergent reading behaviour.* Unpublished doctoral dissertation, University of Auckland, New Zealand.

Clay, M. (1972). *The early detection of reading difficulties.* Portsmouth, NH: Heinemann.

Clay, M. (1985). *The early detection of reading difficulties* (3rd ed.). Portsmouth, NH: Heinemann.

Clay, M. (1993). *An observation survey of early literacy achievement.* Portsmouth, NH: Heinemann.

Cooter, R. B., & Cooter, K. S. (1998). *Miscomprehension analysis: A procedure for conducting and analyzing expository text retellings.* Unpublished research report.

Durrell, D. D. (1940). *Improvement of basic reading abilities.* New York: World Book.

Flynt, E. S., & Cooter, R. B. (1996). *The Flynt/Cooter reading inventory for the classroom,* (2nd ed.). Flagstaff, AZ: Gorsuch Scarisbrick Publishers.

Flynt, E. S., & Cooter, R. B. (1998). *The Flynt/Cooter reading inventory for the* classroom, (3rd ed.). Columbus, OH: Merrill/Prentice Hall.

Gambrell, L. B., Pfeiffer, W., & Wilson, R. (1985). The effects of retelling upon reading comprehension and recall of text information. *Journal of Educational Research, 78,* 216–220.

Goodman, Y. M. (1967). *A psycholinguistic description of observed oral reading phenomena in selected young beginning readers.* Unpublished doctoral dissertation, Wayne State University.

Goodman, Y. M., & Burke, C. L. (1972). *Reading miscue inventory manual: Procedures for diagnosis and evaluation.* New York: Macmillan.

Harris, T. L., & Hodges, R. E. (Eds.). (1981). *A dictionary of reading and related terms.* Newark, DE: International Reading Association.

Heilman, A. W., Blair, T. R., & Rupley, W. H. (1990). *Principles and practices of teaching reading.* Englewood Cliffs, NJ: Merrill/Prentice Hall.

Martorella, P. H. (1985). *Elementary social studies.* Boston: Little, Brown.

Meddaugh, S. (1992). *Martha speaks.* New York: Houghton Mifflin.

Meyer, B. J., & Freedle, R. O. (1984). Effects of discourse type on recall. *American Educational Research Journal, 21*(1), 121–143.

Morrow, L. M. (1985). Retelling stories: A strategy for improving children's comprehension, concept of story structure and oral language complexity. *Elementary School Journal, 85,* 647–661.

Tompkins, G. E. (1997). *Literacy for the 21st century.* Columbus, OH: Merrill, an imprint of Prentice Hall.

Wiener, R. B., & Cohen, J. H. (1997). *Literacy portfolios: Using assessment to guide instruction.* Columbus, OH: Merrill, an imprint of Prentice Hall.

Chapter 4

Cooperative and Collaborative Learning:
Assessing the Learning Opportunities

When school-aged children are asked what they enjoy about school, they typically respond, "being with my friends." Today's students live in an interactive and social world. Collaborative learning activities are acknowledged by educators as an excellent means for spurring achievement and learning. Current thinking about how students learn best in schools is a far cry from old models in which a "quiet classroom was an orderly classroom and a quiet classroom was where learning took place." From the time children enter kindergarten to the time they exit high school, they are learning about life, meeting human dilemmas, solving problems, and constructing knowledge with others in a social network. The importance of learning from and with peers is taking center stage in America's school and university classrooms (Slavin, 1995; Kagan, 1990b; Morrow & Sharkey, 1993; Stevens & Slavin, 1995; Swafford, 1995).

Cooperative learning strategies capitalize on the social nature of human learning (Slavin, 1994; Johnson & Johnson, 1994; Kagan, 1990). Stevens and Slavin (1995) and Palinscar, Parecki, and McPhail (1995) have found that students with diverse abilities and low motivation can be helped to become more successful learners by using cooperative learning approaches. Why is cooperative learning so important? What is it that causes students to learn and achieve more in social settings where interaction is not only permitted but encouraged? Johnson and Johnson (1994, pp. 31–34) suggest the following principles that relate to the importance of peer interaction as a means of increasing learning and motivation to learn:

1. In their interactions with peers, children and adolescents directly learn attitudes, values, skills, and information unobtainable from adults.

2. Interaction with peers provides support, opportunities, and models for "pro-social" behavior.

3. Peers provide models, directions, and reinforcements for learning to control impulses.

55

4. Children and adolescents learn to view situations and problems from per-spectives other than their own through their interaction with peers.

5. Relationships with other children and adolescents are powerful influences on the development of the values and the social sensitivity required for auton-omy.

6. Children need close and intimate relationships with peers with whom they can share their feelings, aspirations, dreams, joys, and pains.

7. It is through peer relationships that a frame of reference for perceiving one-self is developed.

8. Coalitions formed during childhood and adolescence provide help and assis-tance throughout adulthood.

9. The absence of any friendships during childhood and adolescence seems to increase the risk of mental disorder.

10. In both educational and work settings, peers have a strong influence on pro-ductivity.

11. Student educational aspirations may be shaped more by peers than by any other social influence.

This chapter suggests ways of helping readers and writers learn from and with their peers using cooperative learning strategies.

BACKGROUND BRIEFING FOR TEACHERS: THE VALUE OF COOPERATIVE LEARNING STRATEGIES

Research reviews published by Slavin (1995), Johnson and Johnson (1994), New-man and Thompson (1987), and Davidson (1985) conclude that cooperative learn-ing methods are an effective means for increasing students' standardized test scores between 6 and 10%. These effects are achieved with little or no cost, have other far-reaching and important effects on students' self-esteem, and impact on the acceptance of mainstreamed handicapped and special needs students (Slavin, 1995; Stevens & Slavin, 1995; Palinscar, Parecki, and McPhail, 1995).

Cooperative learning strategies promote acceptance and improved relations among students of differing races, linguistic, and cultural backgrounds (Hansell & Slavin, 1981). These students typically represent a group that has been particularly at risk for problems in learning to read and write. Johnson and Johnson (1981) and Stevens and Slavin (1995) found more acceptance of handicapped or special needs students when they were partners in a cooperative learning situation than when they were placed in an individualized learning context. Thus, research on cooperative learning and relations between special needs and normal progress stu-dents generally shows that cooperative learning strategies can overcome obstacles to building meaningful interaction among students (Slavin, 1995).

ESSENTIAL FEATURES OF EFFECTIVE COOPERATIVE LEARNING STRATEGIES

After reviewing more than 60 studies related to the effectiveness of cooperative learning, Slavin (1995) concluded that there is wide agreement that cooperative learning methods result in increased student achievement and motivation. In addition, Slavin (1990) identified three essential features of effective cooperative learning strategies. The first centers on the idea of *group goals.* Groups must work together to form a positive interdependence that assists in the achievement of common goals. Thus, individual success is dependent upon the group member's ability to work together toward the achievement of a common goal or the completion of a common task. A second essential feature of cooperative learning strategies is *individual accountability.* The group's success must depend upon the individual learning and effort of all group members. There are no "free rides" in effective cooperative learning groups. The final essential feature of successful cooperative learning groups is *equal opportunity for success.* According to Slavin (1990), this means students contribute to their groups by improving upon their own past performance. Hence, high, average, and low achievers are challenged to do their best and to value the contributions of everyone in the group.

TYPES OF COOPERATIVE LEARNING STRATEGIES BY PURPOSE

Kagan (1989; 1990a) describes several ways of organizing social interaction in the classroom according to purpose. If, for example, the purpose of the interaction is to build bonds among class members, then *class building or team building* structures can be used to accomplish this aim. Or, if strengthening communication among classmates or between student and teacher is the goal of the cooperative learning experience, then cooperative learning structures designed for *communication building* can be employed. In some instances teachers may seek to help students master specific skills, facts, or procedures. Here, teachers could select *mastery* cooperative learning structures to achieve these objectives.

Of particular use in reading and writing instruction, *concept development* cooperative learning structures may be selected to help learners grasp new, important, and difficult conceptual knowledge. When tasks are assigned to be completed by a cooperative learning team or group, one way of ensuring that students are held individually accountable for completing a task is to use *division of labor* cooperative learning structures. And, finally, projects undertaken by a group or team can be approached with *cooperative projects* structural approaches. Although teachers may design a wide range of activities that are typically content or academic content bound, cooperative learning structures may be used repeatedly with almost any subject matter, a wide range of grade levels, and at various points in any lesson plan (Kagan, 1989; 1990b).

In the next section we will examine various informal assessment tasks related to cooperative learning strategies. Each assessment task is somewhat general and focuses on either group processes or individual accountability within the group.

ASSESSING COOPERATIVE LEARNING PROCESSES AND PRODUCTS

SELF-ASSESSMENT: INDIVIDUAL AND GROUP ACCOUNTABILITY

Purpose

The purpose of self-assessment centers on developing each student's ability to judge the quality of her own contributions to a cooperative team effort (Johnson & Johnson, 1991; Ellis & Whalen, 1990). Students of any age and ability can engage in self-assessment. This is important to cooperative learning because it helps students take responsibility for their own behavior and learning.

Materials

Examples of group and individual assessment forms are shown in Figures 4.1 and 4.2. These, or modified forms, can be duplicated and distributed to teams or individuals to be completed at the conclusion of daily cooperative group activities.

Figure 4.1   Group Self-Assessment

Group: _____   Date: _____

Today:

1. **We offered our ideas to each other.**
   Usually _____ Sometimes _____ Seldom _____

2. **We listened carefully to each other.**
   Usually _____ Sometimes _____ Seldom _____

3. **We offered encouragement to each other.**
   Usually _____ Sometimes _____ Seldom _____

4. **We helped each other with building ideas or solving problems.**
   Usually _____ Sometimes _____ Seldom _____

5. **We completed the assigned tasks well.**
   Usually _____ Sometimes _____ Seldom _____

Signatures

_____   _____

_____   _____

_____   _____

Figure 4.2   Individual Self-Assessment

Name: _____   Date: _____

Today:

1. **I offered my ideas.**
   Usually _____ Sometimes _____ Seldom_____

2. **I listened carefully to others.**
   Usually _____ Sometimes _____ Seldom_____

3. **I offered encouragement to others.**
   Usually _____ Sometimes _____ Seldom_____

4. **I helped others with building ideas or solving problems.**
   Usually _____ Sometimes _____ Seldom_____

5. **I completed the assigned tasks well.**
   Usually _____ Sometimes _____ Seldom_____

Signatures

_____   _____

_____   _____

_____   _____

Procedures

For group assessment, students can independently complete the form shown in Figure 4.1. Then, they can be encouraged to share their responses with the group and to compare with their teammates their perceptions of the group's functioning. At the conclusion of the discussion, the group then fills out a single form representing the consensus of the group. Teammates with dissenting opinions should be given space at the bottom of the form in which to express their differences from the group.

For individual assessment, a student simply completes the form shown in Figure 4.2 independently and places it in her self-assessment file. Teachers can create a file on each student to keep a running account of how that individual rates her own learning and involvement.

TEACHER OBSERVATION: GROUP PROCESSES MATRIX

Purpose

The purpose of group process assessment is to determine how individual students are learning from others and participating in team or group activities. One way to organize assessment of this type is to use a matrix approach such as those suggested

Figure 4.3 Group Processes Matrix

Name of Book or Basal Story: _____

Instructional Goal: _____

Date: _____

Student Names	Makes Predictions	Uses Background Knowledge	Participates in Discussion	Gets the Main Idea	Uses Story Vocabulary	Asks Questions	Answers Questions	Can Retell Story Episodes	Can Retell Entire Story in Sequence	Makes Inferences	Makes Personal Connections
Mario	✓	○	—	✓	✓	✓	✓	—	✓	○	✓
Ethan	—	✓	✓	○	✓	○	✓	✓	○	✓	—
Maria	○	✓	✓	✓	—	○	○	—	✓	✓	○
Reggie	✓	✓	○	✓	○	✓	○	✓	○	—	○
James	✓	○	—	✓	✓	—	○	✓	○	—	✓
Patty	○	○	—	✓	○	—	○		✓	—	○
Chauna	✓	○	—	✓	✓		✓	✓	○	—	○
Michelle	○	○	✓	✓	○	—	○	✓	✓	✓	—

Key: ○ — Usually

✓ — Sometimes

— — Seldom

by Wood (1988) and Paradis and others (1991). By examining the matrix, a teacher can determine when, how, and where the team or group failed to function effectively. By reviewing a particular row, the teacher can determine when, how, and where individual students were effective in their participation and learning.

Materials

A matrix similar to the one shown in Figure 4.3 can be used to assess individual student learning and performance in a group or team cooperative learning situation. The matrix shown is only an example and would be modified to include any subject area, skills, or tasks to be completed.

Procedures

To begin, you will need a videotape or audiotape recorder to record the discussion of the literature books, big books, or basal stories read. This type of group assessment is best used with small groups of between 5 and 8 children. At a later time, preferably after school, replay the tape/video recording. Make a record of each student's participation using the matrix. Careful record keeping and periodic analysis using this type of group process assessment matrix will reveal individual and group strengths and weaknesses. For example, students may never discuss inferences to be made from the story, or some students may not participate at all. Records made from these observations may indicate that future discussions should center on modeling a "think aloud" process to make inferences, or indicate a need to involve specific children to a greater degree. Such records allow teachers to document progress in a group as well as for an individual. Furthermore, this process provides an audit trail for administrators to know what and how you have been teaching.

TEAMMATE FEEDBACK: INDIVIDUAL ACCOUNTABILITY

Purpose

Sometimes it is important for students to see their own learning and participation through the eyes of teammates. For some students, such a process is not only a reality check, but also an opportunity to interact in positive ways to support and extend individuals within the group. By engaging in peer feedback and accountability, cooperative learning teams and individuals create and maintain a spirit of healthy interdependence (Johnson & Johnson, 1991).

Materials

An example of a teammate individual feedback form is shown in Figure 4.4. These, or modified versions, can be duplicated and distributed to teams to be completed at the conclusion of daily cooperative group activities.

Procedures

The Partner or Teammate Feedback Form shown in Figure 4.4 is given on a periodic (usually weekly) basis to students within a group or partnership. The form is to be completed on another individual. Next, partners or teammates share their com-

Figure 4.4   Partner or Teammate Feedback Form

Partner or Teammate Name: _____

Evaluator Name: _____

1. My partner or teammate offers facts, opinions, or ideas to help the group discussion.

   Usually   Frequently   Seldom   Never

2. My partner or teammate expresses a willingness to cooperate with other group members.

   Usually   Frequently   Seldom   Never

3. My partner or teammate supports group members who are struggling to participate in the group.

   Usually   Frequently   Seldom   Never

4. My partner or teammate listens carefully and respectfully to others in the group when they express themselves.

   Usually   Frequently   Seldom   Never

5. My partner or teammate evaluates the contributions of other group members in terms of usefulness and correctness.

   Usually   Frequently   Seldom   Never

6. My partner or teammate takes risks to express new ideas and feelings during a group discussion.

   Usually   Frequently   Seldom   Never

7. My partner or teammate expresses awareness of and appreciation for the gifts, talents, abilities, and skills of other group members.

   Usually   Frequently   Seldom   Never

8. My partner or teammate offers support and help to other team members.

   Usually   Frequently   Seldom   Never

9. My partner or teammate shares materials, books, resources, or information with others to help in the completion of tasks or in problem solving.

   Usually   Frequently   Seldom   Never

10. My partner or teammate is open and willing to share and participate in the group.

    Usually   Frequently   Seldom   Never

ments and rating with the individual whom they evaluated. Students should give one another encouragement in weak areas and offer praise for the many and varied contributions the partner or teammate makes to the successful completion of group goals and tasks. Before using this form, however, teachers should first model the types of oral and written responses to be offered during these feedback discussions.

PERFORMANCE OUTCOME EVALUATION: TEAM ASSESSMENT

Purpose

Although process is important during cooperative learning activities, a quality process should frequently result in a quality product. Assessment of the performance outcome is necessary to maintain accountability. As discussed previously, accountability for task completion is essential in cooperative learning groups.

Materials

The *Performance Outcome Evaluation* is a tool for helping teachers to assess the products of cooperative learning activities. An example form is shown in Figure 4.5. Though much of this sort of assessment is preferably ungraded, you will note that a column is provided in which to insert a grade, if required.

Procedures

Teachers collect student or group projects, papers, or other products for evaluation. We suggest that students be provided a copy of the form shown in Figure 4.5 as a guide for understanding teacher expectations. Upon completing the evaluation, the form should accompany feedback to the group or team about the quality of their product.

BALANCED READING PROGRAM INTERVENTIONS: COOPERATIVE LEARNING

Cooperative learning strategies have many applications and benefits. They are particularly useful in learning settings in which inherent cultural or other differences tend to cause students to label, isolate, or compete with one another. Further, group cooperation and collaboration can result in enhanced understanding for students facing learning and curriculum challenges—especially special needs learners.

TURN TO YOUR NEIGHBOR

Purpose

The purpose of the *Turn to Your Neighbor* cooperative learning strategy is to build a supportive classroom atmosphere in which children have opportunities to share their thoughts and feelings in an emotionally safe and accepting environment. In addition, this strategy allows for higher levels of student participation and interaction as ideas and thoughts are exchanged in student-to-student interactions. This is preferable to following a pattern of student-to-teacher interaction while the majority of other students sit passively listening to the conversation.

Figure 4.5 Performance Outcome Team Evaluation Form

Team Name: _____ Date: _____
Teacher's Name: _____ Class: _____

OUTCOMES	POINTS	GRADE
Completes assigned tasks (assignments, quizzes, reports, work units, homework)		
Applies skills taught in task completion (work units, use in problem-solving situations, homework)		
Understands concepts and principles (team scores, reports, homework, observations)		
Communication		
1. Communicates ideas and feelings effectively (observations, direct discussion)		
2. Participates actively in problem-solving groups		
Writing work (homework, reports)		
Cooperation (observations, team products)		
Competitive ability (observations, performances in competitions)		
Independent work (observations, performances in individualized activities)		
Affective Learning Appreciation of subject areas		
Appreciates learning (receives enjoyment and satisfaction from learning)		
Aware of and appreciates own abilities, achievements, talents, and resources		
Helps others, shares resources, etc., when appropriate		
Accepts and appreciates cultural, ethnic, linguistic, and individual differences		
Values free and open inquiry into all problems		
Total		

Figure 4.6   *Turn to Your Neighbor* Poster

When using Turn to Your Neighbor, remember:

1. Speak just long enough to share your ideas or thoughts.
2. Be sure to be a good listener.
3. Stay on the topic or task assigned.
4. Ask questions of the speaker.
5. Speak quietly so as not to disturb others.
6. Stop sharing when asked to do so by the teacher.

Materials

A poster that describes the expectations and processes of the Turn to Your Neighbor strategy, such as the one shown in Figure 4.6, is a useful classroom tool. This poster is displayed in a prominent location in the classroom.

Procedures

The strategy Turn to Your Neighbor can be applied in a variety of ways in reading and writing classes. This approach can be used for discussing, responding, sharing, or problem solving. For example, as teachers ask a question or assign a task, they instruct students to turn and talk to a neighbor about how to accomplish the task or answer the question. Prompts with open-ended responses can be phrased, "Tell your neighbor about . . ." and can focus on the student's favorite part of a story, or her feelings about a character. Whenever a point is reached in a class discussion in which high levels of involvement would increase thinking, the Turn to Your Neighbor cooperative learning strategy is effective. Indeed, using it increases learning, interaction, and participation in any classroom.

NUMBERED HEADS TOGETHER

Purpose

This approach to cooperative learning is effective in helping students to understand and comprehend knowledge or skill-based activities as well as to provide structured practice and to increase student interaction during class discussions (Kagan, 1990a; Johnson, 1995). In this activity all students feel that they must be involved because they could be called upon at any time to represent their group.

Materials

A poster that describes the expectations and process of the *Numbered Heads Together* strategy, such as the one shown in Figure 4.7, may be helpful for younger students. This poster should be displayed in a prominent location in the classroom.

N **Figure 4.7**   *Numbered Heads Together* Poster

Procedures

Numbered Heads Together is a simple practice or review strategy comprising four major steps. In the first step, Students number off, students number off from 1 to 5. In the second step, Teacher asks a question, a time limit for the group discussion is set. In the third step, Heads together, students literally put their heads together for discussion to make sure that all members in the group know the answer to the teacher's question or problem posed. One student may be appointed group checker to quickly review with the group that each member has and understands the answer. The final step is Teacher calls a number. At this point, the teacher calls out a number at random from 1 to 5. In each group, students with that number raise their hands to answer the question and the teacher chooses one to call upon.

CHECKING IN PAIRS
Purpose

When making cooperative learning group assignments, sometimes special roles may be assigned to help students rely on each other and appreciate what their peers are contributing (Johnson & Johnson, 1991, 1995). In the *Checking in Pairs* arrangement, students are grouped into pairs and each student must assume

Figure 4.8   *Checking in Pairs* Poster

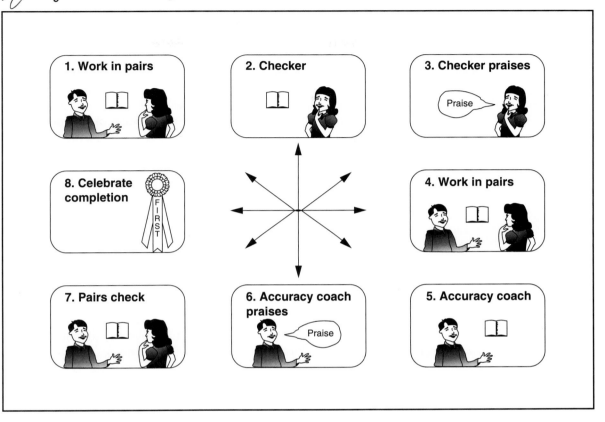

an assigned role for the group as a whole to function effectively. These roles may include a summarizer (one who restates the pair's major conclusions), a checker (one who assures that the other pair member can explain how an answer is reached), and an accuracy coach (one who corrects any mistakes in the other members' work). The Checking in Pairs cooperative learning strategy promotes helping among students and assures that they will stay on task to complete an assignment or solve a problem.

Materials

A poster describing the expectations and processes of the *Checking in Pairs* strategy is shown in Figure 4.8. This poster should be displayed in a prominent location in the classroom.

Procedures

To begin, students are grouped in pairs. Two pairs may work together as a group of four, if desired. One student volunteers to be the checker; the other is the worker. In the second step, the students exchange roles so that the checker becomes the worker, and the first worker becomes the accuracy coach. The checker functions as a critical friend to help writers get their ideas sharpened through revision. The accuracy coach focuses more on product, acting as an editor to help writers get the mechanics correct. In the final step, students share the role of checking before turning in a completed assignment. The pairs should then be encouraged to celebrate their efforts through a "high-five" or some other simple means.

The *Checking in Pairs* cooperative learning strategy is particularly appropriate for reading and writing assignments. For example, let's say students are writing letters to their favorite author. The teacher can model the process of researching the author's publisher, obtaining an address, and writing a letter. An enlarged model of a letter may be displayed at the board or in some other location in the classroom. The teacher may then ask students to help each other write a letter to their favorite author using the *Checking in Pairs* strategy. At the completion of the task, the pair turns in their letters and celebrates. If a pair decides to write to the same author, they can divide the tasks of letter writing into steps such as researching the author's publisher; writing the inside address, the greeting, the body, and the closing; and addressing the envelope.

THREE-STEP INTERVIEW

Purpose

For teachers who want to help their students respond, share, think, and problem solve with others (as well as to reduce management problems among students), Kagan's (1990a) *Three-Step Interview* can be a useful strategy. In typical classrooms the traditional way of sharing information is for the teacher to ask a question or pose a problem, then ask students individually to share with the remainder of the group. This format limits sharing to only a few students, however, and sometimes promotes discipline problems for beginning teachers. The *Three-Step Interview* provides a more creative way of sharing information in classrooms.

Materials

A poster that describes the expectations and processes of the *Three-Step Interview* strategy is shown in Figure 4.9. This poster should be displayed in a prominent location in the classroom.

Procedures

To begin the *Three-Step Interview,* students are placed in groups of four. If an odd number of students remains, the process can be modified for a group of three. Next, students within the groups are paired with another student in the group. One student is initially assigned to be the interviewer, while the other is the interviewee. In the second step, the students reverse their roles. In the final step, students share what they have learned in the interviews. With three students, student 1 interviews student 2, student 2 interviews student 3, and student 3 interviews student 1. Then, students share with groups of 5 or 7.

Applications of the *Three-Step Interview* are particularly appropriate for involving students in discussions or responses to literature stories. For example, suppose

Figure 4.9   *Three-Step Interview* Poster

that the students have read the book *The Indian in the Cupboard.* The teacher may, after reading the first chapter of the book, ask students to meet in groups of four to conduct the interview. This begins by posing the question(s) for the interview: *Have you ever had something so fantastic happen that you wouldn't tell anyone else? What was it? How would you have reacted if you had been Omri and found that your plastic Indian figure had come to life in your toy box?* Next, students interview each other and record their responses by taking notes and sharing the stories or responses from the interview with the other members of the group. Kagan (1990a) indicates that the *Three-Step Interview* is helpful for special needs students who are shy or who have Limited English Proficiency (LEP). These students are often reticent to speak out in a whole class, but feel more comfortable speaking to an individual or in a small group.

THINK-PAIR-SHARE

Purpose

Teachers often want students to share their ideas and feelings with one another. A typical way of accomplishing this end is for the teacher to lead by asking students to volunteer to share ideas one-at-a-time with the remainder of the group. For

Figure 4.10   *Think-Pair-Share* Poster

teachers who want to increase opportunities for their students to respond, share, think, and problem solve with others, the *Think-Pair-Share* strategy (Lyman & McTighe, 1988) provides a successful "across the curriculum" method (Slavin, 1995), especially in reading and learning science texts (Wood & Jones, 1994).

Materials

A poster that describes the expectations and processes of the *Think-Pair-Share* strategy is shown in Figure 4.10.

Procedures

The teacher begins by instructing students to listen to a question or problem. Students are then given time to think of a response. Next, students are told to share their responses with a neighboring peer. Finally, students are encouraged to share their responses with the whole group. A time limit is typically set for each segment of the *Think-Pair-Share* strategy. Students may also be asked to use another cooperative strategy during the *Think* or *Pair* parts of the strategy, such as the word web discussed in the following section on fact storming.

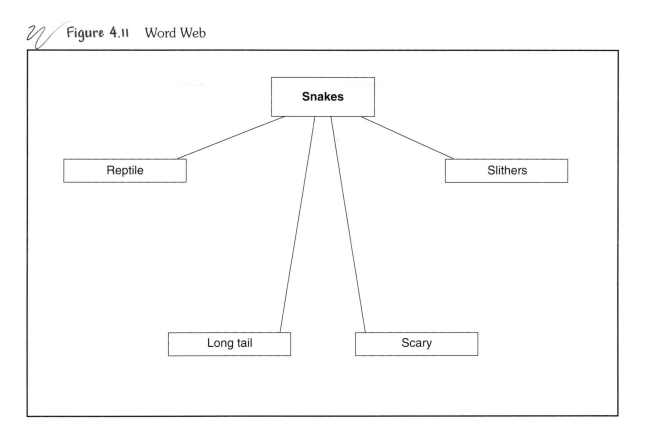

Figure 4.11   Word Web

FACT-STORMING GROUPS

Purpose

Klemp, Hon, and Shorr (1993) describe a cooperative learning activity known as *Fact Storming.* The purpose is to engage students in text previewing, activating prior knowledge, self-monitoring of reading comprehension (metacognition), text-specific vocabulary learning, and summarizing of the lesson. This strategy is particularly well suited to learning new content material from text in science and social studies.

Materials

The materials needed include subject-related trade books or textbooks and poster-sized or larger pieces of paper for each group for fact storming. Prior to reading and discussing snakes in an upcoming science lesson, students produce a word web (like the one shown in Figure 4.11).

Procedures

Students begin by examining an information trade book or textbook assignment to construct a study plan describing how the group will accomplish the reading. This allows the reading of texts that may exceed the individual abilities of a single child but may be within the abilities of a group of children. Students also share study strategies during this initial group discussion. They may discuss how much time it will take to read the assigned materials, for example. An assigned "group writer" completes a *Fact Storm Sheet* on a large piece of paper or poster board. The teacher then asks groups to post their study plans so that other students can see and possibly learn new ideas from their peers for studying the text.

Next, the groups preview the reading selection. Previewing helps readers to consider what they already know about a topic and to identify potentially troubling or important vocabulary words. The group writer records any information deemed important in the group preview on the *Fact Storm Sheet* that they have displayed. This approach allows all students, especially those with special needs, to contribute to the conversation and the study plan. Again, the teacher asks students to post their study plans with previewing information, questions, and vocabulary. This phase allows all groups to benefit from the work of other students and prepares each child for reading the text with greater comprehension.

In the next step, the groups read the assigned text. Each member of the group is assigned a portion of the text to examine carefully. As information is found, questions are answered, or vocabulary is defined, students enter the data on the group's *Fact Storm Sheet*. Afterward, the class reconvenes to post and examine the more elaborated displays of the *Fact Storm Sheets*. At this point the students are ready to reread individually the entire text and to complete comprehension activities. The teacher may elect to provide a study guide containing questions of various types, such as literal, inferential, and evaluative questions. The teacher may also provide vocabulary activities such as semantic mapping, semantic feature analysis, or word maps to help students learn new vocabulary as they read the text.

The final phase of this activity involves reworking the group's *Fact Storm Sheet* to either add, eliminate, or modify information. At this point students should contribute new information to the *Fact Storm Sheet*. Because this sharing occurs after reading, students should be able defend their contributions based upon their knowledge gained in reading the text. The final version of the group's *Fact Storm Sheet* can then be used to guide student's individual summaries to be entered in student learning logs.

COOPERATIVE GROUP ROTATION

Purpose

By using *cooperative group rotation* (Mermelstein, 1994), students have access to a variety of quality literature books and to nonfiction trade books in small group settings. Children participate actively in gathering and using information to create projects that demonstrate their growing knowledge of subject matter.

Materials

You may want to design a poster such as the one shown in Figure 4.12 that describes the expectations and processes of the *Cooperative Group Rotation*. Also needed are sufficient numbers of topic-, subject-, or theme-related trade books for each group.

Figure 4.12   Cooperative Group Rotation

Cooperative Group Rotation

1. Meet with your assigned group or team.
2. Decide who will fill the roles of reader, note taker, and leader for today. *Remember, this should change each day!*
3. The Reader reads the book aloud to the rest of the group.
4. The Leader reminds the reader to stop at the end of each page and asks the group members, "What do you think was important on the page?"
5. The Note taker writes down the group members' answers to the leader's question.
6. Select a project from the following list for today's book:
   * composing different kinds of poetry
   * drawing a picture showing the topic or subject
   * writing a paragraph about the subject
   * creating an adjective word web
   * writing a creative story about the subject
   * making a puppet
   * creating a diorama
7. When all books have been read by each group, choose your favorite project to display.

Procedures

The process begins by dividing the class into groups of four or five students. Next, at the beginning of each daily session, the group assigns the roles of reader, note taker, and leader. The teacher must obtain enough books on a selected subject, topic, or theme for each group to have at least one book per group. The student chosen as the day's reader reads the book aloud to the rest of the group, stopping at the end of each page. The student selected as the day's leader then asks her group members, "What do you think was important on the page?" The student selected to serve as note taker for the day writes down the group members' answers to the leader's question. When the group has finished reading the book, each student selects a project about the book's topic, using the book and the note taker's notes as resources (see Figure 4.12). For the sessions on the following days, the remaining books are rotated among the groups, so that all of the groups will have an opportunity to read all of the books. After a group has read all the books, the students then complete their selected individual projects for each book. Finally, each student selects her favorite project, to be added to a class portfolio or displayed on a bulletin board.

JIGSAW GROUPS

Purpose

The purpose of *Jigsaw Groups* is to create close working relationships among teammates (Aronsen, Blaney, Stephan, Sikes, & Snapp, 1978; Slavin, 1995). One objective for which *Jigsaw* is particularly useful is group projects. For example, in a social studies unit on government, students can be assigned to study one of the three branches of the U.S. government, with each student becoming an expert on each branch. This unit may culminate in a group presentation to the class, using diagrams, information sheets, and so on.

Materials

The materials tend to be unique to each project assigned to a *Jigsaw Group*.

Procedures

The least complex approach to *Jigsaw Groups* is the *within-team* approach. Each team member is assigned a bit of new knowledge to research and master. After information is sought, recorded, and organized, students move into a round-robin sharing process within their teams. Once sharing is complete, children are assessed on all the knowledge produced and shared within the team. The object of within-team *Jigsaw* is for students to learn how to best master information, report the information to teammates, and teach or tutor teammates to ensure their understanding. Students can become experts on assigned information in a variety of ways, such as silent reading, homework, learning centers, computer programs, experimentation, and interviews. *Jigsaw* allows individuals to become experts through developing and using good reading study skills for mastery of a body of information. In addition, it allows each group member to feel that she has contributed to the knowledge and learning of each of her teammates.

COOPERATIVE INTEGRATED READING AND COMPOSITION (CIRC)

Purpose

Designed by Slavin (1989; 1995), a major purpose of Cooperative Integrated Reading and Composition (CIRC) is to improve reading and writing instruction by engaging students in three major program elements: 1) oral reading, 2) reading comprehension skills, and 3) writing and language arts. These three aims are operationalized through mixed ability reading groups, teams, basal-related activities, partner checking, tests, direct instruction in reading comprehension skills, integrated writing and language arts, and independent reading and book reports.

Materials

Materials are teacher-generated using a basal reader.

Procedures

CIRC consists of three major components: basal-related activities, direct instruction in reading comprehension, and integrated language arts and writing. Students work in heterogeneous learning teams in all activities and these activities, follow a regular cycle involving teacher presentations, team practice, independent practice, peer assessment, and other practice and testing.

Reading Groups. Students are assigned to one of two or three reading groups, depending upon their measured reading level or as determined by the teacher.

Teams. Student pairs are designated within their reading groups, and the pairs are assigned to teams composed of partnerships from two reading groups—a high reading group and a low reading group. Teams receive points during the week for individual performance on activities. Teams that receive 95% on all work are designated as Super Teams.

Basal Related Activities. Basal stories are introduced and discussed in teacher-led reading groups that meet daily for 20 minutes. A typical Directed Reading Lesson (DRL) is conducted with the basal reader teacher's manual. Emphasis is upon learning and demonstrating the use of vocabulary words, as well as on predicting story outcomes and discussing narrative elements in each story such as setting, problem, events, and resolutions. After the story is introduced, children are given a packet of activities to do in their teams when they are not working with the teacher in a reading group. The sequence of activities is described by Slavin (1995) as follows:

Partner Reading. Students read the story silently, then take turns reading the story aloud with a partner by alternating paragraphs.

Story Grammar and Story Related Writing. Students are given questions for each story related to major story grammar elements. At the end, students are to respond to the story by writing a few paragraphs on a topic related to the story.

Words Out Loud. Students are given a list of new or difficult words used in the story. They must be able to read the words aloud correctly and without hesitation, practicing with a partner until they can be read fluently.

Word Meaning. Students are given a list of story words that they are to look up in the dictionary, paraphrase the meaning of, and write a sentence for that shows the meaning of the word as it is used in the story.

Story Retell. After reading, students summarize the story orally to their partner in a retelling.

Spelling. Students are given a list of spelling words weekly. A pretest is followed by practice until all words can be spelled correctly on a weekly posttest.

Partner Checking. Students work in pairs to check one another's work until they achieve the desired criteria level. Students are given a daily list of activities to be completed each day.

Tests. At the end of three class periods, students are given a story comprehension test, asked to use the vocabulary words in a sentence, and asked to read the list words aloud to the teacher.

Direct Instruction in Reading Comprehension. One day each week, students receive specific reading comprehension skill instruction such as cause and effect, main ideas, and summarizing. After each lesson students work on worksheets or games as a team. Following this, other worksheets are worked through in pairs and individually on other worksheets to practice and assess comprehension skill.

Integrated Language Arts and Writing. In this part of CIRC, students engage in a "Writers Workshop" in which they author compositions of their own choosing. Minilessons are conducted on grammar and mechanics as well as peer editing and conferencing. Final, polished compositions are shared in team or class books.

Independent Reading and Book Reports. Students are asked to read a trade book every evening for 20 minutes and parents are asked to sign off on this task each week. Students also complete one book report every two weeks, for which they receive team points. If students complete other assigned activities early, they can read their independent reading books.

Research reported on CIRC in 1987 by Stevens, Madden, Slavin, and Farnish found that CIRC students performed significantly better on standardized measures of reading, comprehension, vocabulary, language mechanics, language expression, and spelling, as well as on writing samples and oral reading measures, than did students who were taught using published reading and language arts programs.

CHAPTER SUMMARY

In this chapter, the benefits and essential features of cooperative learning strategies were described. The purpose of specific cooperative learning strategies were categorized into several types: *team building, communication building, mastery, concept development, division of labor,* and *cooperative learning projects.* Specific assessment strategies were presented to help teachers and students determine the extent to which cooperative learning strategies improve individual and collective learning processes and products. Next, a discussion of cooperative learning strategies that support learners in a variety of task categories was presented. Research asserts that judicious use of cooperative learning strategies for purposes intended can lead to measurable improvement in learning to read and write effectively.

REFERENCES

Aronsen, E., Blaney, N., Stephan, C., Sikes, J., & Snapp, M. (1978). *The jigsaw classroom.* Beverly Hills, CA: Sage.

Davidson, N. (1985). Small-group learning and teaching in mathematics.: A selective review of the research. In R. E. Slaving, S. Sharan, S. Katan, R. Hertz-Lazarowithz, C.Webb, and R. Schmuck (Eds.), *Learning to cooperate, cooperating to learn.* (pp. 211–230). New York: Plenum.

Ellis, S. S., & Whalen, S. F. (1990). *Cooperative learning: Getting started.* New York, NY: Scholastic.

Hansell, S., & Slavin, R. E. (1981). Cooperative learning: The structure of interracial friendships. *Sociology in Education, 54,* 98–106.

Johnson, D. W., & Johnson, R. T. (1981). The integration of the handicapped into the regular classroom: Effects of cooperative and individualistic instruction. *Contemporary Educational Psychology, 6,* 344–355.

Johnson, D. W., and Johnson, R. T. (1994). *Learning together and alone: Cooperative, competitive, and individualistic learning.* Boston, MA: Allyn and Bacon.

Johnson & Johnson, (1995)

Kagan, S. (1989). The structural approach to cooperative learning. *Educational Leadership, 47*(4) 12–15.

Kagan, S. (1990a). *Cooperative learning.* San Juan Capistrano, CA: Resources for Teachers.

Kagan, S. (1990b). On cooperative learning: A conversation with Spencer Kagan. *Educational Leadership,* 8–11.

Kagan, (1991a)

Klemp, R. M., Hon, J. E., & Shorr, A. A. (1993). Cooperative literacy in the middle school: An example of a learning-strategy-based approach. *Middle School Journal, XX,* 19–27

Lyman, F.T., & McTighe, J. (1988). Cueing thinking in the classroom: The promise of theory-embedded tools. *Educational Leadership, 45,* 18–24.

Mermelstein, B. (1994). Cooperative group rotation. *The Reading Teacher, 48*(3), 281–282.

Morrow, L. M., & Sharkey, E. A. (1993). Motivating independent reading and writing in the primary grades through social cooperative literacy experiences. *The Reading Teacher, 47*(2), 162–165.

Newman, F. M., & Thompson, J. (1987). *Effects of cooperative learning on achievement in secondary schools: A summary of research.* Madison: University of Wisconsin, National Center on Effective Schools.

Palinscar, A. S., Parecki, A. D., & McPhail, J. D. (1995). Friendship and literacy through literature. *The Journal of Learning Disabilities, 28*(8), 503–510.

Paradis, E. E, Chatton, B., Boswell, A., Smith, M., & Yovich, S. (1991). Accountability: Assessing comprehension during literature discussion. *The Reading Teacher, 45,* 8–17.

Slavin, R. E. (1989). Research on cooperative learning: Consensus and controversy. *Educational Leadership, 47*(4) 52–54.

Slavin, R. E. (1990). Learning together. *The American School Board Journal, 177*(8) 22–23.

Slavin, R. E. (1995). *Cooperative learning: Theory, research, and practice.* Needham Heights, MA: Allyn and Bacon.

Slavin, R. E., Madden, N. A., & Stevens, R. J. (1989). Cooperative learning models for the 3 R's. *Educational Leadership,* 22–28.

Stevens, R. J., Madden, N. A., Slavin, R. E., & Farnish, A. M. (1987). Cooperative integrated reading and composition: Two field experiments. *Reading Research Quarterly, 22,* 433–454.

Stevens, R. J., & Slavin, R. E. (1995). Effects of a cooperative learning approach in reading and writing on academically handicapped and nonhandicapped students. *Elementary School Journal, 95*(3), 241–262.

Swafford, J. (1995). I wish all my groups were like this one: Facilitating peer interaction during group work. *Journal of Reading, 38*(8), 626–631.

Wood, K. D. (1988). Techniques for assessing student potential for learning. *The Reading Teacher, 41,* 440–447.

Wood, K. D., & Jones, J. P. (1994). Integrating collaborative learning across the curriculum. *Middle School Journal, XX,* 19–23.

Chapter 5

Concepts About Print
Children's Insights into Reading and Writing

Many children enter school already knowing a good bit about books and written language. They know the difference between a word and a letter, for instance, and on which page a story begins. Such elements of reading are known as **print concepts** (also concepts about print). There are other students, however, who enter school knowing very little about basic print concepts. Sometimes the difference in knowledge is due to a lack of exposure to books and other print material in the home. Attention to these basic building blocks of reading in the early years is important so that children coming to school without prior learning opportunities will not develop reading problems (Clay, 1991; Durkin, 1989).

A number of studies have shown that some children require in-depth assistance in learning print concepts. For example, Yaden (1982) found that even after a year of reading instruction, some readers' concepts of letters, words, and punctuation marks have not yet developed to a level that is functionally useful. Johns (1980) also learned that good and poor readers can consistently be identified based on their knowledge of written language conventions at the conclusion of first grade. Furthermore, Morrow (1989) has found that mastery of certain characteristics, conventions, and details associated with printed language is necessary for successful literacy development. As a result of these and other findings, some (Yaden, 1986; Taylor, 1986) have called for teachers, administrators, curriculum developers, and publishers to focus their efforts on assessing and developing print awareness among learners with reading problems. The focus of the next section, then, is defining and explaining print concepts and conventions of written language and teaching them to children.

BACKGROUND BRIEFING FOR TEACHERS: HOW DO CHILDREN LEARN TO LOOK AT PRINT?

Print concept knowledge that children need to acquire to become successful readers and writers may be divided into four aspects (Taylor, 1986): 1) schemas about print, 2) functions of print, 3) mapping principles, and 4) technical aspects of print. We discuss these separately to help teachers clarify their understanding of each.

SCHEMAS ABOUT PRINT

Students' understanding of how texts are constructed or crafted by authors relates to **schemas about print**. Even very young students who have read books with their parents or caregivers understand how authors create a story. Each kind of story, or literary genre, involves certain kinds of information organized in fairly predictable and specific ways. For example, many fairy tales begin with the phrase, "Once upon a time . . ." and close with "and they lived happily ever after. The End." Children who understand schemas about print also know that narrative, or story, structure differs from expository, or informational text, structure. Many an intermediate grade teacher has been perplexed by students who experience difficulties when they begin to read expository text in content area textbooks (such as science and social studies). Because schemas about print are so important to successful reading, we discuss this print concept in chapters 10 and 11 of this book.

FUNCTIONS OF PRINT

Children learn early that written language is useful for a variety of purposes. Halliday's (1975) landmark research describes how language functions in our daily lives. The purposes for using language can be divided into three aspects: 1) *Ideational,* or expressing one's thoughts, 2) *Interpersonal,* or intimate social language, and 3) *Textual,* or informational language. Smith (1977) expanded and explained in greater detail Halliday's three language aspects by describing ten functions or purposes for which language can be used. Each of the ten purposes or functions for using language (Smith, 1977, p. 640) are detailed below with related examples of written language uses.

1. *Instrumental:* "I want." (Language is used as a means of getting things and satisfying material needs.)
   Examples in Written Language: Classified ads, notes, sign-up sheets, applications, bills, invoices, etc.
2. *Regulatory:* "Do as I tell you." (Language is used to control the attitudes, behaviors, and feelings of others.)
   Examples in Written Language: traffic signs, procedures, policies, traffic tickets, prompts, etc.
3. *Interactional:* "Me and you." (Getting along with others, establishing relative status) Also, "Me against you." (establishing separateness)
   Examples in Written Language: love notes, invitations, dialogue journals, friendly letters, etc.
4. *Personal:* "Here I come." (Expressing individuality, awareness of self, pride)
   Examples in Written Language: opinion papers, letters to the editor, etc.

5. *Heuristic:* "Tell me why." (Seeking and testing world knowledge)
Examples in Written Language: letters of inquiry, requests, and registration forms, etc.

6. *Imaginative:* "Let's pretend." (Creating new worlds, making up stories, poems)
Examples in Written Language: stories, tall tales and yarns, etc.

7. *Representational:* "I've got something to tell you." (Communicating information, descriptions, expressing propositions)
Examples in Written Language: arguments, lists, problem solving, etc.

8. *Divertive:* "Enjoy this." (Language for humor and fun)
Examples in Written Language: Puns, jokes, riddles

9. *Authoritative/contractual:* "How it must be." (Rules)
Examples in Written Language: Statutes, laws and regulations, etc.

10. *Perpetuating:* "How it was." (Records)
Examples in Written Language: Personal histories, diaries, journals, scrapbooks, etc.

Children understand the varied uses for *oral* language in their own lives, at least in a subconscious way. As teachers help students become aware of these language functions they readily apply this knowledge in their written language. Success in reading and writing are very much dependent upon the quality and creativity of the oral and written language that children encounter in their early reading and writing experiences. Any reading or writing program that is confined strictly to basals or textbook instruction represents a very limited written language experience base for students. Knowing this, balanced reading teachers give students authentic reading and writing experiences within the varied world of printed language, such as songs and raps, poetry, exposure to environmental print, logos, newspapers, signs, schedules, displays, tables, and so forth.

MAPPING PRINCIPLES

The ability to match, or map, speech sounds and printed symbols (sound-symbol relationships) develops rather slowly. Some researchers believe that a knowledge of mapping principles and a knowledge of the sound-symbol code, or phonics knowledge, may develop simultaneously. Several important mapping principles are listed below as goals for balanced reading classrooms.

The student . . .

1. understands that speech can be written down and read, and what is written down can be spoken

2. is aware of print in the environment and can read at least some signs and logos

3. understands that the message of the text is constructed from the print more than the pictures

4. knows written language uses different structures (see Halliday, 1975, and Smith, 1977, mentioned above) from spoken language

5. comprehends that the length of a spoken word is usually related to the length of the written word

6. demonstrates that one written word equals one spoken word
7. identifies some correspondences between spoken sounds and written symbols
8. uses context and other language-related clues to construct meaning and identify words

Mapping principles help students become successful readers and benefit from experiences with written language. However, adults often take the learning of mapping principles for granted and may make the mistake of assuming that children already know these principles (Reutzel, Oda, & Moore, 1989; Johnston, 1992). For some readers, failing to acquire an understanding of mapping principles can seriously impede progress in reading and writing development (Ehri & Sweet, 1991; Clay, 1991; Johns, 1980).

TECHNICAL ASPECTS

A knowledge of the technical aspects of print refers to the conventions that govern written language. Examples of these technical aspects of written language include directionality (left to right/top to bottom progression across the page in reading), spatial orientation, and instructional terms used in classrooms to refer to written language as an object. Since many of these concepts are commonsense matters for adults, it is little wonder that sometimes teachers and parents mistakenly assume that children already possess these understandings prior to the onset of formal reading instruction. There is, however, ample evidence that a knowledge of the technical aspects of written language develops slowly among learners who are young, inexperienced, or who have reading problems (Johns, 1980; Clay, 1979; Day & Day, 1979; Downing & Oliver, 1973; Meltzer & Himse, 1969). A listing of these terms and concepts follows:

Levels of Language Concepts
- Book
- Paragraph
- Sentence
- Word
- Letter

Ordinal
- First, second, third, etc.
- Last

Location Concepts
- Top
- Bottom
- Left
- Right
- Beginning (front, start, initial)
- Middle (center, medial, in between)
- End (back, final)

Visual Clues Embedded in Print
- Cover, spine, pages
- Margins, indentations
- Print size
- Punctuation
- Spacing

A knowledge of these concepts about print is extremely important for balanced reading teachers interested in assessing and guiding learning experiences related to the conventions and concepts associated with written language.

ASSESSING STUDENTS' KNOWLEDGE OF CONCEPTS ABOUT PRINT

The assessment strategies that follow were selected to provide teachers with greater insights into children's understanding of some of the concepts and conventions associated with written language. Much of what we describe here relates to reading, since writing assessment is discussed in greater detail in chapter 12, "Connecting Reading and Writing."

CONCEPTS ABOUT PRINT TEST

Purpose

The Concepts About Print Test (CAP) was designed by Marie Clay (1985) to assess children's knowledge of such instructional terms as *letter, word, sentence, story, directionality, text versus picture,* and *punctuation.* The CAP test is based upon two small booklets, *Sand* and *Stones,* which the teacher and student read together. One booklet may be used as a pretest early in the year and the other may be used as a posttest to measure growth after teaching has occurred.

Instructions for administering the *Concepts About Print Test* can be found in Clay's (1993) book, entitled, *An Observation Survey of Early Literacy Achievement* published by Heinemann Educational Books.

Materials

You will need the following items, authored by Marie M. Clay: *Concepts About Print Tests; Sand* or *Stones* booklets, and *An Observation Survey of Early Literacy Achievement.*

Procedures

Procedures for administering this test are found in *An Observation Survey of Early Literacy Achievement,* pages 47–52. The concepts tested include: front of book; proper book orientation to begin reading; beginning of book; print rather than pictures carry the message; directional rules of left to right; top to bottom on a page; return sweep to the beginning of a line of print; matching spoken words with written words; concepts of first and last letters in a word; beginning and ending of a story; punctuation marks; sight words; identifying printed letters, words, and upper- versus lowercase letters.

To test these concepts, the *Sand* and *Stones* booklets include some rather unusual features. At certain points the print or pictures are upside down, letter orders are changed or reversed (*saw* for *was*), and line order is reversed as well as paragraph indentions. The test has established a long and excellent record as an early reading screening test to be used as part of a battery of screening tasks for young, inexperienced, or at-risk readers. A major limitation of this test, however, is that it is based on error-detection tasks that require the child to find problems and explain them. Because of the somewhat tedious nature of this test and its tasks, children need to be tested in a calm environment and to have a trusting relationship with the examiner in order to obtain reliable results on the CAP.

READING ENVIRONMENTAL PRINT

Purpose

This task is designed to assess students' ability to read commonplace or "high frequency" print found in their daily environment, such as STOP, EXIT, NO SMOKING, McDonalds, Cheerios, Diet Coke, and so forth. Information gained can be used to assess the extent to which a child has been exposed to printed language in the environment. Further, teachers can discover ways that environmental print may be used to help each child develop successful reading and writing behaviors. An added advantage of environmental print is that it encourages beginning readers to develop an "I can read!" attitude.

Materials

Three sets of ten 5″ × 7″ plain index cards (30 total) are needed to construct this task. The first set of ten cards is used to display traffic signs or informational logos found on roads and in public buildings. The second set of ten cards is used to display logos of restaurant chains, television shows, gasoline stations, and national chain shores such as K-Mart. The third set of ten cards is used to display food product logos such as Pepsi, Alphabits, and Butterfinger.

Procedures

The classification procedures shown in the *Written Language Knowledge Taxonomy* are found in Figure 5.1 and are used to clarify student responses to the sets of 30 cards. (Harste, Burke, and Woodward, 1981; McGee, LoMax, and Head, 1988) This taxonomy has been used to help reading researchers determine how well children process print in their environment. This task can also help teachers gain insights into students' growing understanding of print concepts and terminology from environmental language. Children who show little awareness of print in the environment are also likely to have had few experiences with printed text in other contexts, such as books and personal writing. In order to provide the best possible instruction, teachers in balanced reading classrooms need to know what children do and do not understand and why some children are not progressing.

MOW MOTORCYCLE TASK

Purpose

As children learn to read and write, they discover how spoken words are mapped in writing using printed words in books and other written language sources. One concept students discover is that the length of the *printed* word is related to the length of the same *spoken* word. The Mow Motorcycle Task (Rozin, Bressman, & Taft,1974) seems to tap students' awareness of this basic relationship between speech and print. The task is one of several print awareness assessment methods

Figure 5.1   Written Language Knowledge Taxonomy

Response Category	Level	Examples
Pragmatic perspective	Attempts to Read	
	Maintains Communication Contract	
	single word or name (with no article)	"potato chips," "bread"
	phrases (not beginning with article "a")	"trouble with the foot-ball team"
	letters	"A" to telephone (index letter)
	numbers	"7:30" to TV Guide
	Renegotiates Communication Contract	
	names print object (usually with article)	"a newspaper"
	describes something in picture of print item	"a man"
	describes what can be found on the print item	"words," "telephone numbers," "pictures"
	describes what can be done with the print item	"take it to the store"
	Refuses to respond	no response or "I don't know"
Inclusion of text from print item	Attempt to read includes text of print item	"State Times" to paper
	Attempt partially includes text of print item (at least one word of response is included in text of print)	"Gulf State" for "State Times" in text
	Attempt does not include text of print item	"gum, candy" not in text of grocery list
Meaning	*Meaningful*	
	Attempt includes print text central in meaning	"eggs" to grocery
	Attempt does not include text but makes sense	"tomato" to grocery list (not in text)
	Nonmeaningful	
	Attempt includes print text not central in meaning	"by," "is" to newspa-per
	Attempt does not include text and does not make sense	"redfish" to book (not in text)
	Naming letters embedded in words	"S" "T" to "State" text

continued

Figure 5.1   Continued

Attention to graphic detail	Evidence of attention to graphic detail	
	Attempt includes print text for item with no picture	"dog food" to grocery list
	Attempt includes print text when child points to correct text	"potato chips" and points to text "potato chips"
	Attempt practically includes print text (1 word plus 1 letter same)	"Sunday Times" for text "State Times"
	Attempt does not include text, but it's obvious child referred to text	"the" and child points to "to"
	Attempt includes identification of letters in text	"S" "T" to newspaper

Note: Reprinted with permission from the National Reading Conference and Lea McGee, from, "Young Children's Written Language Knowledge: What Environmental and Functional Print Reading Reveals" by L. McGee, R. Lomax, and M. Head, 1988, *Journal of Reading Behavior 20*(2) pg. 105. Copyright 1988 by the National Reading Conference.

that can be used to provide teachers with insights into how children are developing as readers and writers in this important area.

Materials

Prepare ten pairs of word cards to be used for this task. Each pair of word cards should contain two words beginning with the same letter and differing in written and spoken length as shown in the example below. As shown in Figure 5.2, print each word card neatly with all uppercase manuscript or printed letters (transitional alphabets, such as D'Nealian, work just as well).

Procedures

Seat the child comfortably next to you at a table or desk of appropriate height. Displaying only one pair of cards at a time, show the child ten pairs of cards bearing printed words beginning with the same letter. For example, tell the student, "One of these words is *mow* and the other is *motorcycle*. Which one is *mow*?" The child responds by pointing. The total score is the number of correct responses, with 0 to

Figure 5.2   Mow Motorcycle Task

One of these words is *mow* and the other is *motorcycle*. Which one is *mow*?

MOTORCYCLE	MOW

10 points possible. Items should be varied so that the "target" word (the one you name) and the foil (the incorrect choice) are not always in the same position. This helps prevent the possibility that mere guessing on the student's part—always choosing the left-hand word, for example—will result in a high number of false correct responses.

METALINGUISTIC INTERVIEW (MI)

Purpose

The Metalinguistic Interview is a set of questions designed to assess children's understanding of the language that teachers use in instruction and their understanding of the way books are designed. For example, researchers (Clay, 1966; Downing, 1970, 1971–72; Reid, 1966; Denny & Weintraub, 1966) interviewed young children and found that they often do not have a clear understanding about many of the common terms used in beginning reading instruction, such as *alphabet, letter, word,* and *sentence.* Obviously, knowledge of these terms is most likely linked to how well children understand early reading and writing instruction.

Items in the Metalinguistic Interview include demonstrating an understanding of the following:

- that the term *alphabet* and/or *ABCs* refers to letters
- that the actual location on a page of a single letter, word, or sentence is an indication of directionality L–>R (left to right), T–>D (top/down), and so on
- punctuation
- how to differentiate upper- and lowercase letters
- terms such as the *front* and *back* of a book, and an understanding of *page(s).*

Children are given a book and asked to demonstrate where one would begin reading, including where on the page, the direction one's eyes should move, and where to go next when the reading of a page is finished. A full-page picture should usually be included on some pages as a foil. Scores on the interview range from a low of 0 to a high of 12. This activity is much like the CAP test described earlier, except that the teacher is using a trade book instead of the *Sand* and *Stones* books.

Materials

Any children's trade book or literature book containing both pictures and print may be used. For the best assessment, locate a book that has print on one page and a full-page picture on an adjoining page. A scoring sheet can be easily constructed by duplicating the tasks shown in Figure 5.3. For scoring, write a 0 or 1 following each question.

Procedures

Seat the child comfortably next to you. Hand the student a picture book, such as *The Gingerbread Man* (Schmidt, 1985) or *The Little Red Hen* (McQueen, 1985) upside down, with the spine of the book facing the child. Once the child takes the book, tell him that the two of you are going to read the book together. Then ask him to respond to the following tasks and observe the responses.

𝒲 **Figure 5.3**   The Metalinguistic Interview

1. "What are books for? What do books have in them?"
2. "Show me the front cover. Show me the back cover."
3. "Show me the title of the story."
4. "Show me the author's name."
5. "Open the book to where I should begin reading."
6. "Show me which way my eyes should go when I begin reading."
7. "Show me the last line on the page."
8. Begin reading. At the end of the page ask, "Now where do I go next?"
9. "Show me where to begin reading on this page. Will you point to the words with your finger as I say them?"
10. "Show me a sentence on this page."
11. "Show me the second word in a sentence."
12. "Show me a word."
13. "Show me the first letter in that word."
14. "Show me the last letter in that word."
15. "Show me a period on this page."
16. "Show me a question mark on this page."
17. Show the child a quotation mark and ask, "What is this?"
18. Ask the child to put his fingers around a word.
19. Ask the child to put his fingers around a letter.
20. Ask the child to show you an upper- and lowercase letter.

Correct responses are given a 1 and incorrect responses are scored 0.

THE BURKE READING INTERVIEW

Purpose

The purpose of the *Burke Reading Interview* (Burke, 1980) is to help teachers discover what students understand about the reading process and the strategies they use. Children are asked to describe how they learned to read, as well as what they can do to become better readers (Burke, 1980; DeFord & Harste, 1982). Teachers can determine whether students recognize that the goal of reading is to understand the author's message, or if they mistakenly think that the only goal of reading is to decode letters to sounds.

Materials

The Burke Reading Interview (Burke, 1980) and a cassette tape recorder to record the child's responses to the interview questions.

Procedures

Seat the child comfortably near you and the cassette recorder. Visit with the student for a moment to establish rapport. Tell the student that you will be asking a few questions and that you will be recording his answers to help you remember

Figure 5.4   The Burke Reading Interview

Name: _____ Age: _____ Date: _____
Occupation: _____ Educational level: _____
Sex: _____ Interview setting: _____

1. When you are reading and come to something you don't know, what do you do? Do you ever do anything else?
2. Who is a good reader you know?
3. What makes _____ a good reader?
4. Do you think _____ ever comes to something he/she doesn't know?
5. "Yes" When _____ does come to something he/she doesn't know, what do you think he/she does?
   "No" Suppose _____ comes to something he/she doesn't know. What do you think he/she would do?
6. If you knew someone was having trouble reading, how would you help that person?
7. What would your teacher do to help that person?
8. How did you learn to read?
9. What would you like to do better as a reader?
10. Do you think you are a good reader? Why?

Note: From Reading Miscue Inventory: Alternative Procedures by Y. Goodman, D. Watson, C. Burke, 1987, New York: Richard C Owen, Publisher, Inc.

what was said. Then, turn the recorder on and begin asking the questions found in the Burke Reading Interview in Figure 5.4. The tape recording can be used later to recall student responses.

BALANCED READING PROGRAM INTERVENTIONS: HELPING STUDENTS LEARN CONCEPTS ABOUT PRINT

INDICATORS THAT READERS HAVE LEARNING NEEDS*

- Below-age norms on the *Concepts About Print Test* (CAP)
- Majority (over 50%) of Environmental Print Reading scored in the Pragmatic Response Category (see *Reading Environmental Print* assessment strategy)
- Majority (over 50%) of responses to Mow Motorcycle Task demonstrate low awareness of spoken-written word length
- Majority (over 50%) of responses to Metalinguistic Interview evidence poorly developed book and mapping principle concepts
- Majority (over 50%) of responses to Burke Reading Interview indicate a vague understanding of the purposes, processes, and functions of reading

*Reminder: No one single indicator should be considered conclusive, but should be compared to other classroom evidence gathered in student portfolios and through Individual Reading Conferences.

In the next part of the chapter we offer ideas for assisting teachers in developing greater understanding of print concepts in their balanced reading classrooms. These activities can often be adapted for use with younger students developing quite normally, or with children with special needs, such as ESL students.

SOME TIPS FOR DEVELOPING CONCEPTS ABOUT PRINT

After a careful assessment of a student's reading progress, one or more of the following strategies may be appropriately applied. Perhaps the most important thing to remember is that children with poorly developed print concepts must be immersed in a multitude of print-related activities in a "print-rich" classroom environment. Authentic reading and writing experiences coupled with the informed guidance of a caring teacher or other literate individuals (e.g., parents, peers, and volunteers) can do much to help students learn necessary print-related concepts. Activities mentioned elsewhere in this book, such as the Shared Book Experience, can be used with the *voice pointing* and the *LAPS* strategies described in this chapter to help learners acquire much-needed print and language concepts in motivating ways!

ENVIRONMENTAL PRINT: "I CAN READ" BOOKS

Environmental print commonly found in students' daily lives can be collected to make *I Can Read* books about such topics as *My Favorite Foods, Signs I See, A Trip to the Supermarket, My Favorite Things,* and so on. Children choose a topic, then use the materials assembled by the teacher to construct their *I Can Read* books. For example, toy catalogues gathered by the teacher could be used by students for making a book called *My Favorite Toys*. Collected logos are another source of print for these books. An example of an *I Can Read* book is shown below.

Because students select logos they can already read, these books are easily read by learners still acquiring print concepts and become a source of confidence building and enjoyment. By reading these books, students very quickly develop an "I can do this . . . I can read!" attitude.

LANGUAGE EXPERIENCE APPROACH (LEA): VARIATIONS FOR READERS LEARNING PRINT CONCEPTS

The **Language Experience Approach** (LEA) is an approach for developing children's reading and writing abilities through the use of firsthand and/or vicarious experiences. Children learn about print conventions and concepts in LEA by seeing their oral speech written down in printed form. They learn story schemas, functions for written language, ways of mapping speech onto print, and the technical aspects of print (i.e., directionality, punctuation marks, etc.). The essence of this approach is to use children's oral language and personal experiences as the catalyst for creating personalized reading materials. Teachers who use LEA have found that children's dictated stories about personal experiences can be recorded in at least three different ways: The Group Experience Chart, The Individual Language Experience Story, and The Key Vocabulary Word Bank. Each of these LEA variations is described below.

Creating Group Experience Charts

The *Group Experience Chart* is a means of recording the experiences of a group of children. In all LEA activities it is essential that students have a shared experience in common about which they can write. The typical steps associated with the creation of a Group Experience Chart are listed below:

1. The children participate in a shared experience, such as a field trip, an experiment, a guest speaker.
2. Teachers and children discuss the shared experience.
3. Children dictate the story while the teacher transcribes the dictation on chart paper.
4. Teachers and children share in reading the chart.
5. The chart is used to teach about words and other important language concepts.

The selection of an interesting and stimulating experience or topic for children can spell the success or failure of an LEA activity. Topics and experiences must capture the interest of children in order to provide the motivation necessary for learning. Some examples of previously successful topics and themes follow:

Our classroom pet had babies last night.

Let's describe our field trip.

Writing a new version of a favorite book

What we want for Christmas

Planning our Valentine's Day party

What did Martin Luther King do?

Scary dreams we've had . . .

Once I got into trouble for . . . .

A classmate is ill. Let's make a get well card from the class.

Be sure to discuss the experience or topic carefully. This helps children to self-assess what they know about the topic and to make personal connections. Also, it motivates them to share their knowledge, experiences, and personal connections with others. Be careful not to dominate the discussion, however. Asking too many focused questions can turn what would otherwise be an open and exciting discussion into an interrogation. Questions should invite discussion, instead of encouraging short and unelaborated responses. Be careful not to make the mistake of beginning dictation too early in the discussion, as this may lead to a dull, even robotic, recounting of the experience or topic.

After plenty of discussion, ask children to dictate the ideas they wish to contribute to the chart. With special needs learners in the early grades, you may want to record each child's dictation in different colored markers to help him identify his contribution to the chart. Later in the year, write the child's name by his dictation rather than using different marker colors. When the chart is complete, read the children's composition aloud in a natural rhythm, pointing to each word as you read. After the first reading, invite students to read along on the second reading. Next, ask volunteers to read aloud portions of the story. Other strategies for reading the composition include the following:

- Read aloud a selected dictation line from the chart and ask a child to come up to the chart and point to the line you just read aloud.
- Copy several lines of the chart onto sentence strips and have children pick a sentence strip and match it to the line in the chart.
- Copy the LEA story onto a duplicating master and make copies to go home with students for individual practice.
- Put copies of favorite words in the chart story onto word cards for word banks and matching activities.

Creating Individual Language Experience Stories

For most students, no single individual is more important and exciting to talk or read about than themselves. *Individual Language Experience Stories* provide an excellent opportunity for learners to talk about their own experiences and to have these events recorded in print.

We suggest that the child tell his story into a tape recorder and listen to it. Listening and editing on tape can have a very positive transfer value for the writing process. This encourages children to retell or edit their stories until they are satisfied with the final product. We also suggest, where circumstances will permit, that parent volunteers be invited to transcribe students' Individual Language Experience Stories from audiotapes to paper copy.

An additional step in this activity might include turning these Individual Language Experience Stories into books. Formalize students' Individual Language Experience Stories by placing a card pocket and library card in each child's book. These books can then be added to the classroom library for other children to read. A story reader's chair can be established to encourage children to read their Individual Language Experience Stories aloud to peers in their own classroom and other classrooms in the school.

One variation of Individual Language Experience Stories that children particularly like is *shape stories*. As shown in the photo below, the cover and pages of the dictated Individual Language Experience Story are drawn and cut into the shape of the book topic. For example, if a child has just created a story about a recent family trip to Disneyland, the book could be cut into the shape of Mickey Mouse's head; a trip to Texas may be recorded in a book cut into the shape of the state of Texas.

LEARNING ABOUT PRINT STRATEGIES (LAPS)

The Learning About Print Strategies (LAPS) developed by Reutzel (1995) are intended to help emergent readers learn certain written language conventions and concepts. While the strategy called voice pointing may be adapted for use with most students, note that the remaining strategies have special uses and may not be appropriate for all learners. Teacher observation and assessment will make it clear which strategy is best in a given situation.

Voice Pointing

Clay (1972) indicates that pointing to the print while reading, or *voice pointing*, is a critical strategy to develop during the early stages of learning to read. To help emergent readers make the connection that the print is guiding the speech

of the reader, teachers should point to the print as they demonstrate reading. From these demonstrations, children learn where words begin and end on the page, how print moves from left to right and top to bottom on a page, and mapping principles. Voice pointing can also be used to identify specific print features such as lines, phrases, words, letters, or punctuation for discussion and attention.

Mapping Speech onto Print

Sometimes emergent readers and readers with learning needs have not yet grasped the idea that a given word is the same every time it appears in print. For instance, the word *football* is always *football* whenever it appears in print, whether it is handwritten text or text appearing in a book. Understanding this basic concept is a major milestone in reading development. *Mapping Speech onto Print* is one strategy that can help students grasp this important print concept.

The basic blueprint for teaching follows closely the *whole to parts to whole* format described in chapter 1 for balanced reading programs: begin by highlighting aspects of written language in a real book, zoom in on the words you wish to emphasize, then help children to use the new knowledge by applying it in new books.

Begin by reading aloud an enlarged text several times without interruption or discussion about print features. This can be text from an LEA Group Chart or a copy of a big book such as *Brown Bear, Brown Bear* (Martin, 1983). Remember to voice point to the text as you read. Next, copy a few high interest phrases, words, or word parts from the enlarged text onto sentence strips or chart paper. Then, demonstrate for students the exact match between the print in the book or LEA chart and the print copied onto the strips or chart paper, as shown in Figure 5.5. This is accomplished by pointing and framing the two sets of print between your

Figure 5.5   Matching Print in the Predictable Book with Print on a Sentence Strip

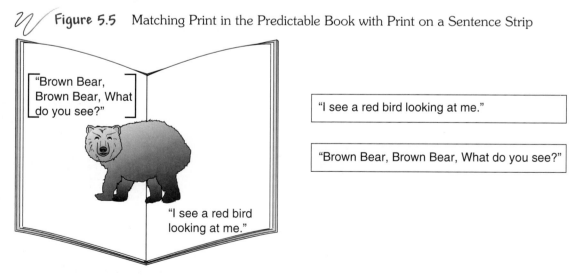

Note: From "Fingerpoint Reading and Beyond: Learning About Point Strategies (LAPS)" by D. Ray Reutzel, 1995, *Reading Horizons, 35* (4), pp. 310–328. Copyright 1995 by Western Michigan University.

hands. For example, you may first frame the enlarged text from the book which asks "Brown Bear, Brown Bear, What do you see?" and then frame the sentence strip version of the same words, one by one. Finally, point out each highlighted word (e.g., *brown, bear, what, do, you, see*) in other books. After several demonstrations, children can be asked to match the text on sentence strips or charts that contain the same print as framed in the book. By observing and participating in this process, emergent readers and readers with learning needs begin to make a visual connection or match between the print in the book and the same print displayed on sentence strips, or other print displays.

An extension of this idea involves children selecting a sentence strip, or sentence cut from a chart, and placing it beneath the matching print in the book or LEA chart. After making a match, students explain to a peer how the two sets of print are the same. If children are invited to match words in charts or books to words on cards, it is best if structure words, such as *the, and, a,* and *there,* are not used. Only concrete nouns, action words, and descriptive words that are easy to see in the mind's eye should be highlighted for this exercise.

Clozing In

Cloze passages are excerpts from books in which certain words are deleted and replaced with blanks. Students are usually asked to decide which word would make sense and fill in the blank, thus bringing closure to the passage. Cloze passages emphasize the differences between words and sentences as well as basic concepts about print, while also demonstrating the importance of context clues in understanding the author's message.

Two variations of cloze that can be used to focus young readers' attention on either content or structure words in predictable books are progressive and regressive cloze. In *progressive cloze,* the text is read aloud. Next, several words are deleted using stick-on notes as shown in Figure 5.6, then the text is read aloud again. Each time a deleted word is encountered, children are asked to identify the missing word. When the deleted word is correctly identified, it is uncovered. For example, in the story *The Gingerbread Man,* the entire text of the book may be read and then several pages used for a progressive cloze procedure.

In *regressive cloze,* the process is also begun by reading the entire text aloud. Next, the text is reduced to only its structure words by covering all content words with stick-on notes. Children are then asked to identify the missing words. As each content word is identified, it is uncovered. By using these cloze variations, children begin to focus on identifying individual words within the context of familiar stories. Teachers can repeat these cloze variations in another context such as on charts, sentence strips, or a chalkboard, as shown in Figure 5.7.

What Else Could We Say Here?

Students who need additional learning opportunities to discover the role of individual words can profit from word substitution activities. Children read a text selection with the teacher and are asked what other words or phrases might be substituted in the text. Stick-on notes can be used for students to substitute other words that

Figure 5.6   Progressive Cloze Covering the Content, Action, or Descriptive Words

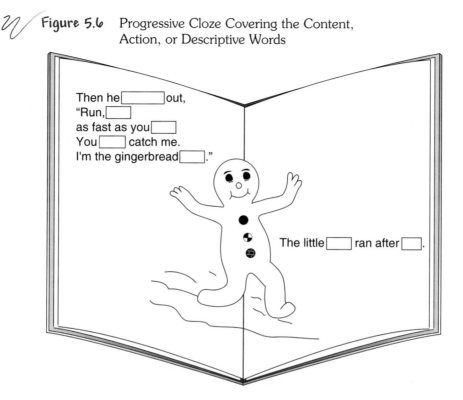

Then he ⬜ out,
"Run, ⬜
as fast as you ⬜
You ⬜ catch me.
I'm the gingerbread ⬜."

The little ⬜ ran after ⬜.

Note: From "Fingerpoint Reading and Beyond: Learning About Point Strategies (LAPS)" by D. Ray Reutzel, 1995, *Reading Horizons, 35* (4), pp. 310–328. Copyright 1995 by Western Michigan University.

Figure 5.7   Moving the Text to Sentence Strips for Progressive or Regressive Cloze Activities

Then he ⬜ out,

"Run, ⬜

as ⬜ as you can.

⬜ can't ⬜ me.

I'm the gingerbread ⬜."

The little ⬜ ran after him.

Note: From "Fingerpoint Reading and Beyond: Learning About Point Strategies (LAPS)" by D. Ray Reutzel, 1995, *Reading Horizons, 35* (4), pp. 310–328. Copyright 1995 by Western Michigan University.

Figure 5.8   Substituting Words to Draw Attention to Print Detail

Original Text	Substitution Text
And on that cat	And on that chicken
there is a mouse,	there is a worm,
a slumbering mouse	a slimy worm,
on a snoozing cat	on a snoozing chicken
on a dozing dog	on a lazy lamb
on a dreaming child	on a dreaming child
on a snoring granny	on a snoring granny
on a cozy bed	on a cozy bed
in a napping house,	in a napping house,
where everyone is sleeping.	where everyone is sleeping.

Note: From "Fingerpoint Reading and Beyond: Learning About Point Strategies (LAPS)" by D. Ray Reutzel, 1995, *Reading Horizons, 35* (4), pp. 310–328. Copyright 1995 by Western Michigan University.

make sense. For example, text copied from, *The Napping House* (Wood & Wood, 1984) could be displayed as shown in Figure 5.8.

In this example, children are asked to substitute other words for the original words *dog, cat,* and *mouse* in the text. These words, along with the words found in the original text, can be interchanged during subsequent rereadings. Exchanging these words helps children carefully focus on print details to determine which words have been switched in the text and how such word play can drastically change the author's message.

What Has Been Changed Here?

Word variations can be inserted into familiar text (books already well known to the students) prior to rereading parts of the story to encourage students to pay close attention to print detail. For example, in the text of a book entitled *Mrs. Wishy-Washy* (Cowley, 1980), the word *dud* can be inserted into the text in place of the original word, *mud,* using a white sticky note.

"Oh, lovely dud," said the pig, and he rolled in it.

Children are reminded that this text should say, "Oh, lovely <u>mud</u>, said the pig, and he rolled in it," but something is wrong here. The teacher then asks, "Can you find what has been changed?" Volunteers are invited to explain what is wrong and how the error can be corrected. Once the concept is grasped from this example, other familiar books having word substitutions can be presented for students to analyze.

Figure 5.9 Identifying Unknown Words in Print

I am a seal and I☐lap my hands.

☐an you do it?

I ☐an you do it.

Note: From Carle, E. (1997). *From head to toe.*
New York: HarperCollins Publishers

Clozing In on Sounds

To draw students' attention to individual letters in printed text, teachers can choose an enlarged text, chart, or book and cover selected letters with stick-on notes. Specific sounds for letters can be discussed in the context of real text. There is some research evidence that students benefit most from voice pointing and finger-point reading when they have developed a sense of letter names and sounds (Ehri & Sweet, 1991). For example, stick-on notes can be used to "cloze in" on selected sounds and letter-sound patterns in a familiar book or song for discussing how the sound-symbol system can help students identify unknown words in print (see Figure 5.9).

Word Rubber-Banding

Word rubber-banding (Calkins, 1986, 1994) is a simple technique that can be used to help students create invented spellings (we prefer "temporary spellings") of words and improve their ability to "sound out" unfamiliar words in print. Children verbally stretch out the word they wish to write, like stretching a rubberband. As explained in chapter 1, teacher modeling is needed in the beginning to help children understand the process. For example, students may want to write about their favorite animals or pets. The teacher could offer the following model after explaining the concept of word rubber-banding:

Teacher: Listen while I stretch out the name of my favorite animal, *snake,* as I say it aloud. *Ssssnnnaaaakkkke.* I sounded kind of like a snake slithering along, didn't I? Now, watch as I write the word *snake* while saying it.

Observations: As the teacher rubber-bands the word *snake* again orally, he writes the following letters that are easily heard. *s-n-a-k-e.*

Teacher: Now I have written the word *snake*. If I want, I can check how I wrote *snake* with the way others write *snake*. I could look in one of the books in our classroom.

In this way children attend carefully to the way words in printed language are constructed as well as learning to use print in their immediate environment to discover conventional spellings.

CHAPTER SUMMARY

In this chapter, the concepts and conventions of printed language—schema, function, mapping principles, and technical aspects of print—have been described to bolster teachers' understanding of these critical learning milestones. Specific assessment ideas have been presented for use in determining students' understanding and growth of print concepts and to inform instructional practice. Likewise, several approaches have been explored for helping learners acquire and refine their understanding of the concepts and conventions of printed language. The use of these strategies will help learners internalize print concepts and prepare them for more advanced decoding and comprehension instruction.

REFERENCES

Burke, C. (1980). The reading interview: 1977. In B. P. Farr and D. J. Strickler (Eds.), *Reading comprehension: Resource guide.* Bloomington, IN: School of Education, Indiana University.

Calkins, L. (1986). *The art of teaching writing.* Portsmouth, NH: Heinemann Educational Books.

Calkins, L. (1994). *The art of teaching writing* (new ed.). Portsmouth, NH: Heinemann Educational Books.

Clay, M. (1966). *Emergent reading behavior.* Unpublished doctoral dissertation, University of Auckland.

Clay, M. (1979). *Reading: The patterning of complex behaviour.* Exeter, NH: Heinemann Educational Books, Inc.

Clay, M. (1993). *An observation survey of early literacy achievement.* Portsmouth, NH: Heinemann.

Cowley, J. (1990). *Mrs. Wishy-washy.* San Diego, CA: The Wright Group.

Day, K. C., & Day, H. D. (1979). Development of kindergarten children's understanding of concepts about print and oral language. In M. L. Damil and A. H. Moe (Eds.), *Twenty-eighth yearbook of the National Reading Conference* (19–22). Clemson, SC: National Reading Conference.

Denny, T. P., & Weintraub, S. (1966). First graders' responses to three questions about reading. *Elementary School Journal, 66,* 441–448.

Downing, J. (1970). The development of linguistic concepts in children's thinking. *Research in the Teaching of English, 4,* 5–19.

Downing, J. (1971–72). Children developing concepts of spoken and written language. *Journal of Reading Behavior, 4,* 1–19.

Downing, J., & Oliver, P. (1973). The child's concept of a word. *Reading Research Quarterly, 9,* 568–582.

Durkin, D. (1989). *Teaching them to read* (5th ed.). New York, NY: Allyn and Bacon.

Ehri, L. C., & Sweet, J. (1991). Fingerpoint-reading of memorized text: What enables beginners to process the print? *Reading Research Quarterly, 26,* (4), 442–462.

Halliday, M. A. K. (1975). *Learning how to mean: Explorations in the development of language.* London: Edward Arnold.

Harste, J. C., & DeFord, D. (1982). Child language research and curriculum. *Language Arts, 59* (6), 590–600.

Harste, J. C., Burke, C., & Woodward, V. A. (1981). *Children, their language and world: The pragmatics of written language use and learning.* NIE Final Report #NIE-G-80-0121. Bloomington, IN: Indiana University, Language Education Department.

Johns, J. L. (1980). First graders' concepts about print. *Reading Research Quarterly, 15,* 529–549.

Johnston, P. H. (1992). *Constructive evaluation of literate activity.* New York, NY: Longman Publishers.

Martin, B. (1983). *Brown bear, brown bear what do you see?* Pictures by Eric Carle. New York: Henry Holt.

McGee, L. M., Lomax, R. G., & Head, M. H. (1988). Young children's written language knowledge: What environmental and functional print reading reveals. *Journal of Reading Behavior,* 20 (2), 99–118.

McQueen, L. (1985). *The little red hen.* New York, NY: Scholastic Books Inc.

Meltzer, N. S., & Himse, R. (1969). The boundaries of written words as seen by first graders. *Journal of Reading Behavior, 1,* 3–13.

Morrow, L. M. (1989). *Literacy development in the early years: Helping children read and write.* Englewood Cliffs, NJ: Prentice Hall.

Reid, J. (1966). Learning to think about reading. *Educational Research, 9,* 56–62.

Reutzel, D. R. (1995). Fingerpoint reading and beyond: Learning about print strategies (CAPS). *Reading Horizons,* 35(4) 310–328.

Reutzel, D. R., Oda, L. K., & Moore, B. H. (1989). Developing print awareness: The effect of three instructional approaches on kindergartners; print awareness, reading readiness, and word reading. *Journal of Reading Behavior, 21*(3), 197–217.

Rozin, P., Bressman, B., & Taft, M. (1974). Do children understand the basic relationship between speech and writing? The mow-motorcycle test? *Journal of Reading Behavior, 6,* 327–334.

Schmidt, K. (1985). *The gingerbread man.* New York, NY: Scholastic Books.

Smith, F. (1977). The uses of language. *Language Arts, 54*(6), 638–644.

Taylor, N. E. (1986). Developing beginning literacy concepts: Content and context. In D. B. Yaden, Jr. & S. Templeton (Eds.), *Metalinguistic awareness and beginning literacy* (pp. 173–184). Portsmouth, NH: Heinemann Educational Books.

Wood, A., and Wood, D. (1984). *The napping house.* Illustrated by Don Wood. San Diego: Harcourt Brace Jovanovich.

Yaden, D. B., Jr. (1982). A multivariate analysis of first graders' print awareness as related to reading achievement, intelligence, and gender. *Dissertation Abstracts International, 43,* 1912A. (University Microfilms No. 8225520)

Yaden, D. B., Jr. & S. Templeton (Eds.) *Reading Research in Metalinguistic awareness: A classification of finding according to focus and methodology* (pp. 41–62). Portsmouth, NH: Heinemann Educational Books.

Chapter 6

The Alphabetic Principle and Phonemic Awareness

An excited kindergarten child came rushing home at the end of her first day of school. When met at the door by her mother, she blurted out with enthusiastic insight, "Mom! Today we learned all about the *albaphet*. You know, it's just like the *ABC's!*"

As young children learn to talk, they use basic speech sounds. When children speak, their goals are, of course, to make themselves understood to others and to be understood. However, for children to develop to the next stage of language use—reading and writing—they must realize: 1) that words in books are composed of the same speech sounds (phonemes) used when speaking, and 2) that these sounds are represented in written words by letters (graphemes).

BACKGROUND BRIEFING FOR TEACHERS: UNDERSTANDING THE PREREQUISITES TO SUCCESSFUL PHONICS INSTRUCTION

The understanding that words are composed of individual sounds is known as **phonemic awareness** (Cunningham, 1990; Yopp, 1992; Stahl & Murray, 1994; Harris & Hodges, 1995; Richgels, Poremba, & McGee, 1996; Strickland, 1998). Phonemic awareness, or the ability to hear and "segment" individual sounds in spoken words, must occur before children can begin to understand how letters represent speech sounds. We call this latter skill of matching written letters with spoken speech sounds the **alphabetic principle** (Adams, 1990; Anderson, Hiebert, Scott, & Wilkinson, 1985; Harris & Hodges, 1995).

Many reading teachers and researchers believe that the alphabetic principle represents a major milestone in learning to read (Juel, 1991; Mason, 1980; Chall, 1996; Holdaway, 1979; Goodman, 1986). After children become *aware* of the alphabetic principle, they develop the ability to *manipulate* letters and sounds. This helps them to decode new words they encounter in books and to create temporary spellings in their writing. According to several researchers (Yopp, 1988; Adams, 1990), phonemic awareness and alphabetic principle skills develop concepts from least difficult to most difficult, as shown:

1. Rhyming
2. Hearing sounds in words
3. Sound substitution and additions
4. Isolating sounds in words
5. Segmentation of sounds in words

In this chapter we suggest assessment ideas related to phonemic awareness and the alphabetic principle. We then provide a number of classroom-proven teaching strategies to assist emergent readers and readers with special learning needs.

ASSESSING STUDENTS' UNDERSTANDING OF THE ALPHABETIC PRINCIPLE AND PHONEMIC AWARENESS

Phonemic awareness is very often preceded by *concepts about print* knowledge (e.g., knowing where to start reading on a page, differentiating a word from a letter, etc.), which was covered in detail in chapter 5. Next, children develop the ability to recognize, name, and manipulate letters. At about the same time that children learn letter shapes and names, the understanding that spoken words are composed of individual sounds develops. For example, the word *me* is composed of two individual sound units or *phonemes*—/m/ and /e/. When the word *me* is stretched out (what we call "word rubber-banding") it sounds like *mmmmmeeeeeeeeeeee*. The ability to hear and manipulate sounds in language, known as *phonemic awareness*, leads to the next level of reading development: an understanding that letters and sounds connect in systematic ways to help us decode written language. This connection is known as the *alphabetic principle*.

Assessment of children's understanding of the alphabetic principle begins by determining whether readers are aware of the alphabet itself, can name or write letters of the alphabet, can identify the sounds represented by each alphabet sound, are aware of sounds in speech, and understand that letters and sounds go together in systematic ways (Byrne & Fielding-Barnsley, 1989, 1993). Following are several informal strategies based on the work of Yopp (1988, 1992) and Griffith and Olson (1992) for phonemic awareness, knowledge of the alphabetic principle, and assessing simple alphabet knowledge.

LETTER IDENTIFICATION

Purpose

Similar to the activity described above, this task based on the work of Marie Clay (1993) determines whether readers with special learning needs can identify letters of the alphabet.

Figure 6.1   Alphabet Letter Display

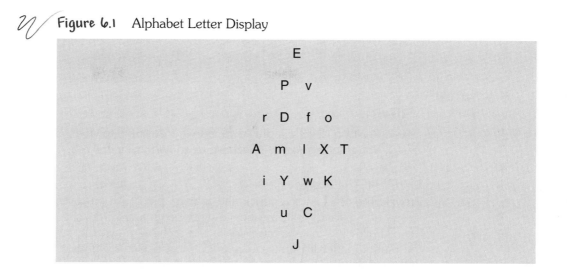

Materials

Reproduce the randomized alphabet letter display (shown in Figure 6.1) on a sheet of paper or a chart for use in this exercise.

Procedures

Invite the student to be seated next to you and explain that you would like to find out which letters of the alphabet she can name as you point to them on a chart. Begin pointing at the top of the alphabet letter display. Work line by line and left to right to the bottom of the display, keeping letters below your line of focus covered. Using a photocopy of the display, mark the letters that were correctly named. Next, ask the child to point to the letter you named in the display. Record this information. Most children, even readers with special learning needs, will be able to identify at least 50% of the letters requested. However, students who have little familiarity with letters may perform poorly.

LETTER PRODUCTION

Purpose

This task is designed to determine whether students know and can write letters of the alphabet. Unlike simple letter identification, this task requires that students be able to produce letters from memory. Letter knowledge is an indication of how well students have sorted out sound/symbol processes, but it is not logically necessary for successful reading. It does, however, make learning to read easier (Venezky, 1975). Letter naming/production can be likened to a bridge that helps children cross the river of early reading and writing.

Figure 6.2   Random Letters

1. b	2. m	3. e	4. f	5. t
6. i	7. p	8. o	9. s	10. h

Materials

Create a list of 10 letters drawn randomly from the alphabet. Be sure to include at least 3 vowel letters in the selection, as shown in Figure 6.2.

Procedures

Provide the child with a pencil and a blank piece of paper. Ask the student if she knows any letters. Next, ask her to write down any letters she knows and to name them. Following this exercise, invite her to write down the letters you name from the random letter list that you created. Most students in Grade 1 will score at least 70% on this task. However, students who have little familiarity with letters may perform poorly. A low score should be interpreted as a need to engage in strategies and activities outlined later in this chapter.

RECOGNIZING RHYMING WORDS

Purpose

Students are asked to recognize whether pairs of words rhyme to assess levels of basic phonemic awareness. According to Adams (1990), the ability to determine rhyme is the easiest of all phonemic awareness tasks.

Materials

A list of 20 word pairs. At least 50% of the word pairs should rhyme.

Procedures

Model the concept of rhyming by giving several examples, including some word pairs that do not rhyme. Explain that rhyming words end with the same sound(s). Then, using the word pairs shown in Figure 6.3, pronounce aloud each pair of words and ask the child if they rhyme. Note her response to each pair. According to Yopp (1988), kindergarten children usually achieve a mean score of 75%. That is, they correctly identify 15 out of the 20 target word pairs. If students score poorly on this task, teachers should provide contextual reading and writing experiences to hear sounds in words, placing particular emphasis upon rhyming texts.

WHAT AM I SAYING? (AUDITORY BLENDING OF SOUNDS)

Purpose

Students are asked to recognize words by blending the sounds that teachers stretch out into segmented units, such as, *m-an* or *sh-i-p* (we call this "word rubber-banding"). According to Griffith and Olson (1992), the ability to guess what the word is from its

Figure 6.3   Rhyming Word Pair Task List

plate	dog
fat	cat
book	hook
desk	shelf
fish	swish
shoe	ball
tree	grass
flower	power
key	lock
pen	tape
swing	thing
sat	rat
box	clock
bark	smart
berry	hairy
cow	milk
brick	thick
malt	halt
wall	call
toy	love

blended form demonstrates a slightly higher level of phonemic awareness than recognizing rhyming sounds.

Materials

As shown in Figure 6.4, prepare a list of 30 words divided into three sets of 10 each.

- The first set of 10 words should have 2 phonemes.
- The second set of 10 words should have 3–4 phonemes that are divided before the vowel, demonstrating the onset and rime, such as *c* (onset) - *ap* (rime).
- The third set of 10 words should have 3–4 phonemes that are segmented completely, such as *ch-i-p*.

Procedures

Tell the child that you will be stretching words out like a rubber band, saying each sound. Model several of these stretched words and tell her the word you have stretched. For example, stretch the word *s-i-t*. Then say the word *sit*. Do this several times. Next, stretch a word and ask the child to tell you the word. Once this has been accomplished, tell the child you are going to play a game in which you

Figure 6.4   Blended Word Lists

at	l-ap	l-o-ck
two	t-ip	s-t-e-m
in	m-an	b-ea-k
if	st-ate	h-i-de
be	b-ox	c-a-sh
as	sc-ab	m-i-c-e
sea	r-ug	sh-ee-t
now	m-ind	f-r-o-g
go	th-ink	j-u-m-p
sew	p-ig	t-ur-key

say a stretched-out word and she is to answer the question. What am I saying? According to Yopp's (1988) research, kindergarten children achieve a mean score of 66% correct, identifying 20 of the 30 target words correctly. If students score poorly on this task, teachers should provide reading and writing experiences that help children hear sounds in words. Creating invented spellings for writing new words and using word rubber-banding to sound out new words found in trade books are just two examples.

NAME THAT SOUND

Purpose

Students are asked to listen to and isolate sounds in the initial, medial, and final positions in a word. A child's ability to isolate sounds in words is an excellent indication of whether she can profit from decoding instruction.

Materials

Construct a list of 15 words consisting of 3 phonemes each. Target sounds in the beginning, middle, and end of the words as in Figure 6.5.

Figure 6.5   Segmenting Sounds in a Word List

d ime	*f* ool	*k i* ss
hu *sh*	l *oo* p	g *e* t
fi *ve*	*r* ode	raf *t*
clo *ck*	*h* ome	*b* ike
c *u* t	yar *d*	mu *g*

Procedures

Model how phonemes can be pronounced by showing how *sit* starts with /s/, *hike* has the /i/ sound in the middle, and *look* ends with the /k/ sound. Next, tell the child you are going to play a quick game together. You will say a word, then you will ask her to tell you the sound she hears in a specific place in the word—the beginning, middle, or end. For example you may say: "*Slam*. Say the sound at the end of the word *slam*." The child responds correctly by articulating the sound /m/. Now continue, using the list of words shown in Figure 6.5. Record each response.

According to Yopp's (1988) research study, kindergarten children achieve a mean score of 9% correct, giving 1 to 2 correct responses in 15 target words. If students score poorly on this task, teachers should provide reading and writing experiences focusing on hearing sounds in specific locations within words.

DICTATION: WRITING PHONEMES IN WORDS

Purpose

Students are asked to listen to several words stretched out or "rubber-banded". Next, students are asked to rubber-band the word(s) as the teacher dictates them, writing the sounds they hear in each word. Calkins (1986) relates how word rubber-banding is used in her teacher's college writing project to help children learn how to listen for sounds. Carnine, Silbert, and Kameenui (1990) refer to a similar approach for stretching words called *auditory telescoping*. Yopp (1992) indicates that the ability to speak the phonemes within a word is a very difficult level of phonemic awareness to achieve. The ability to both speak and write phonemes in words indicates an advanced level of phonemic awareness that can be used effectively in reading and writing instruction.

Materials

Compile a list of 22 words of 2 or 3 phonemes each. Be sure to include a variety of words with varying consonant and vowel patterns (i.e., some that begin with consonants, others that begin with vowel sounds). An example list is shown in Figure 6.6.

Procedures

Demonstrate how several words can be stretched or rubber-banded into sounds—both orally and in writing. Next, invite the child to rubber-band and write the words in the list as you did. This task assesses whether children have developed an ability to hear and map sounds through writing by using invented spellings. Yopp (1988) found the response rate for kindergartners to this task was 12 out of 22, or about 55% correct. Griffith and Olson (1992) indicate that the word rubber-banding task has been shown to be a highly reliable, authentic measure of phonemic awareness, and a good indication of whether a child is ready for decoding instruction.

Figure 6.6   Word List

page	did
live	my
big	this
sat	have
men	some
no	back
me	say
can	now
get	but
on	come
at	tile

ALPHABET AWARENESS TEST

Purpose

The purpose of this task is to determine whether children can in some way identify the concept of an alphabet in written and spoken language. Walsh, Price, and Gillingham (1988) found that letter naming was strongly related to early reading achievement for kindergarten children. Simple awareness that an alphabet exists is necessary for understanding any alphabetic language system.

Materials

One copy of the alphabet awareness task form shown in Figure 6.7.

Figure 6.7   Alphabet Awareness Test

> **Alphabet Awareness Test**
>
> 1. Have you ever heard of the alphabet or *abc's*?   Yes ____   No ____
>
> 2. Can you tell me what this is?   Answer_____
>
>   A B C D E F G H I J K L M N O P Q R S T U V W X Y Z
>
> 3. Can you tell me any alphabet letters you know?
>
> 4. Do you know any songs, poems, books, or rhymes about the alphabet?
>
>   Yes____   No____   Give me an example:
>
> 5. Can you tell me the order of the alphabet letters beginning with the letter *A*?   Yes__   No____
>
>   Answer _____

Procedures

Begin this task by seating the child next to you. Ask each question on the Alphabetic Awareness Task form. On Question 3, if another alphabet display is available in the immediate area (such as those typically displayed over classroom chalkboards), point to that display and ask the same question. Results of this task should give teachers a sense of a student's alphabetic awareness. Teachers should view these results as a means to inform and direct their selection of alphabetic and phonemic awareness activities discussed later in this chapter.

Balanced Reading Program Interventions: Developing Phonemic Awareness and the Alphabetic Principle

Special Needs Indicators and Teaching Strategies for Readers

Teachers may observe several significant learning needs related to simple alphabet knowledge, phonemic awareness, or the alphabetic principle. Common special needs indicators are listed below:

- Little or no knowledge of the alphabet
- Inability to name letters when presented
- Inability to produce letter or letterlike forms in writing
- Inability to recognize rhyming sounds
- Inability to recognize or identify specific letter sounds in words
- Inability to map spoken sounds onto letters

Several effective strategies for helping readers with special learning needs in the areas of simple alphabet knowledge, the alphabetic principle, and phonemic awareness are described below.

Language Watching

Purpose

As teachers get to know their student's phonemic awareness and alphabetic principle needs, they often search in books for opportunities to teach to these needs. When just the right book, song, chant, or other print opportunity is found by the teacher, it is used to teach to the student's need. This act is called *language watching*—the search for and creative use of print materials to teach phonemic awareness and alphabet principle skills (Reutzel, 1992). Following are several language watching ideas that may be helpful.

Materials

Any texts, stories, or poems that can be used to highlight sounds or sound-letter connections in language.

Procedures

Option 1: Select a poem, for instance, "Sister for Sale" (Silverstein, 1976), for a shared reading experience. Next, read the poem, looking for language patterns useful in furthering the student's knowledge of the alphabetic principle. After reading and analyzing this poem, the teacher determines that "Sister for Sale" provides an excellent opportunity to demonstrate one sound associated with the letter /s/.

Option 2: Teachers may wish to highlight certain sounds by verbally emphasizing them while reading a poem, text, or story. Using stick-on notes to cover or mask certain letters representing selected sounds can draw attention to the relationship between letters and spoken sounds.

Option 3: A frame with a sliding window, as shown in Figure 6.8, can be used to help children blend letter sounds from left to right to apply letter-sound knowledge to *sounding out* words.

Figure 6.8 Language Frame with Sliding Window

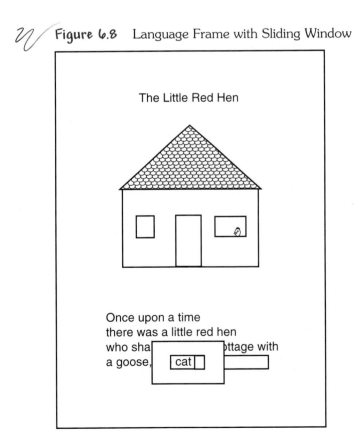

USING ENVIRONMENTAL PRINT

Purpose

The purpose of this strategy is to use familiar examples of writing from the students' environment (such as cereal boxes, signs, bumper stickers, and candy wrappers) to help them begin to understand how sounds and letters go together (the alphabetic principle). Hiebert and Ham (1981) have found in their research that children who were taught the alphabetic principle using environmental print learned significantly more letter names and sounds than did children who learned alphabet letters without using environmental print. Familiar print in the environment can be used in interesting ways to give children confidence in reading and writing and to help them understand how print works.

Materials

The only materials needed for this strategy are collectibles from home and school. Can labels, empty cereal boxes, bumper stickers, advertisements from the local papers, and other old boxes or containers are usually available in large quantities.

Procedures

Begin by setting aside a classroom display area, bulletin board, or wall that is designated as an *Environmental Print* wall. Children may be asked to bring environmental print or product logos from home to put on this display wall in random order. Next, environmental print can be taken down and rearranged in an alphabet display, with 26 blocks or areas reserved for each alphabet letter, as shown in Figure 6.9. For example, specific print items such as *Butterfinger, Baby Ruth,* and *Batman* can be placed in a block for the letter *B*.

In some cases, children can be asked to bring environmental print to school for a specific letter name or sound. These activities maintain an authentic language context for learning the alphabetic principle through readings of complete stories, poems, chants, or songs. After discussing and displaying letter-specific environmental print, teachers and children can cut and paste environmental print items onto 5" × 7" plain index cards. These letter name and sound environmental print collections may be bound together on a ring to be read in small groups or by individuals in an alphabet center (see Figure 6.10).

Selected letter/word patterns, such as the final silent *e*, also can be taught from known environmental print items to illustrate various phonic rules. Environmental print logos can be collected and bound together to represent selected letter/word patterns, such as the silent *e* found in *Sprite, Coke, Tide,* etc. Other possibilities for using environmental print include: producing classroom signs using product logos to substitute for written word(s); cutting up environmental print to compose notes between teachers and children; or making word collages for an art activity.

Figure 6.9   Environmental Print Chart

Alphabet Wall			Butterfinger	Coca-Cola	

PLAYING WITH THE ALPHABET

Purpose

Morrow (1993) has suggested that children can learn the alphabetic principle by enjoying playful activities centering around letter naming, letter sounds, and the connection between letter names and sounds. Providing relaxed and gamelike learning opportunities can often spark the desire to learn the letters and sounds.

Figure 6.10   Environmental Print Ring

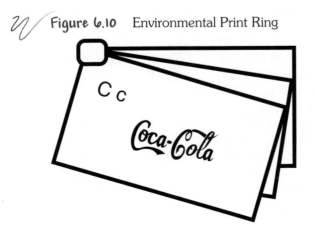

Materials

Alphabet puzzles, magnetic letters, sandpaper letters, alphabet games, letter stencils, letter flash cards, alphabet charts, dry-erase boards, clay trays, paper, pencils, markers, painting easels, alphabet logos, cereals and foods, and commercially published alphabet books all may be used in constructing alphabet play games.

Procedures

An alphabet station or center stocked with alphabet puzzles, magnetic letters, sand paper letters, alphabet games, stencils, flash cards, and alphabet charts can be a part of every kindergarten or first-grade classroom station or learning center. Children can be invited to write, trace, or copy alphabet letters. Individual-sized chalkboards, dry-erase boards, clay trays, tracing paper, and painting easels naturally draw children into copying, tracing, and experimenting with letters.

Delicious possibilities can be periodically added to this rich alphabet activity menu. Samples of alphabet soup, animal crackers, and Alphabits cereal may be provided. Children may be encouraged to sort the letters or animals into alphabet letter categories prior to eating. Children can eat in pairs or small groups and talk about which letter they are eating. This playful interaction increases children's awareness of letters, sounds, and alphabetical order. In teaching the alphabetic principle, other playful experiences may be used as well. To emphasize specific letter sounds found in the course of language watching, activities involving a sip of Sprite, a bite of a Snickers candy bar, a long spaghetti noodle to munch on, and a handful of Skittles to taste may be used successfully to emphasize /s/. Art experiences can be designed in which children create pictures using a given alphabet letter as the beginning point. Collages of things that begin with /s/, for example, such as a sack, screw, safety pin, salt, silver, or sand can be created and displayed.

Further, environmental print logos can be used to make *I Can Read Alphabet Pattern* books. These books are often patterned after well-known alphabet books such as *The Z was Zapped* (Van Allsburg, 1987) and *On Market Street* (Lobel, 1981). Children select one product to represent the /c/ sound from a group of alphabetized logos such as Coca-Cola, Cocoa Puffs, Cap'n Crunch, etc. Other alphabetized product labels are selected to represent the remaining letters of the alphabet in child-produced *I Can Read Alphabet Pattern* books. Because children select logos they can already read, these books are easily read by every child. They become a source of confidence building and enjoyment.

SONGS, CHANTS, AND POETRY
Purpose

The purpose of using songs, chants, and poetry is to explore and discover how letter sounds combine to create words, word parts, and, when combined, written and oral language. Weaver (1988, 1990) suggested that many teachers use songs, poetry, raps, and chants to convey the alphabetic principle as an alternative to the more tedious direct teaching and drill of phonic generalizations and letter sounds.

Materials

Select songs, chants, and poems according to the needs and interests of your students. Your media specialist/school librarian can assist you in making choices.

Procedures

When using poetry, songs, and chants, teachers can watch for specific letters that are repeated in texts to be used as examples for learning the alphabetic principle and developing phonemic awareness. For example, to emphasize the letter /s/ for a day or so, teachers might select and enlarge onto chart paper the text of the chants "Sally go round the sun" or "Squid Sauce" to be read aloud by the group. Songs such as "See Saw, Margery Daw" or "Sandy Land" may be selected and the lyrics enlarged onto charts for practice and group singing. Shel Silverstein's (1976) "Sister for Sale" or Jack Prelutsky's (1984) "Sneaky Sue" poems could be likewise enlarged and used to emphasize the name and sound of the letter /s/ through repeated group readings.

ALPHABET BOOKS

Purpose

The purpose of using alphabet books is to assist young and special needs readers in discovering the order and elements of the alphabet, both names and sounds. To do this, teachers may wish to acquire collections of quality alphabet trade books. *On Market Street* (Lobel, 1981), *Animalia* (Base, 1986), and *The Z was Zapped* (Van Allsburg, 1987) are just a few of the many delightful books that can be used to teach children the alphabet.

Materials

Commercially published alphabet books.

Procedures

After multiple readings of commercially produced alphabet books, teachers and children can construct their own highly predictable alphabet books using the commercial books as patterns. In an established writing center, young students can create both reproductions and innovations of commercial alphabet books shared in class. A *reproduction* is a student-made copy of an original commercially produced alphabet book. Children copy the text of each page exactly and draw their own illustrations for a reproduction. *Innovations* borrow the basic pattern of commercially produced alphabet books, but change the selected words. For instance, one group of first-grade students made innovations on the book *The Z Was Zapped* (Van Allsburg, 1987). Each child chose a letter and made a new illustration as an innovation. One child, Kevin, picked the letter /d/ and drew a picture of the letter in the shape of a doughnut being dunked into a cup of hot chocolate. The caption underneath the picture read THE "D" WAS DUNKED. Reproductions and innovations of alphabet books help students take ownership of familiar text and encourage them to learn about the alphabetic principle through experimentation. Reproductions and innovations of alphabet books also help children sense that they can learn to read successfully.

WRITING EXPERIENCES

Purpose

Marie Clay (1993) suggests that children practice many of the skills of reading in another form when they write, and vice versa. As a rule, writing activities should not take the form of copying or tracing. Instead, they should grow naturally from the child's *thoughts* to *saying* words to *writing* words.

Materials

Plain unlined paper, lined paper, construction paper (multiple colors), drawing paper, poster paper, crayons, watercolors, water-based markers, colored pencils, pencils, felt-tip pens, felt-tip calligraphy pens, scissors, staplers, staples, brass fasteners, card stock, hole punch, yarn, wallpaper and wrapping paper for book covers, glue stick, tape, paper clips, ruler, and letter stencils all are useful.

Procedures

Since chapters 5 and 12 have several useful tips for using writing activities to enhance special needs readers' knowledge of language, we mention writing as a strategy again at this point to remind teachers that writing plays an important part in helping special needs or younger readers become successful readers and writers.

WORD RUBBER-BANDING

Purpose

As mentioned earlier in the chapter, the purpose of word rubber-banding is to help children hear sounds in words and be able to represent these sounds in writing. Listening to words in text or attempting to write one's own words with invented spellings are direct ways to enhance phonemic and alphabetic awareness. Not only can word rubber-banding be used in assessment, it is also a helpful means of developing young or special needs readers' alphabetic and phonemic awareness.

Materials

Some materials that might be useful include texts that play with words, such as *Jamberry* (Degen, 1983); a list of words taken from a recently read story such as *The House That Jack Built* (Stevens, 1985); or a collection of words germane to students' learning and interests, such as colors, numbers, days of the week, and holiday words.

Procedures

Teacher modeling is needed in the beginning to help children understand the process. For example, during the Christmas season students may want to write stories about Santa Claus. The teacher could offer the following model for her students for *Scrooge* after explaining the concept of word rubber-banding:

Teacher: Listen while I stretch out the name *Scrooge* as I say it aloud. *Ssssccr-rooooogggge.* I sounded kind of like Marley's ghost when I said it like that, didn't I? Now, watch as I write the name *Scrooge* while saying it like Marley's ghost.

Observations: As the teacher rubber-bands the name *Scrooge* again orally, she writes the following letters that are easily heard. *S-c-r-o-o-g.*

Teacher: Now that I have written the word, *Scrooge,* I can begin to check it to see if I spelled it accurately. Where could I find the correct spelling of *Scrooge,* class?

Children: Maybe in a dictionary. Maybe in the book, *A Christmas Carol.*

By stretching words out phoneme by phoneme, sound clues are provided to students. These sound clues can help in both hearing and writing the sounds in a word that often result in an invented spelling for a word. When children have an opportunity to practice these word rubber-banding strategies in the context of real writing, the connection between letters and their sounds becomes even clearer.

HEARING SOUNDS IN WORDS

Purpose

Learning to use graphophonic cues requires that students orchestrate two different modalities: listening and seeing. Students need to develop the ability to hear sounds in words in sequence and to match these sounds in a left-to-right visual sequence to the letters (Yopp & Troyer, 1992). A version of this activity has been used successfully for a number of years in holistic intervention programs, such as Reading Recovery.

Materials

Prepare 5 to 10 cards with pictures as shown in Figure 6.11 using words already familiar to the student.

Procedures

This activity uses a card with a picture clue, such as the one shown in Figure 6.11 for the word *cat.* The teacher begins by pronouncing the word very slowly while pushing a chip into a box for each letter/sound, progressing sound by sound

Figure 6.11   Word Rubber-Banding Chart ("Pushing Sounds")

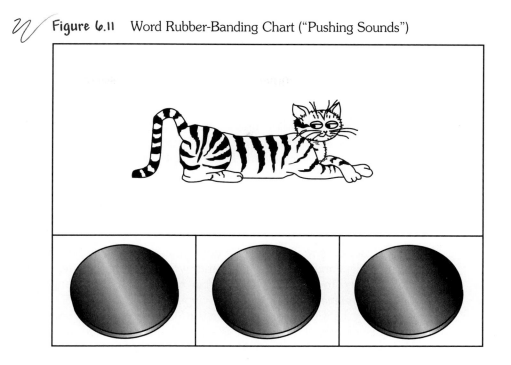

(CCCCC—AAAAAAA—TTTTT). After an initial demonstration, the child is encouraged to join in the activity by saying the next word slowly while the teacher pushes a chip into a box for each letter/sound. Note: This activity is sometimes called "pushing sound."

The teacher gradually releases responsibility to the child by exchanging roles. For example, the teacher can pronounce the word and the child can push chips into the boxes for each letter/sound. Finally, the child can both say the word and push a chip into a box for each letter/sound entirely on her own. Eventually, children should be able to count the number of sounds in a word and answer questions about the order of sounds in words (Griffith & Olson, 1992).

An extension of this idea involves drawing boxes and asking a child how to write a word by filling in the boxes. This approach can be connected with word rubber-banding and the notion of invented spellings.

Sound Addition or Substitution

Purpose

Adding or substituting sounds in words in familiar songs, stories, or rhymes may help special needs and younger readers attend to the sounds in their speech. The ability to add or substitute sounds in words in familiar language is easier than segmenting sounds and benefits students in many of the same ways.

Materials

Any song, rhyme, or chant will be useful.

Procedures

Two strategies add enjoyment to developing awareness of phonemes and the alphabetic principle. The first of these is *consonant substitution.* When using this strategy, initial, final, or medial consonants in words found in a phrase or sentence can be exchanged. For example, in the Shel Silverstein poem "Jimmie Jet and His TV Set," change the consonants from /j/ to /n/ or /b/ to produce:

"Nimmie Net and His TV Set"
"Bimmie Bet and His TV Set"

Special needs readers find the nonsensical result to be both humorous and helpful in understanding how consonants work in connected text. Other consonants may be used to vary both the number of consonants exchanged and the position of the exchanged consonants in the words.

A second strategy is *vowel substitution.* When using a vowel substitution strategy, a single vowel (and sound) is selected and substituted in key words in the text. For example, in the poem *Mary Had a Little Lamb,* the vowel sounds can be changed to produce a completely nonsensical version with *Miry hid a little limb* by substituting the /i/ short vowel sound in place of the vowels in the original poem.

Children find that adding, changing, or substituting sounds in this way turns learning about letters and sounds into a game. One first-grade, chapter 1 student who had been working with his teacher late one afternoon using these strategies remarked on his way out the door to catch his bus, "Teacher, can we play some more games tomorrow?" This statement sums up the enthusiasm these two strategies generate among young children as they learn to focus their attention on the graphophonic cues embedded in print to develop alphabetic and phonemic awareness.

SOUND SEGMENTATION

Purpose

Segmenting refers to isolating individual sounds in a spoken word. Segmenting can be one of the more difficult phonemic awareness tasks for students. It is, however, an important skill for children to develop if they are to profit from implicit or indirect instruction related to letter names, sounds, and the connections between the two. Segmenting is basically an oral version of word rubber-banding. One strategy used to develop the ability to segment sounds is called *iteration* and is described below.

Materials

Any song, poem, rhyme, chant, or story may be used.

Procedures

Begin by singing a favorite song such as "Old MacDonald Had a Farm." Next, ask the children to repeat the first sounds of selected words as follows: "Old m-m-m-MacDonald had a f-f-f-farm, e i e i o, and on this f-f-f-farm he had a c-c-c-cow, e i e i o. With a m-m-m-moo here and a m-m-m-moo there, here a moo, there a moo, everywhere a moo moo . . . ." Children's names can be used in this fashion such as J-J-J-Jason, or K-K-K-Kate. Still another variation on iteration involves drawing a sound out or exaggerating the sound, for example, MMMMMaaaaarrrrryyyy had a little llllllllaaaaammmmm. Beyond this iterative technique, children can be asked to segment entire words. Griffith and Olson (1992) recommend a song set to the tune of "Twinkle, Twinkle Little Star" for this purpose.

> *Listen, Listen*
> *To my word*
> *Tell me all the sounds you heard:* race (pronounce this word slowly)
> */r/ is one sound*
> */a/ is two*
> */s/ is last in race*
> *It's true.*

When working with the segmentation of entire words, it is best to use words of no more than three to four sounds because of the difficulty of these tasks for young children or special-needs learners. However, with careful guidance, children can experience high levels of success as they develop phonemic awareness through segmentation tasks.

CHAPTER SUMMARY

In this chapter, the concepts of *phonemic awareness, letter name knowledge,* and the *alphabetic principle* have been explored to inform teachers about how these elements develop and combine to influence special needs learners' ability to progress into successful and skillful readers and writers. Specific informal assessment tasks were presented for use to determine students' letter name knowledge, phonemic awareness, and their understanding of the alphabetic principle. After conducting careful assessment related to these critical components of the graphophonic subsystem in language, several approaches for helping special needs learners understand, develop, and apply phonemic and alphabetic awareness knowledge to reading and writing were presented. Approaches for developing letter name knowledge, phonemic awareness, and the alphabetic principle were embedded in authentic reading and writing opportunities.

REFERENCES

Adams, M. J. (1990). *Beginning to read: Thinking and learning about print.* Cambridge, MA: M.I.T. Press.

Anderson, R. C., Hiebert, E. F., Scott, J. A., & Wilkinson, I. A. G. (1985). *Becoming a nation of readers: The report of the commission on reading.* Washington, D.C.: The National Institute of Education.

Base, G. (1986). *Animalia.* New York: Harry N. Abrams.

Byrne, B., & Fielding-Barnsley, R. (1989). Phonemic awareness and letter knowledge in the child's acquisition of the alphabetic principle. *Journal of Educational Psychology, 81,* 313–321.

Calkins, L. (1986). *The Art of Teaching Writing.* Portsmouth, NH: Heinemann Educational Books.

Carnine, D., Silbert, J., & Kameenui, E. (1990). *Direct instruction reading* (2nd ed). Columbus, OH: Merrill Publishing Company.

Chall, J. S. (1996). Stages of reading development. Fort Worth, TX: Harcourt Brace.

Clay, M. M. (1993). *An observation survey of early literacy acheivement.* Portsmouth, NH: Heinemann.

Cunningham, A. E. (1990). Explicit versus implicit instruction in phonemic awareness. *Journal of Experimental Child Psychology, 50,* 429–444.

Degen, B. (1983). *Jamberry.* New York: Harper & Row.

Goodman, K. S. (1986). *What's whole in whole language?* Ontario, Canada: Scholastic.

Griffith, P. L., & Olson, M. W. (1992). Phonemic awareness helps beginning readers break the code. *The Reading Teacher, 45,* 516–523.

Harris, T. L., & Hodges, R. E. (1995). *The literacy dictionary: The vocabulary of reading and writing.* Newark, DE: International Reading Association.

Hiebert, E., & Ham, D. (1981). *Young children and environmental print.* Paper presented at the annual meeting of the National Reading Conference, Dallas, TX.

Holdaway, D. (1979). *The foundations of literacy.* New York: Ashton Scholastic.

Juel, C. (1991). Beginning reading. In R. Barr, M. Kamil, P. Mosenthal, & P. D. Pearson (Eds.), *Handbook of Reading Research* (Vol. 2). New York, NY: Longman.

Lobel, A. (1981). *On market street.* Pictures by Anita Lobel; Text by Arnold Lobel. New York: Scholastic.

Mason, J. M. (1980). When do children begin to read: An exploration of four-year-old children's letter and word reading competencies. *Reading Research Quarterly, 15,* 203–227.

Morrow, L. M. (1993). *Literacy development in the early years: Helping children read and write.* Boston, MA: Allyn and Bacon.

Prelutsky, J. (1984). *The new kid on the block.* New York: Greenwillow Books.

Reutzel, D. R. (1992). Breaking the letter-a-week tradition: Conveying the alphabetic principle to young children. *Childhood Education, 69*(1), 20–24.

Richgels, D. J., Poremba, K. J., & McGee, L. M. (1996). Kindergarteners talk about print: Phonemic awareness in meaningful contexts. *The Reading Teacher, 49*(8), 632–642.

Silverstein, S. (1976). *A light in the attic.* New York: Harper & Row.

Stahl, S. A., & Murray, B. A. (1994). Defining phonological awareness and its relationship to early reading. *Journal of Educational Psychology, 86*(2), 221–234.

Stevens, J. (1985). *The house that Jack built.* New York: Holiday House.

Strickland, D. (1998). *Teaching phonics today: A primer for educators.* Newark, DE: International Reading Association.

Van Allsburg, C. (1987). *The Z was Zapped.* Boston: Houghton-Mifflin.

Venezky, R. L. (1975). The curious role of letter names in reading instruction. *Visible Language, 9,* 7–23.

Walsh, D. J., Price, G. G., & Gillingham, M. G. (1988). The critical but transitory importance of letter naming. *Reading Research Quarterly, 23,* 108–122.

Weaver, C. (1988). *Reading process and practice: From socio-psycholinguistics to whole language.* Portsmouth, NH: Heinemann Educational Books.

Weaver, C. (1990). *Understanding whole language: From principles to prac-tices.* Portsmouth, NH: Heinemann Educational Books.

Yopp, H. K. (1988). The validity and reliability of phonemic awareness tests. *Reading Research Quarterly, 23,* 159–177.

Yopp, H. K. (1992). Developing phonemic awareness in young children. *The Reading Teacher, 45,* 696–703.

Yopp, H. K. & Troyer, S. (1992). *Training phonemic awareness in young children.* Unpublished manuscript.

Chapter 7

Teaching and Assessing Phonics in a Balanced Reading Program

Phonics refers to the relationships between letter sounds and spelling patterns within written language, and to the reader's use of this knowledge to decode unknown words (Rasinski & Padak, 1996). Phonics instruction is an essential part of balanced reading programs in the early grades. As children begin to emerge as readers, phonics knowledge can assist them in approximating the pronunciation of words and, as a consequence, can help readers discover meanings of unfamiliar words in print. Phonics skills are best taught *after* phonemic awareness and alphabetic principle have been learned by students. When phonics rules are used in conjunction with semantic (meaning) and syntactic (grammar) cues in a reading passage, the reader can positively identify unknown words in instructional level reading materials.

Though phonics is an essential tool in a reader's arsenal, there is one important prerequisite to remember: for phonics to help the reader, the word(s) to be decoded must already be known. That is, the words must be in the reader's listening and speaking vocabulary. Thus, for many children, a solid preschool-kindergarten language development program is a crucial part of a balanced literacy program. This is particularly true not only for children learning English as a second language (ESL), but also for children who come from homes in which there is a lack of regular and rich language interaction with siblings and adults.

In this chapter we summarize some of the more recent phonics research and suggest activities that we have found useful in assessing and developing this important constellation of reading skills.

BACKGROUND BRIEFING FOR TEACHERS

Recent surveys conducted by The International Reading Association (IRA) indicate that phonics is one of the most talked about subjects in the field of reading education (second only to the topic of balanced reading). In reviewing the literature, we have concluded that there are two essential areas for you to know about: *which* phonics skills and generalizations you should consider teaching to emerging readers, and *how* you might teach these skills in your classroom.

As a kind of self-awareness check on phonics knowledge, we have included a Phonics Quick Test in Figure 7.1 so that you can determine just how much you already know. (The results may surprise you!) Please complete the exercise below *before* reading on.

A Review of Phonics Skills and Generalizations Commonly Taught

In spite of the fact that many basal reader series feature long lists of phonics skills and generalizations, there are actually only a few skills that have a reasonably high degree of consistency according to the research. Indeed, because of the many exceptions and irregularities of the English language, there are only seven phonics generalizations that are consistent forty-nine percent of the time or better (May & Elliot, 1978)! Nevertheless, when used in conjunction with other decoding strategies, phonics generalizations can be of immense help to readers. Following are the most reliable phonics generalizations and, thus, those that should be taught to students beginning to learn decoding strategies. [We wish to note that some of these explanations are derived from Hull (1989) and cited in our earlier work, *Teaching Children to Read* (Reutzel & Cooter, 1996).]

The C Rule

The letter *c* is an irregular consonant letter that has no phoneme of its own. Instead, it assumes two other phonemes found in different words—*k* and *s*. In general, when the letter *c* is followed by *a, o,* or *u,* it will represent the sound we associated with the letter *k,* also known as the *hard c* sound. Some examples are the words *cake, cosmic,* and *cute.* On the other hand, the letter *c* can sometimes represent the sound associated with the letter *s.* This is referred to as the *soft c* sound. The *soft c* sound is usually produced when *c* is followed by *e, i,* or *y.* Examples of the *soft c* sound are in the words *celebrate, circus,* and *cycle.*

The G Rule

G is the key symbol for the phoneme we hear in the word *get* (Hull, 1989, p. 35). It is also irregular, having a *soft g* and a *hard g* sound. The rules remain the same as they are for the letter *c.* When *g* is followed by the letters *e, i,* or *y,* it represents a *soft g* or *j* sound, as in the words *gently, giraffe,* and *gym.* If *g* is followed by the letters *a, o,* or *u,* then it usually represents the *hard* (or regular) *sound,* as in the words *garden, go,* and *sugar.*

The CVC Generalization

When a vowel comes between two consonants, it usually has the short vowel sound. Examples of words following the CVC pattern include *sat, ran, let, pen, win, fit, hot, mop, sun,* and *cut.*

Figure 7.1   Checking Phonics Knowledge

A Phonics Quick Test*

1. The word *charkle* is divided between _____ and _____. The *a* has an _____-controlled sound, and the *e* is _____.

2. In the word *small,* *sm-* is known as the *onset* and *-all* is known as the _____.

3. *Ch* in the word *chair* is known as a _____.

4. The letter *c* in the word *city* is a _____ sound; in the word *cow,* the letter *c* is a _____ sound.

5. The letters *bl* in the word *blue* are referred to as a consonant _____.

6. The underlined vowels in the words *author, spread,* and *blue* are known as vowel _____.

7. The words *tag, run, cot,* and *get* have which vowel pattern? _____

8. The words *glide, take,* and *use* have the _____ vowel pattern.

9. The single most powerful phonics skill we can teach to emergent readers for decoding unfamiliar words in print is _____ sounds in words. We introduce this skill using _____ sounds first because they are the most _____.

10. The word part *work* in the word *working* is known as a _____.

11. The word part *-ing* in the word *working* is known as a _____.

12. Cues to the meaning and pronunciation of unfamiliar words in print are often found in the print surrounding the unfamiliar, also known as the _____.

*Answers to the *Phonics Quick Test* are found at the end of this chapter.

Vowel Digraphs

When two vowels come together in a word, usually the first vowel is long and the second vowel is silent. This occurs especially often with the *oa, ee,* and *ay* combinations. Some examples are *toad, fleet,* and *day.* A common slogan used by teachers, which helps children remember this generalization, is "when two vowels go walking, the first one does the talking."

The VCE (Final E) Generalization

When two vowels appear in a word and one is an *e* at the end of the word, the first vowel is generally long and the final *e* is silent. Examples include *cape, rope,* and *kite.*

The CV Generalization

When a consonant is followed by a vowel, the vowel usually produces a long sound. This is especially easy to see in two-letter words such as *be, go,* and *so.*

R-Controlled Vowels

Vowels that appear before the letter *r* are usually neither long nor short, but tend to be overpowered or "swallowed up" by the sound. Examples include *person, player, neighborhood,* and *herself.*

OTHER COMMON PHONICS SKILLS WORTH TEACHING

Moore (1951) and Black (1961) performed exhaustive reviews of words in English to determine the most predictable phonics rules. The following are selected phonics patterns they discovered (other than those described previously), along with a few other patterns that we have found may be worth teaching to students.

Consonant Rules

- *Single consonants* Single consonants nearly always make the same sound. It is recommended that they be taught in the following order due to their frequency in our language: *T, N, R, M, D, S (sat), L, C (cat), P, S, F, V, G (got), H, W, K, J, Z, Y.*
- *Consonant digraphs* Two consonants together in a word that produce only one speech sound (*th, sh, ng*).
- *Initial consonant blends or clusters* Two or more consonants coming together in which the speech sounds of all the consonants may be heard are called *consonant blends* (*bl, fr, sk, spl*). Consonant blends that come at the beginning of words are the most consistent in the sounds they make. It is recommended that they be taught in the following order due to their frequency in English:

Group 1	Group 2	Group 3	Group 4
ST	PL	SC	SM
PR	SP	BL	GL
TR	CR	FL	SN
GR	CL	SK	TW
BR	DR	SL	
	FR	SW	

- *Double consonants* When two consonants come together in a word, they usually make the sound of a single consonant (e.g., *all, apple, arrow, attic*, etc.).
- *PH and the F sound* Ph always is pronounced as F (e.g., *phone, phoneme, philosophy, phobia, phenomenon*, etc.).

Vowel Rules

- *Schwa* Vowel letters that produce the *uh* sound (*a* in *America*). The schwa is represented by the upside-down *e* symbol (ə)
- *Diphthongs* Two vowels together in a word that produce a single, glided sound (*oi* in *oil, oy* in *boy*).
- *The y Rules* When the letter *y* comes at the end of a long word (or a word having at least one other vowel), it will have the sound of long *e* as in *baby*. When *y* comes at the end of a short word or in the middle of a word, it will make the sound of long *i* as in *cry* and *cycle*.

ONSET AND RIME: A PHONICS-RELATED SUBJECT

There has been significant research in recent years that suggests that word elements known as *onset* and *rime* are much more reliable sound/symbol patterns for children to learn and can have a high degree of utility. Because onset and rime can be useful as both word identification and vocabulary-building tools, we have elected to place this important information in chapter 8, on teaching and assessing vocabulary development.

Syllabication

The ability to segment words into syllables is yet another form of "phonic awareness" that can be useful when encountering unknown words. The research has been very inconclusive indeed as to whether teaching syllabication actually helps students with identifying unknown words in print. Nevertheless, we include in Figures 7.2 and 7.3 the syllabication rules that seem to be the most reliable for 1) dividing words, and 2) pronouncing words (Manzo & Manzo, 1993). (Note: We tend to favor teaching students to use common onset and rime knowledge whenever possible to segment words in print, as discussed in chapter 8.)

Figure 7.2   Syllabication Rules for Dividing Words
(Manzo & Manzo, 1993)

1. When two identical consonants come together, they are divided to form two syllables. Examples: *ap / ple, but / ter, lit / tle*
2. The number of vowel sounds that occur in a word usually indicate how many syllables there will be in the word. Examples: *slave* (one vowel sound/one syllable); *caboose* (four vowels, but only two vowel sounds, hence, two syllables—*ca / boose*).
3. Two unlike consonants are also usually divided to form syllables, unless they form a consonant digraph. Example: *car / pet*
4. Small words within a compound word are syllables (as with onset/rimes). Examples: *book / store, fire / fly*

Structural Analysis

Structural analysis refers to the study of words to identify their meaning-bearing units (called *morphemes*). Words are made up of two classes or morphemes—free and bound. *Free morphemes* are word parts (words, really) that can stand alone. They are also known as "root words." For example, in the word *working, work* is the root word or free morpheme. In contrast, *bound morphemes* must be attached to a root word to have meaning. Prefixes and suffixes (together referred to as *affixes*) are usually bound morphemes. Common prefixes, which come *before* a root word, include: *intro-, pro-, post-, sub-,* and *dis-.* Some of the more common suffixes, which come after the root word, include: *-ant, -ist, -ence, -ism, -s,* and *-ed.* As you are attending to students' reading miscues, you may sometimes note problems with root words or affixes that may require minilessons.

Figure 7.3   Syllabication Rules for Pronouncing Words
(Manzo & Manzo, 1993)

1. *le* is pronounced as *ul* when it appears at the end of a word. Examples: *shuttle, little, remarkable.*
2. Syllables that end with a vowel usually have a long vowel sound. Examples: *bi / lingual, re / read.*
3. When a vowel does not come at the end of a syllable, and it is followed by two consonants, it will usually have a short sound. Examples: *let / ter, all, attic.*

RECENT RESEARCH ON PHONICS AND RELATED SKILLS

In 1990, Marilyn J. Adams published a research summary derived from her doctoral dissertation on beginning reading instruction. Adams essentially reviewed a century of reading research on emergent literacy and arrived at several important conclusions. According to numerous studies, it now seems clear, for instance, that letter knowledge is one of the single best predictors of early reading success in young children, with their ability to auditorily discriminate phonemes (i.e., phonemic awareness) a close second (Adams, 1990). This latter conclusion regarding phonemic awareness has taken on such significance in the field that we have dedicated an entire chapter to the subject. In sum, a knowledge of letter sounds and the rules governing our sound-symbol relationships in written English (i.e., phonics) is essential for reading success.

As a result of more recent phonics research (Bear, Templeton, Invernizzi, & Johnston, 1996; Eldredge, 1995; Moustafa, 1997; Blevins, 1997), we have been able to define a logical sequence for teaching phonics skills to most children. This knowledge of *what* to teach and *when* to teach can be extremely helpful in 1) assessing phonics knowledge in students, and 2) planning instruction and grouping effectively to meet their needs. The *Developmental Instruction Sequence of Phonics and Related Skills* we find most constructive in classrooms, as supported by the research, should proceed in a kind of hierarchy from 1) phonemic awareness, to 2) the development of alphabetic principle, to 3) explicit phonics instruction. In the next section, we list the various subskills to be taught within each of these major categories in the developmental instruction sequence.

HOW ARE PHONICS SKILLS COMMONLY TAUGHT?

There have traditionally been two primary methods for teaching phonics skills: explicit and implicit. Beginning reading instruction that depends on the teaching of isolated letters, letter sounds, and phonics generalizations is known as the *alphabetic,* or *explicit phonics method* (Reutzel & Cooter, 1996). Explicit phonics methods are based on "bottom-up" theories of learning, indicating that readers mentally process information letter by letter, word by word, and sentence by sentence until comprehension occurs. With explicit phonics methods, children are first taught regular sounds and sound patterns in words. Then, examples of words having those patterns are shown, followed by reading texts that include words having those patterns. If, for example, the explicit phonics teacher is emphasizing the "consonant-vowel-consonant" (CVC) pattern, then he will first explain that "when a vowel comes between two consonants, it will usually have the short vowel sound." Next, he may write on an overhead transparency the following words so that the students may discuss the sound represented by the underlined vowel:

p<u>e</u>t

p<u>i</u>n

f<u>a</u>t

m<u>o</u>p

Finally, some explicit phonics teachers may have students read from books containing what is known as "decodable text" (Shefelbine, 1997). These are books with language contrived to prominently display a given phonics pattern. For example, for the short *a* sound in CVC patterns, a sentence might read, "The fat cat sat on the mat." Other explicit phonics teachers, once the phonics rule and examples have been offered, may choose standard children's literature that has the given pattern appearing frequently. Using poetry and songs that rhyme is one way that this can be done.

Implicit phonics methods advocates, on the other hand, call for the teaching of whole words at the outset of beginning reading instruction, then help children to deduce letter sounds in words that are similar. For example, suppose the students have already been introduced to the following whole words:

car

candy

cake

Through implicit phonics instruction, they can be helped to deduce the hard *c* sound.

In recent years, many teachers have revised their thinking as to the most effective way to teach phonics skills to children. The explicit versus implicit debate is slowly giving way to a revised view that is discussed briefly in the next section.

MORE RECENT APPROACHES TO TEACHING PHONICS

The ultimate goal of phonics instruction, in our view, is to cultivate students' knowledge about phonics relationships and to provide classroom practice with letter sounds and symbol decoding, later generating unknown printed words through writing. A more comprehensive way of viewing phonics instruction is what we term the *contextual in-out-in explicit* approach. This model is based on the writings of a number of researchers (Bear, et al., 1996; Eldredge, 1995; Moustafa, 1997; Blevins, 1997) and mirrors our own "whole to parts to whole" approach discussed in chapter 1. In the "contextual in-out-in explicit" approach, students are first introduced to the phonic elements to be emphasized as parts of words in stories or other connected text (i.e., poems, songs, chants, etc.). This is the "context-in" or, in other words, "in-context" reading. In the "context-out" phase of the lesson, students are helped to zoom in on the word part to be emphasized in the phonics lesson (e.g., VCE patterns, selected rimes, digraphs, etc.). The phonics rule to be learned is taught directly and explicitly to students, and examples illustrating the rule are drawn from the text. This helps students to see the relevance of the rule to real reading tasks. We recommend 7 to 15 practice examples to make sure that learning has occurred, based on the seminal research and writings of Lev Vygotsky (Cooter & Cooter, 1998).

Once the phonics skill or rule has been practiced sufficiently, the learner then sees the phonics rule applied in other (new) whole text examples. This final "context-in" step helps students to recognize that the rule works in many reading situations. We have developed Table 7.1 to illustrate how "whole to parts to whole" in-

Table 7.1   Comparing Phonics Teaching Approaches

"Whole to Parts to Whole" Teaching	"Contextual In-Out-In Explicit" Approach
Whole text introduction	*Contextual-In* step
Parts (Input, modeling, guided practice activities)	*Context-Out*
Whole text reapplication (in new and varied texts)	*Context-In*

struction for reading skills (review chapter 1 for details) and the "contextual in-out-in explicit" approach are comparable.

THE KEY TO SUCCESSFUL PHONICS INSTRUCTION

Thus far in this chapter, we have explored *which* phonics skills might be taught in your classroom and, to an extent, *how* these skills might be taught via "contextual in-out-in" instruction. We conclude this discussion by explaining how phonics instruction can be consistently successful in your classroom.

Many teachers fail to help students achieve their potential because they offer illogical and disjoint instruction. How can this be avoided? The solution is relatively simple: instruction in phonics, and most everything else for that matter, should proceed from easier skills (developmentally speaking) to more difficult or complicated skills. In the previous section, we explained that there is a developmental sequence that should be followed in teaching phonics and related skills. This sequence proceeds logically from easy skills to more difficult ones, as suggested, and helps students easily develop phonics and related skills. Figure 7.4 is our recommended Developmental Instruction Sequence of Phonics and Related Skills.

As you can see in Figure 7.4, we begin instruction at the lower level of phonemic awareness with rhyming and alliteration. These activities are much simpler than, say, "oral segmentation" activities (see Item 5 in Level 1 of the Developmental Instruction Sequence of Phonics and Related Skills chart) and lay the necessary developmental groundwork for later learning. After the students acquire greater phonemic awareness, they are ready for the more difficult alphabetic principle tasks (see Level 2), which ultimately help students consistently map letters and sounds. The final developmental stage in sound/symbol instruction is explicit phonics instruction (Level 3). As Figure 7.4 shows, there are increasing developmental levels within this category, ranging from basic acquisition of knowledge related to consonants/onsets, common rimes, vowels, and so forth, to word play with rimes, to segmentation of sounds in words (sounding out) and writing-related tasks.

Once the skills involved are taught, the natural application of the Developmental Instruction Sequence of Phonics and Related Skills is clear. When students come to a word in print that they do not know, they will use context to help reduce the universe of possibilities, then break the word into syllables (i.e., *pronunciation units*). Breaking words into syllables is the natural and logical application of onset and rime knowledge. Students will find great success in their phonics applications

Figure 7.4

Developmental Instruction Sequence of Phonics and Related Skills

Level 1: Phonemic Awareness

1. Rhyming
2. Alliteration
3. Oddity tasks*
4. Oral blending: syllables, onset/rime, phoneme by phoneme
5. Oral segmentation: syllables, onset/rime, phoneme by phoneme
6. Phonemic manipulation: substitution (*i, f, v*); deletion (*s, i, f*)

Level 2: Alphabetic Principle

7. Making the connection between sounds and symbols

Level 3: Explicit Phonics Instruction

8. Specific letter sounds/Specific letter names
   a. Onset/consonants and rimes
   b. Continuous consonants
   c. Short vowel sounds
   d. Continue teaching both vowels and consonants
   e. Consonant digraphs: *wh, ch, th, sh*, etc.
   f. Vowel diphthongs: *oi, oy, ou*
   g. Vowel digraphs: *ee, ea, ai, ay*, etc.
9. Word play with onset and rime blending
10. L → R blending of letters-sounds in words
11. Segmentation of sounds in words, and writing segmented sounds

*Oddity tasks are those that contrast an "odd" word/sound pattern with others that fit a given pattern (i.e., *sat, fat, ball, rat*—Which one doesn't fit?—a rhyming oddity task).

Note: Based on W. Blevins (1997). *Phonemic Awareness Activities for Early Reading Success.* New York: Scholastic.

when they can chunk words into syllables using onset (consonant and consonant blends or digraphs) and rimes, then blend the sound units to pronounce the word. Individual letter sounding and blending should be used only as a kind of last resort, since there are so many variations in the English language.

In summary, there is a definite developmental sequence recommended for teaching phonics and related skills. Proceeding developmentally from easy to harder skills in the sequence will help assure success for most students. Teaching methods should include explicit instruction, implicit instruction, and phonics by analogy. The "contextual in-out-in" approach was suggested as a kind of "whole to parts to whole" orientation that has been demonstrated to be successful through reading research.

ASSESSING PHONICS KNOWLEDGE

As with all assessment activities, one of the goals is to try to discover a pattern of consistent reading behaviors. By knowing what a student can and cannot do, it soon becomes clear what your course of action should be in the classroom. There are a number of basic strategies that one can use to discover which phonics skills have been learned and which need attention. In this section, we share the knowledge assessment strategies that have worked best in our classrooms.

In general, assessment should proceed developmentally according to the sequence in which skills are learned. In this case, the assessment should proceed from phonemic awareness activities to alphabetic principle assessment activities to phonics skills. Methods for assessing phonemic awareness and alphabetic principle knowledge are reviewed extensively in chapter 6.

A most important and effective means for beginning your assessment of phonics skills is the running record (see our earlier discussion in chapter 3). Using real words in context, running records permit teachers to observe how well a student's phonics skills are developing. A second procedure uses nonsense or "made up" words in a list (without context). These two procedures will provide a great deal of useful information. To help you sort it all out, we provide you with Figure 7.5, a *Phonic Analysis Form*. Note that it includes all of the phonics skills listed earlier for your convenience.

ASSESSING VIA RUNNING RECORDS: ORAL READING PHONICS MISCUES

Purpose

Listening to a student read aloud is one of the ways we attempt to monitor the reading process. It is an imperfect assessment strategy, however, because oral reading ability differs somewhat from silent reading. Nevertheless, oral reading is suggestive of skills the student may be using. The goal in this instance is to use running records (as described in chapter 3) as a means for identifying phonics-related miscue patterns.

Materials

See chapter 3 for a description of how to set up running record passages using the "miscue grid" system. This will make your analysis much easier in a classroom situation in which you may have only five to ten minutes to listen to a child read aloud. Also, you may want to make copies of the Phonic Analysis Form for Oral Reading Miscues (see Figure 7.5) to help determine phonics needs for each student.

Procedure

Listen to the student read the passage(s) you have prepared that are on his instructional reading level (about 95–97% word call accuracy). Record any miscues, using the grid system to begin to look for patterns (recurring problems related to

Figure 7.5   Phonic Analysis Form

Phonics Generalizations	Oral Reading Miscue Examples	Data from Other Sources (e.g., The R/C Word Attack Survey)
Vowel Rules		
CVC rule (*sat, ran*)		
Digraphs (*ee, ea, oa*)		
VCE (*cape, rope*)		
CV (*go, so*)		
R-controlled (person, her)		
Schwa sound (*America*)		
Diphthongs (*oi, oy*)		
Y rules (*baby; fly*)		
Consonant Rules		
C rule ("hard"- *cake, cute;* "soft"- *city, cycle*)		
G rule ("hard"- *go, sugar;* "soft"- *gym*)		
Single consonant sounds		
Digraphs (*this, she, black, from*)		
Ph (*f* sound)		
Double consonants (*apple, letter*)		
Syllabication Rules		
Two identical consonants (*ap/ple*)		

continued

Phonics Generalizations	Oral Reading Miscue Examples	Data from Other Sources (e.g., The R/C Word Attack Survey)
Vowel sounds in a word (*slave, ca/boose*)		
Unlike consonants (*car/pet*)		
Compound word (*without*)		
Structural Analysis		
Root words [*work(er)*]		
Affixes [*work(er)*, (pre)set]		

phonics). Study the miscues and pay careful attention to those classified as word call errors, attempted decoding, and self-corrections. To identify recurring patterns of phonics miscues, use the Phonic Analysis Form in Figure 7.5. Once you have identified phonic generalizations that require attention, you can plan minilessons accordingly. Be sure to begin instruction with skills that have the greatest utility.

THE REUTZEL/COOTER WORD ATTACK SURVEY

Purpose

For many years, *nonsense words* ("made up words" having common phonics patterns) have been used in reading assessment to determine students' knowledge of English spelling patterns. These nonsense words are usually read in a list and the teacher records any miscues. Critics say that nonsense words, because they are not real words, do not permit students to use their prior knowledge—a primary reading tool used in decoding unfamiliar words in print. Advocates counter that nonsense words, *because* they deny the student the ability to use background knowledge, force the student to use only those phonics skills that he has internalized. We support the limited use of nonsense words as simply one tool in a teacher's toolbox of assessment ideas that may shed some light on a student's phonics skills development. Thus, we have prepared Figure 7.6, *The Reutzel/Cooter Word Attack Survey*, which uses nonsense words for this diagnostic purpose.

Figure 7.6   The Reutzel/Cooter Word Attack Survey Form

Student name: _____   Date: _____

Part 1: Vowel Generalizations

Sample Item:	sim cip sar

A. CVC/Beginning Consonant Sounds
1. tat   _____
2. nan   _____
3. rin   _____
4. mup   _____
5. det   _____
6. sim   _____
7. loj   _____
8. cal   _____
9. pif   _____
10. fek   _____

B. Vowel Digraphs
11. geem   _____
12. hoad   _____
13. kait   _____
14. weam   _____

C. VCE Pattern
15. jape   _____
16. zote   _____

17. gipe   _____
18. tope   _____

D. CV Pattern
19. bo   _____
20. ka   _____
21. fi   _____
22. tu   _____

E. *R*-Controlled Vowels
23. sar   _____
24. wir   _____
25. der   _____
26. nur   _____

F. Schwa Sound
27. ahurla   _____
28. thup   _____
29. cremon   _____
30. laken   _____

Part 2: Consonant Generalizations

G. Hard and Soft *C*
31. cale   _____
32. cose   _____
33. cimmy   _____
34. cyler   _____

H. Hard and Soft *G*
35. gare   _____
36. gob   _____
37. gime   _____
38. genry   _____

I. Consonant Digraphs
39. chur   _____
40. thim   _____
41. shar   _____
42. whilly   _____
43. thar   _____

J. Double Consonants
44. nally   _____
45. ipple   _____

continued

46. attawap _____   L. **Single Consonants***

47. urrit _____

K. ***Ph* (*f* sound)**   M. **Syllabication Rule***

48. phur _____   51. lappo _____

49. phattle _____   52. pabute _____

50. phenoblab _____   53. larpin _____

54. witnit _____

*See section A

**Besides Items 51–54, there are many other syllabication examples throughout the *R/CWAS*.

Comments:

Materials

You will need to reproduce the word cards provided at the end of this chapter for the students to read. Also, make copies of the survey (see Figure 7.6) for use in noting student responses.

Procedure

Directions for administering The Reutzel/Cooter Word Attack Survey:

1. Seat the student across from you at a small table.

2. Begin by showing him the examples provided using the premade flash cards (see word cards at the end of the chapter). Say, "I would like for you to read aloud some words on these flash cards. These are not real words, but are make-believe words, so they may sound kind of funny to you. Just try to say them the way you think they should be pronounced. For example, this first word (*sim*) is pronounced 'SIM.'" (Note: The teacher pronounces the word for the student). "Now I'd like for you to pronounce the next word for me." (Show the word *cip*.) Praise the child for saying the word correctly (or explain again the instructions, if necessary). After asking the student to do the third example word (*sar*), go ahead to the next step.

3. Say, "Now I would like for you to say each word as I show it to you. These are also make-believe words, so they will not sound much like any word you know. Just say them the way you think they should be pronounced." Then, work your way through the words and note any mispronunciations on the survey form provided (see Figure 7.6).

Figure 7.7   Student Phonics Knowledge Checklist

Student Phonics Knowledge Checklist

Student's name: _____

Skill(s)   **Date Observed**

Level 1: Phonemic Awareness

   1. Rhyming   _____

   2. Alliteration _____

   3. Oddity tasks _____

   4. Oral blending: syllables, onset/rime, _____
phoneme by phoneme

   5. Oral segmentation: syllables, onset/rime, _____
phoneme by phoneme

   6. Phonemic manipulation: substitution _____
(*i, f, v*); deletion (*s, i, f*)

Level 2: Alphabetic Principle

   7. Making the connection between sounds and symbols _____

Level 3: Explicit Phonics Instruction

   8. Specific letter sounds/Specific letter names
     a. Onset/consonants and rimes _____
     b. Continuous consonants _____
     c. Short vowel sounds _____
     d. Continue teaching both vowels and consonants _____
     e. Consonant digraphs : *wh, ch, th, sh,* etc. _____
     f. Vowel dipthongs: *oi, oy, ou* _____
     g. Vowel digraphs: *ee, ea, ai, ay,* etc. _____

   9. Word play with onset and rime blending _____

 10. L → R blending of letters-sounds in words _____

 11. Segmentation of sounds in words, and writing _____
segmented sounds

Sequence based on W. Blevins (1997). Phonemic Awareness Activities for Early Reading Success. New York: Scholastic.

4. Once the student has completed reading through the word cards, praise him for his hard work and allow him to go on to other activities. Tally up the miscues using the Phonic Analysis Form provided in Figure 7.5.

5. Determine areas of phonic knowledge the student may be having difficulty with, based on repeated miscues. We recommend that your instructional decisions be based on a pattern of errors repeated over time. Thus, you will

need to hear the child read more than once before deciding which areas must be addressed in your minilessons.

One of the challenges for busy classroom teachers is organizing assessment information so that you can make enlightened teaching decisions and group effectively for instruction. To help you in this process, we offer a *Student Phonics Knowledge Checklist,* shown in Figure 7.7. It is based on the Developmental Instruction Sequence of Phonics and Related Skills presented in Figure 7.4.

BALANCED READING PROGRAM INTERVENTIONS: HELPING STUDENTS INCREASE PHONICS KNOWLEDGE

Indicators That Readers Have Learning Needs

- Problems correctly identifying vowel sounds and their variant sounds in words
- Problems correctly identifying consonant sounds and their variant sounds in words
- Problems correctly identifying sounds represented by digraphs (consonant and/or vowel) in words
- Problems correctly identifying syllable breaks in words
- Problems with the identification of structural analysis elements in words

In the remainder of this chapter we suggest a number of activities that can be used to teach many of the phonics generalizations. They tend to be one of two major types: implicit or explicit methods.

Implicit methods help students draw phonic conclusions about words having similar spelling patterns. Using words already in their sight vocabulary, students are often able to deduce sounds in words and sound out remaining elements to correctly identify the unknown word in print. When used with context clues, analytic phonics can be quite powerful. For example, if a student knows the words *cake* and *take,* then these words can be used to deduce the sounds represented by *-ake.* With this knowledge in mind, trying to decode words such as *make, rake,* and *lake* becomes a fairly simple matter of matching the word's beginning sound with the known sound represented by *-ake,* especially when combined with meaning cues from the context of a sentence. Some of the activities in this section use analytic phonics as the underlying word attack approach.

Explicit methods are the reverse of implicit methods. They use inductive reasoning. Here, students are taught the letter sounds in words, then how to blend sounds together to decode an unfamiliar word in print. For example, students may be taught the short *a* sound one hears in the word *fan*, along with the usual sounds associated with the letter *m, c,* and *n.* By blending sounds in different combinations, students can be shown how to sound out the words *man* and *can.* This inductive or word-building method dates back to the famous *McGuffey Readers* of the 19th century. Again, the method works reasonably well when used in conjunction with context clues. As you might surmise, some of the activities presented in this section are more "synthetic" in nature.

Which approach is best: implicit or explicit? Frankly, they both have merit and they both are inadequate as a "best" approach. We feel that students should be shown both approaches within the strategic and meaningful context of "contextual in-out-in" skill instruction, as with "whole to parts to whole" instruction as described in chapter 1. Sometimes, in education, we tend to look for "magic bullets" and one-size-fits-all approaches to teaching students. Because, as human beings, we all have differing needs, this viewpoint is not an appropriate one. (As Dr. Kathleen Spencer Cooter, a principal for many years, has said about one-size-fits-all teaching approaches, "The only thing I recommend for *all* children is good oral hygiene!"

In this section we recommend several activities that may be used—often with many or most of the phonics skills we have enumerated earlier. Hence, please understand that if we recommend an activity that is useful in teaching, say, consonant sounds, it may be just as useful in teaching consonant digraphs, or, for that matter, many of the phonics skills and generalizations.

Letter Sound Cards

Purpose

Letter sound cards are intended as prompts to help students remember individual and combination (i.e., digraphs and blends) letter sounds that have been introduced during minilessons or other teachable moments.

Materials

You will need to have a word bank for each child (children's shoe boxes, recipe boxes, or other small containers in which index cards can be filed), alphabetic divider cards to separate words in the word bank, index cards, and colored markers.

Procedure

This is essentially the same idea as the word bank activity shown in chapter 8 on vocabulary instruction. The idea is to provide students with their own word cards on which you (or they) have written a key letter sound or sounds on one side and a word that uses that sound on the other. Whenever possible, it is best to use nouns or other words that can be depicted with a picture, so that, for emergent readers, a drawing can be added to the side having the word (as needed). Two examples are shown in Figure 7. 8.

Phonics Fish (or Foniks Phish?) Card Game

Purpose

Based on the age-old children's card game, *Fish,* sometimes called *Go Fish,* this review activity helps students use their growing visual awareness of phonics sounds and patterns to construct word families (i.e., groups of words having the same phonetic pattern). This game can be played in small groups, at a learning center with two to four children, or during reading groups with the teacher.

Materials

You will need a deck of word cards. The words can be selected from the students' word banks or chosen by the teacher or parent/teaching assistant from among those familiar to all students. The word cards should contain ample examples of at least three or four phonetic patterns that you wish to review (e.g., beginning consonant sounds, *r*-controlled vowels, clusters, digraphs, rime families, etc.).

Procedure

Before beginning the game, explain which word families or sound patterns are to be used in this game of Phonics Fish. Next, explain the rules of the game:

1. Each child will be dealt five cards.
2. The remaining cards (deck of about fifty) are placed facedown in the middle of the group.

Figure 7.8   Letter Sound Card Examples

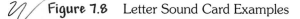
dog

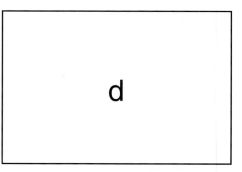
d

boat

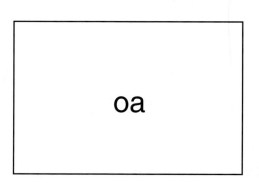
oa

3. Taking turns in a round-robin fashion, each child can ask any other if he or she is holding a word having a particular sound or pattern. For example, if one of the patterns included is the /sh/ sound, then the first student may say something like, "Juanita, do you have any words with the /sh/ sound?" If the student being asked does not have any word cards with that pattern, he or she can say "Go Fish!" The student asking the question then draws a card from the deck.

4. Cards having matching patterns (two or more) are placed faceup in front of the student asking the question.

5. The first student to get rid of all his or her cards wins the game.

SOUND SWIRL

Purpose

Sound Scramble is a simple activity that is used to 1) help students think of "words in their head" that have a certain sound element, and 2) to then use invented or "temporary" spellings to construct the words they have recalled. This helps students learn to sound out words and to notice particular word sounds as their phonics awareness grows. This activity is usually best applied as a Guided Practice or for review.

Materials

You will need some chart paper and markers in different colors.

Procedure

Gather a group of children around you with whom you wish to review a phonics sound pattern (for our example here, we will use the beginning sound represented by the letters *ch* as in *church*). Write the letters representing the sound you wish to emphasize (*ch* in our example) on the chart paper using a colorful marker. Say, "Boys and girls, I want us to see just how many words we can think of that begin with the sound made by the letters *ch*—which make the /ch/ sound. So, get your mouth ready to make the /ch/ sound, swirl around all the letters in your head (Note: Here, the teacher makes a grand gesture of a swirling motion above her head), and say the first words that come to your mind, *right now*!!!" At this point, the students will call out such words as *church, chump, change, child, chirp,* etc. Select a few of the words they called out and, in whole group fashion (using volunteers), have them sound out the written words (beginning each time with *ch* in a different color from the rest of the word) so they can recognize visually how words can be sounded out and written.

"BUTTON" SOUNDS

Purpose

Children often enjoy wearing buttons that are unique. Similarly, many schools have button-making machines that can inexpensively produce buttons for special projects. "Button sounds," as we call them, take advantage of children's attraction to buttons to help cement their understanding of introductory sounds in words. (Note: This is recommended only as an adjunct to other more comprehensive mini-lessons.)

Materials

You will need access to a button-making machine and materials, or a local vendor who can make the buttons for you inexpensively.

Procedure

Identify the phonics sounds/symbols you wish to emphasize. For example, we first used this activity with first-grade students to help them learn alphabet letters as initial sounds in words (e.g., *Bb* together with a picture of a butterfly, *Cc* with a picture of a cat, *Gg* with a picture of a goat, etc.). However, any sound/symbol relationship can be used that can be illustrated with a picture. Once you have introduced the "sound for the day" and linked it to a key illustration (e.g., a witch for the letters *Ww,* or a ship for the digraph *sh*), distribute the buttons to all students in the group or class. You should instruct the children that whenever they are asked by anyone about their button, they should respond with a statement such as "This is my /sh/ and *ship* button." An example of a button is shown in Figure 7.9.

STOMPING, CLAPPING, TAPPING, AND SNAPPING SOUNDS
Purposes

Helping children hear syllables and words enables them to segment sounds. This knowledge can be used in myriad ways to improve writing/spelling, increase awareness of letter combinations used to produce speech sounds, and apply knowledge of onsets and rimes. All these skills and more enable students to sound out words in print more effectively. For ages, teachers have found success in helping children hear syllables by clapping them out when reading nursery rhymes, such as "Mar-y had a lit-tle lamb, lit-tle lamb, lit-tle lamb . . . ."

Materials

We prefer to use rhyming poetry, songs, chants, or raps for these syllabication activities. Use an enlarged version produced for an overhead projector, a big book version, or simply rewrite the text on large chart paper using a colored ink marker.

Procedures

First, model read the enlarged text aloud in a normal cadence for your students. Reread the selection at a normal cadence, inviting students to join in as they wish. Next, explain that you will reread the selection, but this time you will clap (or snap, or stomp, etc.) the syllables in the words. (Note: If you have not already explained the concept of *syllables,* you will need to do so at this point.) Finally, invite students to clap (or make whatever gesture or sound that you have chosen), as you reread the passage.

Figure 7.9   Button from "Button Sounds" Activity

TONGUE TWISTERS

Purpose

Many students enjoy word play. Tongue twisters can be a wonderful way of reviewing consonants (Cunningham, 1995) in a way that is fun for students. We have found that Tongue Twister activities can combine reading and creative writing processes to help children deepen their understanding of phonic elements.

Materials

There are many traditional tongue twisters in published children's literature that may be used. However, we find that children enjoy creating their own tongue twisters perhaps even more. All you need to do is decide which sounds/letter pattern families are to be used.

Procedure

Cunningham (1995) suggests that you begin by simply reciting some tongue twisters aloud and inviting students to join in. We recommend that you produce two or three examples on chart paper and post them on the wall as you introduce the concept of tongue twisters. For example, you might use the following:

Silly Sally sat in strawberries.

Peter Piper picked a peck of pickled peppers.
If Peter Piper picked a peck of pickled peppers,
Then how many peppers did Peter Piper pick?

Peter Piper panhandles pepperoni pizza,
With his pint-sized pick-up he packs a peck
 of pepperoni pizzas,
For Patti his portly patron.

Simple Simon met a pieman going to the fair,
Said Simple Simon to the pieman,
"Let me taste your wares!"
Said the pieman to Simple Simon,
"Show me first your penny!"
Said Simple Simon to the pieman,
"I'm afraid I haven't any."

Children especially love it when teachers create tongue twisters using names of children in the class, such as the following example:

Pretty Pam picked pink peonies for Patty's party.

Lastly, challenge students to create their own tongue twisters to "stump the class." It may be fun to award students coupons that can be used to purchase take-home books for coming up with clever tongue twisters.

CREATING POETRY NONSENSE WORDS WITH WORD FAMILIES

Purpose

Many of the most popular poets, such as Shel Silverstein and Jack Prelutsky, have tapped into children's fascination with word play in their very creative poetry. For instance, when Silverstein speaks of "gloppy *glumps* of cold oatmeal," we all understand what he means, even though *gloppy* and *glumps* are really nonsense words. Getting students to create nonsense words and apply them to popular poetry is a motivating way to help students practice phonic patterns.

Materials

First decide which phonic sound/letter pattern families you wish to emphasize. For instance, it may be appropriate to review the letter/sound families represented by

-ack, -ide, -ing, and -ore. Also needed are books of poetry or songs with rhyming phrases, chart paper or overhead transparencies, and markers.

Procedure

As with all activities, begin by modeling what you expect students to do. On a large sheet of chart paper or at the overhead projector, write the word family parts that you wish to emphasize (for this example, we used -ack, -ide, -ing, and -ore). Illustrate how you can convert the word parts into nonsense words by adding a consonant, consonant blend, or consonant digraph before each one, such as shown by the following:

-ack	-ide	-ing	-ore
gack	spide	gacking	zore
clack	mide	zwing	glore
chack	plide	kaching	jore

In the next phase of the demonstration, select a poem or song that rhymes and review it with students first (use enlarged text for all of your modeling). Next, show students a revised copy of the song or poem in which you have substituted nonsense words. Here is one example we have used with the song "I Know An Old Lady Who Swallowed a Fly." We show only the first verse here, but you could use the entire song, substituting a nonsense word in each stanza.

Original version:

I know an old lady who swallowed a fly,
I don't know why,
she swallowed the fly,
I guess she'll die.

Nonsense word version:

I know an old lady who swallowed a zwing,
I don't know why,
she swallowed the zwing,
I guess she'll die.

"MAKING WORDS" LESSON

Cunningham and Cunningham (1992) describe making words as a hands-on manipulative activity in which students look for patterns in words. Students also learn how new words can be created by simply changing one letter or letter combination. Making words can be useful for either vocabulary building or for developing phonetic understanding. For a complete explanation of making words, please see the discussion of this activity in chapter 8.

ODDITY TASKS

Purpose

Oddity tasks are implicit learning tasks that help students discover similarities and differences among words. Oddity tasks can be quite useful in developing phonemic awareness through rhyming and alliteration, as well as through phonics patterns such as rimes.

Materials

You will need to have a means for sharing enlarged text examples (word lists) if you are using this strategy for phonic awareness (rimes); otherwise, no special materials are needed beyond examples you wish to use for instruction.

Procedure

For Phonemic Awareness: Rhyming (using common rimes)* Say: "I would like for you to listen carefully to the words I am about to say. See if you can tell me which word does not rhyme with the others." (Note: The oddity word below appears in italics.)

sing	wing	*them*	sting
back	sack	crack	*will*
ash	stash	crash	*make*
stove	wheat	eat	neat

A Brief Statement About Building Decoding Fluency

John J. Pikulski (1998), a recent president of the International Reading Association, has noted the importance of massive amounts of reading in high-quality texts as a tool for developing decoding fluency. Specifically, he points out that children can benefit from three main types of practice: wide reading, independent level reading, and multiple rereadings of texts.

Wide reading simply refers to the notion of encouraging children to read in a variety of topics and genre. Teachers can encourage wide reading by regularly conducting "book talks." With book talks, the teacher reads aloud a particularly interesting portion of a great book or other text form, but leaves the students "hanging" at a particularly suspenseful point in the narrative. This often makes students mad with desire to finish reading the selection!

Independent level reading refers to helping children find many and varied books of interest that are easy for them to read. In this case, "easy" reading refers to books in which students will be able to read about 98% or more of the words without difficulty. In addition to improving phonics fluency, research shows that independent level reading for at least twenty minutes each day will also greatly improve reading rate.

Multiple rereading of texts means just what the words imply—rereading favorite books, poems, or other text forms. Multiple rereadings will essentially provide the same benefits as independent level reading.

*Note: This activity could just as easily be done as a phonics level activity if presented in worksheet form during the "context-out" portion of the lesson sequence.

A Phonics Quick Test (Answer Key)

1. The word *charkle* is divided between r̲ and k̲. The *a* has an r̲- controlled sound, and the *e* is <u>silent</u>.

2. In the word *small,* sm- is known as the *onset* and -all is known as the <u>rime</u>. (See chapter 8 for a full explanation.)

3. *Ch* in the word *chair* is known as a <u>consonant digraph</u>.

4. The letter *c* is the word *city* is a <u>soft</u> sound; in the word *cow,* the letter *c* is a <u>hard</u> sound.

5. The letters *bl* in the word *blue* are referred to as a consonant <u>blend</u>.

6. The underlined vowels in the words *au̲thor, spre̲ad,* and *blu̲e* are known as vowel <u>digraphs</u>.

7. The words *tag, run, cot,* and *get* have which vowel pattern? <u>consonant - vowel - consonant (CVC)</u>

8. The words *glide, take,* and *use* have the <u>vowel - consonant - "e"</u> vowel pattern.

9. The single most powerful phonics skill we can teach to emergent readers for decoding unfamiliar words in print is <u>beginning</u> sounds in words. We introduce this skill using <u>consonant</u> sounds first because they are the most <u>constant (or "dependable" or "reliable")</u>.

10. The word part *work* in the word *working* is known as a <u>root (or "base" or "unbound morpheme")</u> word.

11. The word part *-ing* in the word *working* is known as a <u>suffix (or "bound morpheme")</u>.

12. Cues to the meaning and pronunciation of unfamiliar words in print are often found in the print surrounding the unfamiliar, also known as the <u>context</u>.

Grading Key for Teachers

Number Correct	Evaluation
12	Wow, you're good! (You must have had no social life in college.)
10–11	Not too bad, but you may need a brushup. (Read this chapter.)
7–9	Emergency! Take a refresher course, quick! (Read this chapter.)
0–6	Have you ever considered a career in telemarketing?! (Just kidding, but read this chapter . . . right away!)

To make wide reading, independent level reading, and multiple rereadings happen every day, we recommend that you institute DEAR time (Drop Everything And Read) in your classroom. For about 20 to 30 minutes each day, have students stop at a designated time and read a book of their choosing. DEAR can be broken into two shorter time segments just as effectively, if you wish. The teacher *must* also participate and read a book for fun (*Warning:* Do *not* grade papers or do other teaching chores during DEAR time, or you will sabotage its effectiveness. Besides . . . reading is fun!). So, set your egg timer and enjoy DEAR time in your classroom daily. You will love the results.

CHAPTER SUMMARY

In this chapter we have summarized several crucial aspects of phonics instruction. First, we have identified the specific skills that should be taught in most classrooms. Relatedly, we have also described in some detail the order in which phonics and related skills should be offered: *phonemic awareness → alphabetic principle knowledge → explicit phonics.* Second, we have described how instruction should be carried out. The "contextual in-out-in" approach is an effective method that corresponds perfectly with the "whole to parts to whole" model described in chapter 1. Finally, we have listed in some detail procedures for assessing and teaching the sundry phonics skills. The assessment process and accompanying student checklist can help teachers identify student needs and group effectively for instruction. The balanced reading activities can also help teachers infuse their students with phonics knowledge via explicit and implicit instruction.

REFERENCES

Adams, M. J. (1990). *Beginning to read: Thinking and learning about print.* Cambridge, MA: MIT Press.

Bear, D. R., Templeton, S., Invernizzi, M., & Johnston, F. (1996). *Words their way: Word study for phonics, vocabulary, and spelling instruction.* Columbus, OH: Merrill/Prentice Hall.

Black, M. C. (1961). *Phonics rules verification by a thirteen hundred word count.* Unpublished master's thesis project, Loyola University of Los Angeles.

Blevins, W. (1997). *Phonemic Awareness Activities for Early Reading Success.* New York: Scholastic.

Cooter, R. B., & Cooter, K. S. (1998). *Using classroom assessment to inform teaching: Focus on K–3.* Texas State Reading Association Annual Conference, El Paso, Texas, March 7, 1998.

Cunningham, P. M. (1995). *Phonics they use* (2nd ed.). New York: HarperCollins.

Cunningham, P. M., & Cunningham, J. W. (1992). Making words: Enhancing the invented spelling-decoding connection. *The Reading Teacher, 46,* 106–107.

Eldredge, J. L. (1995). *Teaching decoding in holistic classrooms.* Columbus, OH: Merrill/Prentice Hall.

Manzo, A. V., & Manzo, U. C. (1993). *Literacy disorders: Holistic diagnosis and remediation.* Fort Worth, TX: Harcourt Brace Jovanovich College Publishers.

Moore, J. T. (1951). *Phonetic elements appearing in a 3000-word spelling vocabulary.* Unpublished doctoral dissertation, Stanford University.

Moustafa, M. (1997). *Beyond traditional phonics: Research discoveries and reading instruction.* Portsmouth, NH: Heinemann.

Pikulski, J. J. (1998). *Improving reading achievement: Major instructional con-*

siderations for the primary grades. Commissioner's Reading Day Statewide Conference, Austin, Texas, February 25, 1998.

Rasinski, T., & Padak, N. (1996). *Holistic reading strategies: Teaching children who find reading difficult.* Columbus, OH: Merrill/Prentice Hall.

Routman, R. (1996). *Literacy at the crossroads.* Portsmouth, NH: Heinemann.

Wilson, R. M., & Hall, M. (1997). *Programmed word attack for teachers* (6th ed.). Columbus, OH: Merrill/Prentice Hall.

Word Cards for The Reutzel/Cooter Word Attack Survey

tat
nan
rin
mup

det
sim
loj
cal
pif

fek
geem
hoad
kait

weam
jape
zote
gipe
tope

bo
ka
fi
tu

sar
wir
der
nur
ahurla

continued

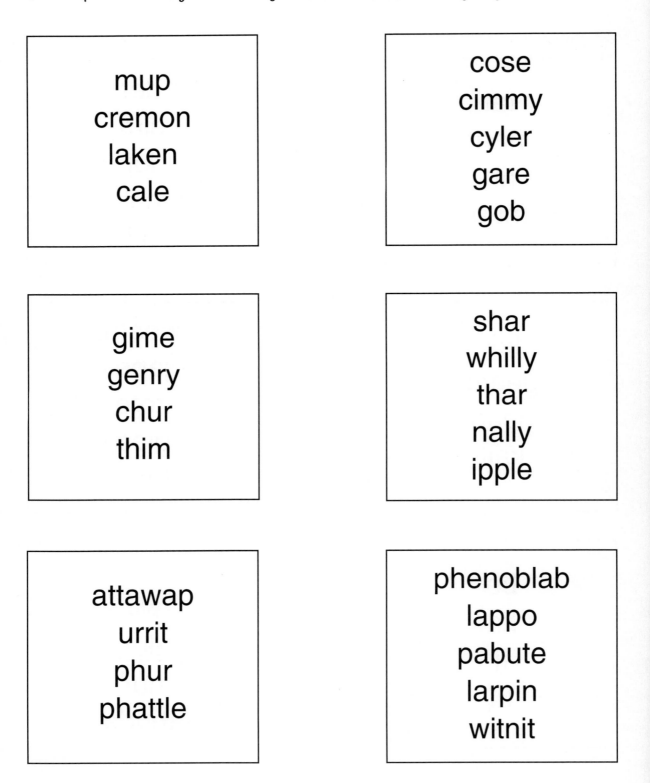

mup
cremon
laken
cale

cose
cimmy
cyler
gare
gob

gime
genry
chur
thim

shar
whilly
thar
nally
ipple

attawap
urrit
phur
phattle

phenoblab
lappo
pabute
larpin
witnit

Chapter 8

Teaching and Assessing Vocabulary Development

Words are the symbols we use to express ideas. Said another way, words are the "captions" that describe our life experiences. Vocabulary development is a process that goes on throughout life and can be enhanced in the classroom through enticing learning experiences. Frank Smith (1987) stated the following:

> All children except the most severely deprived or handicapped acquire a vocabulary of over 10,000 words during the first four or five years of their lives. At the age of four they are adding to their vocabulary at the rate of twenty words a day. By seven this rate may have increased to nearly thirty words . . . By late adolescence the average vocabulary is at least 50,000 words.

Since the latter part of the nineteenth century in America, there has been much research and debate about the role of vocabulary knowledge in learning to read. James M. Cattell in 1885 argued that children should learn entire words as a method of beginning reading. Though learning "sight words" alone is no longer recommended as an *effective* beginning reading approach, most teachers still believe that the acquisition of a large number of sight words should be part of every child's beginning reading program.

BACKGROUND BRIEFING FOR TEACHERS

There are actually several different "vocabularies" housed in one's mind and usable for language transactions. The largest vocabulary is known as one's **listening vocabulary**. These are words you are able to hear and understand, but not necessarily use in your own speech. For example, when the famous Hale-Bopp comet visited our solar system in 1997, most children in the middle and upper elementary grades were quite capable of watching news telecast about the comet and understanding most of what was reported. However, if you were to ask many of these same children to explain what they had just learned, many of the technical words and factual bits of information would not be included. It's not that the children somehow forgot everything they had just learned, but simply that they do not yet "own" the words for speech purposes—they can only hear and understand the technical words. It has been estimated that many first grade students have a listening vocabulary as large as 20,000 words!

Words that a student can hear, understand, *and* use in her speech are known as her **speaking vocabulary**. It is a subset of the listening vocabulary and, thus, is smaller. The gap between peoples' listening and speaking vocabularies is greatest in youth. The gap tends to narrow as adulthood approaches, though the two vocabularies are never equal. The next largest vocabulary is the **reading vocabulary**. As you might guess, it is a subset of one's listening and speaking vocabularies and consists of words one can read and understand. The smallest vocabulary that one acquires is the **writing vocabulary**—words that one can understand when listening, speaking, and reading, *and* can reproduce when writing.

Cooter and Flynt (1996) group listening and reading vocabularies into a collective category known as the *receptive vocabulary* and writing and speaking vocabularies into a category known as the *expressive vocabulary*. These descriptors reflect the broader language functions of these vocabularies for the student as either information receiver or spoken or written language producer.

For a student to be able to read and understand a word, she must have first acquired it at a listening and speaking level. Teachers, then, must somehow find out which words are already "owned" by their students as listening and speaking vocabulary and teach the unknown words that may be critical in their assigned reading. Without this kind of knowledge, adequate context for word identification will be missing and can threaten further reading development and, of course, damage comprehension.

The primary way of increasing vocabulary should be through wide reading on a daily basis (Irwin, 1990). This helps readers gain greater fluency and improves their ability to use context from the passage to interpret word meanings. Effective readers can maintain satisfactory comprehension when up to 15% of the words in a passage are unknown or new. On the other hand, research shows that students who are learning English as a second language (Johnson & Steele, 1996) and, we believe, others having weak vocabularies, tend to be word-by-word readers and are much less able to tolerate unknown vocabulary. The teacher's role is to help these learners with special needs, as well as normally developing readers, to learn the largest possible vocabularies.

ASSESSING VOCABULARY KNOWLEDGE

In truth, most vocabulary assessment done by master teachers is through careful classroom observations of student reading behaviors. As teachers work with their pupils each day in needs-based group instruction they discover high-utility words that seem to cause trouble for one or more students. Teachers can work these words into vocabulary instruction activities like those featured later in this chapter. But this is not to suggest that more cannot be done early in the school year to discover which words most of your students may need to learn. Following are a few classroom-proven ideas to help with that process.

ORAL READING ASSESSMENT

Purpose

Oral reading assessment is a method by which problem vocabulary words in print can be distinguished by the teacher in a quick and efficient manner. It is drawn from the running record style of assessment frequently used to note reading miscues.

Materials

You will need photocopies (two copies each) of three or four passages for the student to read that you believe to be at the student's *instructional* or *frustration* reading level. The passages should be drawn from reading materials commonly used in your classroom curriculum. Ideally, the passages are sufficiently challenging so that students will have trouble with about 5 to 10% of the words. It will be necessary for you to do a quick word count to determine if the passages are appropriate once they have been read by the student. It is also essential that you have a range of passages, in terms of difficulty, to account for the vast differences between students' reading ability. (Note: If the student calls less than 10% of the words correctly, she may not be getting enough context from the passages for adequate comprehension.)

Procedure

Give the student a copy of the first passage you want him to read and keep one for yourself. Ask the student to read the passage aloud. While he does, note any words that he either doesn't know or mispronounces. Repeat the procedure until the student has read all of the passages. We recommend that you discontinue a passage if the student consistently has trouble with more than one or two words in any one sentence. After the student has finished, tally the number of miscalled words and determine if the passage is acceptable for analysis (no more than about 10% miscalled or unknown words). List any words that seem to be problematic for the student.

Repeat this procedure with all of your students during the first week or so of the new school year and (1) create a master list of words that seem to be problematic, and (2) determine the number or percentage of the class who seem to find each word difficult or unknown. Use the more frequent problem words as part of your vocabulary instruction program.

CLOZE PASSAGES

Cloze passages are short (250 words) passages drawn from typical reading materials found in your instructional program. These passages have certain words deleted (usually every fifth word) and replaced with a blank. Students are asked to read the cloze passage(s) and fill in the missing words based on what they believe makes sense using context clues. Cloze tests cause students to use their "schema knowledge" of a subject, understanding of basic syntax (word order relationships), and/or word and sentence meaning (semantics) knowledge to guess what a missing or familiar word in print might be. We encourage teachers to administer cloze passages to the whole class at once as a starting point to determine vocabulary needs.

Vocabulary Flash Cards

Purpose

One of the most traditional ways to do a quick assessment of a student's vocabulary knowledge is the flash card technique. High-frequency words, those appearing most in print, as well as other high-utility words for specific grade levels, are printed individually on flash cards and shown to students for them to identify. Though some reading researchers argue that flash cards are not a valid assessment tool—because the words are presented in isolation instead of in complete sentences and paragraphs—flash cards continue to be used by many master teachers as one way to determine the direction of classroom instruction.

Materials

Obtain a list of high-frequency sight words (Note: we provide a copy of the Fry [1980] word list in Figure 8.8). Copy each word, one word each, on to index cards using a bold marker. An alternative is to type the words into a classroom computer and print them in a large font size onto heavy paper stock. Then, cut the words into a uniform flash card size. For recording purposes, you will also need a photocopy/master list of the words for each student in your class.

Procedure

"Flash" each card to the student one at a time and ask him to name the word. Allow about five seconds for the student to identify each word. Circle any unknown or mispronounced words on a copy of the master sheet you are using for that student (simply note the student's name at the top of the photocopy along with the date of testing). After you have shown the flash cards to all students, compile a master list of troublesome words for whole-class or small-group instruction. The *Word Banks* activity found later in this chapter is one way to use this information that we highly recommend. The flash cards can be reused periodically to determine if students have learned the words being taught.

Balanced Reading Program Interventions: Helping Students Increase Their Reading Vocabularies

Indicators That Readers May Have Vocabulary Learning Needs

- The student has difficulty correctly calling enough words when reading orally for good fluency.
- When trying to identify an unknown word in a sentence, the student cannot call the word even when the student has sufficient context (listening/speaking vocabulary deficiency).
- The student seems to have a limited English proficiency (LEP) according to standardized tests (e.g., IDEA Proficiency Test, etc.) or teacher recommenda-

tions (Cox & Boyd-Batstone, 1997). Note: This usually applies to those learning English as a second language (ESL).

- The student has limited language ability according to standardized tests (such as the reading and/or language subtests of the MAT 6).

MORPHEMIC ANALYSIS

Purpose

Morphemic analysis is the process of using one's knowledge of word parts to deduce meanings of unknown words. A *morpheme* is the smallest unit of meaning in a word. There are two types of morphemes: free and bound. A **free morpheme** is a freestanding root or base of any word that cannot be further divided and still have meaning. In the word *farmer, farm* is the root word or free morpheme. The -*er* portion of the word *farmer* is considered to be a bound morpheme. *Bound morphemes* carry meaning, but must be attached to a free morpheme to do so. The most common bound morphemes are prefixes (*in-, pre-, mono-*), suffixes (*-er, -ous, -ology*), and inflectional endings (*-s, -es, -ing, -ed, -est*).

There are several ways that teachers commonly introduce morphemic analysis to students as a way of learning the meaning of new words. Sometimes it is possible to use students' unconscious knowledge of morphemes to determine the meanings of a new word by putting it into the context of a list of similar words (e.g., words ending in the morpheme *-phobia* or *-er* to decipher meaning). Other times, teachers can simply offer students the meanings of certain morphemes and allow them to figure out new word meanings on their own or in small groups.

Materials

The essential activity for teachers is to research the meanings of morphemes and, in the case of activities involving word family lists, examples of other words having the morphemes to be used. A resource we have found helpful in planning many vocabulary activities is *The Reading Teacher's Book of Lists* (Fry, Polk, & Fountoukidis, et al., 1984).

Procedures

Preselect words to be learned from the reading selection, then do the necessary background research and planning about the morphemes found in the new words. One activity is to construct *word family lists* that help students determine morpheme meanings. For example, a middle school teacher might decide to focus on the word *claustrophobia*. Her research into the morpheme *-phobia* might lead to the construction of the following list:

claustrophobia
cardiophobia
olfactophobia
telephonophobia
verbaphobia

This activity causes students to use *compare and contrast methods* of morphemic analysis. That is, they must look at the unfamiliar word and use their prior knowledge of other words that look like parts of the unfamiliar word to figure out what each word probably means. For example, *cardio-* probably reminds you of *cardiac* which deals with the heart, and *-phobia* means "fear of." Therefore, *cardiophobia* must mean a fear of heart disease. To use this compare-and-contrast technique with students, first select words that have morphemes that can be compared to other words students are likely to know, and present both the new word and other words that begin or end like the unfamiliar word. Look at the following example from Cooter and Flynt (1996):

Because of my expansive vocabulary, my teacher called me a verbivore.

verbi-	vore
verbal	carnivore
verbose	herbivore
verbalize	omnivore

The teacher would write the sentence on the chalkboard and list below it examples of words that begin and end like the unfamiliar word. Then, through questioning, the teacher would lead students to specify the word's meaning by comparing and contrasting the known words to the unfamiliar one, thus concluding: A verbivore is a person who loves (eats) words.

Another way of using morphemic analysis to help students deduce meaning is to present unfamiliar terms along with explanations of the morphemes that make up the unfamiliar terms. The following procedure might be used as part of an introduction to a new text containing the words listed.

Step 1: Identify the terms that need preteaching.

pro-life

illegal

pro-choice

rearrest

unable

forewarn

Step 2: Along with these terms, write on the board a list of appropriate morphemes and their meanings.

pro = in favor of

il = not

fore = earlier

re = to do again

un = not

Step 3: Engage students in a discussion of what each term means and how the terms are interrelated. When there is confusion or disagreement, direct students to the terms in the text and/or the glossary for verification.

As useful as morphemic analysis can be, Cooter and Flynt (1996) offer a word of *caution* concerning morphemic analysis:

> Although we encourage the teaching of how to use context and morphemic analysis, we in no way advocate the overuse of these two techniques nor the memorization of lists of morphemes or types of context clues. Teachers who make students memorize common prefixes and suffixes run the risk of having students view the task as an end and not a means to help them become better readers. The story is told of a student who memorized the prefix "trans-" as meaning "across." Later the same week, the student was reading a science text and was asked what the word "transparent" meant. He replied confidently "a cross mother or father." The point being that all vocabulary instruction in the upper grades should be meaning-oriented, connected to text, functional, and capable of being used in the future. (p. 154)

FIVE-STEP METHOD

Purpose

Smith and Johnson (1980) suggested a five-step direct method of teaching new vocabulary for instant recognition. It uses multiple modalities to help students bring new words into the four vocabularies: listening, speaking, reading, and writing.

Materials

A variety of materials may be used in the five-step method, including a dry-erase board or chalkboard, an overhead projector, flash cards, and different color markers.

Procedure

1. Seeing — The new vocabulary word is shown on the overhead projector, chalkboard, or dry-erase board in the context of a sentence or (better) a short paragraph.

2. Listening — The teacher next discusses the word with students and verifies that they understand its meaning.

3. Discussing — Students are asked to create their own sentences using the new word, or, perhaps, to think of a synonym or antonym for the word. This is done orally.

4. Defining — Students try to create their own definitions for the new word. This is often much more difficult than using it in a sentence, and may not even be possible for some words (i.e., *is, the, if,* etc.). Sometimes it is helpful to ask students questions such as "What does this word mean?" or "What does this word do in the sentence?"

5. Writing   We advocate using word banks or similar strategies in grades K–3. Students, sometimes requiring help, add each new word to their word bank and file it in alphabetical order. List the word in isolation on one side of an index card and in the context of a sentence on the reverse side. Emergent readers may want to draw a picture clue on the word bank card to remind them of the word's meaning.

FRAYER MODEL

Purpose

The *Frayer Model* (Frayer, Frederick, & Klausmeir, 1969) helps students understand new vocabulary and concepts in relation to what is already known. This strategy is especially useful for nonfiction terms—especially in the sciences—because it presents essential and nonessential information related to the term, as well as examples and nonexamples.

Materials

A blank Frayer Model form on a transparency and an overhead projector for demonstration purposes. Students will need paper and pencils for notetaking.

Procedure

The teacher presents or helps students determine essential and nonessential information about a concept, find examples and nonexamples of the concept, and recognize coordinate and subordinate relationships of the concept. This classification procedure can be done as a group, in dyads, or individually. Figure 8.1 is an example for the concept of mammals.

CUBING: THE DIE IS CAST!

Purpose

Cubing (Cowan & Cowan, 1980) is a postreading activity requiring students to analyze, discuss, and write about important new terms. By so doing, they activate prior knowledge or schemata that relate to the new term, which in turn helps the new information to become part of their long-term memory.

Materials

You will need a large foam or wooden cube covered with contact paper. On each side of the cube is written a different direction or question. Here are some examples that might be used for the term *wheelchair*:

1. Describe what it looks like.
2. What is it similar to or different from?
3. What else does it make you think of?
4. What is it made of?

2/ **Figure 8.1**   Frayer Model: Mammals

Concept: MAMMALS

Essential Information or Attributes: **Examples:**

1. higher-order vertebrates   1. dogs
2. nourish young with milk from   2. humans
   mammary glands   3. monkeys
3. warm blooded   4. whales
4. have skin covered with hair

Nonessential Information or Attributes: **Nonexamples:**

1. size of the mammal   1. spiders
2. number of young born   2. fish
3. where the mammal lives (i.e., water,   3. reptiles
   land, etc.)

5. How can it be used?
6. Where are you likely to find one?

Once the cube is rolled and the direction facing the class or group is seen, each student is given a set number of minutes to record her answer. All six sides of the cube can be used in the activity, or, if you prefer, only a few. Once the cubing has ended, students can share their responses with the class or in small groups.

VOCABULARY BINGO!

Purpose

Vocabulary Bingo! (Spencer, 1997) is a whole group word review activity in the format of the popular game bingo. This activity is an especially useful review for students learning English as a second language (ESL) and students in language enrichment programs, as well as for students whose first language is English.

Materials

For all students, make Vocabulary Bingo! boards on which you have printed new words learned in reading and writing activities during the year. The Vocabulary Bingo! cards can all be the same or can differ from one another, depending on the size of the group and the abilities of the learners. These words can be chosen from a classroom word bank, if one is being kept. For each word found on the cards, you will also need definitions written on slips of paper for the "caller" to read aloud during the game.

Procedure

Unlike traditional bingo games in which participants cover spaces on their boards when a number such as "B23" is called, students playing Vocabulary Bingo! cover board spaces upon which are printed review vocabulary words matching the definition that is read aloud by a caller. When all spaces in a row are covered, they call out bingo! An example of a Vocabulary Bingo! card is shown in Figure 8.2.

ONSET AND RIME

Purpose

For many decades, reading teachers have understood the utility of teaching children about what have been termed "word families." These are typically collections of words having the same parts, such as *-ight, -ing,* and *-ack.* Word families might be presented thus:

-ight	-ing	-ack
sight	sing	back
might	wing	sack
right	ring	whack
tight	sting	tack

For a time, word families were no longer emphasized to the extent they once were. Then, a research summary (Adams, 1990) found that teaching about some word elements was a highly reliable practice for recognizing many words in print. The word parts were differentiated into onsets and rimes. An **onset** is the word part (or syllable part) that comes before a vowel, and the **rime** is the rest. For example, in the word families example *sight,* s- is the onset, and *-ight* is the rime. In the word *sack,* s- is the onset, and *-ack* is the rime.

Teaching onset and rime helps students recognize new words in print, and helps students spell words that have common elements (rimes).

Materials

The materials needed really depend on the purpose of the lesson. For awareness of the most common and reliable rimes (listed in the next section), the teacher

Figure 8.2   Vocabulary Bingo Card

VOCABULARY BINGO!				
silo	desert	umpire	dromedary	elevator
aviatrix	conifer	photography	precious	caravan
financier	meteoric	flank	declaration	cleats
maladjusted	payee	odoriferous	seizure	oasis
biannual	proceed	semicircle	humorous	proverb

should consider a "Rime Chart" to display in the classroom. For practice exercises, one will need quality literature that has many words that rhyme (note that rimes rhyme!), such as Shel Silverstein's or Jack Prelutsky's poetry.

Procedure

When emphasizing rimes in grades K–3, the teacher should begin by sharing fun poetry with many rhyming words—the more the better! The poems should be shown in enlarged text (big books, or overhead transparencies). Highlighting first the rhyming words, then the word parts (rime) that cause the words to rime, is a second level of awareness. Posting a language chart displaying some of the most common and sound-reliable rimes as a reference tool is also helpful for student development. Following are 37 rimes that, when different consonants and consonant clusters are added, can be used to create nearly 500 primary-level words (Adams, 1990), not to mention many syllables in more complex words:

-ack	-ank	-ay	-ide	-ink	-or
-ain	-ap	-eat	-ight	-ip	-ore
-ake	-ash	-ell	-ill	-ir	-uck
-ale	-at	-est	-in	-ock	-ug
-all	-ate	-ice	-ine	-oke	-ump
-ame	-aw	-ick	-ing	-op	-unk
-an					

SUBJECT AREA VOCABULARY REINFORCEMENT ACTIVITY (SAVOR)

Purpose

The Subject Area Vocabulary Reinforcement activity (SAVOR) (Stieglitz & Stieglitz, 1981) is an excellent postreading vocabulary learning procedure. As its name implies, SAVOR is intended for use with factual readings. Students combine research and rereading skills to identify similarities and differences between new terms.

Materials

Construct a SAVOR grid on a bulletin board or worksheet to be photocopied. Base it on a topic being studied in science, social studies, mathematics, health, history, or another content area. Make a content analysis of the unit of study and select new terms, to be listed in the left-hand column of the SAVOR grid, and characteristics related to the terms, to be listed across the top row. An example is shown in Figure 8.3.

Procedure

SAVOR is intended to be used as a postreading activity to reinforce learning of new vocabulary. After students have completed their initial reading of the subject matter text, introduce the SAVOR grid bulletin board or photocopied worksheet. Discuss how to complete each grid space with either a plus (+) or minus (–), based on whether the term has the trait listed across the top of the grid. As with all minilessons, the teacher should first model the thinking process she is using to determine whether to put a plus or minus in the space provided. In Figure 8.3 we show an example of a SAVOR grid that was completed by children in a school in southern Texas as they studied the solar system.

PEER TEACHING

Purpose

An activity that has been proven to be effective with ESL students is called *peer teaching* (Johnson & Steele, 1996). It is considered to be a *generative strategy*, or one that is student-initiated and monitored and can be used in different situations. Peer teaching first has individual students choosing from the reading selection a word that they feel is new and important. Next, one child teaches her term to another student, then vice versa.

Materials

Materials needed include only a reading selection to be shared with the whole group and the kind of supplies usually found in a writing center for students to use as they wish. It is also helpful to list several ways of teaching new vocabulary words to others, like those techniques found in this chapter, that you commonly use with the students in your class.

Figure 8.3   SAVOR Grid: Solar System

Planets	Inner planet	Outer planet	Made up of gas	Has more than one moon	Longer revolution than Earth's 365 days	Has rings	Has been visited by a space probe	Stronger gravity than Earth's
Venus	+	−	−	−	−	−	+	−
Neptune	−	+	+	+	+	?	+	+
Saturn	−	+	+	+	+	+	+	+
Mercury	+	−	−	−	−	−	+	−

Procedure

First, conduct a one- or two-session minilesson in which you model how you might choose a word from the reading selection that seems to be important to understanding what the author is saying. As an example, in Betsy Byars's Newbery Award-winning book *The Summer of the Swans* (1970), the main character, Sara, has a "grudging tolerance" of her Aunt Willie. Since this is important to understanding Sara and her feelings, you might select "grudging tolerance" as a term to teach someone reading the book. Next, model how you would choose one of the common strategies you use in class (on a list you post for all to see) and demonstrate how you would plan to teach your term to another. Finally, ask someone to role play with you as you teach *grudging tolerance*.

PERSONAL WORD LISTS

Purpose

Most words are learned through repeated encounters in a meaningful context in spoken and written forms. All too often, however, when students come to a word they don't know they simply run to the dictionary or to someone else for a quick definition, instead of using sentence or passage context to figure out for themselves the word's meaning. While, certainly, we want students to develop dictionary skills, the first line of attack for gaining word meaning should be sentence or passage context. *Personal word lists,* as described in this section, have been around elementary and secondary classrooms for a very long time and have recently found success with ESL learners (Johnson & Steele, 1996). A personal word list is a structured way of helping students develop the habit of using context to determine vocabulary meaning and to permanently fix the vocabulary in long-term memory.

Materials

Multiple blank copies of the personal word list, as shown in Figure 8.4, and a transparency version for demonstrations on the classroom overhead projector.

Procedure

Distribute blank copies of the personal word list sheet for students to review as you explain its function. Using a passage read recently by the class, model two or three examples of how you would complete the form for words you found in the passage that seemed important. Next, do a guided practice exercise with the whole group in which you provide several more words from the passage. Ask them to complete the form for each word and have volunteers share what they found with the class. Once students seem secure with the personal word list form, ask them to make several new entries with words of their own choosing in the next reading assignment. This will serve as a kind of individual practice exercise. Further use of the personal word list will depend on your class needs and how well you feel it works with your students. An example of a personal word list for the book *Lincoln* (Donald, 1995) is shown in Figure 8.4.

Figure 8.4   Personal word list: *Lincoln* (Donald, 1995)

New Word	What I think it means . . .	Clues from the book or passage . . .	Dictionary definition (only when I needed to look)
1. abolitionists	people against slavery	John Brown was called one and was the leader of the Harper's Ferry raid.	
2. Republican	the party that Lincoln joined and ran for President	Lincoln went to the first meeting in 1855 (page 187) and later became its candidate in 1860.	
3. dispatches	a telegraph	Lincoln and Lee sent dispatches to people during the Civil War.	a message sent with speed

SEMANTIC MAPS

Purpose

Semantic maps are useful in tying together new vocabulary with prior knowledge and related terms (Johnson & Pearson, 1984). Semantic maps are essentially a kind of "schema blueprint" in which students map what is stored in their brain about a topic and related concepts. Semantic maps help students relate new information to schemata already in the brain, integrate new information, and restructure existing information for greater clarity (Yopp & Yopp, 1996). Further, for students having learning problems, using semantic maps prior to reading a selection has also proven to promote better story recall than traditional methods (Sinatra, Stahl-Gemake, & Berg, 1984). Writing materials are the only supplies needed.

Procedure

There are many ways to introduce semantic mapping to students, but the first time around you will likely want to use a structured approach. One way is to introduce semantic maps through something we call "wacky webbing." The idea is to take a topic familiar to all, such as the name of one's home state, and portray it in the center of the web, inside an oval. Major categories related to the theme are connected to the central concept using either bold lines or double lines. Details that relate to the major categories are connected using single lines. Figure 8.5 shows a semantic web for the topic "Tennessee."

Semantic webs can also be constructed that relate to a story or chapter book the students are reading. In Figure 8.6 we share one example of a semantic web from

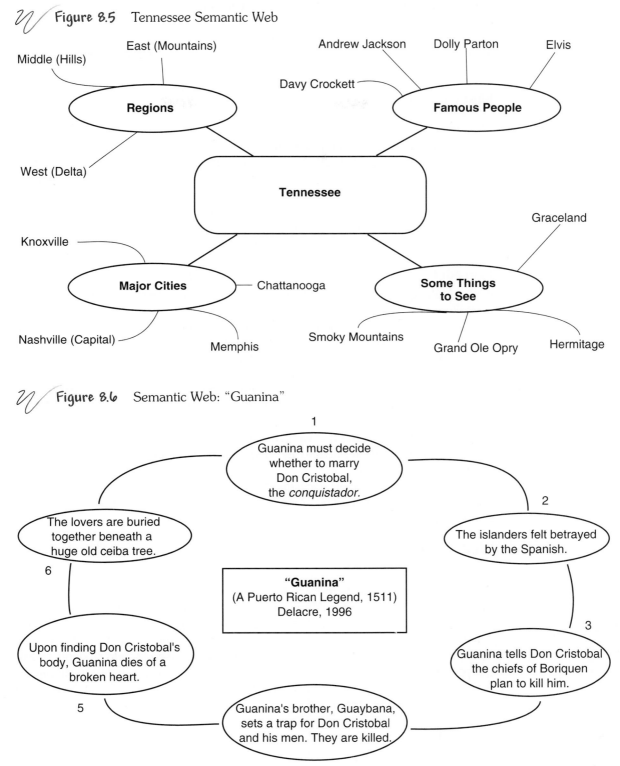

Figure 8.5 Tennessee Semantic Web

Middle (Hills)

East (Mountains)

Andrew Jackson

Dolly Parton

Elvis

Davy Crockett

Regions

Famous People

West (Delta)

Tennessee

Graceland

Knoxville

Major Cities — Chattanooga

Some Things to See

Nashville (Capital)

Memphis

Smoky Mountains

Grand Ole Opry

Hermitage

Figure 8.6 Semantic Web: "Guanina"

1

Guanina must decide whether to marry Don Cristobal, the *conquistador*.

The lovers are buried together beneath a huge old ceiba tree.

6

"Guanina"
(A Puerto Rican Legend, 1511)
Delacre, 1996

2

The islanders felt betrayed by the Spanish.

3

Guanina tells Don Cristobal the chiefs of Boriquen plan to kill him.

Upon finding Don Cristobal's body, Guanina dies of a broken heart.

5

Guanina's brother, Guaybana, sets a trap for Don Cristobal and his men. They are killed.

4

a story in the book *Golden Tales: Myths, Legends, and Folktales from Latin America* (Delacre, 1996).

MAKING WORDS

Purpose

Making Words (Cunningham & Cunningham, 1992) is a word learning strategy that might fit just as well in our chapter on phonics. It is a strategy that helps children improve their phonetic understanding of words through invented or "temporary spellings" (Reutzel & Cooter, 1996) while also increasing their repertoire of vocabulary words they can recognize in print. Making Words will be a familiar strategy for anyone who has ever played the crossword board game Scrabble. You will need a pocket chart, large index cards, and markers.

Procedure

In the Making Words activity, students are given a number of letters with which to make words. They begin by making two- or three-letter words using the letters for a set amount of time, then progress to making words having more letters until they finally arrive at a specific word that uses all the letters. This final word can be the main word to be taught for the day, but the other words discovered during the activity may also be new for some students. By manipulating the letters to make words of two, three, four, and more letters using temporary spellings, students have an opportunity to practice their phonemic awareness skills. Making words is recommended as a 15-minute activity when used with first and second graders. In Tables 8.1 and 8.2 we summarize and adapt the steps in planning and teaching a Making Words lesson as suggested by Cunningham and Cunningham (1992).

Table 8.3 provides details necessary for making two more Making Words lessons suggested by Cunningham and Cunningham (1992) that may be useful for helping students learn the procedure.

WORD BANKS

Purpose

It is important for students to learn to recognize a number of words on sight to facilitate the decoding process. Many words carry little meaning (*the, of,* and, *a*), but provide the "glue" of language that helps us represent thoughts. One question for teachers is *how* to go about helping students increase the numbers of words they can recognize immediately on sight. **Word banks** are used to help students collect and review these "sight words." Word banks also can be used as personal dictionaries. A word bank is simply a student-constructed box, file, or notebook in which newly discovered words are stored and reviewed.

Materials

In the early grades, teachers often collect small shoe boxes from local stores to serve as word banks. The children are asked at the beginning of the year to deco-

Table 8.1   Planning a "Making Words" Lesson

1. Choose the final word to be emphasized in the lesson. It should be a key word from a reading selection, fiction or nonfiction, to be read by the class, or it may be of particular interest to the group. Be sure to select a word that has enough vowels and/or one that fits letter-sound patterns useful for most children at their developmental stage in reading and writing. For illustrative purposes, in these instructions we will use the word *thunder* that was suggested by Cunningham and Cunningham (1992).

2. Make a list of shorter words that can be spelled using the main word to be learned. For the word *thunder,* one could derive the following words: *red, Ted, Ned/den/end* (Note: these all use the same letters), *her, hut, herd, turn, hunt, hurt, under, hunted, turned, thunder.*

   From the You Were Able To list, select 12–15 words that include such aspects of written language as a) words that can be used to emphasize a certain kind of pattern, b) big and little words, c) words that can be made with the same letters in different positions (as with *Ned, end, den*), d) a proper noun, if possible, to remind students about using capital letters, and especially e) words that students already have in their listening vocabularies.

3. Write all of these words on large index cards and order them from the smallest to the largest words. Also, write each of the individual letters found in the key word for the day on large index cards (make 2 sets of these).

4. Reorder the words one more time to group them according to letter patterns and/or to demonstrate how shifting around letters can form new words. Store the 2 sets of large single-letter cards in 2 envelopes—one for the teacher, and one for children participating during the modeling activity.

5. Store the word stacks in envelopes and note on the outside of each the words/patterns to be emphasized during the lesson. Also, note clues you can use with the children to help them discover the words you desire. For example, "See if you can make a three-letter word that is the name of the room in some people's homes where they like to watch television." (*den*)

rate the boxes in order to make them their own. In the upper grades, more formal-looking word banks are used. Notebooks or recipe boxes are generally selected. Alphabetic dividers can also be used at all levels to facilitate the quick location of word bank words. In addition, use of alphabetic dividers in the early grades helps students rehearse and reinforce knowledge of alphabetical order. Figure 8.7 on page 171 shows an example of a word bank.

Procedure

Once students have constructed word banks, the next issue for the teacher is helping students decide which words should be included and from what sources. At least four sources can be considered for sight-word selection and inclusion in word banks (Reutzel & Cooter, 1996): basal reader sight word lists; "key vocabulary" words that

Table 8.2   Teaching a "Making Words" Lesson

1. Place the large single letters from the key word in the pocket chart or along the chalkboard ledge.
2. For modeling purposes, the first time you use Making Words, select one of the students to be the "passer" and ask that child to pass the large single letters to other designated children.
3. Hold up and name each of the letter cards and have students selected to participate in the modeling exercise respond by holding up their matching card.
4. Write the numeral 2 (or 3, if there are no two-letter words in this lesson) on the board. Next, tell the student "volunteers" the clue you developed for the desired word. Then, tell the student volunteers to put together two (or three) of their letters to form the desired word.
5. Continue directing the students to make more words using the clues provided and the letter cards until you have helped them discover all but the final key word (the one that uses all the letters). Ask the student volunteers if they can guess the key word. If not, ask the remainder of the class if anyone can guess it. If no one is able to do so, offer students a meaning clue (e.g., " I am thinking of a word with _____ letters that means . . . .").
6. As a guided practice activity, repeat these steps the next day with the whole group using a new word.

Table 8.3   Making Words: Additional Examples
(Cunningham & Cunningham, 1992)

Lesson Using One Vowel:

Letter cards: u k n r s t
Words to make: us, nut, rut, sun, sunk, runs, ruts/rust, tusk, stun, stunk, trunk, *trunks* (the key word)
You can sort for . . .   rhymes, "s" pairs (run, runs; rut, ruts; trunk, trunks)

Lesson Using Big Words:

Letter cards: a a a e i b c h l l p t
Words to make: itch, able, cable, table, batch, patch, pitch, petal, label, chapel, capital, capable, alphabet, *alphabetical* (the key word)
You can sort for . . .   el, le, al, -itch, -atch

students have self-selected for learning (Ashton-Warner, 1963); "discovery" words (i.e., words that are discovered during class discussions); and "function words" (words that supply structure to sentences, but carry little or no meaning, such as

Figure 8.7   A Word Bank

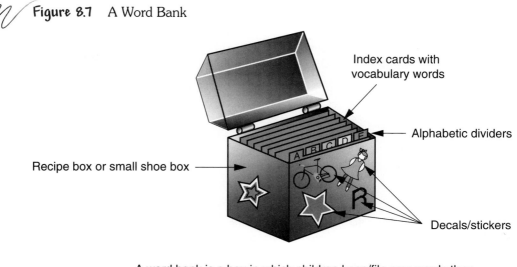

Index cards with vocabulary words

Alphabetic dividers

Recipe box or small shoe box

Decals/stickers

A word bank is a box in which children keep/file new words they are learning. The words are usually written in isolation on one side of the card, and in a sentence on the back of the card (usually with a picture clue).

Example:

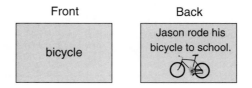

Front

Back

bicycle

Jason rode his bicycle to school.

with, were, what, is, of). A more complete list of high-frequency sight words is supplied in Figure 8.8.

CONTEXTUAL REDEFINITION (FOR TECHNICAL VOCABULARY)
Purpose
While there has been some debate over the years about the extent to which context should be emphasized, it is clear that learning from context is a very important component of vocabulary acquisition (Adams, 1990, p. 150). An excellent method of introducing terminology in context, such as that found in informational readings, as well as demonstrating to students why they should use context whenever possible to figure out unfamiliar words, is a strategy called *contextual redefinition* (Cunningham, Cunningham, & Arthur, 1981).

W **Figure 8.8** High-Frequency Sight Words

The first 10 words make up about 24% of all written material, the first 100 words about 50% of all written material, and the first 300 about 65%.

1. the	44. each	87. who	130. through	173. home	216. never	259. walked
2. of	45. which	88. oil	131. much	174. us	217. started	260. white
3. and	46. she	89. its	132. before	175. move	218. city	261. sea
4. a	47. do	90. now	133. line	176. try	219. earth	262. began
5. to	48. how	91. find	134. right	177. kind	220. eyes	263. grow
6. in	49. their	92. long	135. too	178. hand	221. light	264. took
7. is	50. if	93. down	136. means	179. picture	222. thought	265. river
8. you	51. will	94. day	137. old	180. again	223. head	266. four
9. that	52. up	95. did	138. any	181. change	224. under	267. carry
10. it	53. other	96. get	139. same	182. off	225. story	268. state
11. he	54. about	97. come	140. tell	183. play	226. saw	269. once
12. was	55. out	98. made	141. boy	184. spell	227. left	270. book
13. for	56. many	99. may	142. following	185. air	228. don't	271. hear
14. on	57. then	100. part	143. came	186. away	229. few	272. stop
15. are	58. them	101. over	144. want	187. animals	230. while	273. without
16. as	59. these	102. new	145. show	188. house	231. along	274. second
17. with	60. so	103. sound	146. also	189. point	232. might	275. later
18. his	61. some	104. take	147. around	190. page	233. close	276. miss
19. they	62. her	105. only	148. form	191. letters	234. something	277. idea
20. I	63. would	106. little	149. three	192. mother	235. seemed	278. enough
21. at	64. make	107. work	150. small	193. answer	236. next	279. eat
22. be	65. like	108. know	151. set	194. found	237. hard	280. face
23. this	66. him	109. place	152. put	195. study	238. open	281. watch
24. have	67. into	110. years	153. end	196. still	239. example	282. far
25. from	68. time	111. live	154. does	197. learn	240. beginning	283. Indians
26. or	69. has	112. me	155. another	198. should	241. life	284. really
27. one	70. look	113. back	156. well	199. American	242. always	285. almost
28. had	71. two	114. give	157. large	200. world	243. those	286. let
29. by	72. more	115. most	158. must	201. high	244. both	287. above
30. words	73. write	116. very	159. big	202. every	245. paper	288. girl
31. but	74. go	117. after	160. even	203. near	246. together	289. sometimes
32. not	75. see	118. things	161. such	204. add	247. got	290. mountains
33. what	76. number	119. our	162. because	205. food	248. group	291. cut
34. all	77. no	120. just	163. turned	206. between	249. often	292. young
35. were	78. way	121. name	164. here	207. own	250. run	293. talk
36. we	79. could	122. good	165. why	208. below	251. important	294. soon
37. when	80. people	123. sentence	166. asked	209. country	252. until	295. list
38. your	81. my	124. man	167. went	210. plants	253. children	296. song
39. can	82. than	125. think	168. men	211. last	254. side	297. being
40. said	83. first	126. say	169. read	212. school	255. feet	298. leave
41. there	84. water	127. great	170. need	213. father	256. car	299. family
42. use	85. been	128. where	171. land	214. keep	257. miles	300. it's
43. an	86. called	129. help	172. different	215. trees	258. night	

Note: From "The New Instant Word List," by Edward Fry, *The Reading Teacher,* December 1980, pp. 284–289. Reprinted with permission of Edward Fry and the International Reading Association.

Materials

This is an activity that can be conducted mainly at the chalkboard, overhead projector, and/or by using teacher-constructed activity sheets.

Procedure

The steps in this procedure, as adapted by Cooter and Flynt (1996), follow:

Step 1: Select 5 or 6 terms that are unfamiliar or probably known by only a few students in the class. Introduce the topic and display the new terms on the chalkboard or overhead. Ask each student or pair of students to predict a brief definition for each term. Encourage students to guess at word meanings, reminding them that the goal is to try to come up with logical ideas and not to worry about being "right." After the students have had an opportunity to discuss probable definitions, call for individuals to share their ideas and write them on the chalkboard or overhead projector transparency. Briefly discuss *why* the students were unable to do much more than guess at the word's meanings.

Step 2: Next, tell the students that you have these same words written in sentences or short paragraphs and that you want them to read each passage to see if they want to revise their original guesses. Be sure to present each word in a contextually rich sentence. During the ensuing discussion, encourage students to explain *why* they think the word means what they now think it means. Record varying responses next to each term as they occur.

Step 3: Finally, if there are differences, have students find the word in either the text or the glossary and read its definition. Then have students copy the finalized sentences in their notebooks/journals.

Contextual redefinition provides students with opportunities to share their skills in using context and can be helpful in promoting independent use of context clues. Teachers find it an invigorating means for preteaching terms and showing that the glossary is not the first tool readers can use in figuring out the meaning of new words: context usually is.

SUMMARY

Reading is language. Reading is comprehension. A student's success in reading and understanding the words of others is necessarily linked to her development of vocabulary. We discussed the four major vocabularies that students learn throughout life. They are, in order of largest to smallest, *listening, speaking, reading,* and *writing/spelling.* Students can read and understand only words they are able to hear, understand, and use in their own speech.

REFERENCES

Adams, M. A. (1990). *Beginning to read: Thinking and learning about print.* Cambridge, MA: MIT Press.

Ashton-Warner, S. (1963). *Teacher.* New York: Simon & Schuster.

Byars, B. (1970). *The summer of the swans.* New York: Puffin Books.

Cattell, J. M. (1885). Veber die Zeit der Erkennung und Bennenung von Schriftzeichen, Bildem und Farben. *Philosophische Studien, 2,* 635–650.

Cooter, R. B., & Flynt, E. S. (1996). *Teaching reading in the content areas: Developing content literacy for all students.* Columbus, OH: Merrill, an imprint of Prentice Hall.

Cowan, E., & Cowan, G. (1980). *Writing.* New York: John Wiley & Sons.

Cox, C., & Boyd-Batstone, P. (1997). *Crossroads: Literature and language in culturally and linguistically diverse classrooms.* Columbus, OH: Merrill/Prentice Hall.

Cunningham, P. M., & Cunningham, J. (1992). Making words: Enhancing the invented spelling-decoding connection. *Reading Teacher, 46*(2), 106–115.

Cunningham, J., Cunningham, P., & Arthur, S. V. (1981). *Middle and secondary school reading.* New York: Longman.

Delacre, L. (1996). *Golden tales: Myths, legends, and folktales from Latin America.* New York: Scholastic.

Donald, D. H. (1995). *Lincoln.* New York: Simon & Schuster.

Flynt, E. S., & Cooter, R. B., Jr. (1998). *The Flynt/Cooter Reading Inventory for the Classroom* (3rd ed.). Columbus, OH: Merrill/Prentice Hall.

Frayer, D., Frederick, W. C., & Klausmeir, H. J. (1969). *A schema for testing the level of concept mastery* (Working paper No. 16). Madison: University of Wisconsin, Wisconsin Research and Development Center for Cognitive Learning.

Fry, E., Polk, J. K., & Fountoukidis, D. (1984). *The reading teacher's book of lists.* Englewood Cliffs, NJ: Prentice Hall.

Irwin, J. L. (1990). *Vocabulary knowledge: Guidelines for instruction. What research says to the teacher.* Washington, D.C.: National Education Association (ERIC Document Reproduction Service No. ED 319 001).

Johnson, D., & Steele, V. (1996). So many words, so little time: Helping college ESL learners acquire vocabulary strategies. *Journal of Adolescent & Adult Literacy, 39*(5), 348–357.

Johnson, D. D., & Pearson, P. D. (1984). *Teaching reading vocabulary.* New York: Holt, Rinehart and Winston.

Meddaugh, S. (1992). *Martha speaks.* Boston: Houghton Mifflin.

Reutzel, D. R., & Cooter, R. B., Jr. (1996). *Teaching children to read: From basals to book* (2nd ed.) Columbus, OH: Merrill/Prentice Hall.

Sinatra, R., Stahl-Gemake, J., & Berg, D. (1984). Improving reading comprehension of disabled readers through semantic mapping. *The Reading Teacher, 38,* 22–29.

Smith, F. (1987). *Insult to intelligence.* Portsmouth, NH: Heinemann.

Smith, R. J., & Johnson, D. D. (1980). *Teaching children to read.* Reading, MA: Addison-Wesley.

Spencer, K. M. (1997). *Vocabulary bingo!: A language review activity.* Unpublished manuscript, Texas Christian University.

Stieglitz, E. L., & Stieglitz, V. S. (1981). SAVOR the word to reinforce vocabulary in the content areas. *Journal of Reading, 25,* 46–51.

Yopp, H. K., & Yopp, R. H. (1996). *Literature-based reading activities.* Boston: Allyn and Bacon.

Chapter 9

Assessing and Enhancing Reading Comprehension

Comprehension is what reading is all about. Elements of language, such as words and letter sounds, exist only to recreate the author's message. We must never lose sight of the purpose for reading—to comprehend. As teachers, we should help students understand from the beginning of reading instruction that comprehension is always the reader's goal.

Until the 1980s, reading comprehension was taught in school classrooms by asking students questions about the material and by assigning practice skill sheets. Basal readers included (and still do, in many cases) lengthy lists of unrelated reading comprehension skills. During the 1980s, however, reading comprehension was the focus of unparalleled research attention, which resulted in new insights on how to teach comprehension skills. This chapter provides a summary of recent advances in reading comprehension, offers focused assessment strategies, and suggests successful instructional strategies for helping special needs readers.

BACKGROUND BRIEFING FOR TEACHERS: THE PROCESS OF MEANING CONSTRUCTION

Reading comprehension instruction has been profoundly influenced by **schema theory,** which explains how people store information in their minds, and how what we already know helps us gain new knowledge. A **schema** (plural is *schemata* or *schemas*) can be thought of as a kind of file cabinet of information in the brain containing related 1) concepts (chairs, birds, ships), 2) events (weddings, birthdays, school experiences), 3) related emotions (anger, frustration, joy, pleasure), and 4) roles (parent, judge, teacher) drawn from the life experiences of a reader (Rumelhart, 1981).

Researchers have sketched schemas as networks of associated meanings (Collins & Quillian, 1969; Lindsay & Norman, 1977). Each schema is connected to other related schemas, forming an individual's vast interconnected network of knowledge and experiences. The size and content of each schema is influenced by past opportunities to learn. Thus, younger children generally possess fewer, less developed schemas than mature adults.

Why Students Often Have Comprehension Difficulties

Difficulties in comprehending can be traced typically to four schema-related problems (Reutzel & Cooter, 1996). Each is discussed below with examples to help you understand the difficulties your students may encounter in comprehending.

Difficulty 1: Students may not have the necessary schema to understand a specific topic. Without a schema for a particular event or concept, they simply cannot construct meaning for the text.

For example, without the necessary schema, readers cannot appropriately interpret individual word meanings in the following passage:

Machine-baste interfacing to WRONG side of one collar section 1/2″ from raw edges. Trim interfacing close to stitching. Clip dress neck edge to stay stitching. With RIGHT sides together, pin collar to dress, matching center back and small dots. Baste. Stitch. Trim seam; clip curve. Press seam open. (Gibson & Levin, 1975, p. 7)

While those individuals who possess a sewing schema can readily interpret this passage, those without a sewing schema experience great difficulty in making any sense out of selected words (*baste, interfacing*) in the text, or even out of the text as a whole.

Difficulty 2: Readers may have well-developed schemata for a topic, but authors may fail to provide enough information for readers to locate or select appropriate schema.

In some cases, readers know a great deal about the topic to be read, but some authors fail to provide enough information in the text to help students connect their schema to a specific topic. For example, read the following text to see if you can locate your schema on this well-known topic:

Our hero bravely defied all scornful laughter that tried to prevent his scheme. "Your eyes deceive," he had said. "An egg, not a table, correctly typifies this planet." Now three sturdy sisters sought proof, forging along sometimes through calm vastness. (Bransford & Johnson, 1972)

The authors, by failing to include relevant clues in the text, such as the terms *explorer, ships,* and *America,* make selecting the *Christopher Columbus* schema extremely difficult. Why? Because these key clues call up specific memory "files" (associations) found in the Columbus schema. In order for the Columbus schema to be located and selected for interpreting this text, enough of these key clues must be found in the text.

Difficulty 3: Readers may prematurely select one schema or interpretation while reading, only to discover later that the selected schema doesn't fit the text meaning.

When this happens, readers may shift from using one schema to using another to interpret a text. Read each sentence, stop, and form a picture in your mind about what you read.

John was on his way to school.
He was terribly worried about the math lesson.

Now read the next sentence and notice what happens as you process the new information:

He thought he might not be able to control the class again today.

Did you notice a change in the schema you accessed to interpret the text? Did your schema shift from that of a young boy on his way to school, worried about his math lesson, to that of a concerned teacher? Now, read the final sentence:

It was not a normal part of a janitor's duties. (Sanford & Garrod, 1981, p. 114)

Did you experience still another change in selecting an appropriate schema? Now you can easily see how an author's writing style can sometimes lead young readers into comprehension miscues.

Difficulty 4: The cultural experiences that a reader possesses may affect his perspective when selecting a schema to interpret a text. This leads to an "understanding" of the text, but sometimes a misunderstanding of the author.

To illustrate this point, Lipson (1983) conducted a study and found that Catholic and Jewish children comprehended texts better that were compatible with their own religious beliefs than those that conflicted with their religious schemata. Alvermann, Smith, and Readence (1985) found that readers' own understandings (schemas) that conflicted with text information were sometimes strong enough to override text information. Reutzel and Hollingsworth (1991) found that attitudes toward a particular schema were strong enough to influence comprehension of incompatible texts about a fictitious country called *Titubia*. Likewise, Read and Rosson (1982) found that attitudes influenced recall of compatible and incompatible texts read about nuclear power. Thus, information represented in schemata can act to facilitate or to inhibit assimilating new information from text. To illustrate this difficulty, Anderson, Reynolds, Schallert, and Goetz (1977) asked people to read the following paragraph:

> Tony slowly got up from the mat, planning his escape. He hesitated a moment and thought. Things were not going well. What bothered him most was being held, especially since the charge against him had been weak. He considered his present situation. The lock that held him was strong, but he thought he could break it. He knew, however, that his timing would have to be perfect. Tony was aware that it was because of his early roughness that he had been penalized so severely—much too severely from his point of view. The situation was becoming frustrating; the pressure had been grinding on him for too long. He was being ridden unmercifully. Tony was getting angry now. He felt he was ready to make his move. He knew that his success or failure would depend on what he did in the next few seconds.

Most people thought the passage is about a convict planning his escape. There *is,* however, another possible interpretation. When physical education majors read the foregoing passage, they sometimes thought the passage was about wrestling! Thus, the background experiences of the readers influenced their perspectives by leading them to select entirely different schemata for interpreting the text.

INSTRUCTIONAL IMPLICATIONS OF SCHEMA THEORY

While schema theory has provided researchers with powerful explanations about how readers comprehend text, these discoveries can benefit children only when teachers clearly understand the instructional implications that arise from schema theory. There are three different types of learning that are possible in a schema-based learning system: 1) accretion, 2) tuning, and 3) restructuring (Rumelhart, 1980).

Accretion refers to learning new information and adding it to existing information in a schema. For a "bird" schema, children learn that the bones in a bird's body are hollow. This information is then added to the bird schema. *Tuning* involves modifying an existing schema to fit new information. A schema may be "tuned" to the point that students can begin to understand a larger class of concepts or events. For example, the bird schema can be changed to include the idea that birds are not the only creatures whose young are hatched from eggs. Another schema change in connection with the concept of tuning relates to altering the schema structure to fit conflicting information. For example, not all birds have the ability to fly; penguins are one example. Finally, *restructuring* relates to the idea of creating new schema from old. For example, the bird schema may be used to create a schema for a pterodactyl—a flying dinosaur. These three learning modes suggest several implications for the teacher of reading.

First, teachers should assess the background knowledge of their students in order to provide meaningful learning experiences. Second, the teacher can help students choose the appropriate schema for interpreting a text—particularly important for special needs learners (Carr & Thompson, 1996). Third, if teachers find that some students need to create a new schema for an unfamiliar concept, they should build the necessary background before asking students to read. Fourth, if teachers find that some students need to tune or modify their schemas to include other unfamiliar or incompatible concepts, they may provide examples and discussion to help those students make the necessary changes. Finally, if teachers discover that students possess a fairly complete understanding of a concept or event, then reading may be assigned with relatively brief background-building discussions or lessons.

ASSESSMENT STRATEGIES FOR READING COMPREHENSION

THINK ALOUDS

Purpose

Unlike asking students questions after reading, *think alouds* help teachers understand how students comprehend as they read (Maria, 1990; Irwin, 1991; Brown & Lytle, 1988). Students are asked periodically to stop during their reading and share their thoughts. Myers and Lytle (1986) suggest that "think alouds" are an important comprehension assessment tool.

Materials

Any book, chapter, story, or textbook can be selected to be used with the *Think Aloud Checklist* shown in Figure 9.1.

Procedures

Lytle (1982) has suggested six categories of possible statements students may make during a "think aloud" process assessment that can be constructed into a student assessment checklist for think alouds. However, before asking students to

Figure 9.1   Assessing Student Comprehension: A Think-Aloud Checklist

Student name: _____   Date: _____

Title of selection: _____   Teacher: _____

1. Monitoring of doubts (I don't get it. It isn't making much sense to me.)
   Number _____   Indicators_____
2. Signaling understanding (Oh, I get it now. Ah, now it makes sense!)
   Number _____   Indicators_____
3. Analyzing text structures (This is organized a lot like the story we read yesterday.)
   Number _____   Indicators_____
4. Elaboration of text (This reminds me of when I . . . . I remember what it was like to . . . .)
   Number _____   Indicators_____
5. Judgments of text (I really don't like this story. Wow, that was weird.)
   Number _____   Indicators_____
6. Reasoning with text (I think if I read on I'll figure this out.)
   Number _____   Indicators_____

Summary:

MD _____   ATS _____   JT _____
SU _____   ET _____   RT _____

Comments:

engage in think alouds as an assessment strategy, teachers should model the think aloud process first. Then, students should be allowed to practice the "think aloud" process a few times before expecting that the "think aloud" assessment process will accurately reflect a student's comprehension. Assessment of student comprehension using "think aloud" processes should be performed with individual students.

Lytle's (1982) six categories can be used effectively to informally assess the types of thinking students engage in during reading that reflect their comprehension of text. The categories may also point out the need to focus on certain aspects of comprehension, such as text elaboration, making self-connections with text and personal experience, and organization of texts. If students fail to use a specific category of thinking in their think alouds, then this may signal a need for future instructional attention.

FREE RECALL

Purpose

For many years, psychologists have measured learning and memory using Free Recall (FR) techniques. Asking a student to tell you in his own words what he has read is superior to traditional questioning techniques for at least two reasons. First, free recall allows students to explain their recollections of the text more completely than does answering specific questions. Second, free recall tasks allow students to share their recall of a text in the order of the events in the text. It also occurs to us that free recall enables students to link their understanding of the text with their prior knowledge and life experiences. Thus, free recall is a more natural and holistic approach to assessing comprehension than is the traditional practice of asking students to respond to a string of questions (Irwin, 1991).

Materials

Any book, chapter, story, or textbook may be used, though we always prefer those chosen by students themselves so that interest is reasonably high.

Procedures

Because students are used to being questioned after reading a selection, the tendency is for them to offer very short free recall responses. Therefore, it is important for teachers to ask students to tell as much about the selection as possible. After the student seems to have offered all that he can, we have found that it helps to ask, "What else can you remember?" Students will almost invariably recall more information. Ask the "what else" question two or three times, or until the student seems finally to run out of information. Once complete, use the checklist shown in Figure 9.2 to assess the student's retelling. Note that this checklist focuses on many of the aspects of comprehension that were typically probed in the past through comprehension questioning.

Scores derived by using the Free Recall Comprehension Assessment Checklist can be averaged across the five questions to get an informal summary rating of the free recall comprehension of a student. We also recommend that teachers probe a student's areas of poor comprehension to determine whether he actually compre-

Figure 9.2   Free Recall Comprehension Assessment Checklist

Evaluate the student's retelling immediately following the retelling. If you find it helpful, you may want to audio record the retelling to review later. Answer each of the questions below using the rating scale shown at the bottom of the checklist.

1. Did the student recall the story in temporal sequence?   _____

2. Did the student recall the major events or ideas in the text?   _____

3. Did the student follow the author's or text pattern in recalling the text?   _____

4. Did the student select the most relevant details to recall?   _____

5. Did the student draw reasonable inferences from the text?   _____

What is your impression of the comprehension? Was it effective and complete? Why?

If there were problems, what were these problems? What strategies do you recommend?

Scale

1. Complete
2. Incomplete, but more than adequate
3. Adequate
4. Inadequate

hended a part of the text, but simply failed to include this information in his free recall of the selection.

SELF-RATINGS OF UNDERSTANDING

Purpose

Sometimes we can overlook the obvious when trying to find out what students are able to do—simply ask them! Forest and Waller (1979) have successfully used self-assessments in research to explore how students rate their own understanding. For assessment to fully represent how well readers comprehend, teachers should ask students to rate their own comprehension abilities.

Figure 9.3   Self-Rating Comprehension Checklist

Name: _____   Date: _____

Title of selection: _____

1. Three things I did today to help myself understand the selection I was reading were:
   _____ I looked at the pictures.
   _____ I thought about what I already knew.
   _____ I thought about what might happen.
   _____ I began reading and stopped to think about what might happen.
   _____ I looked quickly through the book, chapter, or story to get an idea.
   _____ I tried to imagine a picture in my head of what was going to happen.
   _____ I asked someone who had read it what it was about.

2. What I did well in reading today:
   _____
   _____
   _____

3. What I need to work on in reading:
   _____
   _____
   _____

4. The ways I like to demonstrate my understanding are:
   _____
   _____

Materials

The *Self-Rating Comprehension Checklist* shown in Figure 9.3 may be used with most reading passages selected.

Procedures

The procedures for using the Self Rating Comprehension Checklist are rather simple. Begin by reading a text aloud and then model for your students how you would complete the checklist. A "think aloud" process in which you communicate your own thinking about how to fill out the checklist can be very helpful for less able readers. Some teachers have also found that the checklist can be used effectively as an interview guide as students work in pairs to complete the checklist.

METACOGNITIVE EVALUATION

Purpose

Metacognition refers to two important concepts related to reading comprehension: 1) a reader's knowledge of strategies for learning from texts and one's own strengths and weaknesses as a learner, and 2) the control a reader has over these strategies as he reads. For many readers, problems in successful comprehension result from failures in one or both of the two areas of metacognition. The purpose of metacognitive evaluation is to gain insight into the types of strategies that students use to read, as well as the degree to which they can control the selection of reading strategies.

Materials

The *Metacognitive Interview* shown in Figure 9.4 can be used with most text selections.

Procedures

Begin by asking students to read an assigned selection silently. Next, write and distribute to students a list of questions to answer that are based on the selection. Once these questions have been answered, invite individual students to a teacher-student conference. With each student, consider the items in the Metacognitive Interview in Figure 9.4. By using this interview on a periodic basis, teachers can gain insights into the strategies students know, how frequently they use these strategies, and how well chosen these strategies are for the comprehension task at hand. Areas for improvement can be identified and then become the subject of future lessons and demonstrations to help special needs students improve their comprehension.

BACKGROUND KNOWLEDGE

Purpose

Among the most important contributors or inhibitors of comprehension are a student's background information and experiences. Researchers have determined that students who know a great deal of background information about a subject tend to recall greater amounts of information more accurately from reading than do students with little or no background knowledge (Pearson, Hansen, & Gordon, 1979; Carr & Thompson, 1996). We also know that well-developed background information can actually inhibit the comprehension of new information that conflicts with prior knowledge and assumptions about a topic. Thus, knowing how much knowledge a reader has about a concept can help teachers better prepare students to read and comprehend text successfully. One way that teachers can assess background knowledge and experience is to use a procedure developed by Langer (1982) for assessing the amount and content of students' background knowledge about selected topics, themes, concepts, and events.

2/ **Figure 9.4**   Metacognitive Interview

Name: _____   Content question # _____

Group A (Right or Wrong)
If the student gives a right or wrong answer
to the question, ask the following:

I. Do you think that is the right
   answer?
   _____ Yes
   _____ No

2a. How do you know that is the right
    answer?
    _____ It makes sense.
    _____ It says so in the story.
    _____ It's a part of my background
    knowledge.
    _____ I know from both the story and
    my background knowledge.
    _____ I don't know.
    _____ Another answer

2b. Why do you think it's the wrong
    answer?
    _____ It doesn't make sense.
    _____ It doesn't say so in the story.
    _____ I don't know.
    _____ Another answer

Group B (I Don't Know)
If the student responds with "I don't know" to
the question, ask the following:

I. Why do you think you don't know the
   answer to the question?
   _____ It isn't in the story.
   _____ I don't know anything about
   this subject.
   _____ I didn't read well enough.
   _____ I don't know.
   _____ Another answer

2. What do you think you could do to
   come up with the right answer?
   _____ I look for clues in the text.
   _____ I think about what I might al-
   ready know about this subject.
   _____ I try an answer and then ask
   myself if it makes sense.
   _____ I don't know.
   _____ Another answer

Materials

The checklist and materials represented in Figure 9.5.

Procedures

Once a chapter, book, poem, song, or story has been selected for children to read, the teacher constructs a list of specific vocabulary terms related to the topic, message, theme, concept, or event to be experienced through reading. For example, students may be reading a selection about the Great Smoky Mountains and the variety of winter sports, such as snow skiing, enjoyed in the mountains. The teacher constructs a list of 5 to 10 specific vocabulary terms related to snow skiing. This list is used by the teacher to probe background knowledge and experiences of the students about snow skiing. Such a list might include the following:

I. bindings
2. lift

Figure 9.4   Continued

(Don't forget to ask the student Question 4 at the end of the interview.)

3a. (Optional) If the student says that the answer is in the story, ask:
Do you know where in the story the answer is?
_____ Yes (Have him show you the clues and check _____ if he can do so)
_____ No

3b. (Optional) If the student says that the answer is in his head (background knowledge), ask:
Do you usually ask yourself what you know about something when you need to answer a question about material you've read?
_____ Yes (Ask him what he knows about the topic and check _____ if he can tell you.)
_____ No

3c. (Optional) If the student says that the answer came from both his background knowledge and the story, ask him the two optional questions given above.

4. (The student should be asked this question only once—at the end of the interview.)
When you need to think of an answer to a question during reading, what do you do?
_____ I think about what I already know about the subject.
_____ I think of an answer and then ask myself if it makes sense.
_____ I don't know.
_____ I reread, go back, and look it over again.
_____ Another answer

Note: From "Effects of Inference Training on Comprehension and Comprehension Monitoring" by P. Dewitz, E.M. Carr, and J.P. Patberg, 1989, 22 (1) pp. 99–121. Copyright 1987 by the International Reading Association.

3. snowplow
4. stem christie
5. moguls

Students are asked to respond to each of these terms in writing. This is accomplished by using one of several stem statements, as shown in Figure 9.5 such as, "What comes to mind when you think of *skiing* and hear the term *bindings*?" Students then respond. Once students have responded to each of the specific terms, the teacher can score the responses using the information in Figure 9.5 to survey the extent and nature of the class's and the individual's knowledge and experience with, in this case, snow skiing. Each item is scored by giving the number of points that most closely represents the knowledge level of the response. Then the score is divided by the number of vocabulary terms (5 in our example) to determine the average knowledge level of individual students. These average scores are registered in the Checklist of Levels of Prior Knowledge in Figure 9.5 by each student's name. By scanning the x's in the checklist, a teacher can get a sense of the class's overall level of prior knowledge. Information thus gathered can be used to inform both

Figure 9.5   Checklist of Levels of Prior Knowledge

Phrase 1	What comes to mind when . . . .?	
Phrase 2	What made you think of . . . .?	
Phrase 3	Have you any new ideas about . . . .?	

Stimulus used to elicit student background knowledge _____

(Picture, word, or phrase, etc.)

	Much - (3)	Some - (2)	Little - (1)
	category labels	examples	personal associations
	definitions	attributes	morphemes
	analogies	defining char-	sound alikes
	relationships	acteristics	personal experiences
Student name			
Maria	_____	__X__	_____
Jawan	__X__	_____	_____
_____	_____	_____	_____
_____	_____	_____	_____
_____	_____	_____	_____

the content and nature of whole group comprehension instruction to prepare students to read the passage with an optimal chance of successfully constructing meaning from information in text.

BALANCED READING INTERVENTIONS: READING COMPREHENSION

Special Needs Indicators*

- Failure to understand a new word or a familiar word in a new context
- Failure to understand a sentence because of new or conflicting information
- Failure to understand how one sentence relates to another sentence
- Failure to understand how the entire text fits together
- Failure to identify and follow the structural organization of the text

* Based on the work of Collins and Smith (1980), the *Special Needs Indicators* should be used as a general guide for recognizing students who require help with a variety of comprehension failures.

SENTENCE COMPREHENSION: MAZE

Purpose

Maze is an approach for improving readers' use of syntax clues (word order and grammar) to aid comprehension. Although many texts allow children to predict deleted content words successfully, some do not. This is particularly true for first-grade and second-grade reading instructional materials. The Maze procedure proposed by Guthrie, Seifert, Burnham, and Caplan (1974) helps to compensate for this problem. When using Maze, only nouns and verbs are deleted, and three carefully prescribed choices are provided for each deletion.

Materials

A 100-word passage from a popular text with selected nouns and verbs deleted is needed. A Maze example of such a passage is shown in Figure 9.6.

Procedures

To use Maze, locate a popular 100-word passage at or near the estimated reading level of your students. Next, delete only selected nouns or verbs from the passage. For each word deleted, provide three choices as follows: one choice provided is the word deleted from the text, the second choice is a word that is the same part of speech as the word deleted, and the third choice is a word that is a different part of speech than the word deleted. You should randomly arrange the order of the Maze stack each time. Students may wish to complete Maze activities as individuals or in small cooperative groups. Sometimes, Maze activities can be placed on an overhead projector and teachers and students can work together in a teacher-directed lesson with the whole class. Further, Maze emphasizes the use of one of the three major cueing systems in reading—syntax. Teaching special needs readers to use syntactical cues is an important part of a balanced reading program.

Figure 9.6   Maze Sample

father
Sylvester Duncan lived with his mother and **dog** at Acorn Road in
jump

friends
Oatsdale. One of his **hobbies** was collecting pebbles of unusual shape
red

color
and **telephone**. On a rainy Saturday during vacation he found . . . .
quickly

Note: From Steig, W. (1969). *Sylvester and the Magic Pebble.* New York: Simon and Schuster.

USING GRAPHIC ORGANIZERS WITH EXPOSITORY TEXTS

Purpose

Students often have difficulty comprehending informational or *expository* texts. A *graphic organizer* is essentially a visual display summarizing and organizing information to be learned that is distributed to students prior to reading a new unit of study. It is a way of presenting new vocabulary in an expository text, showing relationships of the vocabulary to larger concepts and generalizations, and helping teachers clarify teaching goals (Tierney, Readence, & Dishner, 1990). Graphic organizers vary in appearance, but they always show vocabulary in relation to more inclusive vocabulary or concepts (Cooter & Flynt, 1996).

Materials

An expository or informational text to be used as part of a new unit of instruction; paper and pencil, or a computer drawing program; an overhead projector and transparency; chalkboard, white board, or large piece of display paper; and access to a copying machine.

Procedures

A graphic organizer is constructed in essentially three steps:

1. Identify all facts, concepts, generalizations, and vocabulary that you feel are essential to understand the expository text to be read. This forms the foundation layer of information, or subordinate concepts (Thelen, 1984; Cooter & Flynt, 1996).

2. After listing the above information, group related facts, concepts, and generalizations into clusters. These clusters form the next layer of understanding.

3. Finally, relational clusters should be grouped under the main idea, title, or superordinate concept for the text.

Format.   Teachers may wish to use a variety of graphic formats to depict the same text. One style is not particularly better than another, but using a different style for various texts may help hold the attention of students. Several popular formats are shown in Figures 9.7 through 9.9 for an elementary unit pertaining to the structure of the United States government.

DISCUSSION WEBS

Purpose

To cement comprehension or correct miscomprehension of text *after* reading, you may want to conduct a class discussion. Most class discussions tend to center around the teacher and a few vocal children, with the rest of the class passively listening, or worse, completely inattentive. A *discussion web* (Alvermann, 1991) is a practical technique for enhancing student participation and thought during class discussions after reading. Recent research has shown the usefulness of webbing, mapping, and other visual organizational approaches on the comprehension of special needs students (Boyle, 1996).

Figure 9.7   Structured Overview Graphic Organizer

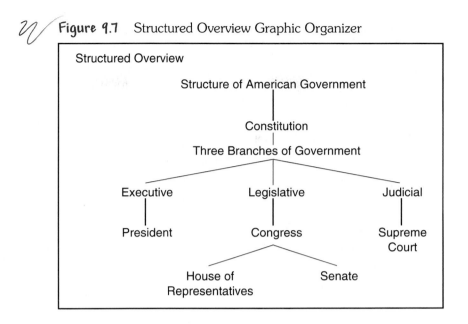

Figure 9.8   Pyramid Outline Graphic Organizer

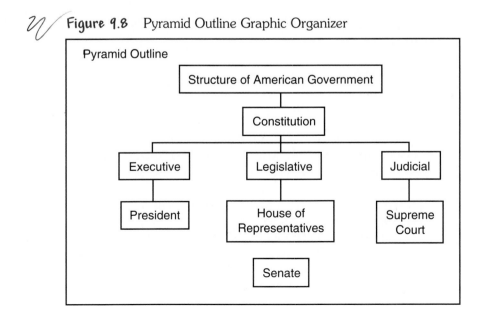

Figure 9.9   Semantic Web Graphic Organizer

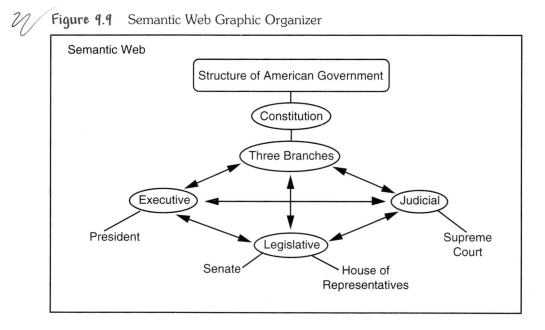

Materials

You will need a popular book or story to be read aloud by the class or group and a discussion web diagram drawn on the chalkboard or on an overhead transparency. After students have read the story with you, write the question you wish to emphasize in the center box, along with a line drawn to the left of the box for "No" reasons and one to the right for "Yes" reasons, as shown in an example in Figure 9.10 for the book *The Widow's Broom* by Chris Van Allsburg (1992).

Procedures

To use a discussion web after reading a story, begin by preparing students to read a text selection or book as you normally would. Help them think of related background experiences and invite them to set a purpose for reading the story. You may want to ask an open-ended question about the story. For example, for *The Widow's Broom* by Chris Van Allsburg (1992), you might ask, "Do you think the widow Minna Shaw should have tricked her neighbors?" Group students in pairs and ask them to answer the question according to their own feelings and the facts they remember from the story. Help them focus on *why* a certain answer could be true. Ask students to think also of some reasons the opposite answer could be true. For example, one student may say, "Yes, they were trying to take her magic broom away." A partner may add, "Yes, those rotten Spivey kids were the ones who needed to be taken away." In this example, these students have voiced two "yes" answers. Next, the teacher should ask the students to think of some "no" answers, as well.

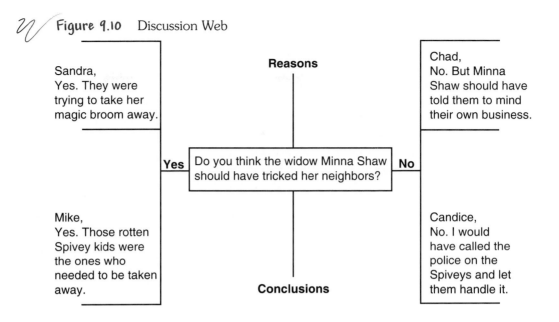

Figure 9.10   Discussion Web

Reasons

Sandra,
Yes. They were
trying to take her
magic broom away.

Chad,
No. But Minna
Shaw should have
told them to mind
their own business.

Yes | Do you think the widow Minna Shaw should have tricked her neighbors? | **No**

Mike,
Yes. Those rotten
Spivey kids were
the ones who
needed to be taken
away.

Candice,
No. I would
have called the
police on the
Spiveys and let
them handle it.

Conclusions

After students have discussed their ideas in pairs, you may want to ask them to share their thinking with another pair of students. Ask each pair to choose their *best* answer to the question, as well as the strongest reason supporting their thinking. Then, bring the children together and ask one student from each pair to report their best answer and the reason supporting that answer. As each student speaks, include the reason in the diagram. After each pair reports, invite others to suggest additional ideas for the discussion web. You may want to reach a class conclusion, or you may want to stop just before a conclusion is reached to avoid a "right" or "wrong" feeling for the answers. (Note: Some teachers of very young students use the discussion web strategy in a whole class setting, rather than grouping students in pairs. Vary the approach according to your teaching style and class needs.)

K-W-L

Purpose

K-W-L has been shown to be effective in improving reading comprehension of all students by causing them to activate, think about, and organize their prior knowledge as an aid to reading comprehension. Ogle (1986), the originator of K-W-L, asserts that this strategy is best suited for use with expository text, although we see no reason it cannot be applied to stories, with minor modifications.

Materials

An expository, or informational, text to be used as part of a new unit of instruction; paper and pencil, or a computer drawing program; an overhead projector and transparency; chalkboard, white board, or large piece of display paper; and access to a copying machine.

Procedures

A K-W-L strategy lesson is accomplished in three steps, as shown:

Step K: What I Know   K-W-L strategy lessons begin with Step K, what I *know*. This step comprises 1) brainstorming and 2) categorizing information. Begin by asking children to brainstorm about a particular topic (in the case of a narrative, brainstorm a particular theme or message). For instance, children may be asked what they know about *bats*. A list of associations is formed through brainstorming. When students make a contribution, Ogle (1986) suggests asking them where or how they got their information in order to challenge students into higher levels of thinking.

Next, teachers should help students look for ways in which the brainstorming list can be reorganized into categories of information. For example, teachers may notice that the brainstorming list shows three related pieces of information about how bats navigate. These can be reorganized into a category on navigation. Children are encouraged to look at the information and think about other categories represented in the brainstorming list.

Step W: What Do I Want to Learn?   During Step W, students begin to recognize gaps, inaccuracies, and disagreements in their prior knowledge. Teachers can play a central role in pointing out these problems and helping students frame questions for which they would like to have answers. Questions can be framed by having students use the question stem, "I wonder." After the group generates a series of questions to be answered before reading, they are directed to write down questions for which they would like answers personally. These can be taken from questions generated by the groups as well as those generated by individuals.

Step L: What I Learned   After reading, have students write down what they learned. This can take the form of answers to specific questions they asked or a concise written summary of their learning. These questions and answers may be discussed as a group or shared between pairs of students. In this way, other children benefit from the learning of their peers as well as from their own learning.

METACOGNITION: CLICK OR CLUNK

Purpose

Readers must learn to monitor the state of their own ongoing comprehension and know when their comprehension of text breaks down. The act of monitoring one's unfolding comprehension of text is called **metacognition** or, sometimes, **meta-comprehension**. The ability to plan, check, monitor, revise, and evaluate one's unfolding comprehension is of particular importance for special needs readers. If these children fail to detect comprehension breakdowns, they will often take no action to correct misinterpretations of the text. However, if special needs children are helped to expect that text should make sense and develop the ability to strategically self-correct comprehension problems, then their reading ability can progress.

Materials

You will need a book or text that children have read collectively or individually and a poster of the repair strategies such as the one shown in Figure 9.11 (adapted from Babbs, 1984).

Procedures

To help students develop the ability to monitor their own comprehension processes, Carr (1985) suggested a strategy called *Click or Clunk.* This strategy urges readers to reflect at the end of each sentence, paragraph, or section of reading by stopping and asking themselves if the meaning or message "clicks" for them or goes "clunk." If it clunks, what is wrong? What can be done to make sense of it?

Once a comprehension breakdown has been detected, it is important to know which strategies to select in repairing broken comprehension, as well as when to use these strategies. In fact, students may know that they need to take steps to repair comprehension, but they may not know which steps to take or when to take them. As a consequence, children should be introduced to several well-known repair options for repairing broken comprehension.

To demonstrate the use of a "fix up" poster, model for students using a "think aloud" process to help them develop a sense for when to select certain repair strategies for failing comprehension. Read part of a text aloud, and as you proceed, comment on your thinking. Reveal to students your thinking, the hypotheses you have formed for the text, and anything that strikes you as difficult or unclear. By doing so, you demonstrate for students the processes that successful readers use to comprehend a text. Next, remind them of the Click or Clunk strategy. Gradually release the responsibility for modeling metacognitive strategies to the children during follow-up lessons on metacognitive monitoring. Display the repair strategies shown above in a prominent place in your classroom. Be sure to draw your students' attention to these strategies throughout the year.

Figure 9.11   Metacomprehension "Repair" Strategies

Broken Comprehension Repair Strategies

• **Read on.**
• **Reread** the sentence.
• **Go back** and reread the paragraph.
• **Seek** information from glossary or reference materials.
• **Ask** someone near you who may be able to help, like one of your peers.

THINK ALOUD: INFERENCE MODELING

Purpose

Simply put, making inferences is necessary when reading. One way to help students make inferences is to model the inferring process through "thinking aloud," as described by Gordon (1985). It is important when modeling "thinking aloud" that the teacher place the emphasis upon the comprehension process and not the content, however, because the intent is to make visible for students the mental processes necessary for making an inference from text. Effective modeling of "thinking aloud" for inference making is characterized by a) the teacher taking a proactive role during the initial stages of learning and b) the teacher using explicit talk to explain the comprehension processes.

Materials

A reading selection, an overhead projector and transparency, and a chalkboard or large piece of display paper are needed.

Procedure

To begin, the teacher defines for students what making an inference involves: using clues from the text along with one's own background knowledge to make a reasonable guess about something the author never puts into writing, but expects his reader to figure out. Next, the teacher reads a portion of the selected text and asks an inference question, then gives the answer. At this point, the teacher "thinks aloud" for the students by explaining how he arrived at the answer to the question (See Figure 9.12: Think Aloud Lesson).

The teacher may want to continue reading the text. At a predetermined point the teacher then stops reading, asks another inference question, and provides the answer. Now, the teacher asks the students to provide the evidence from the text and their own background knowledge to support the inference answer given by the teacher. Once the evidence is provided during the discussion, the teacher may focus on what information is relevant or irrelevant. In this phase of the lesson, students are asked to "think aloud" and to justify the teacher's inference. The reading of the text continues to another predetermined point. Next, the teacher asks the inference question and the students answer. Finally, the teacher justifies the students' answer to the inference question.

SUMMARY WRITING

Purpose

The purpose of writing a summary is to extract main ideas from a reading selection. Good readers are constantly stopping themselves during reading to think about their comprehension and to take corrective action when necessary. Summaries are important because they help form memory structures that readers can use to select and store relevant details from their reading. Some readers do not spontaneously summarize their reading, and, as a result, have poor understanding and recall of what they read (Brown, Day, & Jones, 1983).

Figure 9.12   Think Aloud Lesson

Inference Awareness Think Aloud Lesson

Teacher reads text: Nylon is a plastic that is best known in the form of a fiber. It was the first synthetic fiber and is still the most important. It is used in all kinds of clothing, from stockings and shirts to anoraks and furs. Like all synthetic fibers, nylon resists creasing and, being waterproof, "drip dries" quickly. A great deal of nylon is used in making carpets.

Teacher asks inference question: What makes nylon waterproof?

Teacher answers inference question: Nylon, because it is made of a plastic, repels water.

Teacher thinks aloud to justify answer: When I think about plastics, I think of how plastic bags keep water out or hold water in. In any case, plastics seem to keep water in control.

Teacher continues reading text: Nylon is exceptionally strong and rot-proof. These properties make it ideal for fishing nets, which have to take the strain of a heavy catch and resist the rotting action of the sea water. For these nets, nylon is used in the form of a thick, solid thread. In this form, too, it is used for stringing tennis rackets.

Teacher asks inference question: Why is nylon rot-proof?

Teacher answers inference question: Because nylon resists water.

Students think aloud to justify answer: When water gets on or in things and stays, it makes things soggy and soft. If things stay soggy and soft, they begin to fall apart. That is what makes things rot. So, because nylon won't let water in, it doesn't get soggy or soft and can't rot.

Teacher continues reading text: Nylon is also widely used in the form of a solid plastic. Many machines, including home food-mixers and beaters, have nylon gears and bearings. Moving nylon parts need no oiling. They are also much quieter than moving metal parts.

Teacher asks inference question: Why don't you need to oil nylon parts?

Students answer inference question: Nylon parts, unlike metal parts that create heat through friction, slide easily over one another without creating friction or heat.

Teacher thinks aloud to justify answer: Because nylon is made of petroleum, or oil, nylon parts do not need additional oil.

Materials

A tradebook, basal, or textbook selection is needed, along with a chart displaying the rules for summary writing. An example based on the work of Hare and Borchardt (1984) is shown in Figure 9.13.

Procedures

Begin by distributing copies of the tradebook or textbook selections to be read by the group. Have the students silently read the first few passages. Next, on an overhead transparency, model for the children how you would use the five summary rules in Figure 9.13 to write a summary. After modeling how you would write a summary, instruct the children to finish reading the entire chapter or passage. Next, organize students into cooperative learning groups, or teams of five, to work on writing a summary together. Each student is assigned to take charge of one of the five summary writing rules. Move about the classroom to assist the groups as needed. You may want to have students use different colored transparency pens for each of the five summary rules to record their work. For example, green may be used for lists, red for eliminating unnecessary details, and so on. Share each

Figure 9.13   Five Rules for Writing a Summary

1. *Collapse lists.* If there is a list of things, supply a word or phrase for the whole list. For example, if you saw *swimming, sailing, fishing, and surfing,* you could substitute *water sports.*

2. *Use topic sentences.* Sometimes authors write a sentence that summarizes the whole paragraph. If so, use that sentence in your summary. If not, you'll have to make up your own topic sentences.

3. *Get rid of unnecessary detail.* Sometimes information is repeated or is stated in several different ways. Some information may be trivial and unnecessary. Get rid of repetitive or trivial information. Summaries should be short.

4. *Collapse paragraphs.* Often, paragraphs are related to each other. For example, some paragraphs simply explain or expand on other paragraphs in a selection. Some paragraphs are more important than others. Join the paragraphs that are related. Important paragraphs should stand alone.

5. *Polish the summary.* When you collapse a lot of information from many paragraphs into one or two paragraphs, the resulting summary sometimes sounds awkward and unnatural. There are several ways to remedy this: add connecting words such as *like* or *because,* or write introductory or closing statements. Another method is to paraphrase the material; this will improve your ability to remember what you read and enable you to avoid plagiarism—using the exact words of the author.

Note: From "Direct Instruction of Summarization Skills" by V.C. Hare and K.M. Borchordt, 1984, *Reading Research Quarterly 20* (1) pp. 62–78. Copyright 1984 by the International Reading Assiociaton.

group's summary writing processes and products with the entire class on the over-head projector. Be sure to provide additional practice on summary writing through-out the year with other stories, passages, or texts.

QUESTION-ANSWER-RELATIONSHIPS (QARs)

Purpose

Raphael (1982, 1986) identified four Question-Answer-Relationships (QARs) to help children identify the connection between the type of questions asked of them by teachers and textbooks and the information sources necessary and available to them for answering questions: 1) *Right There,* 2) *Think and Search,* 3) *Author and You,* and 4) *On My Own.* Research by Raphael and Pearson (1982) provided evidence that training students to recognize question/answer relationships (QARs) results in improved comprehension and question answering behavior. In addition, using the QARs question-answering training strategy is useful for another purpose: helping teachers examine their own questioning with respect to the types of questions and the information sources that students need to use to answer their questions. By using QARs to monitor their own questioning behaviors, some teacheres may find that they are asking only *Right There* types of questions. This discovery very often leads teachers to ask other questions that require the use of additional or seldom-used information sources.

Materials

The materials needed include a variety of texts for asking and answering questions, a poster displaying the information in Figure 9.14 in the classroom to heighten children and teachers' awareness of the types of questions asked, and the informa-tion sources available for answering those questions. The illustration below provides examples of each of the four types of Question Answer Relationships (QARs).

Procedures

Instruction using QARs begins by explaining to students that when they answer ques-tions about reading there are basically two places they can look to get information: *In the Book* and *In My Head.* This concept should be practiced with the students by reading aloud a text, asking questions, and having the students explain or show where they found their answers. Once students understand the two-category ap-proach, expand the *In the Book* category to include: *Right There* and *Putting It To-gether.* The distinction between these two categories should be practiced by reading and discussing several texts. For older students, Raphael (1986) suggests that stu-dents be shown specific strategies for locating the answers to *Right There* questions. These include looking in a single sentence or looking in two sentences connected by a pronoun. For *Putting It Together* questions, students can be asked to focus their attention on the structure of the text, such as cause-effect, problem-solution, listing-example, compare-contrast, and explanation.

Next, instruction should be directed toward two subcategories within the *In My Head* category: *Author and Me,* and *On My Own.* Here again, these categories can be practiced as a group by reading a text aloud, answering the questions, and

Figure 9.14   Illustrations to Explain Question-Answer Relationships (QARs) to Students

In the Book QARs

Right There

The answer is in the text, usually easy to find. The words used to make up the question and words used to answer the question are **Right There** in the same sentence.

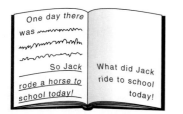

In My Head QARs

Author and You

The answer is *not* in the story. You need to think about what you already know, what the author tells you in the text, and how it fits together.

**Think and Search
(Putting It Together)**

The answer is in the story, but you need to put together different story parts to find it. Words for the question and words for the answer are not found in the same sentence. They come from different parts of the text.

On My Own

The answer is *not* in the story. You can even answer the question without reading the story. You need to use your own experience.

Note: From "Teaching Question Answer Relationships, Revisited" by Taffy E. Raphael, *The Reading Teacher,* February 1986. Reprinted with permission of Taffy E. Raphael and the International Reading Association.

discussing the sources of information. To expand this training, students can be asked to identify the types of questions asked in their basal readers, workbooks, content area texts, and tests; in addition, they can determine the sources of information needed to answer these questions. Students may be informed that certain types of questions are asked before and after reading a text. For example, questions asked before reading typically ask students to activate their own knowledge. Therefore, questions asked before reading will usually be *On My Own* questions. However, questions asked after reading will make use of information found in the text. Thus, questions asked after reading will typically focus on the *Right There, Putting It Together,* and *Author and Me* types of questions. As a culminating training activity for QARs, children are asked to write their own questions for each of the QAR categories and to answer these questions.

EXPERIENCE-TEXT-RELATIONSHIPS (ETRs)

Purpose

Au (1993) has had unusual success helping special needs students improve their comprehension of text by making their background experiences integral to the entire reading instructional process. The purpose of the ETR method is to give special needs learners a general approach to text comprehension that emphasizes the importance of connecting personal experiences with the text to be read. The ETR lesson is composed of three major phases: 1) an experience-eliciting discussion or activity, 2) a discussion about the students' reading of the text, and 3) a discussion relating students' experiences to the content of the text.

Materials

A tradebook, basal, or textbook selection and a lesson plan for ETR as shown in Figure 9.15 are needed.

Procedures

The process for using the ETR reading lesson structure begins with planning. You should preview the text to be read, looking for themes, major topics, and important information or significant messages. Determine how you might help students relate the topic and/or message to their own personal experiences. Next, invite students to share their experiences with you about the topic or message. By using the illustrations, title page, or a short excerpt that you read aloud, invite children to make predictions about the story or text. Then have them read an assigned portion of the story silently or in a dyad, or buddy-reading, setting (see chapter 4). When children have finished their reading, ask them to talk about the text and their predictions. Then have children make predictions about the next segment of the text to be read. Alternate periods of discussion and reading until the entire text or story has been completed.

To end the lesson, reopen the discussion by asking children to make connections between the events and characters in the story and their personal experiences. This can be accomplished by asking children to respond to some question that you pose as the teacher. To provide ample opportunity for as many children to participate as possible, sharing of connections can be achieved by using a *Turn to Your Neighbor* process, as outlined in chapter 4.

Figure 9.15   ETR Sample Lesson

An Example Experience-Text-Relationship (ETR) Lesson for *Tales of a Fourth Grade Nothing* (Blume, 1972)

Planning

Preview *Tales of a Fourth Grade Nothing* by Judy Blume (1972). The story is about Peter Hatcher's trials of living with his younger brother, Fudge. After previewing, the teacher notes that the book has fairly typical story structure: setting, theme, problem, and resolution. Knowing this, the teacher selects a story frame (see chapter 10) to elicit students' predictions about the story. To engage children's experiences, the teacher decides to share a personal story about problems with a younger brother or sister.

Experience

The teacher begins by showing the children the book they will be reading. She reads the title. She asks, "How many of you have an older or younger brother or sister?" Children respond. The teacher then relates her personal story about when she was young and had problems with her younger brother. Next, the teacher tells the children to *Turn to their Neighbor* and tell him or her a problem story about their brother, sister, or younger friend who is troublesome. After sharing these personal experiences, the teacher distributes copies of the book to the class. She asks students to study very carefully the illustration on the cover as she unveils the story frame prediction chart at the board. Children are then asked to make a prediction for the trouble that might happen between Peter and Fudge.

Text

Students are asked to read chapter 1 silently or quietly in dyads. After reading, the teacher asks students to choose a partner. Next, they are to use a *Three-Step Interview* with their partner about his or her predictions and what he or she learned from reading the text. The students alternate in their roles as interviewer and respondent throughout the reading of the book.

Relationship

At the conclusion of the book, children might be asked to discuss and write a list about the personal connections they made as they read the story. These listed items could be displayed on a bulletin board showing the title of the story and student reactions and connections to *Tales of a Fourth Grade Nothing.*

RECIPROCAL TEACHING

Purpose

Palincsar and Brown (1985) designed and evaluated an approach for improving the reading comprehension and comprehension monitoring of special needs students who scored two years below grade level on standardized tests of reading comprehension. Their results suggest a teaching strategy called *Reciprocal Teaching* that is useful for helping students who have difficulties with comprehension and comprehension monitoring. Although Reciprocal Teaching was originally intended for use with expository text, we can envision using this intervention strategy with narrative texts by focusing discussion and reading on the major elements of stories. By using Reciprocal Teaching with narrative texts, teachers can intervene earlier with those who are experiencing difficulties with comprehension and comprehension monitoring, rather than delaying intervention until the intermediate years, when expository text is typically encountered.

Materials

A tradebook, basal, or textbook selection is needed for this activity.

Procedures

Essentially, this strategy lesson requries teachers and students to exchange roles, much like the *ReQuest* lesson, which is intended to increase student involvement in the lesson. The Reciprocal Teaching lesson comprises four phases or steps. These are described below:

- *Prediction:* Students predict from the title and pictures the possible content of the text. The predictions are recorded by the teacher.
- *Question Generation:* Students generate purpose questions after reading a predetermined segment of the text, such as a paragraph, page, etc.
- *Summarizing:* Students write a brief summary (see Figure 9.13) for the text by starting with "This paragraph was about . . ." Summarizing helps students capture the gist of the text.
- *Clarifying:* Students and teacher discuss various reasons a text may be hard or confusing, such as difficult vocabulary, poor text organization, unfamiliar content, or lack of cohesion. Students are then instructed in a variety of comprehension fix-up or repair strategies.

Once teachers have modeled this process with several segments of text, the teacher assigns one of the students (preferably a good student) to assume the role of teacher for the next segment of text. The teacher may also, while acting in the student role, provide appropriate prompts and feedback when necessary. When the next segment of text is completed, the student assigned as teacher assigns another student to assume that role.

Teachers who use Reciprocal Teaching to help students with comprehension difficulties should follow four simple guidelines suggested by Palincsar and Brown (1985). First, assess student difficulties and provide reading materials appropriate to students' decoding abilities. Second, use Reciprocal Teaching for at least 30 minutes a day for 15 to 20 consecutive days. Third, model frequently and provide corrective feedback. Finally, monitor student progress regularly and individually to determine whether the instruction is having the intended effect. Palincsar and Brown (1985) have reported positive results for this intervention procedure by demonstrating dramatic changes in students' ineffective reading behaviors.

CHAPTER SUMMARY

In this chapter, selected assessment strategies are described to help teachers understand the nature and quality of each student's abilities before, during, and after reading comprehension processes. We also offered instructional strategies for helping students understand, develop, and improve reading comprehension strategy selection and application in students' daily reading. To improve reading comprehension at the micro or sentence level, we offered the Maze strategy to help students use surrounding contextual information within and between sentences. To help students prepare to read a selection with greater comprehension, we proposed using graphic organizers and KWL. During reading comprehension monitoring, we suggested the use of comprehension repair strategies coupled with the use of the "Click or Clunk" strategy and "Inference Modeling." For comprehension elaboration and discussion following the reading of a selection, we suggested the use of discussion webs, ETR, summary writing, and Question-Answer-Relationships (QARs). For students who have difficulties comprehending texts, we suggested the implementation of the Reciprocal Teaching strategy. In this chapter, assessment and instructional strategies bridge the before, during, and after nature of reading comprehension as well as providing teachers with a specific, well researched, strategy in Reciprocal Teaching for those hard to teach students who struggle with reading comprehension.

REFERENCES

Alvermann, D. E. (1991). The discussion web: A graphic aide for learning across the curriculum. *The Reading Teacher, 45,* 92–99.

Alvermann, D. E., Smith, L. C., & Readence, J. E. (1985). Prior knowledge activation and the comprehension of compatible and incompatible text. *Reading Research Quarterly, 20*(4), 420–436.

Anderson, R. C., Reynolds, R. E., Schallert, D. L., & Goetz, E. T. (1977). Frameworks for comprehending discourse. *American Educational Research Journal, 14,* 367–382.

Au, K. (1993). *Literacy instruction in multicultural settings.* Fort Worth, TX: Harcourt Brace College.

Babbs, P. J. (1984). Monitoring cards help improve comprehension. *The Reading Teacher, 38,* 200–204.

Blume, J. (1972). *Tales of a fourth grade nothing.* New York: Dell Publishing.

Boyle, J. R. (1996). The effects of cognitive mapping strategy on the literal and inferential comprehension of students with mild disabilities. *Learning Disability Quarterly, 19*(3), 86–98.

Bransford, J. C., & Johnson, M. K. (1972). Contextual prerequisites for understanding: Some investigations of comprehension and recall. *Journal of Verbal Learning and Verbal Behavior, 11,* 717–726.

Brown, A. L., Day, J. D., & Jones, R. S. (1983). The development plans for summarzing texts. *Child Development, 54,* 968–979.

Brown, C. S., & Lytle, S. L. (1988). Merging assessment and instruction: Protocols in the classroom. In S. M. Glazer, L. W. Searfoss, & L. M. Gentile (Eds.), *Reexamining reading diagnosis: New trends and procedures.* Newark, DE: International Reading Association, 94–102.

Carr, E. (1985). The Vocabulary Overview Guide: A metacognitive strategy to improve vocabulary comprehension and retention. *Journal of Reading, 28*(8), 684–689.

Carr, S., & Thompson, B. (1996). The effects of prior knowledge and schema activation strategies on the inferential reading comprehension of children with and without learning disabilites. *Learning Disabilities Quarterly, 19*(2), 48–61.

Collins, A. M., & Quillian, M. R. (1969). Retrieval time from semantic memory. *Journal of Verbal Learning and Verbal Behavior, 8,* 240–247.

Collins, A., & Smith, E. (1980). Teaching the process of reading comprehension (Tech. Rep. No. 182). Urbana, IL: University of Illinois, Center for the Study of Reading.

Cooter, R. B., & Flynt, E. S. (1996). *Content area reading: Content literacy for all students.* Columbus, OH: Merrill/Prentice-Hall.

Forest, D. L., & Waller, T. G. (1979). Cognitive and metacognitive aspects of reading. Paper presented at the meeting of the Society for Research in Child Development. San Francisco, CA.

Gibson, E. J., & Levin, H. (1975). *The Psychology of Reading.* Cambridge, MA: The MIT Press.

Gordon, C. J. (1985). Modeling inference awareness across the curriculum. *Journal of Reading, 28*(5), 444–447.

Guthrie, J. T., Seifert, M., Burnham, N. A., & Caplan, R. J. (1974). The maze technique to assess and monitor reading comprehension. *The Reading Teacher, 28*(2), 161–168.

Hare, V., & Borchardt, K. M. (1984). Direct instruction of summarization skills, *Reading Research Quarterly, 20,* 62–78.

Irwin, J. W. (1991). *Teaching reading comprehension processes.* Englewood Cliffs, NJ: Prentice Hall.

Langer, J. A. (1982). Facilitating text processing: The elaboration of prior knowledge. J. A. Langer & M. Smith-Burke (Eds.), *Reader meets author: Bridging the gap.* Newark, DE: International Reading Association.

Lindsay, P. H., & Norman, D. A. (1977). *Human information processing: An introduction to psychology.* New York: Academic Press.

Lipson, M. Y. (1983). The influence of religious affiliation on children's memory for text information. *Reading Research Quarterly, 18*(4), 448–457.

Lytle, S. (1982). Exploloring comprehension style: A study of twelfth-grade readers' transactions with text. Ann Arbor, MI: University Microfilm.

Maria, K. (1990). *Reading comprehension instruction: Issues & Strategies.* Parkton, MA: York Press.

Myers, J., & Lytle, S. L. (1986). Assessment of the learning process. *Exceptional Children, 53,* 138–144.

Ogle, D. (1986). K-W-L: A teaching model that develops active reading of expository text. *The Reading Teacher, 39*(6), 564–570.

Palincsar, A., & Brown, A. (1985). Reciprocal teaching: A means to a meaningful end. In J. Osborn, P. T. Wilson, & R. C. Anderson (Eds.), *Reading education: Foundations for a literate America* (pp. 299–310). Lexington, MA: D. C. Heath and Company.

Pearson, P. D., Hansen, J., & Gordon, C. (1979). The effect of background knowledge on children's comprehension of implicit and explicit information. *Journal of Reading Behavior, 11*(3), 201–209.

Raphael, T. E. (1982). Question-answering strategies for children. *The Reading Teacher, 36,* 186–191.

Raphael, T. E., & Pearson, P. D. (1982). *The effect of metacognitive training on children's question-answering behaviors.* ERIC Document Reproduction Service No. ED215315. Urbana, Ill: Center for the Study of Reading.

Raphael, T. E. (1986). Teaching question answer relationships, revisited. *The Reading Teacher, 39*(6), 516–523.

Read, S. J., & Rosson, M. B. (1982). Rewriting history: The biasing effects of attitudes on memory. *Social Cognition, 1,* 240–255.

Reutzel, D. R., & Cooter, R. B., Jr., (1996). *Teaching children to read: From basals to books (2nd ed.).* Columbus, OH: Merrill/Prentice-Hall.

Reutzel, D. R., & Hollingsworth, P. M. (1991). Investigating the development of topic-related attitude: Effect on children's reading and remembering text. *Journal of Educational Research, 84*(5), 334–344.

Rumelhart, D. E. (1981). Schemata: The building blocks of cognition. In J. T. Guthrie (Ed.), *Comprehension and teaching: Research Reviews* (pp. 3–26). Newark, DE: International Reading Assocation.

Sanford, A. J., & Garrod, S. C. (1981). *Understanding written language.* New York: John Wiley & Sons.

Steig, W. (1969). *Sylvester and the magic pebble.* New York: Simon and Schuster.

Thelen, J. (1984). *Improving reading in science.* Newark, DE: International Reading Association.

Tierney, R. J., Readence, J. E., & Dishner, E. K. (1990). *Reading strategies and practices: A compendium* (3rd ed.). Boston: Allyn & Bacon.

Van Allsburg, C. (1992). *The witch's broom.* Boston, MA: Houghton Mifflin.

Voss, J. F., & Silfies, L. N. (1996). Learning from history text: The interaction of knowledge and comprehension skill with text structure. *Cognition and Instruction, 14*(1), 45–68.

Chapter 10

Assessing and Developing a Sense of Story

Reading and listening to stories are key developmental experiences for children. From the time children first experience *Peter Cottontail* in kindergarten to the time they experience *Romeo and Juliet* in high school, students are learning about life, human dilemmas, and the triumph of the human spirit. Stories capture moral principles, provide escape from the problems of the moment, and allow imagination to soar beyond the bounds of the here and now. Children begin to internalize how stories are written and told from their first encounters in the early years. They learn, for example, that stories begin with vivid descriptions of when and where a story takes place, called *setting.* A knowledge of setting is often followed by an understanding of problems, goals, attempts to solve problems, and the resolution of the problems by the central characters. Internalization of story language, such as *Once upon a time . . .* and *. . . they lived happily ever after,* is often our first clue that children are attending carefully to story parts and structure. This chapter deals with helping readers attend to, learn about, and use their knowledge of story structure to increase reading comprehension and fluency.

How can teachers assess what students understand about story structures? Further, once story structure knowledge has been assessed, how can teachers help students use the structure of stories to increase reading enjoyment and comprehension? First, it is important that teachers understand how children develop a sense of story structure. Similarly, teachers building effective balanced reading programs must understand methods available to *assess* story structure knowledge in order to determine what readers need to know in order to develop a sense of story. Finally, teachers need to have a repertoire of successful and proven instructional alternatives available to assist children in developing a sense of story structure. These are the three main areas of focus of this chapter, presented to help teachers assist readers in developing a sense of story.

BACKGROUND BRIEFING FOR TEACHERS: UNDERSTANDING THE STRUCTURE OF STORIES

During the 1970s, cognitive psychologists began to study how stories, or *narratives,* were constructed and how children developed an understanding of these story structures (Applebee, 1979). It became clear that authors, usually subconsciously, crafted stories by following a set of patterns, frameworks, or schemas for how stories should be constructed. Researchers then developed a generalized set of rules to describe how stories are composed. These rules for describing how stories are formed became known as *story grammars* (Mandler & Johnson, 1977; Stein & Glenn, 1979; Thorndyke, 1977).

The elements typically found in story grammars include:

1. Setting
2. Problem
3. Events
4. Resolution
5. Moral or Theme

A story typically begins with a description of the setting. A *setting* includes information about the story location and the introduction of the main character(s). Setting also establishes the general time frame of the events in the story. Watson (1991) explains that setting involves more than just describing *when* and *where* a story takes place. Setting usually begins by introducing characters, who in turn reveal the time and place of the story, which drives the plot into action and sets the mood or tone of the story, and which finally leads to disclosing the main theme of the story. Discussions of setting should probe this chain of events carefully.

The *problem* propels the story characters into action. This is often followed by the main character devising some sort of plan to solve the problem set up in the early part of the story. Attempts to solve the problem or achieve some goal as outlined, are called *events.* Stories may be composed of a single event, but more complex stories may contain several events that may use such stylistic devices as flashbacks, dream states, and so on. Results of the character's attempts are revealed as the story progresses. Finally, the story reaches a point of *resolution,* with some hint of the character(s) current and future state. A moral or theme of the story is sometimes also evident, such as in the classic tales "The Boy Who Cried Wolf" and "The Little Red Hen."

While labels used to describe these story grammar elements may vary slightly, all stories contain these essential parts. Next, we consider some ways of assessing students' knowledge of story grammar elements.

ASSESSING STUDENTS' SENSE OF STORY

To assess a student's sense of story structure, several approaches may be taken. One method involves having students construct a story from scrambled story elements. Another approach is to ask students to read a story and indicate what was remembered and understood through retellings and questioning. Finally, students may be asked to complete a partial outline or "frame" of a story. By using a variety of approaches, teachers can successfully determine what students specifically know (or don't know) about story structure. The assessment strategies that follow utilize versions of these three formats for assessing students' story structure knowledge.

ORAL STORY RETELLINGS

Purpose

One of the most effective ways to find out if a child understands story structure is through the use of oral story retellings (Gambrell, Pfeiffer, & Wilson, 1985; Morrow, 1985; Brown & Cambourne, 1987). Asking children to retell a story involves reconstruction of the entire story by sequencing the story, recalling important elements of the plot, making inferences, and noticing relevant details. Thus, oral story retellings assess story comprehension and story structure knowledge in holistic, sequenced, and organized ways.

Materials Needed

For this activity, you will need the following materials:

1 blank audiotape

1 portable audiocassette recorder with internal microphone

1 brief story

1 parsing of the story

1 scoring sheet

Procedures

Select a brief story for students to listen to or read. For example, *The Carrot Seed* by Ruth Krauss (1945) could be selected. Next, type the text of the story onto a separate piece of paper for parsing. *Parsing,* in this instance, refers to dividing a story into four major and somewhat simplified story grammar categories: setting, problem, events, and resolution, as shown.

Story Grammar Parsing of "The Carrot Seed"*

Setting

A little boy planted a carrot seed.

Problem (Getting the seed to grow)

His mother said, "I'm afraid it won't come up."
His father said, "I'm afraid it won't come up."
And his big brother said, "It won't come up."

Events

Every day the little boy pulled up the weeds around the seed and sprinkled the ground with water.

*From *The Carrot Seed* by R. Krauss, 1945, New York: Scholastic, Inc.

But nothing came up.
And nothing came up.
Everyone kept saying it wouldn't come up.
But he still pulled up the weeds around it every day and sprinkled the ground with water.

Resolution

And then, one day, a carrot came up just as the little boy had known it would.

Oral retellings may be elicited from children in a number of ways. One way involves the use of pictures or verbal prompts from the story. As pictures in the story are flashed sequentially, the child is asked to retell the story as remembered from listening or reading. Morrow (1985) suggests that teachers prompt children to begin story retellings with a statement such as: "A little while ago, we read a story called [Name the story]. Retell the story as if you were telling it to a friend who has never heard it before." Other prompts during the recall may be framed as questions:

- "How does the story begin?" Or, "Once upon a time . . . ."
- "What happens next?"
- "What happened to [the main character] when . . . ?"
- "Where did the story take place?"
- "When did the story take place?"
- "How did the main character solve the problem in the story?"
- "How did the story end?"

Morrow (1989) says that teachers should offer only general prompts like those listed above rather than asking about specific details, ideas, or a sequence of events in the story. Asking questions like those listed above is a form of *assisted recall* and may be especially useful with special needs students.

A second way to elicit oral story retellings from students is to use *unaided recall,* in which students retell the story without picture or verbal prompts. This approach is begun by simply asking the child to orally retell a story as if she were telling it to someone who had never heard or read the story before. To record critical elements of the child's recalled story structure, use an audiotape recording and coding sheet like the one shown in Figure 10.1. The information gleaned from an oral retelling may be used to help teachers focus their instruction in the future to enhance students' understanding of story structure.

STORY FRAMES

Purpose

A story frame (Cudd & Roberts, 1987; Fowler, 1982; Nichols, 1980) is a summary of the structure of a story with specific elements deleted. Story frame assessment is typically accomplished *during* or *after* the reading of a story. If an assessment of the students' ongoing understanding of a story is desired, story frames can be filled in as students complete the reading of an assigned part of a story. If the purpose for assessment is to determine the elements of a story that have been internalized after reading a text, then the story frame assessment can be filled in after reading.

Figure 10.1   Oral Retelling Coding Form for Narrative or Story Structure

Student's name: _____   Grade: _____
Title of story: _____   Date: _____

General directions: Give 1 point for each element included, as well as for "gist." Give 1 point for each character named, as well as for such words as *boy, girl,* or *dog.* Credit plurals (*friends,* for instance) with 2 points under characters.

Setting
   a. Begins with an introduction _____
   b. Indicates main character _____
   c. Other characters named _____
   d. Includes statement about time or place _____

Problem
   a. Refers to main character's goal or problem to be solved _____

Events
   a. Number of events recalled _____
   b. Number of events in story _____
   c. Score for "events" (a/b) _____

Resolution
   a. Tells how main character resolves the story problem _____

Sequence
Retells story in order: setting, problem, events, and resolution. (Score 2 for correct order, 1 for partial order, 0 for no sequence.) _____

Possible Score: _____   **Student's score:** _____

In either case, story frames offer teachers one means of assessing *what, how,* and *how much* of a story structure students understand and use to help them comprehend narrative text.

Materials

For this activity, you will need a brief story or passage that represents an entire narrative or story, one of the types of story frames described below, and a *Story Frame Assessment and Analysis Form.*

Procedures

Because not all stories—especially those found in early basal primers—are well-formed stories, meaning they do not contain all of the elements of a story in the usual order, several types of story frames can be designed to assess students' understanding of narrative structure. For most stories, the basic story frame shown in Figure 10.2 is useful.

Figure 10.2   Basic Story Frame

Title:_____

This story takes place _____.
The problem in this story starts when _____
_____.
After that, _____.
Next, _____. Then,
_____. The
problem in the story is solved when _____.
The story ends when _____.

Other story frames may be designed to focus on the sequence of events or on a character's problem and the solution. Figures 10.3 and 10.4 illustrate these kinds of story frames.

We have also found story frames helpful in assessing children's attention to specific story elements. In Figure 10.5, a story frame is used to assess attention to key sequencing word clues (i.e., *first, next, then,* etc.) embedded in the text.

Teachers begin assessing children's attention to story elements by first deciding the purpose of the assessment, the type of story frame to be selected and prepared, when (during or after reading) the story frame will be completed, and whether the frame(s) will be completed orally or in written form. Next, students are asked to listen to or read an assigned story. Once the story frame has been com-

Figure 10.3   Story Frame with a Simple Sequence of Events

Title: _____

The story takes place _____.
The problem in this story starts when _____
_____. This was a
problem because _____.
The problem in the story was finally solved when _____.
The story ends when _____.

Figure 10.4   Story-Specific Story Frame (*The Carrot Seed*)

Title: _____

In this story _____ had a problem. His problem was that he
_____. This was a problem for him because _____
_____. Then one day, a _____
came up just as he thought it would.

Figure 10.5 Story-Specific Story Frame (*The Little Red Hen*)

Title: _____

A little red hen found a _____ to plant.
First, she _____.
Next, she asked her friends to help her _____.
Then, she asked her friends to help her _____.
After that, she asked her friends to help her _____.
Finally, she asked her friends to help her _____.
In the end, the little red hen ate the _____ all by herself because her friends didn't help her.

pleted by the reader, the Story Frame Assessment and Analysis Form shown in Figure 10.6 can be used to analyze the results.

In summary, story frames can be adapted to many narrative texts for assessing students' ongoing development of a sense of story. Specific elements of story structure, as well as elements of language such as sequence words, can be assessed to determine the extent to which story structure knowledge has been successfully developed among readers of all ages.

SCRAMBLED SCHEMA STORY TASK

Purpose

A scrambled schema story task requires that readers reconstruct the order of a story based on their comprehension and story grammar knowledge. In this task, a story is divided into its components, such as setting, problem, events, and resolution, and

Figure 10.6 Story Frame Assessment and Analysis Form

1. The setting of the story was described. _____
2. The problem, gist, or main idea of the story was named. _____
3. The events or episodes in the story were told. _____
4. The resolution of the story was explained. _____
5. Episodes or events were told in sequence. _____

Total score: _____   % of total: _____

• Strengths

_____
_____

• Needs

_____
_____

• Instructional intervention ideas

_____
_____

then scrambled. Students are asked to read each element of the story and then organize the story elements in order. Results from this analysis can be used to help teachers emphasize either the increased experience with story reading or direct instruction in story parts to help readers build a better sense of story structure.

Materials

You will need a short narrative selection divided into story parts, an envelope for mixing the story parts, and a scoring sheet for recording and analyzing student responses.

Procedures

Begin by choosing a simple story for this activity. The next step is to parse the story into story grammar elements as shown previously on pages 207–208 in the "Oral Story Retellings" assessment activity. After parsing the story, transcribe the text to plain white paper. Print the transcribed text and, with scissors, cut the text into the parts of the story. Scramble the pieces and place them into a plain white envelope. Hand the child the envelope and ask her to read each part of the story. You may want to assist her with any decoding problems. Next, ask her to put the pieces of the scrambled story in order and to reread the pieces to check that her ordering of the story makes sense. Record on a copy of the form shown in Figure 10.7 the child's responses to the task. Poor performance on this task is typically due to limited reading practice of complete stories. Thus, daily sustained reading activities such as DEAR (*Drop Everything And Read*) with stories would be a logical means of helping regular and special needs readers who perform poorly on this task to develop an improved sense of story.

STORY GRAMMAR QUESTIONING

Purpose

Questions are an integral part of life in and out of school. From birth we learn about our world by asking questions, and then by testing our answers against the confines of reality. Beck and McKeown (1981) and Sadow (1982) suggested that

Figure 10.7   Scrambled Story Task Summary

Student name: _____   Date _____

Mark an X for correct placement. Mark an O for incorrect placement.*
   1. Setting _____
   2. Theme _____
   3. Episode(s) _____ _____ _____ _____ _____ _____ _____
   4. Resolution _____

*"O" responses should be carefully examined and questioned. Such responses may indicate lack of opportunities to experience complete stories.

teachers should follow a logical model of questioning. Research (Mandler & Johnson, 1977) indicates that story grammars provide such a model, and that developing questions for stories using a story grammar produced improved reading comprehension (Beck, Omanson, & McKeown, 1982). Other evidence from research on story grammars suggests that good readers have well-developed understanding of story structure, while poor readers do not (Whaley, 1981). Therefore, using a story grammar to guide questioning can help teachers to assess readers' understanding of story structure and to provide a logical framework for guiding teacher questioning.

Materials

You will need a short narrative selection (story) to read, a story grammar map, a set of questions that deal with each element of the story map and are sequenced in the order of the story map, and a summary scoring sheet based on the story map.

Procedures

Begin by identifying a simple story or narrative. Construct a story grammar map for the story, as shown in Figure 10.8 for the story of "Jack and the Beanstalk." Next, write a question for selected major elements represented in the story grammar map, as shown in the example questions listed in Figure 10.9. Students can be asked, depending on their level of writing development, to answer the questions orally or in written form. Answers to each question are evaluated for accuracy and completeness.

SUMMARY WRITING

Purpose

Having students prepare a written summary for assessment purposes can provide teachers with revealing insights into a student's decisions about important (and unimportant) information used to retell the story. In writing summaries, students organize text information in a manner that is meaningful to them; therefore, they reveal how they selected information to construct their comprehension of a text (Bromley, 1985). By examining the elements of story that students include or exclude in their summary writing, teachers can adjust their instruction to highlight specific story elements accordingly. Much like oral retellings, teachers can examine written summaries for both inclusion of major story grammar elements and the sequence in which these elements were presented to inform their instruction and interactions with children and stories.

Materials

You will need a brief story, a "parsing" of the story (see Figure 10.10), a scoring sheet, one to two lined sheets for the written summary, and two pencils/pens for summary writing.

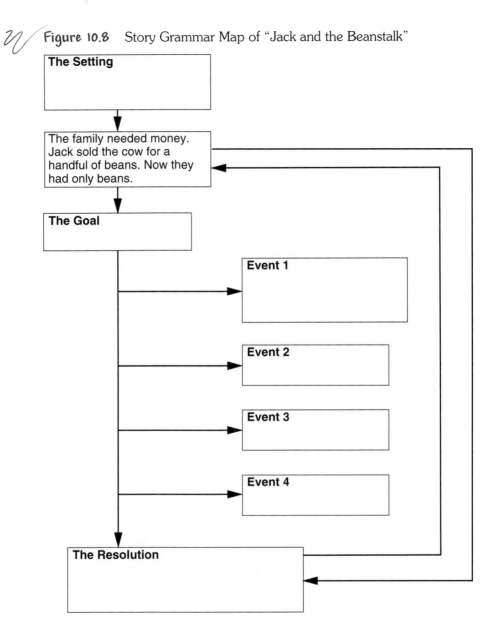

Figure 10.8   Story Grammar Map of "Jack and the Beanstalk"

Procedures

Select a brief story for students to listen to or read. For example, *The Day Jimmy's Boa Ate the Wash* by Trinka Hakes Noble (1980) could be selected. Next, type the text of the story onto a separate piece of paper for parsing. Divide the story into the four major story grammar categories mentioned earlier: setting, problem, events, and resolution (see Figure 10.10).

Figure 10.9   Story Grammar Questioning for "Jack and the Beanstalk"

Setting:	In the beginning of the story, why did Jack's mother want him to sell the cow?
Problem:	When Jack traded the cow for a handful of beans, what kind of a problem did this decision create for Jack and his mother?
Events:	When Jack climbed the Beanstalk the first time, relate what happened to him.
	Why did Jack climb the Beanstalk a second time?
Resolution:	At the end of the story, what had happened to Jack and his mother to solve the problem of trading the cow for a handful of beans?

Figure 10.10   Story Grammar Parsing of *The Day Jimmy's Boa Ate the Wash*

The Setting

"How was your class trip to the farm?"

The Problem

"Oh . . . boring . . . kind of dull . . . until the cow started crying."

The Events

"A cow . . . crying?"

"Yeah, you see, a haystack fell on her."

"But a haystack doesn't just fall over."

"It does if a farmer crashes into it with his tractor."

"Oh, come on, a farmer wouldn't do that."

"He would if he were too busy yelling at the pigs to get off our school bus."

"What were the pigs doing on the bus?"

"Eating our lunches."

"Why were they eating your lunches?"

"Because we threw their corn at each other, and they didn't have anything else to eat."

"Well, that makes sense, but why were you throwing corn?"

"Because we ran out of eggs."

"Out of eggs? Why were you throwing eggs?"

"Because of the boa constrictor."

"THE BOA CONSTRICTOR!"

"Yeah, Jimmy's pet boa constrictor."

"What was Jimmy's pet boa constrictor doing on the farm?"

"Oh, he brought it to meet all the farm animals, but the chickens didn't like it."

"You mean he took it into the hen house?"

"Yeah, and the chickens started squawking and flying around."

"Go on, go on. What happened?"

"Well, one hen got excited and laid an egg, and it landed on Jenny's head."

"The hen?"

continued

Figure 10.10   Continued

> "No, the egg. And it broke—yucky—all over her hair."
> "What did she do?"
> "She got mad because she thought Tommy threw it, so she threw one at him."
> "What did Tommy do?"
> "Oh, he ducked and the egg hit Marianne in the face."
> "So she threw one at Jenny but she missed and hit Jimmy, who dropped his boa constrictor."
> "Oh, I know, the next thing you knew, everyone was throwing eggs, right?"
> "Right."
> "And when you ran out of eggs, you threw the pigs' corn, right?"
> "Right again."
>
> **Resolution**
>
> "Well, what finally stopped it?"
> "Well, we heard the farmer's wife screaming."
> "Why was she screaming?"
> "We never found out, because Mrs. Stanley made us get on the bus, and we sort of left in a hurry without the boa constrictor."
> "I bet Jimmy was sad because he left his pet boa constrictor."
> "Oh, not really. We left in such a hurry that one of the pigs didn't get off the bus, so now he's got a pet pig."
> "Boy, that sure sounds like an exciting trip."
> "Yeah, I suppose, if you're the kind of kid who likes class trips to the farm."
>
> Based on *The Day Jimmy's Boa Ate the Wash* by Trinka Hakes Noble.

Next, ask the child to prepare a written summary of the story just completed. Written summaries may be elicited from children in a number of ways. One way involves the use of pictures or verbal prompts from the story. As pictures in the story are flashed sequentially, students write a summary of the story as remembered from listening or reading. Morrow (1985) suggests that teachers prompt children to begin writing story summaries with a statement such as: "A little while ago, we [or you] read a story called [Name the story] . . . [W]rite a story summary as if you were telling it to a friend who has never heard it before" (p. 659). Other prompts during the recall and summary writing may be framed as questions:

- "How does the story begin?" Or, "Once upon a time . . . ."
- "What happens next?"
- "What happened to [the main character] when . . . ?"
- "Where did the story take place?"
- "When did the story take place?"
- "How did the main character solve the problem in the story?"
- "How did the story end?"

As noted earlier with oral retellings, teachers may use both aided and unaided re-call prompts to help students produce written story summaries. To record and ex-amine critical elements of the child's story summary, try using a coding sheet like the one shown in Figure 10.11.

The information gleaned from a written story summary may be used to help teachers focus their instruction on enhancing students' understanding of story structure, the sequence of events in a story, or important story information. Story summary analyses may also indicate the nature of information to be focused upon in future story summary writing instructional sessions, or the nature of the prompts to be given during summary writing. Assessment of children's written story summaries can reveal much about their understanding of story structure, story sequence, and the major elements of the story plot from a reading and writ-ing perspective.

Figure 10.11   Written Story Summary Coding Form

Student's name: _____   Grade: _____
Title of story: _____   Date: _____

General directions: Give 1 point for each element included, as well as for "gist." Give 1 point for each character named, as well as for such words as *boy, girl,* or *dog.* Credit plurals (*friends,* for instance) with 2 points under char-acters.

Setting

   a. Begins with an introduction   _____
   b. Indicates main character   _____
   c. Other characters named   _____
   d. Includes statement about time or place   _____

Objective

   a. Refers to main character's goal or problem to be solved   _____

Events

   a. Number of events recalled   _____
   b. Number of events in story   _____
   c. Score for "events" (a/b)   _____

Resolution

   a. Tells how main character resolves the story problem   _____

Sequence

Summarizes story in order: setting, objective, episodes, and resolution. (Score 2 for correct order, 1 for partial order, 0 for no sequence.)   _____

Possible score: _____   **Student's score:** _____

BALANCED READING PROGRAM INTERVENTIONS: STUDENTS WITH A POORLY DEVELOPED SENSE OF STORY

Reading Problem Indicators

- Incomplete or inaccurate recall of stories
- Confused story order during recall
- Inability to recall important story elements

After a careful assessment of each student's current understanding of story structure, teachers may find one or more of the following instructional strategies helpful in developing greater story sense. Perhaps the most important thing to keep in mind is that children who have a poorly developed sense of story structure must be given numerous opportunities to read and discuss well-formed stories. We begin this section with an activity known as the Shared Reading Experience, which can be used as the central model around which all story structure instruction may be built.

THE SHARED READING EXPERIENCE

Purpose

We highly recommend a strategy called the *Shared Reading Experience* for developing students' sense of story. This strategy involves teachers and students in guided readings and discussions with authentic stories and literature—the key to developing an understanding of story structure. When used as a primary activity complemented by one or more of the other eight demonstration and instructional strategies offered in the following pages, the Shared Reading Experience provides an effective and interesting way to help learners develop, apply, and understand story structure.

Materials

The success of the Shared Reading Experience, also called the Shared Book Experience (Holdaway, 1979), is naturally dependent upon the selection of high quality predictable books. Several criteria need to be observed. First of all, books and stories that are proven favorites of children need to be chosen. Any book or story to be shared (including those in basal readers) should have literary merit and engaging content. Pictures should augment the text and support the telling of the story in proper sequence. The text should be characterized by repetition and a logical and cumulative sequence. Sometimes it is also helpful to select books having rhyme and rhythm to entice and "hook" children on the language patterns. Further, books should put reasonable demands on the reader or, put another way, the amount of print should not overburden the reader.

In books for emergent readers, pictures should carry the story. Later, books can be selected in which the print and the picture carry nearly equal shares of the story. With practice and increased independence in reading, books can be chosen in which the print carries the story and the illustrations simply augment the text (Peterson, 1991). Big books are used when available so that groups of students are able to see the print and pictures about as well as they would if sharing a book one-on-one with an adult. When these conditions are observed, children share the discovery of good books, an awareness of how print works, and the power and humor of language. What's more, they gain a growing confidence in their ability to read (Barrett, 1982).

Procedures

A Shared Reading Experience is begun by introducing a book. For instance, if the book *The Napping House* (Wood, 1984) was selected for sharing, the introduction might begin with children looking at the book cover as the teacher reads the title aloud. Talk about the front and back covers of the book, and attend to certain features of the book, such as the author and illustrator names, publisher, copyright, table of contents, etc. Next ask, "What do you think this story might be about?" After looking at the cover and reading the title aloud, children may want to make predictions about the contents of the book. The intent of the introduction is to heighten children's desire to read the story and help them draw upon their own experiences to enjoy and interpret the story.

Next, read the story with "full dramatic punch, perhaps overdoing a little some of the best parts" (Barrett, 1982, pg. 16). If the story possesses the characteristics outlined above that make the text predictable, children will begin chiming in on the repetitive and predictable parts. In *The Napping House,* children may join in on the phrase, ". . . in the Napping House, where everyone is sleeping." At key points, teachers may pause during reading to encourage children to predict what is coming next in the book. Be sure to tell students that making predictions that seem to "make sense" is the goal. In other words, avoid the notion of "right" and "wrong" predictions.

After completing the book, a discussion usually ensues. Children often want to talk about their favorite parts, share their feelings and experiences, and discuss how well they were able to make logical predictions. The same story can be reread on subsequent days and will eventually become a part of the stock of favorite stories children request for rereading. During subsequent rereadings, hand movements or rhythm instruments can be used to add variety to the routine for early readers.

STORY RETELLINGS

Purpose

Seldom do children spontaneously produce quality oral retellings (Morrow, 1985). However, they can quickly learn to retell stories with the help of teacher demonstrations and individual or group practice. Story retelling is a strategy that helps students achieve that important developmental milestone.

Materials

Any predictable book, picture book, short story, poem, or book that follows a logical story structure and sequence of events is appropriate.

Procedures

Begin by introducing the story and any important concepts or vocabulary. Next, read the story aloud to the children with enthusiasm and expression. Following the reading, demonstrate a quality retelling of a favorite story for your students. Explain that the best retellings include key story elements such as a description of characters, setting, and so forth. When you feel the students are ready to begin producing their own oral retellings of a story, be sure to let them know *before* they read the story that you will want them to give retelling a try (Morrow, 1989). We have also found that it is best that students be allowed to read a story at least three times before they are asked to retell it on their own. This helps children learn how to produce a quality retelling while also attending to important story elements.

SCHEMA STORIES

Purpose

Watson and Crowley (1988) describe *schema stories* as a reading strategy lesson that helps readers "reconstruct the order of a text based on meaning and story grammar" (p. 263). This strategy helps students learn to anticipate such elements as setting, problem to be addressed by the characters, key events in the story, and resolution of the story.

Materials

For emergent readers or students having reading problems, the key is to select texts that contain familiar phrases such as *Once upon a time* and *They lived happily ever after.* After choosing an interesting text, prepare the schema story strategy lesson by making a photocopy of the text and physically cutting the photocopy into sections that are long enough to contain at least one main idea. Usually, one or two paragraphs will be a sufficient length to accomplish this purpose.

Procedures

To begin the lesson, distribute a section of the story to each small group of students (4 to 8 students in each group is about right). Typically, one student is selected in each group to read the text aloud. Addressing the group, ask the child who believes she was given a section with the beginning of the story on it to raise her hand. Members of the group must state *why* they believe they have the beginning. After a majority of the students agree as to which section of text is first, the group proceeds to the next segment of the text. This procedure continues as described until all of the segments have been placed in order.

Schema story lessons make excellent small group or individual activities that can be located at a classroom center or station devoted to developing a sense of story. All of the segments of a text can be placed into an envelope and filed in the center. Small groups of children or individuals can come to the center and select an envelope, working individually or collectively on reconstructing a story. A "key" for self-checking can be included in the envelope, as well, to reduce the amount of teacher supervision necessary in the center.

As children work through a schema story strategy lesson, they talk about how language works, ways authors construct texts, and how meaning can be used to make sense out of the scrambled elements of a text or story.

USING WORDLESS PICTURE BOOKS AND STORY FRAME BOARDS

Purpose

Wordless picture books are books in which the illustrations tell the entire story (Norton, 1991). Wordless picture books are ideal for helping children learn about how stories are formed without having to focus attention on decoding the print.

Materials

Donna Norton (1991, p. 185) offers several questions to guide the selection of wordless picture books for sharing and instruction:

1. Do the pictures follow a sequentially organized plot?
2. Is the depth of detail appropriate for the children's age levels?
3. Do the children have enough experiential background to interpret the illustrations?
4. Is the size of the book appropriate for group sharing?
5. Is the subject one that will appeal to children?

Procedures

We suggest that you initially select a picture book such as *The Three Little Pigs.* Physically cut it apart (or cut a photocopy, if you prefer) and temporarily mount the pages on separate pieces of chart paper, or place them inside an acetate story frame board. If the book has text to accompany the pictures, mask the text wth removable adhesive notes or correction tape. An acetate story frame board is shown in Figure 10.12 with pages from *The Three Little Pigs.*

One disadvantage of the story frame board is that two copies of the book are needed to display both sides of the pages. However, this disadvantage is offset by the advantage of providing protection for the pictures in the book as well as the ease of cleanup and the opportunity for repeated usage. A waterbased pen can be used to record children's dictation on the acetate sheets of the story frame board, then cleaned later with water and a dry rag. Chart paper is not as easy to use and provides less protection for the original pages of the book.

When introducing a wordless picture book such as *The Three Little Pigs,* children and teachers can begin by looking carefully at each picture in the book. They may discuss what they think is happening in each of the pictures. After this initial discussion, individual children can be called upon to describe the events in a particular picture. The descriptions dictated by the children to the teacher can be written beneath the wordless picture book pages on the chart or on the story frame board. The text of these dictated wordless picture book stories can then be read and reread.

Figure 10.12 Story Frame Board (*The Three Little Pigs*)

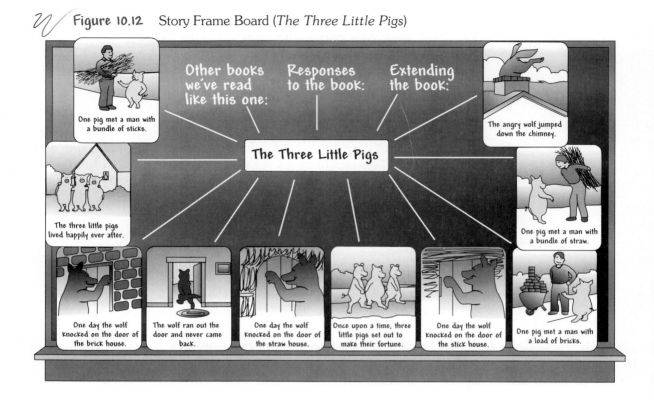

Finally, students can compare their dictated story with another version of the book *The Three Little Pigs* to see how well they were able to construct the story line.

SUPPORTED READING USING READ-ALONG CASSETTES

Purpose

Just as a parent provides support with training wheels and by holding onto the back of the bicycle seat when a child learns to ride a bicycle, teachers also need to provide support to the emergent reader learning to read. *Supported reading* strategies include the use of adult and child volunteers, as well as mechanical support devices and read-along cassette tapes.

Materials

A wide selection of predictable books, as well as prerecorded cassette tapes of selected books is essential. Tapes of books can be recorded by parent volunteers or the teacher at a great savings over commercially prepared prerecorded tapes.

Procedures

Read-along cassettes can be used to effectively support readers through the reading of new or relatively unfamiliar books at all levels. However, this practice seems to make best sense in the emergent or beginning stages of learning to read. Read-along cassettes are now commercially available for a wide variety of predictable books, but, as stated above, parent volunteers can be invited to participate in the production of read-along cassettes. When these tapes are carefully paced, they support children through the reading of a book when the teacher is needed elsewhere in the classroom. Tapes can, for example, be color coded for varying text levels using a system such as the following:

1. emergent
2. easy reading
3. independent reading

The tapes can be stored in specially designated cassette storage cases. Further, the tapes can be checked out for home use to support children at home when parents are unavailable to provide the time and support needed for beginning readers. Not that read-along cassettes should ever supplant human interaction with stories, of course, but, when necessary, read-along tapes can serve as a stopgap aid to children, teachers, and parents.

SMALL GROUP OR ONE-TO-ONE READING

Purpose

While most reading aloud in school takes place with an entire class or group of children, Morrow (1988) reminds us not to overlook the benefits and importance of reading aloud to smaller groups and individuals.

Materials

No special materials are needed, other than books correctly matched to students' interests and reading ability.

Procedures

One of the benefits associated with reading to children at home is the interaction between parent and child. This same benefit can be replicated in the school setting. Children whose reading development is lagging behind their peers can be helped a great deal by teachers and parents who take time to read to them in small group or individual settings. One advantage is that children can stop the teacher to ask questions, make comments, or respond to the story. This seldom happens in whole groups. Morrow (1989) also suggests that individual readings be recorded and analyzed to provide diagnostic information to inform instruction, as described in the discussion of running records in chapter 3.

LITERATURE WEBBING WITH PREDICTABLE BOOKS

Purpose

Reutzel and Fawson (1989) designed a successful strategy lesson to be used with predictable books for building children's understanding of story structure. A literature web is constructed from the major story elements in a predictable book by selecting sentences from a book that tell about each major element of the story (i.e., setting, problem, events, and resolution).

Materials

The following materials are needed for literature webbing: books having clear story structure, sentence strips, hand drawn or copied pictures from the selected book, and a chalkboard or other display area for posting the literature web.

Procedures

The sentences from the strips are written around the title of the book in mixed order on a chalkboard or a large bulletin board (see Figure 10.13 for an example). Prior to reading the story, children read the sentences aloud with the teacher. In the early part of the school year, the sentences selected for the web sentence strips are usually heavily augmented with hand drawn or copied pictures from the book.

Next, children are organized into small groups and each group is given one of the picture/sentence cards from the board. The children are asked which group thinks it has the first part of the story. After discussion and group agreement is reached, the first sentence/picture card is placed at the one o'clock position on the literature web. The remainder of the groups are asked which sentence/word card comes next, and the cards are placed around the literature web in clockwise order. Figure 10.14 shows how one group of students rearranged a literature web to conform with their predictions.

Next, the story is read from a traditional-sized trade book or big book. Children listen attentively to confirm or correct their literature web predictions. After the reading, predictions are revised in the literature web as necessary (see Figure 10.15). Children respond to the story, and these responses are recorded near the end of the literature web. Other books similar to the one read may be discussed and comments recorded on the web. Finally, the children and teacher brainstorm together some ideas about how to extend the reading of the book into the other language arts while recording these ideas on the web.

Reutzel and Fawson (1991) have also demonstrated that children having reading problems who participate in literature webbing of a predictable book learn to read these books with fewer oral reading miscues, fewer miscues that distort comprehension, and greater recall. They attribute this to the fact that children must impose an organization onto their predictions when using literature webs, rather than simply making random predictions from story titles and pictures.

STORY FRAMES

Purpose

Fowler (1982) details a strategy for developing sense of story and improving comprehension of text for readers of all ages called *story frames*. For most stories, the basic story frame shown in Figure 10.2 works quite well. Other story frames (review Figures 10.3 through 10.5 for examples) may be designed to focus on the main idea or plot of the story, or on the comparison and analysis of characters.

Materials

The materials needed include books or stories to be used and story frame boards based on these selected books or stories.

Figure 10.13 Random-Order Literature Web

One pig met a man carrying a bundle of sticks. "May I have those sticks to build myself a house?" asked the pig. "You may," answered the man.

And the three little pigs lived happily ever after in a brick house built for three.

One day the wolf came knocking at the door of the brick house. "Little pig, little pig, let me come in." "Not by the hair of my chinny chin chin," said the pig. "Then I'll huff and I'll puff and I'll blow your house in." But the house would not fall down.

The wolf fell, kersplot, into a kettle of hot water. He jumped out with a start and ran out the door and never came back again.

One day the wolf came knocking at the door of the straw house. "Little pig, little pig, let me come in." "Not by the hair of my chinny chin chin," said the pig. "Then I'll huff and I'll puff and I'll blow your house in." And he blew the house down.

Once upon a time, three little pigs set out to make their fortune.

The Three Little Pigs

The wolf got so angry that he climbed to the top of the house and jumped down the chimney.

One pig met a man with a load of bricks. "May I have those bricks to build myself a house?" asked the pig. "You may," answered the man.

One pig met a man carrying a bundle of straw. "May I have that straw to build myself a house?" asked the pig. "You may," answered the man.

One day the wolf came knocking at the door of the stick house. "Little pig, little pig, let me come in." "Not by the hair of my chinny chin chin," said the pig. "Then I'll huff and I'll puff and I'll blow your house in." And he blew the house down.

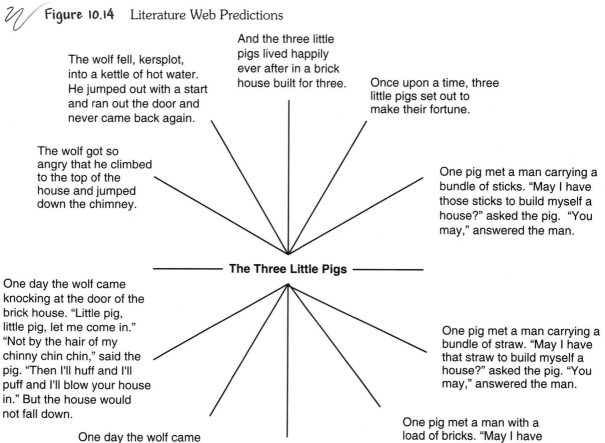

Figure 10.14   Literature Web Predictions

The wolf fell, kersplot, into a kettle of hot water. He jumped out with a start and ran out the door and never came back again.

And the three little pigs lived happily ever after in a brick house built for three.

Once upon a time, three little pigs set out to make their fortune.

The wolf got so angry that he climbed to the top of the house and jumped down the chimney.

One pig met a man carrying a bundle of sticks. "May I have those sticks to build myself a house?" asked the pig. "You may," answered the man.

The Three Little Pigs

One day the wolf came knocking at the door of the brick house. "Little pig, little pig, let me come in." "Not by the hair of my chinny chin chin," said the pig. "Then I'll huff and I'll puff and I'll blow your house in." But the house would not fall down.

One pig met a man carrying a bundle of straw. "May I have that straw to build myself a house?" asked the pig. "You may," answered the man.

One day the wolf came knocking at the door of the straw house. "Little pig, little pig, let me come in." "Not by the hair of my chinny chin chin," said the pig. "Then I'll huff and I'll puff and I'll blow your house in." And he blew the house down.

One day the wolf came knocking at the door of the stick house. "Little pig, little pig, let me come in." "Not by the hair of my chinny chin chin," said the pig. "Then I'll huff and I'll puff and I'll blow your house down. And he blew the house down.

One pig met a man with a load of bricks. "May I have those bricks to build myself a house?" asked the pig. "You may," answered the man.

Procedures

To use story frames, write the major story elements such as setting, problem, events, and resolution on the story frame board after reading a story. Next, cut parts of the story frame "chart" apart and scramble them. Individual students or small groups are then given one of the pieces of the story frame chart. Ask students which part of the story schema they might have in their hands. This can be done by pointing to a card at the board, such as a card that reads *setting,* then asking children to raise their hands if they think that they have this part of the story.

Figure 10.15 Completed Literature Web

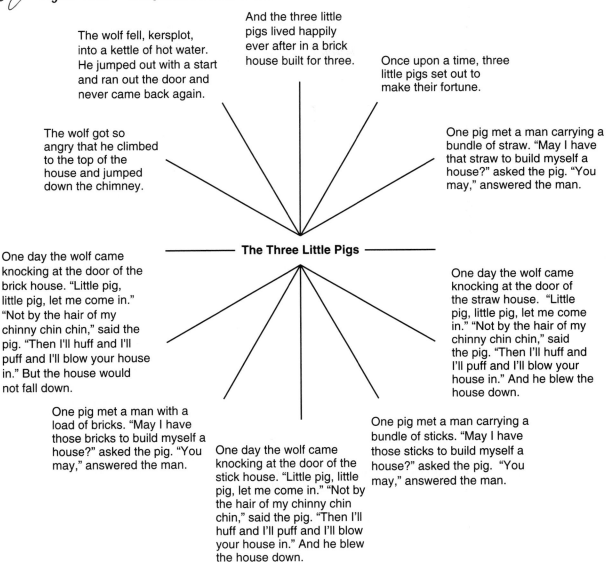

The wolf fell, kersplot, into a kettle of hot water. He jumped out with a start and ran out the door and never came back again.

And the three little pigs lived happily ever after in a brick house built for three.

Once upon a time, three little pigs set out to make their fortune.

The wolf got so angry that he climbed to the top of the house and jumped down the chimney.

One pig met a man carrying a bundle of straw. "May I have that straw to build myself a house?" asked the pig. "You may," answered the man.

One day the wolf came knocking at the door of the brick house. "Little pig, little pig, let me come in." "Not by the hair of my chinny chin chin," said the pig. "Then I'll huff and I'll puff and I'll blow your house in." But the house would not fall down.

The Three Little Pigs

One day the wolf came knocking at the door of the straw house. "Little pig, little pig, let me come in." "Not by the hair of my chinny chin chin," said the pig. "Then I'll huff and I'll puff and I'll blow your house in." And he blew the house down.

One pig met a man with a load of bricks. "May I have those bricks to build myself a house?" asked the pig. "You may," answered the man.

One day the wolf came knocking at the door of the stick house. "Little pig, little pig, let me come in." "Not by the hair of my chinny chin chin," said the pig. "Then I'll huff and I'll puff and I'll blow your house in." And he blew the house down.

One pig met a man carrying a bundle of sticks. "May I have those sticks to build myself a house?" asked the pig. "You may," answered the man.

Progress through the entire story structure until all of parts of the story frame have been classified under one of the story structure headings on the board.

A useful side benefit from using story frames as a discussion guide is that story discussions end up being sequenced in the typical order of story elements. Another benefit associated with using story frames is that students having reading problems begin to ask themselves questions about their reading based on story structure knowledge. They are also able to use their knowledge of story structure to read new books more logically resulting in increased recall and enjoyment of stories.

Perhaps the greatest benefit associated with using story frames is that students begin to read more like writers. They pay more attention to structure, sequence, and story sense in reading, and expect stories to be well formed and logical.

STORY GRAMMAR INSTRUCTION

Purpose

Developing a sense of how stories are formed through story grammar instruction helps students having reading problems predict with greater facility, store information more efficiently, and recall story elements with increased accuracy and completeness.

Materials

Well-formed stories and a visual organizer (see Figures 10.8 and 10.13) to guide the introduction of story grammar concepts are the materials needed for this activity.

Procedures

A number of reading researchers have described instructional procedures for developing readers' story schema or *story grammar* awareness. Gordon and Braun (1983) recommend several guidelines for teaching story grammar. We have adapted these recommendations below.

1. Story grammar instruction should use well-formed stories such as "Jack and the Beanstalk." A visual organizer can be used to guide the introduction of the concept of story grammar. For the first story used in story grammar instruction, read the story aloud, stop at key points in the story, and discuss the information needed to fill in the diagram. For stories read after introducing the concept of story grammar, use the visual organizer to introduce the story and make predictions about the story prior to reading. During and after reading, a visual organizer can be used to guide a discussion.

2. Set the purposes for reading by asking questions related to the structure of the story. Questioning developed to follow the structure of the story will focus students' attention on major story elements.

3. After questioning and discussing story structure, specific questions about the story content can be asked.

4. For continued instruction, gradually introduce less well-formed stories so that students will learn that not all stories are "ideal" in organization.

5. Extend instruction by encouraging children to ask their own questions using story structure and to apply this understanding in writing their own stories.

CHAPTER SUMMARY

In this chapter, selected assessment strategies were introduced to help teachers determine students' understanding and development of story structure. These ideas help teachers construct a reading portfolio profiling students' current understanding of story structure to help inform future teaching. This chapter also offered ideas for helping students understand, develop, and apply story structure knowledge in their daily reading. The Shared Reading Experience was offered as a key strategy or model of instruction to develop readers' story structure knowledge in a natural and enjoyable reading context. The Shared Reading Experience, when supplemented by other teaching strategies presented, can be a powerful tool leading students to greater understanding of story structure and deeper comprehension of text.

REFERENCES

Applebee, A. N. (1979). *The child's concept of story: Ages two to seventeen.* Chicago, IL: The University of Chicago Press.

Barrett, F. L. (1982). *A teacher's guide to shared reading.* Richmond Hill, Ontario, Canada: Scholastic-TAB Publications Ltd.

Beck, I. L., & McKeown, M. G. (1981). Developing questions that promote comprehension: The story map. *Language Arts, 58,* 913–918.

Beck, I. L., Omanson, R. C., & McKeown, M. G. (1982). An instructional redesign of reading lessons: Effects on comprehension. *Reading Research Quarterly, 17,* 462–481.

Bromley, K. (1985). Precise writing and outlining enhance content learning. *The Reading Teacher, 38*(4), 406–411.

Brown, H., & Cambourne, B. (1987). *Read and Retell.* Portsmouth, NH: Heinemann Educational Books.

Cudd, E. T., & Roberts, L. L. (1987). Using story frames to develop reading comprehension in a 1st grade classroom. *The Reading Teacher, 41*(1), 74–81.

Fowler, G. L. (1982). Developing comprehension skills in primary students through the use of story frames. *The Reading Teacher, 36*(2),176–179.

Gambrell, L. B., Pfeiffer, W., & Wilson, R. (1985). The effects of retelling upon reading comprehension and recall of text information. *Journal of Educational Research, 78,* 216–220.

Gordon, C. J., & Braun, C. (1983). Using story schema as an aid to reading and writing. *The Reading Teacher, 37*(2), 116–121.

Holdaway, D. (1979). *The foundations of literacy.* New York: Ashton Scholastic.

Krauss, R. (1945). *The Carrot Seed.* New York, NY: Scholastic Inc.

Mandler, J. M., & Johnson, N. S. (1977). Remembrance of things parsed: Story structure and recall. *Cognitive psychology, 9,* 111–151.

Morrow, L. M. (1985). Retelling stories: A strategy for improving children's comprehension, concept of story structure and oral language complexity. *Elementary School Journal, 85,* 647–661.

Morrow, L. M. (1988). Young children's responses to one-to-one story reading in school settings. *The Reading Teacher, 23*(1) 89–107.

Morrow, L. M. (1989). *Literacy development in the early years: Helping children read and write.* Englewood Cliffs, NJ: Prentice Hall.

Nichols, J. (1980). Using paragraph frames to help remedial high school students with written assignments. *Journal of Reading, 24,* 228–231.

Noble, T. (1980). *The day Jimmy's boa ate the wash.* Illustrated by Steven Kellogg. New York, NY: Dial Books.

Norton, D. E. (1991). *Through the eyes of a child: An introduction to children's literature* (3rd ed.). Columbus, OH: Merrill Publishing Company.

Peterson, B. (1991). Selecting books for beginning readers. In D. DeFord, C. Lyons, and G. S. Pinnell (Eds.) *Bridges to literacy: Learning from reading recovery.* Portsmouth, NH: Heinemann Educational Books.

Reutzel, D. R., & Fawson, P. C. (1989). Using a literature webbing strategy lesson with predictable books. *The Reading Teacher, 43*(3), 208-215.

Reutzel, D. R. & Fawson, P. C. (1991). Literature webbing predictable books: A predication strategy that helps below-average, first-grade readers. *Reading Research and Instruction, 30*(4), 20–30.

Sadow, M. W. (1982). The use of story grammar in the design of questions. *The Reading Teacher, 35,* 518–523.

Stein, N. L., & Glenn, C. G. (1979). An analysis of story comprehension in elementary school children. In R. O. Freedle (Ed.), *New directions in discourse processing* (pp. 53–120). Hillsdale, NJ: Lawrence Erlbaum Associates.

Thorndyke, P. N. (1977). Cognitive structure in comprehension and memory of narrative discourse. *Cognitive Psychology, 9*(1) 77–110.

Watson, J. J. (1991). An integral setting tells more than when and where. *The Reading Teacher, 44*(9), 338–347.

Watson, D., & Crowley, P. (1988). How can we implement a whole-language approach? In C. Weaver, *Reading Process and Practice* (pp. 232–279). Portsmouth, NH: Heinemann Educational Books.

Whaley, J. F. (1981). Readers' expectations for story structures. *Reading Research Quarterly, 17,* 90–114.

Wood, A. (1984). *The napping house.* Illustrated by Don Wood. San Diego: Harcourt Brace Jovanovich.

Chapter 11

Teaching Expository Text Structures

Content classrooms (such as social studies, science, mathematics, etc.) are heavily populated with students for whom reading informational, or *expository* materials is a challenge (Romine, McKenna, & Robinson, 1996). These students, who are otherwise "good readers," must sometimes think to themselves, "Why am I such a lousy reader in my content classes when I am such a good reader otherwise?!"

The answer is relatively simple: expository texts use very different organizational structures and techniques to convey ideas than those used in narrative texts. One of our most important tasks as teachers is to help students learn to strategically organize and construct new knowledge from content texts (Simpson, 1996; Farnan, 1996). Even though a number of effective strategies have been identified for use in content classrooms to help students succeed (e.g., Alvermann & Moore, 1991; Cooter & Flynt, 1996), startlingly few teachers actually use them (Irvin & Connors, 1989, Romine, McKenna, & Robinson, 1996). In this chapter we provide a short tutorial for teachers regarding expository text writing patterns, strategies for assessing reading problems with expository texts, and teaching methods to help students succeed when reading expository texts.

BACKGROUND BRIEFING FOR TEACHERS: THE NATURE OF EXPOSITORY TEXTS

In narrative texts the writer is attempting to tell a story using *story grammar* elements (i.e., setting, characters, problem, resolution, etc.) to construct the text. Expository writing, on the other hand, is intended to inform others about a subject rather than to tell a story (Cooter & Flynt, 1996, p. 226). Just as narrative authors use story grammars to communicate effectively, expository writers use what we call *expository text patterns* to effectively convey information. An important difference in usage exists between story grammars and expository text patterns, however. In narrative texts, all story grammar elements are typically used; in expository texts, only a few of the patterns are generally used in any one content area textbook or passage, depending on the nature of the information to be shared.

Researchers in the field of content area reading (Armbruster & Anderson, 1981; Meyer & Freedle, 1984; Cooter & Flynt, 1996) describe five common patterns for presenting information: *time order* (sequence of events), *cause-effect* (showing how one event happened as a result of another), *problem-solution* (presenting a problem along with its possible solution[s]), *comparison* (also known as compare/contrast), and simple *listing*. Other researchers (McGee & Richgels, 1985; Flood, Lapp, & Farnan, 1986) have discovered that students can be taught about these patterns to help them better comprehend content texts and simultaneously improve their written communication skills.

Because of the varying and rather unique styles used by writers of expository text, students can have difficulties acquiring new or technical vocabulary, comprehending expository texts, retaining information over time, and monitoring their own learning. In this chapter we offer a variety of classroom-proven strategies to help students succeed with expository materials.

A fundamental maxim of effective teaching is for teachers to assess what a student knows (and still needs to know) before offering instruction. In the next section, we offer some suggestions for discerning which expository text patterns are known to students so that instruction can be planned strategically.

ASSESSING KNOWLEDGE OF EXPOSITORY TEXT PATTERNS

The key to effective expository text instruction lies in the accurate identification of the types of content or expository texts that students are able to read effectively, as well as the forms of expository writing that are difficult for them to comprehend. We have discovered that several rather common forms of reading assessment are easily adaptable to expository texts and can help teachers plan instruction. Offered in this section are some examples of each for your consideration.

EXPOSITORY TEXT FRAMES

Purpose

Expository text frames are useful in identifying types of expository text patterns that may be troublesome for students. Based on the "story frames" concept (Nichols, 1980; Fowler, 1982), expository text frames are completed by the student after reading an expository passage. Instruction can be focused much more precisely, based on student needs, as a result of this procedure.

Materials

You will need the textbook, a computer and word processing program, and means by which to copy the expository text frames for students. Abbreviated examples of expository text frames for each of the primary expository text patterns are shown in Figures 11.1 through 11.5.

Figure 11.1   Expository Text Frames: Description

Decimals are another way to write fractions when _____
_____
_____
_____ .

Figure 11.2   Expository Text Frames: Collection

Water Habitats

Freshwater habitats are found in _____, _____, _____, and rivers. Each freshwater habitat has special kinds of _____ and _____ that live there. Some plants and animals live in waters that are very _____ . Others live in waters that are _____ . Some plants and animals adapt to waters that flow _____ .

Figure 11.3   Expository Text Frames: Causation

America Enters the War

On Sunday, December 7, 1941, World War II came to the United States. The entry of the United States into World War II was triggered by _____ . Roosevelt said that it was a day that would "live in infamy." *Infamy* (IN • fuh • mee) means remembered for being evil.

Figure 11.4   Expository Text Frames: Problem/Solution

Agreement by Compromise

Events that led to the Civil War

For a while there were an equal number of Southern and Northern states. That meant that there were just as many Senators in Congress from slave states as from free states. Neither had more votes in the Senate, so they usually reached agreement on new laws by compromise. One way that the balance of power was maintained in Congress was _____
_____ .

Figure II.5   Expository Text Frames: Comparison

> ## Segregation
>
> Many people said that the segregation laws were unfair. But in 1896, the Supreme Court ruled segregation legal if _____. "Separate but equal" became the law in many parts of the country.
>
> But separate was not equal. One of the most serious problems was education. Black parents felt _____. Sometimes the segregated schools had teachers who were not _____ as teachers in the white schools. Textbooks were often _____, if they had any books at all. But in many of the white schools the books were _____. Without a good education, the blacks argued, their children would not be able to get good jobs as adults.

Procedure

Before reading the selection, list the major vocabulary and concepts. Discuss what students already know about the topic and display it on the chalkboard or on chart paper. Next, have students read an expository selection similar to the one you will ask them to read in class. Once the passage has been read, model the process for completing expository text frames using mock examples. Now have them read the actual selection for the unit of study. Finally, have students complete the expository text frame(s) you have prepared for this passage.

For students who have trouble with any of the frames, conduct a one-on-one reading conference to determine the thinking processes going on as the student completed the expository text frame.

CLOZE PASSAGES

Purpose

Cloze passages, from the word *closure,* are short passages (250 words) from expository books commonly used in the teacher's classroom that have certain words deleted (usually every fifth word) and replaced with a blank. Students are asked to read the cloze passages and fill in the missing words based on what they feel makes sense using context clues. If students are reading effectively and with adequate comprehension, usually they are able to accurately guess the missing words—or, at least, a word of the same part of speech. This helps the teacher know whether the student is able to use context clues when reading expository materials in the selected field of study, and whether he has a strong enough vocabulary to cope with the textbook being used. Following are the usual materials and procedures for constructing expository text cloze passages, followed by some examples from selected content texts.

Materials

Materials needed include the textbook, a computer and word processing program, and means by which to copy the cloze passage for students.

Procedure

Cloze tests cause students to use their background knowledge of a subject, their understanding of basic syntax (word order relationships), and their word and sentence meaning (semantics) knowledge to guess what a missing or familiar word in print might be (Cooter & Flynt, 1996). We encourage teachers working with students having reading problems to *first* assess the student's performance using cloze passages created from *narrative* texts as a baseline indicator of general reading ability. This will help you to find out how well the student normally performs at reading narrative books, which are the main focus of reading instruction in the elementary years. This approach also helps students to practice the cloze procedure before being asked to take on the different—and perhaps more difficult—expository cloze passages.

Teachers may choose cloze excerpts that include each of the expository text patterns found in the textbook(s) currently used by students in their content classes. Results inform the teacher as to whether the text is likely to be at what is termed the independent level (easy to read), the instructional level (requiring some assistance from the teacher for student success), or the frustration level (far too difficult for the student). General instructions for the construction and scoring of cloze tests using content area texts are as follows:

1. Choose a passage of about 250 words from the class textbook. It is usually best to choose a passage at the beginning of a chapter or unit so that needed introductory information is included.

2. Prepare the cloze passage, preferably using a computer word processing program. The first sentence should be typed exactly as it is written in the original text. Thereafter, beginning with the second sentence, delete one of the first five words and replace it with a blank, then repeat this procedure every fifth word. The process is complete when you have fifty (50) blanks in the cloze passage. After the fiftieth blank, finish typing the sentence in which the last blank occurred. Then, type at least one more sentence *intact* (no deletions).

3. Have students read the passage all the way through once *without* attempting to fill in any of the blanks, then reread the passage and fill in the blanks to the best of their ability.

4. To score cloze passages, use the one-half/one-third formula. Students who correctly complete one-half (25 of 50) or more of the blanks are considered to be at the independent reading level, at least with the passage selected. Students who complete fewer than one third of the blanks correctly (17 out of 50 blanks) will probably find the text frustrating, or too difficult even with assistance. Those students falling somewhere between the one-third and one-half range will probably be able to succeed with the text if they receive some preparatory assistance from the teacher.

Figure 11.6   Cloze Passage: Diamonds

Diamonds

A diamond is one of the most beautiful treasures that nature has ever cre-ated. And one of _____ rarest. It takes thousands _____ years for nature to _____ a chunk of carbon _____ a rough diamond. Only _____ important dia-mond fields have _____ found in the world, _____ India, South America, and Africa.

_____ first diamonds were found _____ the sand and gravel _____ stream beds. These types _____ diamonds are called alluvial _____ . Later, diamonds were found _____ in the earth in _____ formations called *pipes.* These _____ resemble extinct volcanoes. The _____ in which diamonds are _____ is called *blue ground.* _____ even where diamonds are _____ it takes digging and _____ through tons of rock _____ gravel to find enough _____ for a one-carat _____ .

Gem diamonds' quality is _____ on weight, purity, color, _____ cut. The weight of a diamond is measured by the carat. Its purity is determined by the presence or absence of impurities, such as foreign minerals and uncrystallized carbon.

Note: From *The Flynt/Cooter Reading Inventory for the Classroom,* 3rd ed. by E. S. Flynt, & R. B. Cooter, 1998. Columbus, OH: Merrill/Prentice Hall Publishers. Used with permission.

Figure 11.6 shows a partial cloze passage constructed using an excerpt from *The Flynt/Cooter Reading Inventory for the Classroom,* 3rd ed. (Flynt & Cooter, 1998).

MAZE PASSAGES

Purpose

Maze passages (Guthrie, Seifert, Burnham, & Caplan, 1974) are a modification of cloze strategies that may be easily adapted to content classroom needs. Maze pas-sages tend to be less frustrating to students because the students have three possi-ble answers to choose from; thus, students tend to get a larger percentage of the items correct. The purpose of maze passages is otherwise identical to cloze.

Materials

You will need the textbook, a computer and word processing program, and means by which to copy the cloze passage for students.

Procedure

In our adaptation of maze, the criteria for the independent reading level is 85% or greater, the frustration level is 50 to 85%, and the instructional reading level is less than 50%. The procedure for constructing maze passages is identical to the construction of cloze passages, with the exception that, following each blank, three fill-in choices are included. One choice is a word that is the same part of speech as the missing word, but does not make sense; a second choice is usually one that does not make sense and is a different part of speech from the missing word; and the third choice is, of course, the correct choice. An example of a maze sentence follows (Berger & Berger, 1974, p. 183) using the content area of sociology and discussing the topic of conformity:

	conformist	
A straight _____	control	is the individual who has learned his
	ever	

place, has accepted it, and acts accordingly.

SELF-RATING CHECKLISTS

Purpose

Cooter and Flynt (1996) suggest that quality assessment plans should include direct student input and self-perceptions via *self-rating checklists.* Students complete a checklist matched to specific reading skills especially useful in the content area studied. Students indicate whether they feel that they are *Strong, Good, Getting by,* or *Not very strong* in the areas specified. Figure 11.7 is a sample self-rating (Cooter & Flynt, 1996, p. 45) suggested for use in an Algebra I class.

Materials

You will need to develop a checklist keyed to the basic reading/study skills needed in your content area prepared on a computer using a word processing program, an enlarged version of the checklist (overhead transparency), and copies for all students.

Procedure

Use the overhead transparency to present your checklist to students. Model several examples, demonstrating the kinds of complete responses that you wish to solicit. Then distribute the checklist for students to complete. When the students have finished, collect and analyze their self-assessments.

CONTENT AREA READING INVENTORY (CARI)

Purpose

The *Content Area Reading Inventory* (CARI) (Readence, Bean, & Baldwin, 1992; Farr, Tully, & Pritchard, 1989) is an informal reading inventory assessing whether students have learned sufficient reading/study strategies to succeed with content materials.

Figure 11.7   Self-Rating Checklist

"Reading" Algebra

Name: _____   Class Period/Block: _____

Date: _____

Part I

Directions: Rate yourself according to your ability to do the following in past mathematics classes. Please be completely honest in your assessment, as this will help your teacher to plan the kind of instruction that meets your needs.

Your ability to . . .	Strong	Good	Getting by	Not very strong
Read the introduction of a new chapter and understand what the author is saying the first time.				
Translate familiar and new mathematical symbols into spoken language.				
Translate words in story problems into mathematical symbols.				
Write daily learning log entries that describe what you have learned and how to solve problems.				
Explain mathematical processes to another person orally.				
Perform complex addition problems.				
Perform complex subtraction problems.				
Perform complex multiplication problems.				
Perform complex division problems.				
Overall, how do rate yourself as a student of mathematics?				

Part II

In the space below, please explain what you hope to be able to do as a result of taking this class.

Note: Adapted from *Teaching Reading in the Content Areas: Developing Content Literacy for All Students,* by R. B. Cooter, Jr., and E. S. Flynt, 1996, New York: Merrill/Prentice-Hall. Used with permission.

Materials

The CARI can be administered to groups of students, and typically includes three major sections (Farr et al., 1989) that assess 1) student knowledge of and ability to use common textbook components (i.e., table of contents, glossary, index) and supplemental research aids (card catalog, reference books, periodicals); 2) student knowledge of important vocabulary and skills such as context clues; and 3) comprehension skills important to understanding expository texts. For the last two sections of the CARI assessment, students are asked to read a selection from the adopted text. Readence, Bean, and Baldwin (1992) suggest contents for a CARI, which are described (and slightly adapted) below:

PART I: TEXTUAL READING/STUDY AIDS

    A. Internal Aids

       1. Table of Contents

       2. Index

       3. Glossary

       4. Chapter Introduction/Summaries

       5. Information from pictures

       6. Other aids included in the text

    B. Supplemental Research Aids

       1. Card Catalog

       2. Periodicals

       3. Encyclopedias

       4. Other relevant aids for the content area

PART II: VOCABULARY KNOWLEDGE

    A. Knowledge and recall of relevant vocabulary

    B. Use of context clues

PART III: COMPREHENSION SKILLS AND STRATEGIES

    A. Text-explicit (literal) information

    B. Text-implicit (inferred) information

    C. Knowledge of text structures and related strategies

Procedure

To develop a CARI, follow this process:

Step 1:   Choose a passage of at least three to four pages from the textbook(s) to be used. The passage selected should represent the typical writing style of the author.

Step 2:   Construct about 20 questions related to the text. Readence, Bean, and Baldwin (1989) recommend eight to ten questions for Part I, four to six questions for Part II, and seven to nine questions for Part III. We urge the use of questions based on writing patterns used in the sample selection; they should reflect the facts, concepts, and generalizations in the selection.

Step 3:   Explain to students that the CARI is not used for grading purposes, but is useful for planning teaching activities that will help them succeed. Using a minilesson kind of format, walk students through the different sections of the CARI and model responses.

Step 4:   Administer Part I first, then Parts II and III on separate day(s). It may take several sessions to work through the CARI. We recommend devoting only about 20 minutes per day to administering parts of the CARI, so that other class needs are not ignored during the assessment phase.

Readence, Bean, and Baldwin (1992) suggest the following criteria for assessing the CARI:

Percent Correct   **Text Difficulty**
86%–100%   Easy reading
64%–85%   Adequate for instruction
63% or below   Too difficult

From careful analysis of this assessment, teachers can plan special lessons to help students cope with difficult readings and internalize important information. Students can be grouped according to need for these lessons and practice strategies leading to success.

BALANCED READING PROGRAM INTERVENTIONS: DEVELOPING READERS AND WRITERS OF EXPOSITORY TEXT

Indicators That a Reader Has Learning Needs

- Poor comprehension of reading assignments, even when the student has been on-task and read the materials
- Takes an inordinate amount of time to read passages, which suggests fluency problems
- Seems to read all materials in the same way and using the same strategies (i.e., reads mathematics and social studies materials using the same strategies as when reading a novel)
- Seems to be unaware of such efficient reading strategies as skimming and scanning when searching for factual information
- Ability to persist, persevere, and stay on task (these abilities are known as "conative" factors) when reading content materials seems weak, and he easily feels defeated
- Interest, attitude, and motivation (known as "affective" factors) for reading expository materials seem low

Helping you to help students overcome the above difficulties (and others associated with expository readings) is our objective in this chapter. Following are some activities we have found helpful.

TEACHING EXPOSITORY READING SKILLS THROUGH WRITING

Purpose

Cooter and Flynt (1996), in *Teaching Reading in the Content Areas: Developing Content Literacy for All Students,* suggest that teachers utilize an *expository text pattern writing* process in helping students to become fluent readers and writers of expository text patterns and materials. The belief is that as students learn how to master the different expository text patterns as writers, they will automatically become better readers of the same types of text. As Lucy Calkins (1994) has stated, it is when students become writers that they become "insiders" and, thus, become more perceptive readers. We feel that this applies not only to narrative texts, but to expository texts, as well.

Materials

You will need examples of the expository text pattern(s) to be shared and learned, as well as the usual writing materials and word processing computer programs for this activity.

Procedure

The steps recommended by Cooter and Flynt (1996) are paraphrased and adapted as follows:

Step 1:   The teacher should learn and internalize knowledge about the various expository text patterns.

Step 2:   The teacher should teach students about expository text patterns commonly found in their textbooks.

Step 3:   The teacher should teach students to recognize and correctly identify expository text patterns in the reading materials they use in their content classes.

Step 4:   The teacher should teach students how to write summaries of their learning in content classes using the various expository text patterns.

Most teachers would intuitively move students through Step 1 through Step 4, especially those students having difficulty with content materials. But it is Step 4—learning to *write* expository texts—that causes students to actually internalize their knowledge and to become better expository text readers.

I-CHARTS

Purpose

One of the most common assignments in content classes is the research report. Theoretically, students survey informational texts in a given area (research), read and synthesize the information, then construct a written report detailing their understanding of the subject under study. Many students have a great deal of difficulty going about these activities in a logical, orderly, and sequential manner, however, leading to much frustration and confusion. Information Charts, or *I-Charts*

(Hoffman, 1992; Randall, 1996), provide a structure to help teachers guide students through these explorations. The version we share here was adapted by Randall (1996) for use in her eighth grade language arts classes. It involves three components: preparing the charts, research and notetaking using the charts, and the completion of the final product using the charts (p. 537).

Materials

You will need access to reference materials, ten copies of an I-Chart like that shown in Figure 11.8, and multiple enlarged copies of the I-Chart on poster board.

Procedure

Planning for Your Research

Topic identification and necessary skills   Students spend some time exploring topics related to the unit to be studied, brainstorming subjects of interest to them, and deciding what their individual topics might be. The teacher also offers minilessons on needed research-related skills such as skimming, scanning, paraphrasing, interviewing techniques, library skills, and how to write bibliographic entries.

Writing topic proposals   Students write their topic proposals for the teacher, including an explanation of their interest in their proposed topics. Also included is a tentative strategy for finding needed information. The teacher is then able to confer with students and/or make written suggestions to help guide them in shaping their topic proposals.

Brainstorming questions   Students generate specific questions to be answered. This is a great activity for cooperative learning groups. These questions should then be turned into *subtopics* to help students fine-tune their research efforts.

Figure 11.8   I-Chart

Student: _____   Topic/Subject: _____
Subtopic: _____
What I already know . . . _____
Bibliography #:

Other related information: _____
Important words: _____
New questions to learn about . . .

Setting up I-Charts   Provide students with about ten copies of the I-Chart. Students should write one subtopic/question at the top of each I-Chart, then complete the section titled "What I already know . . ." for each subtopic. Sometimes students may know a good deal about a topic, while at other times they may simply write "Nothing." Their I-Charts should be kept in a loose-leaf notebook for easy access during this process.

Modeling   As with all new learning experiences, it is important that students be able to see someone with expertise (the teacher, usually) modeling the task. Using the large poster board copies of the I-Chart, lead a class simulation pertaining to topics related to the unit of study. Complete each step on the I-Chart with the help of student volunteers.

Research and Notetaking

Finding resources   Randall (1996) advocates spending about a class period each day for a week in the school library. Make "house calls" (Reutzel & Cooter, 1996) on the students to make sure that each is using the I-Charts to guide his searches for information and to provide coaching as needed. Also, as homework, students should be encouraged to continue their quest for information at local public libraries, through governmental agencies that have relevant print information, and in interviews with experts.

Answering research questions   Students should have their I-Chart notebooks in front of them as they skim new information sources, pulling relevant I-Chart/subtopics as they discover information that may be pertinent to their research (Randall, 1996, p. 539). The corresponding I-Chart should be pulled out of the notebook as new information is discovered, then numbered and summarized on the I-Chart in the Bibliography section. A line should be drawn between bibliographic entries and corresponding information to keep things straight.

Making bibliographic entries   For each bibliographic entry made on the various I-Chart forms, the student should make one complete bibliographic entry on a sheet labeled "References" at the end of the notebook. This will save him from having to make the same reference repeatedly on the different I-Chart forms when a reference is used more than once.

Completing the I-Chart   As students come across "Other related information" that is of interest but is not really pertinent to the subtopic or question, they can note it in the appropriate space. Sometimes this information can be included in a research report to make the report more interesting—like adding color to a black-and-white photograph. Likewise, "Important words" related to the subject—especially unusual words previously unknown to the student—should be noted in the space provided. Sometimes these words will require further research for clarity. Finally, "New questions to learn about . . ." that have arisen as a result of the research should be noted and answered before moving on to the final product stage.

Critically evaluating research findings   Sometimes students are not able to locate authoritative sources to complete their I-Charts. If they cannot locate print information or an expert to interview, then that particular I-Chart should be abandoned

(Randall, 1996). Students should constantly evaluate whether they have accumulated enough information to consider a given I-Chart complete before moving on.

Completion of Final Products

Writing research papers   I-Charts create a natural bridge from research to outlining. They should be used (after considerable modeling by the teacher) to construct webs, traditional outlines, or structured overviews of the information. Timelines, maps, flowcharts, bar graphs, lists, and other graphic aids can also be constructed as prewriting tools to aid students in organizing facts, concepts, and generalizations. Each subtopic/I-Chart naturally becomes a category under the primary topic or generalization, with information noted in the "Bibliography" and "Important words" sections becoming concepts and facts in subordinate categories. Once an outline of the information is completed, students can begin their first drafts of their research papers.

EXPOSITORY TEXT FRAMES

Purpose

We know that students internalize reading processes on a much deeper level when they are able to apply their knowledge through writing. For example, students become much stronger readers and comprehenders of cause-and-effect-style texts when they have developed the ability to *write* cause-and-effect texts themselves. Thus, the goals of using *expository text frames* (Cudd & Roberts, 1989) are 1) to encourage the use of writing skills to enhance content area learning, 2) to review and reinforce specific content in the subject area, and 3) to familiarize students with the different ways that authors organize material.

Materials

You will need the adopted content textbook or appropriate nonfiction trade books, expository text frames (such as those shown in the assessment section of this chapter), and writing materials.

Procedure

Step 1: Model the Process

1. Write a simple paragraph organized in the pattern of the content book (i.e., collection, cause-effect, etc.).
2. Copy the sentences on strips or transparency strips.
3. Review the topic and logical order embedded in the text.
4. Have students arrange sentences in the way in which they believe the paragraph should be organized.
5. Read the paragraph aloud, letting the students suggest any necessary changes.
6. Ask students to illustrate the details of the paragraph (optional).
7. After the students are more comfortable with the organization, practice the process with more paragraphs from the text- or trade book.

Step 2: Add a Frame

1. Model the process of using the story frame with another paragraph from the text.
2. Discuss the transition and signal words used.
3. Let the students work through the rest of the process independently.
4. Ask students to illustrate the story frame (optional). Note: This can be an important visual connector for many children, especially those having reading problems.

Step 3: Optional Extensions of Story Frames

Extension A

1. Use a "reaction frame" as an extension of the story frame, letting the students respond to what they have learned.
2. When opinions are divided, the reaction frames lead nicely into group discussions for older students.
3. Reaction frames can either be used to bring in prior background with current knowledge, or they can be used to see how new information can modify or revise old conceptual ideas.

Extension B

1. Students should use the comparison and contrast frames after they have worked with other types of paragraph frames because they are more complex.
2. Make the transition to this type of frame by discussing similarities and differences in a familiar paragraph.
3. Introduce comparison and contrast frames separately for younger children.
4. Illustrations are particularly useful for comparison and contrast.

LEARNING LOGS

Purpose

One of the problems students frequently have with expository texts is monitoring their own comprehension—they often do not know what they know or don't know. Journal writing has been effective with many students, probably because it causes students to be more directly engaged with the subject being studied (Emig, 1983; Strong, 1983). *Learning logs,* as described by Commander and Smith (1996), are a form of structured journal writing that not only can aid a student's ability to gain new information from expository texts, but also can help him develop better awareness of his own comprehension (metacognition).

Materials

You will need to develop a learning log assignment sheet similar to the one shown in Figure 11.9 (adapted from Commander & Smith, 1996) that is keyed to the requirements of the unit of study. Also needed are about ten enlarged examples (overhead transparencies or on poster board) of learning log entries that conform to your expectations for students of this developmental level, for use in modeling activities.

Figure 11.9   Learning Log Assignment Sheet

What is a learning log?

This learning log assignment will help you find out more about how you learn. We all learn in many different ways—listening, doing, thinking about what we already know, and learning from others. You will be able to use all of these ways of learning in your log.

Purpose of the assignment

Your daily entries will help you to know what it is you are learning and what you still need to learn. This will also help you to be able to share what you know with other students and the teacher. You will also learn important steps in knowing more about this subject, and how to be a better student in other subjects, as well.

Grade

Here are the important procedures for using your learning log as part of your grade this term:
- All learning logs will be collected each Tuesday at the beginning of the class period. They will not be accepted late, so be sure to have it ready to turn in.
- You can make log entries either daily or every other day. It is usually easier, though, to do it daily so that you do not fall behind.
- There will be ten separate topics assigned for you to respond to in your learning log each week. They will be awarded anywhere from 0 to 10 points based on the quality of your response. How much thought you put into your answers will be an important factor in determining your grade each time.

Format

Your response to the weekly question should be from one to two pages on notebook paper, or the same number double-spaced using a 12-point "Geneva" font on the computer. Again, *quality* of ideas, not *quantity* of pages, will determine your grade on this assignment.

continued

Figure 11.9   *Continued*

Topics

Topics will be assigned each Tuesday, and your learning log entry must directly address the topic. Your response should include information from class discussions, cooperative learning activities, library assignments, presentations in the multimedia lab, and any other learning experience we have during that week.

Examples of learning logs

We will work through several learning log entries the first week to help you better understand what we are doing. Then, each Tuesday, the teacher will show you another example from the previous week's topic to better help you learn the process. The goal here is to get better at this as we go along. Please do not hesitate to ask a classmate or your teacher for help whenever you have a problem. Together we can learn a great deal this term!

Procedure

Pass out the Learning Log Assignment Sheet you created for this unit. After discussing the assignment sheet, walk students through several examples using the enlarged versions to model the thinking processes. Then distribute the first week's topic and discuss it. Follow the remaining procedure as described in the Learning Log assignment sheet example above.

READER RESPONSE JOURNALS

Purpose

Many reading authorities have indicated in recent years that students need to respond to what they read in order to move them from passive to active learning. Reader response, as it is logically called, frequently involves writing about what has been read. However, many teachers have noted that, in the beginning, students often don't know *what* to write or *how* to respond without some sort of structure. Linda Berger (1996) has developed a structure called the *reader response journal* for getting her junior high students started in more active learning.

Materials

Each student will require a notebook that can serve as his reader response journal (loose-leaf notebooks usually work best). A classroom chart, bulletin board, or handout similar to the one shown in Figure 11.10 to guide the students' early attempts at journal writing will also be needed.

Procedure

For a new chapter or unit of study, conduct usual prereading activities such as the following (see Cooter & Flynt, 1996, pp. 186–203): a structured overview, survey techniques, anticipation guides, prereading questions, semantic maps, or preview guides. Next, introduce the concept of reader response journals and share some teacher-made examples or examples from other classes the previous year. Distribute or display the information shown in Figure 11.10 and walk students through

Figure 11.10   Reader Response Journal: Guide Questions for Expository Tests

Reader Response Journal for Your Social Studies Textbook

DIRECTIONS: Skim your new chapter in social studies once using the methods we discussed in class. Then, as you carefully reread the chapter, write a journal response each day using one or more of the questions below after each five (5) pages. Date each journal entry and be sure to mention the major headings, subheadings, and new vocabulary in bold print. I will collect your journal about every five to ten school days and write back to you. Your chapter and journal should be completed by _____.

What do you notice that is new information for you?

Examples: Did you discover any cause/effect situations as you read? Could you identify a time sequence in what you read? (If so, you may want to sketch a timeline.) What key words or concepts did you come across? Can you compare and contrast with others not related to this unit that we have learned about?

What do you wonder about or question?

Examples: Do you wonder what a certain passage or paragraph might mean? (If so, which one?) Do you question if the author completely and accurately discussed one of the topics? Do you need to know more about something in the chapter to really understand it? Do you think the author may be biased? If so, why?

What do you feel?

Examples: Does any part of this section make you feel interested, confused, happy, annoyed, angry, or horrified? Which part, and why? Do you feel differently about a subject in this section than you did before? If so, why have your feelings changed? Do you want to read more about this subject? Why or why not?

What do you relate to?

Examples: Does anything in this section remind you of something from your own experience, a movie, a T.V. show, a song, or another book you have read? Talk about those ideas.

If your teacher could suggest a great book to read on this subject, such as an historical novel, would you be interested?

If so, write me a note and I'll see what I can find!

Note: Adapted from Berger, L. R. (1996). Reader response journals: You make the meaning . . . and how. *Journal of Adolescent & Adult Literacy, 39*(5).

several more examples using each of the questions and accompanying examples. Each day, conduct a five-minute minilesson in which you highlight one of the questions and relate it to the unit by answering an aspect of that question. This kind of continuous modeling will help students learn and understand the process, and the unit!

VOCABULARY BUILDING: PERSONAL WORD LISTS

Purpose

Researchers have estimated that fluent readers have recognition vocabularies of anywhere from 10,000 to 100,000 words (Nagy & Herman, 1987). Students having reading difficulties, as well as those learning English as a second language (ESL), have much smaller vocabularies—perhaps 5,000 words or fewer (Singer, 1981). This is not nearly enough for success with infrequently used or technical vocabulary. A *personal word list* (Johnson & Steele, 1996) is one strategy that a student can use to build his vocabulary, based on self-need.

Materials

In addition to the reading materials to be used in the content area unit being studied, the student will require multiple copies of the chart shown in Figure 11.11. Each student should also have a notebook in which to keep his new vocabulary for review and as an aid to his writing assignments.

Procedure

Help students put together their vocabulary notebooks using multiple sheets such as the one shown in Figure 11.11. Model the use of the notebook with a practice passage that contains useful words that are not likely already known by the

Figure 11.11   Personal Word List

New Word	What I think it means . . .	Clues from the sentence	Dictionary definition (if needed)	My definition

Note: Adapted from Johnson D., & Steele, V. (1996). So many words, so little time: Helping college ESL learners acquire vocabulary-building strategies. *Journal of Adolescent & Adult Literacy, 39*(5).

students. Demonstrate how these new "dictionaries" they are creating can be useful to them in compositions on the subject being studied, and quite likely in other assignments, as well. For the latter, however, students will need to pursue multiple meanings in the dictionary.

MAKING BIG BOOKS

Purpose

For many years, teachers have understood the value of student-made big books that summarize the content found in a unit of study. Constructing big books requires students to read, comprehend, and then "tell back" what they have learned. Big books can be especially motivating because they provide students with an opportunity to share with others what they have learned, such as when presenting their finished book to the rest of the class, or perhaps to a class of younger students. One school with which we worked in Nevada had an ongoing program wherein sixth-grade students each Friday would visit a first-grade class to share their big books and other literature response projects. This had a very positive effect on both older and younger students and stimulated much interest and reading. The following procedure is based on one offered by Snowball (1989) and is an easy-to-use version of this popular expository text response activity.

Teacher using a big book.

Materials

You will need appropriate content area books, large paper (preferably heavy construction paper), markers, crayons, paints, colored pencils, and lined and unlined paper.

Procedure

1. Select a topic from the text that is likely to stimulate interest for students. As a prereading exercise, to call to mind background knowledge about the subject, write on the chalkboard or overhead projector topic-related words that children brainstorm.

2. Ask students to describe relationships between these words and the topic, and organize the words under headings or categories. A structured overview or semantic web format will work well with this part of the lesson.

3. The first time this process is used, the class should pick one topic to write about and the teacher should model the process. After they are familiar with the process, students may choose their own topic(s) and work in groups. In this stage of writing, the students should list *what they know, what they would like to find out,* and *where they could find that information.* This step is essentially a traditional K-W-L framework.

4. Relate new information to existing information and begin writing using visual displays of information. The teacher should demonstrate how to clarify and classify information using flowcharts, headings, subheadings, etc.

5. Write a first draft of a big book that retells what the students have learned about the topic using the organization described as a guide. Early drafts should be written in pencil on 8½ × 11-inch paper, complete with sketches of illustrations to be used. We have found that this makes drafting and revising relatively quick and painless for the students.

6. Write the final draft in big-book format for presentation to others.

GROUP SUMMARIZING

Purpose

Writing summaries of what has been learned helps make learning permanent. Oftentimes, however, students don't know where to begin in creating summaries. They benefit greatly from an initial structure for organizing ideas, as well as from having these structures modeled by the "classroom writing expert" (you, the teacher)! Following is a simple structure for *group summarizing* adapted from one offered by Olson and Gee (1991).

Materials

The fundamental learning tools include well-written content books and writing materials (paper and pencil, etc.).

Procedure

Prior to reading about a subject, the class should read for descriptions of the key topic(s) for the day. The teacher then divides the chalkboard into four sections relating to the topic. For example, if you are learning about an animal (say, *alligators*), your topics might be "Description," "Food," "Home," and "Interesting Facts." As the groups read, the students can write facts on the chalkboard under the different headings. After reading the text materials carefully, the students can discuss the facts they have listed, erase any duplicates, and write the facts in complete sentences. The class can then draft a summary using the above information as a guide.

RESPONSE CHARTS

Purpose

One of the characteristics of successful readers is that they frequently self-assess what they understand or don't understand, then make adjustments as needed (e.g., rereading sections of a book that they failed to grasp). *Response charts* (Richards & Gipe, 1992) provide an initial "scaffolding" for students that helps them to perform these metacognitive reflection and self-assessment activities. Not only do response charts help students interpret expository texts, they can also help the teacher understand which areas in the curriculum need more attention for planning instruction.

Materials

Aside from content books or other instructional texts, chart paper will be needed for making the response charts. For whole class demonstrations and modeling, you will also need an overhead projector, blank transparencies, and watercolor markers.

Procedure

Using a minilesson format for instruction (remember, this series of activities will likely be spread over several sessions), begin by reading a short excerpt pertaining to the topic you wish to study. Next, explain that good readers regularly monitor their own comprehension. They ask themselves such questions as, "What do I already know about this subject?" "What did I not understand about what I just read?" "Did my mind wander as I read that last paragraph?" Explain that this kind of self-monitoring (metacognition) helps readers know when they need to take corrective actions, such as rereading that last section in which their mind wandered, so that any gaps in their learning can be filled.

Next, using a blank transparency and markers, draw a line down the middle of the transparency and write the headings YES and NO at the top (see Figure 11.12, illustrating a unit on comets). Then, using the passage you read at the beginning of the lesson for context, write under the YES column those things that the reader knows, appreciates, or understands about the topic. Explain as you go along what you know about the topic and how you chose the phrases to represent your knowl-

Figure 11.12   Response Chart

YES	NO
• mostly dirt and ice	• what makes them move?
• Halley's comet	• do they ever strike Earth?
• cause of superstitious tales	• what causes the tail?
• no life on them, most likely	• what's so special about Halley's
• have a "tail"	comet, anyway?

edge. Repeat the parallel process under the NO column, describing points from the passage that you did not understand, any dislikes or disputes, and the strategies you might use to gain the needed information (i.e., ask a friend, reread the passage, ask a designated "classroom expert," check in the library for a clearer explanation, etc.).

As your minilesson series progresses, students will read a small section of the book or text. With your guidance, they should respond to what they do and do not like or understand by filling in an individual response chart labeled "My YES and why" and "My NO and why."

TEXTBOOK ACTIVITY GUIDES

Purpose

Textbook activity guides (Noyce & Christie, 1989) help students learn ways to read strategically and understand new information found in the text.

Materials

A teacher-constructed textbook activity guide pertaining to a new unit of study is needed. Also, a copy of the textbook activity guide on transparency for the overhead projector, blank transparencies, and watercolor markers will be needed for modeling activities.

Procedure

After a thorough content analysis of the new unit of study (see chapter 12 of Reutzel & Cooter, 1996, for a full description of this process), develop questions for all major facts, concepts, and generalizations. For each question, decide whether students will best understand and retain the new knowledge through *discussion with their partner* (DP), *predicting with their partner* (PP), *writing individual responses* (WR), *preparing semantic maps* (MAP), or simply *reading the passage quickly* (SKIM). Write the appropriate abbreviation after each question as a guide to students' reading-study activities. Students should work in dyads or small groups, especially when just learning to use the guide, and should use the abbreviations to direct their efforts in discovering new information. As with all new learning strategies and processes, the first few times you use the textbook activity guide you will need to model the process.

DEFINITION WRITING
Purpose
In *definition writing,* students simply create definitions for specialized content vocabulary using their own language.

Materials
A list of words relating to the content unit being studied is needed.

Procedure
Make a list of new vocabulary words and concepts found in the new unit of study. You may want to ask students to make predictions about word meanings before reading the text in order to assess background knowledge and to focus their attention on the most important elements. After reading the text, make class dictionaries using the revised definitions.

CARTOONS
Purpose
To use *cartoons* as a creative medium for students to demonstrate their understanding of the unit of study. (Note: This activity is especially functional in social studies, literature, and science courses.)

Materials
Textbook and other learning materials, markers, crayons, paints, art paper, and cartoon examples are needed.

Procedure
Prior to reading new text materials, explain to students that they will have an opportunity to complete a text response activity in lieu of taking a traditional test (this usually grabs their interest right off!), and that the activity consists of working in small groups of two to construct a cartoon strip. The cartoon strip is to retell the important information found in the text in a creative way. If they wish, students can create a fictional situation as a context for presenting the information. Prepare and show partial examples of the kinds of products you hope to see (see Figure 11.13). Students should help you to construct an evaluation rubric prior to beginning the unit so that the expectations are clear. At the conclusion of the unit, teams will present their cartoon strips to the class. Many classes enjoy making awards for such aspects as art quality, creativity, and accuracy and completeness of information presented.

FOUR-STEP SUMMARY WRITING
Purpose
Four-step summary writing serves to help students internalize a simple procedure for summarizing information.

Figure 11.13 A Cartoon Created by a Student to Retell Key Points about a Passage

Materials

A content textbook and writing materials are needed.

Procedure

We have found the following procedure by Noyce and Christie (1989) to be easy for most students from grade five on up. (Naturally, the teacher will need to model this process and then guide students as they work in groups discussing how to do it.) It is built on these four easy steps:

Step 1: Write a topic sentence, that is, one that summarizes in general terms what the content is about. Either select one that the author has written or write your own.

Step 2: Delete all unnecessary sentences, words, and other information from the entire passage.

Step 3: After sorting all terms into categories, think of a collective term(s) for those things that fall into the same category.

Step 4: Collapse paragraphs on the same subject down to one when they are largely redundant.

REFERENCES

Alvermann, D. E., & Moore, D. W. (1991). Secondary school reading. In R. Barr, M. L. Kamil, P. B. Mosenthal, & P. D. Pearson (Eds.), *Handbook of reading research* (Vol. 2, pp. 951–983). White Plains, NY: Longman.

Armbruster, B., & Anderson, T. (1981). *Content area textbooks* (Reading Education Report No. 23). Urbana–Champaign: University of Illinois, Center for the Study of Reading.

Berger, L. R. (1996). Reader response journals: You make the meaning . . . and how. *Journal of Adolescent & Adult Literacy, 39*(5), 380–385.

Berger, P. L. (1974). *Sociology: A biographical approach.* New York: Basic Books.

Calkins, L. (1994). *The art of teaching writing* (new ed.). Portsmouth, NH: Heinemann.

Commander, N. E., & Smith, B. D. (1996). Learning logs: A tool for cognitive monitoring. *Journal of Adolescent & Adult Literacy, 39*(6), 446–453.

Cooter, R. B., Jr., & Flynt, E. S. (1996). *Teaching reading in the content areas: Developing content literacy for all students.* New York: Merrill/Prentice-Hall.

Cudd, E. T., & Roberts, L. (1989). Using writing to enhance content area learning in the primary grades. *The Reading Teacher, 42,* 392–403.

Emig, J. (1983). Writing as a mode of learning. In D. Goswami & M. Butler (Eds.), *The web of meaning: Essays on writing, teaching, learning and thinking* (pp. 122–131). Montclair, NJ: Boynton/Cook.

Farnan, N. (1996). Connecting adolescents and reading: Goals at the middle level. *Journal of Adolescent & Adult Literacy, 39*(6), 436–445.

Farr, R., Tulley, M. A., & Pritchard, R. (1989). Assessment instruments and techniques used by the content area teacher. In D. Lapp, J. Flood, & N. Farnan (Eds.), *Content area reading and learning* (pp. 346–356). Englewood Cliffs, NJ: Prentice Hall.

Flood, J., Lapp, D., & Farnam, N. (1986). A reading-writing procedure that teaches expository paragraph structure. *The Reading Teacher, 39* 556–562.

Flynt, E. S., & Cooter, R. B., Jr. (1998). *The Flynt/Cooter reading inventory for the classroom,* 3rd ed. Columbus, OH: Merrill/Prentice Hall.

Fowler, G. L. (1982). Developing comprehension skills in primary students through the use of story frames. *The Reading Teacher, 36*(2), 176–179.

Guthrie, J. T., Seifert, M., Burnham, N. A., & Caplan, R. J. (1974). The maze technique to assess and monitor reading comprehension. *The Reading Teacher, 28*(2), 161–168.

Hoffman, J. V. (1992). Critical reading/thinking across the curriculum: Using I-Charts to support learning. *Language Arts, 69,* 121–127.

Irvin, J. L., & Connors, N. A. (1989). Reading instruction in middle level schools: Results of a U.S. survey. *Journal of Reading, 32,* 306–311.

Johnson, D., & Steele, V. (1996). So many words, so little time: Helping college ESL learners acquire vocabulary-building strategies. *Journal of Adolescent & Adult Literacy, 39*(5), 348–357.

McGee, L. M., & Richgels, D. J. (1985). Teaching expository text structure to elementary students. *The Reading Teacher, 38,* 739–748.

Meyer, B. J., & Freedle, R. O. (1984). Effects of discourse type on recall. *American Educational Research Journal, 21*(1), 121–143.

Nagy, W., & Herman, P. (1987). Breadth and depth of vocabulary knowledge: Implications for acquisition and instruction. In M. McKeown & M. Curtis (Eds.), *The nature of vocabulary acquisition* (pp. 19–35). Hillsdale, NJ: Erlbaum.

Nichols, J. (1980). Using paragraph frames to help remedial high school students with written assignments. *Journal of Reading, 24,* 228–231.

Noyce, R. M., & Christie, J. F. (1989). *Integrating reading and writing instruction.* Boston: Allyn and Bacon.

Olson, M. W., & Gee, T. C. (1991). Content reading instruction in the primary grades: Perceptions and strategies. *The Reading Teacher, 45,* 298–306.

Randall, S. N. (1996). Information charts: A strategy for organizing student research. *Journal of Adolescent & Adult Literacy, 39*(7), 536–542.

Readence, J. E., Bean, T. W., & Baldwin, R. S. (1992). *Content area reading:* *An integrated approach* (4th ed.). Dubuque, IA: Kendall/Hunt.

Reutzel, D. R., & Cooter, R. B. (1996). *Teaching children to read: From basals to books* (2nd ed.). New York: Merrill/Prentice-Hall.

Richards, J. C. & Gipe, J. P. (1992) Activating background knowledge: Strategies for beginning and poor readers. *The Reading Teacher, 45,* 474–475.

Romine, B. G., McKenna, M. C., & Robinson, R. D. (1996). Reading coursework requirements for middle and high school content area teachers: A U.S. survey. *Journal of Adolescent & Adult Literacy, 40*(3), 194–198.

Simpson, M. (1996). Conducting reality checks to improve students' strategic learning. *Journal of Adolescent & Adult Literacy, 40*(2), 102–109.

Singer, H. (1981). Instruction in reading acquisition. In O. Tzeng & H. Singer (Eds.), *Perception of print* (pp. 291–311). Hillsdale, NJ: Erlbaum.

Snowball, D. (1989). Reading and writing in the content areas. *The Reading Teacher, 43,* 266–270.

Strong, W. (1983). Writing: A means to meaning or how I got from the Tastee Donut Shop to the Inn of the Seventh Mountain. *English Journal, 72,* 34–37.

Chapter 12

Connecting Reading and Writing

Reading and writing are two sides of the same coin, or, put another way, they are *reflections* of the same language process (Squire, 1983). Reading is a *receptive* language process in that the reader *receives* the message of a writer for mental processing. Writing, on the other hand, is a *productive* language process such that the author is *producing* a message to be interpreted later by a reader. Reading and writing are even more closely linked than one might think initially, however. This point is further examined later in this chapter in a discussion on teacher knowledge base. In addition, the chapter focuses on specific ways of measuring writing development. Further, it includes suggestions for activities that help foster the strengthening of reading and writing processes simultaneously.

BACKGROUND BRIEFING FOR TEACHERS: WRITING CONNECTIONS TO READING

Reading and writing are reciprocal processes (Goodman & Goodman, 1983; Shanahan, 1984): when teachers build students' skills in one process, the other tends to be strengthened, as well. For example, when students act in the role of writer they also act as readers, since "writers must read, and reread during writing" (Goodman & Goodman, 1983, p. 591). Similarly, when students read, they often notice and learn aspects of writing from the author, such as writing styles, interesting phrases, ways to write dialog, new vocabulary, and methods of punctuation. Lucy Calkins (1994) has stated that one of the great benefits of writing process instruction for students is that it helps them feel like "insiders" or peers with their favorite authors. Tompkins (1994), in summarizing research pertaining to reading-writing connections, concludes

> Reading and writing are both meaning-making processes, and experience with one process provides a scaffold or framework to support the learning of the other . . . . Frank Smith (1983) reminds us that, in order for students to be writers, they must read like writers.(p. 2)

Assessing Writing Development

At least two writing assessment perspectives are commonly thought of when analyzing student compositions: *qualitative* (also known as *descriptive*) and *quantitative* (also known as *numerical*). Each will be briefly described, along with other ideas and an instrument useful in writing assessment.

Qualitative Assessment

Qualitative assessments use written summaries rather than numbers in assessing student work samples. Descriptive assessment is anecdotal in nature, meaning that teachers make "field notes" on a student's work during classroom writing activities which are later placed into the student's portfolio. Additionally, teachers summarize their impressions of student writing samples gathered during learning experiences. By accumulating informal classroom observations and analyses of writing samples over time, teachers develop a more complete picture of students' development in writing.

Purpose

Teachers compile written observations and interpretations of student accomplishments in writing that may be used in conjunction with other pieces of assessment evidence (i.e., quantitative measures) to form a more complete understanding of students' writing development.

Materials

Materials needed are a legal pad for notetaking by the teacher and student work samples.

Procedure

It is very difficult to describe in specific terms how best to carry out this form of assessment; nevertheless, we do have a few suggestions to offer based on our own experiences. Qualitative assessments are based on a thorough understanding of writing development coupled with classroom experience. Many teachers accustomed to performing qualitative writing assessments in their classrooms try to identify two students per day whom they will observe during writing activities (do not alert these students that they are the ones being studied). This permits most teachers to observe each student about once every two weeks or so. At the end of the day the teacher reviews the classroom observations, along with work samples collected by students in their writing folders, and attempts to draw some conclusions as to students' development.

Writing development may be said to encompass several broad abilities, including the capacity to transmit messages effectively and an understanding of the basic mechanics of writing. In the first aspect of writing development, students gain an understanding of the writing process: prewriting, drafting, revising, editing, and sharing or publishing. The mechanics of writing involve such aspects as spelling, punctuation, and appropriate use of reference materials. Of course, students' relative ability in each of these areas varies a great deal and is, by definition, developmental (one gets better at these skills with practice). The best advice we can offer is for teachers to read extensively about the writing process, then meet with colleagues to develop a kind of writing development checklist(s) to help in monitoring student progress. We find that Gail Tompkins' (1994) book titled *Teaching Writing: Balancing Process and Product* is an excellent resource for gaining basic information about the writing process and for developing writing observation checklists.

QUANTITATIVE ASSESSMENT: HOLISTIC SCORING

Quantitative assessments use numbers rather than words to describe student development and performance in writing. There are at least two forms of quantitative assessment: *holistic* and *analytic*. These two forms are closely related, with the chief difference being that holistic scoring seems to work best with a single criterion, while analytic scoring is intended for multiple criteria. In all instances, students should understand the assessment criteria for which they are being held accountable.

Purpose

To develop relatively objective measures of writing products using a numerical system.

Materials

An assessment form that includes a numerical scale for each criterion and student work samples such as that shown in Figure 12.1.

Procedure

Probably the most convenient way to conduct a quantitative assessment is for teachers to first construct an assessment instrument. This makes the process much more time efficient when trying to review more than one work sample. Since only one criterion is being assessed, all that is required is a place for the student's name, date, the criterion specified, and a numerical scale (usually 1 to 5) to rate student performance using the writing skill. *In group settings, we recommend that teachers read all of the student compositions once without grading to get a feel for the range of development in the class before assigning numerical values to each paper.*

Figure 12.1 shows an example of an assessment form for emergent writers in a first-grade classroom focusing on students' use of temporary spellings (also called *invented spellings*) with at least beginning and ending sounds.

QUANTITATIVE ASSESSMENT: ANALYTIC SCORING

As mentioned above, analytic scoring methods are essentially holistic scoring systems for *multiple* criteria. Analytic scoring systems add a "weight" dimension for each criterion being measured, since the criteria tend to be of unequal value. For example, let's say a fifth-grade teacher has been teaching minilessons on *commas correctly, developing characters more fully* in student-created stories, and com-

Figure 12.1   Sample Holistic Scoring Form for Writing: Single Criterion

Student's name: _____					
Date: _____					
Criterion:					
	Not used				Used a great deal
Temporary (invented) spellings: Beginning and ending sounds	1	2	3	4	5
Comments/observations:					

pleting a *prewriting outline or web* before writing a first draft. Let's also assume that, in this instance, the teacher feels that correct usage of commas is not quite as important (or as challenging) as is developing characters more fully. Further, if the teacher feels that developing characters more fully is more important than completing a prewriting outline or web (perhaps because her students have been creating webs and outlines since second grade, and the focus on characters is a newly introduced skill), then the weighting used in scoring a work sample will reflect that priority, as well. In any event, it is easy to see that the teacher feels that certain writing skills are somewhat more important or challenging than others.

When multiple criteria are being used in writing assessment, the teacher usually assigns a weighted value of "1" to the least important skill, "2" for the more important skill, and "3" for the next most important skill. As mentioned previously, the numerical scale frequently ranges from a low rate of 1 to a high rate of 5. Thus, for our example the following assigned weights would apply:

Writing Skill/Criteria	Relative Weight or Value
Using commas correctly	1
Developing characters more fully	3
Prewriting outline or web	2

These teacher-determined weights are to be multiplied by the holistic scoring value (1–5) arrived at in the same way as described in the previous section on holistic scoring for a single criterion (i.e., a score of 1 to 5 is given based on the quality of the student's work on that criterion, say using commas correctly). Figure 12.2 presents an assessment form based on the above example. (Note that the figure for "Total possible points" (30) is arrived at by first multiplying the maximum possible score of 5 for each skill by the weighted value, then adding the total possible scores [5 + 10 + 15 = 30]).

Figure 12.2   Analytic Writing Assessment Form Using Three Criteria

Student's name: _____

Date: _____

Criteria

	Not used				Used a great deal		Weighted value		Total points
Using commas correctly	1	2	3	4	5	×	1	=	_____
Developing characters more fully	1	2	3	4	5	×	3	=	_____
Prewriting outline or web	1	2	3	4	5	×	2	=	_____

A. Total points for assignment   _____

B. Total possible points   30

C. Percentage of points achieved (A divided by B)   _____

Comments/observations:

OTHER ACTIVITIES FOR ASSESSING READING-WRITING CONNECTIONS

In addition to the quantitative and qualitative strategies mentioned previously, the following activities have value as both assessment and writing activities. These activities remind us that good assessment is frequently synonymous with good teaching.

STORY PYRAMIDS

An activity popularized by teachers in the Rio Grande Valley area of south Texas is the *story pyramid*. It combines the use of story grammars as a means for assessing reading comprehension in narrative passages with writing (vocabulary knowledge) assessment. Story pyramids are interesting and simple to use, yet powerful in their assessment potential.

Purpose

The assessment purpose of story pyramids is twofold. First, they require students to recall key information from stories using a modified story grammar scheme (main character, setting, problem, attempts to solve the problem, and solution). Next, students are asked to survey their vocabulary knowledge to find just the right word or words to report the story grammar information in the pyramid.

Materials

The materials needed include paper and pen or pencil, one sheet of poster board, and a narrative book recently read by the student.

Procedure

Teachers usually create a poster or bulletin board depicting a pyramid, such as the one shown in the photograph. It should show the required information needed in a story pyramid and an example based on a book shared during a read aloud experience. The one in the adjacent photograph uses the book *Sally's Room* (Brown, 1992). The following information and pattern for writing are used in the story pyramid:

Line 1:   One word for who the story is about (main character)

Line 2:   Two words describing the main character

Line 3:   Three words describing the setting

Line 4:   Four words stating the problem

Line 5:   Five words describing an event in the story

Line 6:   Six words describing an event in the story

Line 7:   Seven words describing an event in the story

Line 8:   Eight words describing the final solution

This activity not only assesses reading comprehension and vocabulary knowledge, but also encourages economy of language when students compose.

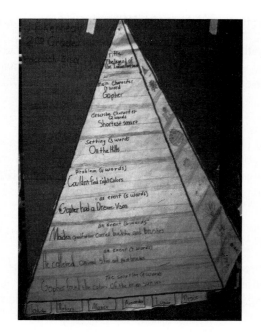

FLIP MOVIES

Flip movies is an activity suggested for assessing students' understanding of a book by having them illustrate and bind a series of scenes together from a story. Flipping through the scenes quickly simulates the action (Pike, Compain, & Mumper, 1994). In our version of this activity, students create a series of pictures and captions that summarize a key story event. Flipping through the book quickly simulates scrolling text that retells part of the story.

Purpose

Flip movies assess students' ability to retell key events in a story using written captions matched to illustrations.

Materials

The student will need a book that she read recently. In addition, you will need to collect the following art materials in order for students to make flip movies:

5″ × 8″ index cards

Writing and illustrating materials

Drawing paper cut to a rectangular pattern of about 3″ × 8″

Access to a photocopier machine

Book-binding tape or a heavy-duty stapler

Procedure

Students begin by choosing a key event in a story that they read recently. Next, they create a single illustration of the setting and characters depicting this key event. The illustration should not be colored in at first, but created to look much like an uncolored coloring book page on a single sheet of 3″ × 8″ paper. On a separate sheet of paper (this can be a "messy copy") the student should write a caption that describes the key event. For example, a student who read *Polar Express* (Van Allsburg, 1985) might draw an illustration depicting the child in the story receiving a bell from Santa's sleigh at the North Pole. Perhaps the caption reads "Santa handed the sleigh bell to me!" Next, take the single uncolored illustration and make the same number of photocopies of the illustration as there are words in the caption. (In our example above, the teacher would make seven copies of the student's illustration, since there are seven words in the caption). The copies of the illustration are then given to the student so that the final phase can be completed.

Next, students carefully trim each photocopy of the illustration to match the size of the original (3″ × 8″) and color each one as desired, making sure to use the same color scheme on each photocopy to produce identical copies. Next, glue each illustration to the upper portion of 5″ × 8″ index cards so that the student now has multiple identical copies of the illustration mounted on index cards. On the first card, the student writes only the *first* word in the caption. She writes the first *two words* of the caption on the second card, the first *three words* of the caption on the third card, and so on. After this process is complete and the cards have been bound together using binding tape or heavy-duty staples, the pages in the flip book can be slowly thumbed through so that the text appears to scroll out across the bottom of the page word by word until the full sentence has appeared. Older students may want to alter this activity, slightly changing the illustrations so that the flipping action simulates movement in the illustration.

COAT-HANGER MOBILES

Coat-hanger mobiles are easy to construct and are an inventive way to combine reader response with writing. Students create illustrations and captions depicting important bits of information from a book they have read. Then, as a form of "publishing," these information bits are displayed on a common coat hanger that is hung from the ceiling as a mobile in the classroom. Coat-hanger mobiles work well with both narrative and expository texts.

Purpose

This activity is useful as a quick assessment of key ideas understood by the student after reading, and as an indirect assessment of descriptive vocabulary in writing (likewise, the acquisition of technical vocabulary in expository books).

Materials

A coat-hanger mobile can be constructed using a wire coat hanger (preferably one that has been coated in colored plastic), string or dark thread, a sheet of poster or tag board, assorted color markers for illustrating and writing captions, and a book that the child has recently read.

Procedure

Using the poster board, ask the student to create at least five illustrations and captions representing key ideas or events found in the book she has recently completed. Students often like to make the illustrations in the shapes of characters, settings, or objects that pertain to the book. Remind them that they will need to illustrate both sides of each shape so that, as the mobile turns, the illustration can be read from any direction. Have students attach each illustration/caption to their coat hanger using thread or string as shown in Figure 12.3. Once it is completed, hang the mobile from the ceiling or from a light fixture.

A CHECKLIST FOR MIDDLE SCHOOL WRITING PROGRAMS

Checklists help teachers maximize the efficiency of their contact time with students because of the checklist's built-in organization and structure. You should be aware, however, that, while checklists may be useful in many situations, they are certainly

Figure 12.3 A Coat-Hanger Mobile

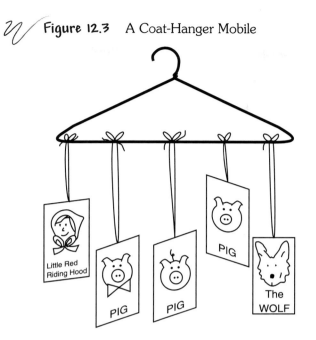

no panacea in writing assessment. In fact, they have somewhat limited use. But, Gail Tompkins (1994), in her book *Teaching Writing: Balancing Process and Product,* offers a number of checklists that we believe teachers find useful. In this section we offer an adaptation of a Tompkins checklist that can be of general use in the middle school.

Purpose

This activity is intended for the assessment of student compositions in order to review their understanding of stages of the writing process.

Materials

A copy of the writing process checklist shown in Figure 12.4 is needed.

Procedure

As the teacher reviews samples kept in students' writing folders, she notes on the checklist evidence of the various writing process activities. Many teachers also note dates when different writing process activities were done. The result is that teachers can determine which writing process activities are being used by class members, and which are not. Thus, the teacher can identify the writing skills that may be needed by some or all of the class members. Figure 12.4 offers a general form for this purpose.

Figure 12.4   Writing Process Checklist Form

Writing Process Checklist: Middle School

Name: _____
Date of writing folder review: _____
Title(s) of compositions: _____

Writing Process Stages and Activities

PREWRITING

1. Student develops a list of possible topics that are of high interest to him/her.

   _____

2. An organizational web or outline is constructed.

   _____

3. Student conducts research to gather necessary facts and information.

   _____

DRAFTING

4. Student produces one or more drafts before the final version.

   _____

5. Drafts are double- or triple-spaced to allow for editorial comments.

   _____

6. Evidence demonstrates that the student is more interested in ideas and content, rather than mechanics at this stage.

   _____

REVISING

7. Student shares the composition with others to obtain useful suggestions.

   _____

8. A new draft of the paper is generated incorporating suggestions offered by peers.

   _____

EDITING

9. Student again reviews composition, looking for ways to improve the mechanics of the piece (e.g., spelling, punctuation, etc.).

   _____

10. After improvements have been made mechanically, the student meets with the teacher for a writing conference.

   _____

SHARING

11. Student produces a final copy suitable for sharing.

   _____

12. An appropriate way of sharing the piece is chosen and carried out (e.g., author's chair, publication area in classroom or library, publishing in the school newspaper, others as appropriate).

   _____

Note: Adapted from *Teaching Writing: Balancing Process and Product* by G. E. Tompkins, 1994, New York: Merrill.

BALANCED READING PROGRAM INTERVENTIONS: DEVELOPING READERS AS AUTHORS

Indicators That Readers Have Learning Needs

- Student has limited written language abilities (i.e., incomplete sentences as the norm, unsophisticated vocabulary, etc.).
- Student has spelling difficulties, coupled with difficulties in decoding unknown words in print while reading.
- Student may demonstrate comprehension difficulties when reading expository (nonfiction) texts.
- Student may demonstrate comprehension difficulties when reading narrative (story) texts.

THE WRITING BRIEFCASE

The *writing briefcase* (Miller-Rodriguez, 1992) is a wonderful idea that helps parents become more involved with their child's literacy learning. In our interpretation of this activity, students periodically take home a briefcase containing materials helpful in the creation of new compositions. We see the writing briefcase as especially useful for emergent writers and readers in the early grades.

Purpose

To involve parents in their child's literacy learning in the home environment and to offer them ideas for assisting in the learning process.

Materials

You will need an old briefcase (a backpack works just as well), stickers and other decorations for the outside of the briefcase, a laminated letter to the family member, markers, crayons, magazine pictures, word cards, picture dictionary, index cards, lined and unlined paper, tape, stapler, paper clips, rubber bands, scissors, and any other writing and illustrating materials of your choice, as well as easy-to-read books of various kinds that might inspire different text types (e.g., poetry, songs, stories, etc.).

Procedure

A different child takes home the briefcase each night and writes (or completes, in some cases) a story and illustrates it. She also reads her story, as well as the other books enclosed, to family members. A letter included in the briefcase is directed to family members explaining the activity and the importance of their involvement. This letter ideally serves as a follow-up refresher course on the writing and other literacy-learning processes previously described by the teacher at the beginning of the school year in a parent meeting expressly held for that purpose. Figure 12.5 is a sample letter to family members.

W **Figure 12.5**   Sample Letter For the Writing Briefcase

Sarah Cannon School
711 Opry Place
Nashville, TN 37211

Dear Family Member:

Children in our class are becoming more and more interested and excited about their abilities as writers and readers. I am interested in helping them realize that writing and reading are not just school activities, but are also skills they can use and enjoy at home and in other places.

This writing briefcase allows your child to experience writing at home using the different tools enclosed. I'd like for you to encourage your child to create a story, poem, song, recipe, rap, or any other composition. You might want to encourage him or her to take the briefcase and write outside, perhaps in a favorite hiding place.

Please allow him or her to try out the enclosed materials. It would be especially helpful if you would take time to listen to your child's finished products. The product may not look like a story or other composition, but you will find that he or she can read and understand it. Please have your child return his or her written composition, along with the writing briefcase, tomorrow.

Sincerely,

Finally, students may wish to have their own writing briefcase or backpack that they can use throughout the year in which to take their compositions and writing materials home. Some students like to emulate adults by "taking work home from the office."

T-Shirts and Tapestries

Students love to make their own T-shirts and tapestries that display something of interest to the student (Pike, Compain, & Mumper, 1994). T-shirts and tapestries are easy to construct and can relate to such things as a student's soccer team, club memberships, favorite book characters, musical groups, or family members. Also, they are great for students who enjoy creating illustrations to accent their writing. Because the text that can appear on either a T-shirt or tapestry is limited by space, students must work with teachers to discover just the right words and thus to develop brevity in written communications.

Purpose

Making T-shirts or tapestries that include illustrations and captions helps students develop brevity in written communications. This activity may also be linked to the usage of such writing tools as the dictionary and thesaurus.

Materials

The materials needed include a plain white T-shirt in the student's size or a sheet of cloth suitable for a tapestry, as well as fabric crayons or paints or liquid embroidery.

Procedure

It is best to begin by having students develop a diagram of their T-shirt or tapestry on paper. The usual steps in the writing process are quite helpful (prewriting, drafting, revising, editing). If this activity is used in a classroom setting, students should be encouraged to take part in peer conferences to share and refine their ideas.

Once the idea has been finalized and approved by the teacher, walk through the steps in creating T-shirt designs or tapestries. If a family member is available who has artistic expertise, by all means put him or her to work teaching the student(s) art skills! Finally, students use the liquid embroidery or fabric crayons or paints to create their final products, as shown in Figure 12.6. "Publishing" is accomplished as students wear their T-shirts or their display tapestries in a place of honor.

TRAVELS OF YOUR FAVORITE STUFFED ANIMAL (OR CLASS MASCOT)

A popular idea with early elementary students, this activity encourages students to write a story about the adventures (usually the student's own experiences that day) of their favorite stuffed animal through the school day, or of a class mascot on an imaginary adventure (Wiseman, 1992).

Figure 12.6   Student-Made T-Shirt

Purpose

The idea is to encourage students to write a creative composition about an imaginary journey or adventure taken by a stuffed animal.

Materials

In order to create an example for students to see, we recommend that you obtain a copy of the book *The Velveteen Rabbit* (Williams, 1922, 1958) and a stuffed animal—preferably one that is showing signs of wear—or a class mascot in the form of a stuffed animal.

Materials needed include the usual writing materials favored by students (markers and crayons), as well as magazine pictures, word cards, picture dictionary, index cards, lined and unlined paper, tape, stapler, paper clips, rubber bands, and scissors. Possibly, these supplies could be collected in a writing briefcase as outlined earlier in the chapter.

Procedure

Begin by reading and discussing *The Velveteen Rabbit* with student(s). Talk about how stuffed animals often seem real to us and how it is fun to fantasize about how our stuffed friends might have real adventures. Bring in a stuffed toy to serve as a class mascot (Wiseman, 1992), such as a teddy bear, and talk about how students could write stories about him—either real-life situations that may take place at school, or fictitious adventures we might choose to create, like the author of *The Velveteen Rabbit* did. You might wish to choose a stuffed friend that is in some disrepair. For example, if an eye is missing, ask the children to create a story about how that could have happened.

Using a large tablet on an easel, begin an outline of the story the children are helping to generate, which will then be fashioned into a story following a kind of language experience format. Next, ask the children to bring in stuffed animals of their own on the following day to write about and share with the class. If a child does not have a stuffed animal, then let her use the class mascot. Completed stories, along with the associated stuffed animal friends, can be displayed in the classroom or school library as part of the publishing process.

SELL-A-BRATION

This activity helps students develop an understanding of persuasive writing (propaganda) strategies used by advertisers through reading and reviewing commercials in print and other media forms, then constructing their own ad campaigns using the writing process.

Purpose

To teach students about persuasive writing while also inspiring interest in reading books, magazines, and other text forms they have not previously considered.

Materials

Materials needed include a variety of magazines and newspapers, video clips recorded on VHS/VCR tape from television commercials* for popular products, radio commercials* recorded on cassette tape, a videocassette recorder/player and television, and a cassette tape player/recorder.

Procedure

Prepare a minilesson about how persuasive writing strategies are used to sell necessities (such as soap, food products, clothing) and nonnecessities (such as computer games, sodas, and designer clothes). Conduct a classroom discussion about specific strategies used in advertising and the common features of each. A comparison grid such as the one shown in Figure 12.7 may be helpful for compare/contrast discussions.

Depending on the age group, you may need to talk about what would or would not be appropriate ways to sell things in your classroom. Some teachers appoint an advertising review committee made up of students who decide whether material is appropriate.

Have students review materials and make notes about the types of advertising strategies used. One strategy sometimes used in persuasive writing involves the use

Figure 12.7   Comparison Grid: Persuasive Writing/Propaganda Types and Examples

Prop. type/ Example	Cigarette ads	Sports car ads	Political ads	Student's choice
Image-makers	Cowboys, athletic-looking people	Racing image, sexy, etc.	Fight-for-right image	
Bandwagon	"Liberated women do it!"	"Join the 'new generation'"	"Come along with us and elect ____."	
Testimonial	(No longer used)	Famous racers	Person-on-the-street testimonials	
Plain folks	Farmers, cowboys, soldiers	Not appropriate to image desired	"I'm just a country lawyer . . . ."	
Name comparisons	"If you *like* Marlboro, then you'll *love* . . . ."	"Audi outperforms Porsche and BMW . . . ."	"Like Lincoln, our candidate stands for . . . ."	

* Permissions required by copyright laws should be secured from companies involved, if applicable. Consult a reference librarian in your locale or the U.S. copyright office in Washington, DC, for restrictions that may apply.

of humor (for instance, TV commercials for the fruit juice Tropicana Twisters, and many of the local commercials for automobile dealerships).

Finally, have students use the writing process to write their own commercials for real or created products. They might also write commercials for their favorite books read during Self-Selected Reading (SSR) periods. The commercials should be presented or performed for the class as a publishing/sharing experience.

Pen Pals

One of the most tried-and-true ways of helping students to become writers on a regular basis is to match them with *pen pals*. Pen pals use informal writing as a vehicle for communicating with others (Harste, Short, & Burke, 1988). The idea is to pair students for an ongoing written dialogue. Pen pals may be matched within the school, the district, other states, or even different nations. For example, students in Virginia may enjoy a dialogue with students in Hawaii. In one university-public school collaboration (Hunter, 1996), students are establishing pen pals over the Internet using e-mail. Opportunities to compare and contrast such real-life differences in cultures, weather patterns, geography, and youth pastimes naturally arise from having written discussions with pen pals.

Purpose

Pen pals provide students with authentic purposes and motivations for ongoing written dialogues with peers. Pen pals also provide a logical instructional link between teachers and students as students realize the need to communicate with others effectively in writing.

Materials

For this activity, writing center materials for final drafts—writing paper, envelopes, pens, and stamps—will be needed, as well as a pen pals list obtained from a cooperative teacher willing to serve as your counterpart and link with other student(s). One idea is to ask the other teacher to serve as *your* pen pal so that these communications can be used for minilessons with the students. Transparency-making equipment and materials for the construction of overhead projector examples of each of the writing process stages as they pertain to the composition of letters are also quite useful.

Procedure

We recommend that pen pals begin with a letter of interest by the collaborating teacher of the other students. This letter should be carefully crafted to appeal to the mutual interests of the students involved, including specific suggestions for the first letter to be sent (such as the desire for a photograph, description of personal interests and friends, family information, etc.), suggested pairings of students (usually of the same gender, but not required), and a target date for first letters to be sent. A schedule for mailing pen pal letters should be constructed so that each participant receives a letter soon after mailing one.

For teachers, pen pals provide an instructional purpose and vehicle for minilessons pertaining to the writing process. Such minilesson themes as topic selection/brainstorming, research and organization of ideas, format for personal letters, writing first drafts, revision and editing, and preparation of final drafts are just a few of the possibilities. Student-selected samples from letter drafts may become part of the student's assessment portfolio.

EDUCATION MAJOR PEN PALS

Education major pen pals (Flickenger, 1991) is a slight variation on the pen pals theme described above that has met with great success in many areas. Its only substantive difference is that, instead of pairing students with other students or peers, education major pen pals matches students (usually elementary level) with students majoring in education at a local college or university. A final book project based on the elementary student is completed jointly between the youngster and the university student.

Purpose

In addition to providing an audience and reason for writing, this form of pen pals gives students other motivational reasons for reading: the anticipation and receiving of letters, personalized books, or other compositions from the student teachers. Education students are likewise given opportunities as new professionals to connect with students in a way that offers valuable insights.

Materials

Begin by obtaining a list of education majors interested in working with your students. This may be obtained from a local college or university professor (usually specializing in reading, literacy and/or language arts education) interested in such a project. Materials needed include writing center materials for final drafts of letters, such as writing paper, envelopes, pens, and stamps; bookmaking materials, such as laminating materials, stiff cardboard for book covers, and art materials for illustrations; first draft (messy copy) writing materials (paper and pencils) for the elementary students; transparency-making equipment and materials for the construction of overhead projector examples of each of the writing process stages as they pertain to the composition of letters; and, if possible, a word processor/computer (such as Macintosh, IBM, etc.) on which students can type letters and other compositions.

Procedure

This activity is essentially the same as with the standard pen pals activity, except that students correspond with student teachers attending education classes at the local college or university. Students in early elementary grades are encouraged to use invented (we prefer the term "temporary") spellings. Elementary students are encouraged to talk and/or draw about families, interests, friends, and special events taking place in their lives at school and at home.

One expectation, which takes the form of a book project, is that university students write books (text only) for their pen pals using what they have learned about their pen pals' interests. The university students bind the nearly finished books, but leave room on each page for illustrations. Then, the elementary students illustrate their personalized books and send them back to the university students. After making one or more copies of the finished books, the university students return the original books to their pen pals.

An additional teacher education benefit is that university students are able to use the letters and other compositions written by their pen pals for analysis of writing development and discovery of children's learning.

"Siskel and Ebert" (Movie Reviews)

One fun way for students to practice analytical reading skills and persuasive writing abilities is through *movie reviews*. In this activity, students read movie reviews and learn about writing styles used by critics, then construct reviews of movies they have recently seen.

Purpose

The movie review activity enables students to practice analytical reading skills, summarization abilities, and persuasive writing skills.

Materials

Collect several copies of past movie reviews, usual writing process materials, and blank comparison grids for compare/contrast.

Procedure

Conduct a minilesson series reviewing a current or popular movie that most students will be aware of and for which reviews can be found. In your minilesson, begin by first reviewing and summarizing the story line through discussions with the students. Next, produce several (3 or 4) authentic movie reviews of the selected film that can be read with the class, either using overhead transparencies or photocopies for students. Organize the differing points of view by completing a blank comparison grid on the chalkboard or on an overhead transparency, then discuss different perspectives and writing styles that each critic seems to use. Next, construct a prewriting outline from information contained on the grid. Finally, draft a new movie review of your own, mimicking the style of your favorite critic. At the conclusion of the minilessons, have each student write a review of a film that he or she has recently seen. The reviews can be displayed on a bulletin board dedicated to the cinema or compiled in a special edition class newspaper.

Capsulization Guides (Summarization)

In this activity, students create their own stories from brief, teacher-created summaries of short books called *capsulization guides* (Gauthier, 1989). Students then read the actual stories and compare.

Purpose

Using capsulization guides helps students learn and practice summarization and writing process skills.

Materials

Writing process materials, short books that the class has not heard before, and teacher- or student-generated capsulation guides are the essential materials for this activity.

Procedure

Step 1:   *Choose a story or other form of text and write a summary or "capsulization guide."* Select a relatively short story or other text type (such as a nonfiction piece pertaining to science or social studies) and write a brief summary (also known as a *capsulization guide*) about the piece. For example, for the story *Gila Monsters Meet You at the Airport* (Sharmat, 1980), your capsulization guide might read: "A boy from New York City is moving to the West with his family. He talks about all the bad things he has imagined about the West and why he won't like living there." The capsulization guide may either be written by the teacher or, better yet, by another student from a different class or grade level. Once you have done this activity with students, you will begin to build a library of capsulization guides.

Step 2:   *Share the capsulization guide with your students and ask them to write a composition.* After reading the capsulization guide with your students, ask them to write their own stories by expanding the information provided in the capsulization guide. Students should be expected to use writing process skills appropriate to their levels.

Step 3:   *Have students share their compositions with peers.* Once compositions are completed, ask students to share their works with a group of students in an "author's chair" format or in pairs.

Step 4:   *Share the original story or nonfiction text.* Now, read the full text of the original story or nonfiction text to the students. Compare and contrast the compositions that students constructed to the original version and discuss similarities and differences. For stories (narratives), it might be helpful to use a story grammar comparison grid such as the one shown in Figure 12.8.

Step 5:   *Have students write their own capsulization guides.* As a final activity, have students select short books or passages of their own and write capsulization guides. Acting as the teacher, they can then be paired with a peer and repeat the cycle above using their own capsulization guides.

THE ILLUSTRATOR'S CRAFT

The *illustrator's craft* encourages students to read and learn all that they can about a favorite illustrator, to create a composition reporting what they have learned, and then to share their report with the illustrator (optional).

Figure 12.8   Story Grammar Comparison Table

	Original story	Your story
Setting		
Characters		
Problem(s)		
Attempts to solve problems		
Conclusion/Resolution		
Theme/Moral		

Purpose

The illustrator's craft activity is intended to cause students to read, use the writing process as a summary tool for the investigation, and then share results with peers. Communications with illustrators may also help students see the importance and purposes of letter-writing skills.

Materials

Materials needed include several books with the same illustrator, writing materials, addresses of the illustrators (optional), and materials such as markers, paints, and colored pencils for making a diary or journal.

Procedure

Spend time with your students discussing different illustrators and looking at some of their work. Tell an interesting fact about each illustrator you have chosen for these activities, in order to show something of the human side and motivations of the illustrators. For example, Rachel Isadora wrote and illustrated a Caldecott

Honor book called *Opening Night* (1984), a story that grew out of her experience as a professional ballerina.

After students select an illustrator whom they would like to learn more about, have them design a portfolio of the illustrator's best work from favorite books. The portfolio might include discussions from the student's perspective as to why this is the illustrator's best work. Students could be creative in their presentation by adding captions to the illustrations or by writing a diary of the illustrator. Students should do some research into the illustrators, exploring how they create their illustrations, settings in which they like to work, and/or what was happening in the world at the time that might have influenced their work. After the portfolio is finished, have students make a copy and send it, along with a letter, to the illustrator.

An alternate version of this activity might be to have students review artwork by older high-school students, to find one person's work they like, and then to interview that person. They could also construct a portfolio of the high-school student's work and present it to the class.

WRITING CONNECTIONS WITH BOOKS AND OTHER TEXTS

CLASSROOM CHARACTERS

Classroom characters (Adams, 1991) has students corresponding with a book character whom they are getting to know during a daily read-aloud activity conducted by the teacher. Letters written to the character are mailed using a classroom mailbox, then the character's response comes back the next class meeting either in the form of a letter, or through cartoonlike "bubble" responses appearing on a special bulletin board depicting the character.

Purpose

The classroom character activity is intended to interest students in writing and reading through interaction with a classroom character, providing a perceived audience for writing.

Materials

Many teachers use a character-for-the-month who appears in a book the student or class has read, letters and stories from the character to the students (provided secretly by older buddy students or the teacher), a bulletin board featuring an illustration of the character, speech "bubbles" with comments from the character to the students to be displayed each day on a bulletin board depicting the character, and writing materials for the students.

Procedure

Select a character—either from a book just read aloud to the class or a book used in a core book unit (Reutzel & Cooter, 1996)—who will interact with the student(s) each day. Sometimes you may decide to use a character associated with a seasonal or classroom theme, but we prefer to use characters from read-aloud or self-selected books (Keiser, 1991). The character should be displayed on a bulletin board or area on the classroom wall throughout the life of this activity. Students are encouraged to write to the character to find out more about him or her, to leave the character books to read, and to respond to letters or captions on the bulletin board each day "written by the character."

WRITING A FAIRY TALE

After careful study of common story grammar patterns found in favorite *fairy tales,* students write their own fairy tales using these same common patterns. It is an interesting introduction to "formula story writing" that offers students yet another writing-reading experience.

Purpose

Writing a fairy tale helps students to develop an understanding of ways an author creates tales and to apply this knowledge in the construction of one's own tales.

Materials

Materials needed include fairy tales with traditional endings; pictures of a mixing bowl, wooden spoon or spatula, old boxes of baking soda, bags of flour or other ingredients used in baking; writing and illustrating materials; a baker's hat; and an artist's beret.

Procedure

Read aloud two or three fairy tales and discuss their common ingredients. For example, tales usually begin with "Once upon a time . . ." or "Long, long ago . . ." Fairy tales also generally have good and bad characters; many contain a commandment or rule, as well as a punishment for breaking the commandment. Sometimes a key incident occurs three times in fairy tales (*Three Pigs* have their homes threatened by the wolf three times). Also, there is often some kind of magic, and most end with a "happily ever after" situation.

Set up a writing center wih a picture depicting a mixing bowl and spoons, along with ingredient boxes labeled *Beginning, Good Character(s), Bad Character(s), 3 Times, Magic,* and *Ending.* An office tray might be placed at the center with an organizational prewriting form using the same labels. Students visiting the center create their own fairy tales (and can wear a baker's hat, if desired). One could also have an illustrator's center, too, where the authors wear an artist's hat or beret and illustrate compositions on an easel.

WRITING A FEATURE STORY ABOUT A CENTRAL CHARACTER

This activity begins by reading several sensationalized "news" accounts of celebrities and other famous people as portrayed in tabloid publications (such as *The National Inquirer*). Students then choose from their free reading a book character and write newspaper articles (*feature stories*) about the character (based on Smith

& Elliot, 1986). The stories are crafted onto a newspaper front page, complete with illustrations created by the student (or several students working in a group), for a fun and motivating writing experience.

Purpose

In writing a feature story, students construct a literature or expository text response in which a character or person from a self-selected book is described using a newspaper or feature story style (who, what, when, where, why, and how).

Materials

Materials needed include newspaper accounts of local or national personalities; a student self-selected book or other text(s) (may be fiction or nonfiction); writing and illustrating materials; and a sheet of poster board to serve as the "newspaper front page."

Procedure

Begin by showing and discussing actual newspaper articles about local or national figures. These may be legitimate press reports, but sometimes it is quite stimulating and fun for students when the teacher uses tabloid or "yellow" journalism. For example, one tabloid story we have used with students proclaims that a "Titanic Survivor Lived 20 Years On Iceberg" and, in the same issue (*Sun,* August 4, 1992), "Head of Goliath Found in Desert." Prepare a minilesson about the typical questions news reporters are interested in learning answers to: *who, what, when, where, why,* and *how.* In your minilesson, choose a character from a well-known book that both the student(s) and you have read, then write a feature story about the character. You may prefer to choose a real person or event to write about from a nonfiction selection.

 As you work through your minilesson, ask students to choose a character from a book they have read and construct their own feature story. The student should write several stories about different events in the books, complete with a title that suggests the main idea of that event. It may be helpful to show the student the front cover of the book *The true story of the Three Little Pigs! By A. Wolf* (Scieszka, 1989) as an example.

WRITTEN RESPONSE TO PICTURE BOOKS FOR OLDER STUDENTS

Upper-grade students *write in response to picture books about sensitive subjects* (Miletta, 1992). The forms of writing vary a great deal based on the subject being studied and the types of response that seem appropriate. Written responses may take the form of poems, songs, letters, essays, debates, one-act plays, video productions, and many more. The key to these writing activities is finding an emotional connection between the theme and the student.

Purpose

In writing in response to picture books about sensitive subjects, students write passionate compositions.

Materials

Materials needed include picture books relating to important and possibly controversial themes and writing supplies.

Procedure

Introduce picture books (those that rely heavily on illustrations to help get ideas across to readers) that portray emotionally powerful themes. Possible themes include war and peace issues, peer pressures, family relationships across generations (such as between grandparents and grandchildren), and health issues (abortion, AIDS, etc.). Try to select books that show different perspectives of the same issue in order to encourage debate. For example, for a theme related to "War and Peace" one might choose *Hiroshima No Pika* by T. Maruki, *The Butter Battle Book* by Dr. Seuss (Geisel), *The Wall* by Edith Bunting, or *The Flame of Peace: A Tale of the Aztecs* by Deborah Nourse Lattimore. For a theme pertaining to "Relationships Between Generations" one might choose *Wilfred Gordon McDonald Partridge* by Mem Fox.

Written responses might take many forms. For controversial issues of the day, students may choose to debate positions and tactics or write letters to congressional leaders or platform positions for political parties. Issues that relate more to personal relationships could take the form of diary entries, letters, or discussions in one-act play format.

It is important, however, to note that these books sometimes contain deep and emotional themes (child abuse and divorce, for instance). They are often controversial, and thus should always be previewed in order to make judgments about the appropriateness of the material.

BOOKMAKING AND PUBLISHING ACTIVITIES

This section presents several highly interesting ways that students can publish their compositions by turning them into books. In each of these activities, teachers stimulate reading and writing in students by showing them easy ways to publish their compositions. Other benefits to bookmaking include promoting creativity and problem-solving and decision-making abilities. Some of the following ideas have been adapted from ideas by Routman (1991) and Yopp and Yopp (1992).

POP-UP BOOKS

In this activity, children produce their own *pop-up books*—a fun and easy activity that stimulates students' interest in writing. An additional benefit is that pop-up books present parents with an impressive product documenting their child's literacy growth.

Materials

Materials needed include construction paper, glue, tape, scissors, and pictures to be used.

Procedure

Begin by sharing several pop-up books that have been commercially produced, as well as a sample the teacher or another student has produced. Next, have students illustrate the background for each page of their story and write in text. This step makes the finished product appear more professional and is less likely to frustrate young authors. It is possible to have one or more pop-up figures on a page by following these simple directions:

Step 1: Fold a sheet of construction paper in half and make two cuts an inch deep each and about an inch apart in the creased part of the paper.

Step 2: Open the paper about halfway, and push through the cut section carefully, and fold it inward.

Step 3: Glue the picture to be used to the protruding cut section.

Step 4: Fold each completed page in the closed position and stack the pages in order. The stack may be either glued or stitched together to complete the process. Don't forget to include an outside cover page.

EIGHT-PAGE BOOKS

This activity produces an *eight-page book* from a single piece of paper. It is quick and easy, yet an inexpensive way to help students transform their compositions into booklike publications.

Materials

Materials needed included a single sheet of paper—preferably 20 lb. bond, scissors, and writing supplies.

Procedure

This is the quickest and easiest of the bookmaking methods. Simply follow these steps:

First, fold a sheet of standard 8-1/2″ × 11″ paper in half (top to bottom).

Second, fold in half again.

Third, fold over.

Fourth, open the sheet of paper back to the first fold position, then cut the paper with scissors halfway up in the center, beginning at the folded edge.

Fifth, open the sheet and fold to the lengthwise position and push in the sides to form a diamond shape.

Finally, push in the sides to form an eight-page book!

ACCORDION BOOKS

Accordion books are easy-to-construct books made of folded tag board that are displayed in special areas in the classroom. This activity has been suggested for group situations not only as a type of problem-solving, but also as a means of putting together a composition in a sequence that makes sense.

Materials

Materials needed include multiple sheets of tag board, tape, and crayons or other colored markers for writing and illustrating.

Procedure

After the teacher shows an example of an accordion book, each group of students selects a composition that it wishes to retell in this format: Groups first decide which student will summarize each of the parts of the selection. Students then write a summary statement and draw an illustration on the tag board. Once group members have completed their assignments, the tag board or transparencies are taped together in sequence. The finished accordion book is then placed on a table in the classroom for other students to read.

INNOVATION BOOKS

Many of the early reading books students encounter have memorable patterns, repeating verses, or other literary devices that make them highly predictable. Dr. Seuss (*Green Eggs and Ham*) and Bill Martin (*Brown Bear, Brown Bear, What Do You See?*) are two authors who have created many such books familiar to most English-speaking children. *Innovation books* are adaptations of popular predictable books using the same basic theme as the original book. They may be created by individual students as literature response projects using the writing process or generated in small group settings with the assistance of the teacher.

Materials

Materials needed include regular 8-1/2″ × 11″ sheets of paper or construction paper, laminating materials, writing and illustrating materials, a hole punch, and metal clasps or rings.

Procedure

Choose a popular book that has a clear pattern. Two popular books that have been used for innovations in the primary grades are *Brown Bear, Brown Bear, What Do You See?* (Martin, 1983) and *If You Give A Mouse A Cookie* (Numeroff, 1985). For example, Miss Tims's first-grade class in Kansas took the *Brown Bear, Brown Bear, What Do You See?* pattern and used it to create a Halloween version using scary words, titled *Brown Spider, Brown Spider* (see Figure 12.9 for a sample page from the book). Innovation books also can be written by older students for younger ones, thus encouraging the older students to practice writing skills and to enjoy a new form of publishing.

The procedure can be followed in either small group or whole class formats. First, read aloud a book, song (such as "On Top of Old Smokey"), poem, rap, or chant that has the desired pattern. Next, challenge the student or group to brainstorm possible new verses. Record them on chart paper, the chalkboard, or on an overhead projector/transparency. Once the new text has been written, each student then writes and illustrates an assigned page that will be laminated upon com-

Figure 12.9   Innovation Book *White Skeleton, White Skeleton*

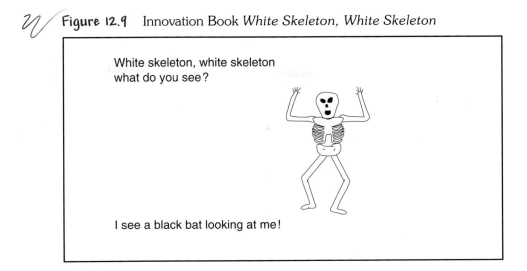

White skeleton, white skeleton
what do you see?

I see a black bat looking at me!

pletion. Assemble all the pages in the desired order, punch three holes along the binding edge of the aligned pages, then bind them with chrome rings or clasps. The innovation book is now ready to be shared.

CHAPTER SUMMARY

In this chapter we have presented a brief summary regarding reading-writing connections and how they may be strengthened simultaneously in the classroom. A number of activities have been suggested that promote writing development in particular, activities linking writing development with published books and other texts, and ideas for bookmaking and publishing.

REFERENCES

Adams, T. (1991). Classroom characters. *The Reading Teacher, 45,* 73–74.

Brown, M. K. (1992). *Sally's room.* New York: Scholastic.

Bunting, E. (1992). *The wall.* Boston: Hougton Mifflin.

Calkins, L. M. (1994). *The art of teaching writing (2nd Ed.).* Portsmouth, NH: Heinemann.

Flickenger, G. (1991). Pen pals and collaborative books. *The Reading Teacher, 45,* 72–73.

Fox, M. (1985). *Wilfred Gordon McDonald Partridge.* Kane/Miller.

Gauthier, L. R. (1989). Using capsulization guides. *The Reading Teacher, 42,* 553–554.

Geisel, T. (Dr. Seuss) (1984). *The butter battle book.* New York: Random House.

Geisel, T. (Dr. Seuss) (1960). *Green eggs and ham.* New York: Random House.

Goodman, K., & Goodman, Y. (1983). Reading and writing relationships: Pragmatic functions. *Language Arts, 60*(5), 590–599.

Harste, J., Short, K. G., & Burke, C. (1988). *Creating classrooms for authors.* Portsmouth, NH: Heinemann.

Isadora, R. (1984). *Opening night.* New York: Green Willow Books.

Keiser, B. (1991). Creating authentic conditions for writing. *The Reading Teacher, 45,* 249–250.

Lattimore, D. N. (1991). *The flame of peace: A tale of the Aztecs.* New York: HarperCollins.

Martin, B. (1983). *Brown bear, brown bear, what do you see?* New York: Henry Holt.

Maruki, T. (1982). *Hiroshuma no pika.* New York: William Morrow.

Miletta, M. M. (1992). Picture books for older children: Reading and writing connections. *The Reading Teacher, 45,* 555–556.

Miller-Rodriguez, K. (1992). Home writing activities: The writing briefcase and the traveling suitcase. *Reading Teacher, 45,* 160–161.

Myers, W. D. (1975). *Fast Sam, cool Clyde, and stuff.* New York: Puffin Books.

Numeroff, L. J. (1985). *If you give a mouse a cookie.* New York: Scholastic.

Pike, K., Compain, R., & Mumper, J. (1994). *New connections: An integrated approach to literacy.* New York: HarperCollins College Publishers.

Reutzel, D. R., & Cooter, R. B. (1996). *Teaching children to read: From basals to books* (2nd ed.). New York: Merrill, an imprint of Prentice-Hall.

Routman, R. (1991). *Invitations.* Portsmouth, NH: Heinemann.

Shanahan, T. (1984). Nature of the reading-writing relation: An exploratory multi-variate analysis. *Journal of Educational Psychology, 76,* 466–477.

Sharmat, M. W. (1980). *Gila monsters meet you at the airport.* New York: Aladdin Books, Macmillan Publishing Company.

Smith, F. (1983). *Essays into literacy.* Portsmouth, NH: Heinemann.

Smith, C. B., & Elliot, P. G. (1986). *Reading activities for middle and secondary schools.* New York: Teachers College Press.

Squire, J. R. (1983). Composing and comprehending: Two sides of the same basic process. *Language Arts, 60*(5), 581–589.

Tompkins, G. E. (1994). *Teaching writing: Balancing process and product.* New York: Merrill.

Tompkins, G. E. (1992). Assessing the processes students use as writers. *Journal of Reading, 36*(3), 244–246.

Van Allsburg, C. (1985). *The polar express.* Boston: Houghton Mifflin.

Williams, Margery. (1922, 1958). *The velveteen rabbit: Or how toys become real.* New York: Doubleday.

Wiseman, D. L. (1992). *Learning to read with literature.* Needham Heights, MA: Allyn and Bacon.

Yopp, R. H., & Yopp, H. K. (1992). *Literature-based reading activities.* Boston: Allyn and Bacon.

Chapter 13

Developing Reading Fluency

For many years, *reading fluency*—the ability to read aloud smoothly at a reasonable rate—has been acknowledged as an important goal in becoming a proficient and strategic reader. However, with a shift in emphasis away from proficient oral reading in the early 1900s toward silent reading for private and personal purposes, the goal of developing fluent *oral* readers all but disappeared from the reading curriculum. This was so much the case that it prompted Allington (1983) to declare reading fluency to be a neglected goal of reading instruction. Most reading methods textbooks and basal reader teacher's manuals today still provide little or no guidance for developing fluency as an important part of reading instruction programs. Visits to many elementary school classrooms likewise reveal little attention to reading fluency in daily instruction.

How can teachers assess and assist at-risk students in becoming fluent readers? First, they must understand *how* children develop fluency in reading. Second, they must be able to *assess* fluency to determine which abilities require attention. And, finally, teachers should know of successful and proven instructional alternatives available to use in assisting children to develop fluency reading behaviors. This chapter discusses reading fluency, describes assessment strategies, and provides successful instructional strategies related to helping at-risk readers develop fluency in reading.

BACKGROUND BRIEFING FOR TEACHERS: THE CHARACTERISTICS OF FLUENT READERS

What makes up the ability to read fluently? While teachers and reading researchers have yet to agree on minor elements of reading fluency, some consensus has been achieved in recent years as to the major aspects. Typically, fluency is described as: 1) accuracy of decoding, 2) appropriate use of pitch, juncture, and stress (prosodic features) in one's voice, 3) appropriate text phrasing or "chunking," and 4) appropriate reading speed or rate. Thus, a fluent reader can decode the words in the text accurately and with relative ease, and can also read the text aloud naturally. In the *Dictionary of Reading*, Harris and Hodges (1981) define reading fluency as expressing oneself "smoothly, easily, and readily, with freedom from word identification problems," and possessing the ability to deal with "words, and larger language units" with quickness (p. 120). Rasinski (1990b) explains that reading fluency contributes to better comprehension.

How readers achieve fluency in their oral reading is a subject of continuing debate. However, several hypotheses help teachers gain insights into the question. In 1983, Allington discussed six hypotheses attempting to explain how readers develop the ability to read fluently. Hypothesis 1 centered on the idea that some children are helped by being exposed to rich and varied models of fluent reading. In this case, parents or siblings spend significant amounts of time reading aloud to these children. Through this process of modeling fluent reading, children learn the behaviors of fluent readers. Other researchers also have documented the significant impact of "modeling" upon the acquisition of fluent reading (Durkin, 1966, 1974; Amarel, Bussis, & Chittenden, 1977). Hypothesis 2 stated that good readers are more likely to get encouragement to read with expression than are students having reading problems (Gambrell, Wilson, & Gnatt, 1981). In comparison, students having reading problems are often directed to focus their attention on "sounding out" rather than on "making sense of the text" when reading orally (Allington, 1980b). Hypothesis 3 centered on the opportunity to learn. Better readers are given more opportunities to read connected text and for longer periods of time than are students having reading problems. This dilemma leads Allington (1977) to muse, "If they don't read much, how they ever gonna get good?"

Hypothesis 4 proposed that proficient readers spend more time reading easier texts than students having reading problems (Gambrell et al., 1981). Reading easy books may help proficient readers make the transition from word-by-word reading to fluent reading, while poorer readers spend more time in reading materials that are relatively difficult. This practice denies students having reading problems access to reading materials that could help them develop fluent reading abilities. Hypothesis 5 proposed that the greater the time a student spends in silent reading, the greater his fluency is likely to be. Here again, proficient readers spend more time reading silently than do students having reading problems (Allington, 1980a). Finally, Hypothesis 6 related to the idea that fluent readers seem to view the reading process itself differently than less fluent readers. Children who believe that reading is simply a process of decoding symbols to sounds, blending sounds together, and pronouncing words tend to be far less fluent in their reading than students who believe reading should be meaningful, enjoyable, and, above all, make sense. Awareness of these six hypotheses can help teachers create optimal conditions for students to become fluent readers.

Rasinski (1989) describes six instructional principles of effective fluency instruction: 1) repetition, 2) modeling, 3) direct instruction and feedback, 4) support or assistance, 5) phrasing practice, and 6) easy materials. Fluency is achieved when students practice a single text repeatedly until the oral reading is perfected. The acts of observing, listening to, and acting like fluent reading models help students having reading problems learn how to become fluent readers themselves. Modeling fluent reading for students and pointing out specific behaviors as texts are read aloud, as well as providing constructive feedback, can also help students become fluent readers. Supporting students using such strategies as choral reading, buddy or dyad reading, and computer-assisted reading can be most effective in a well-conceived reading fluency program. Finally, providing readers with easy reading materials for oral reading is essential for developing fluency.

TEACHER FEEDBACK

Understanding the nature, quantity, and quality of teacher feedback during oral reading is a crucial part of helping students become fluent readers. The following self-assessment questions are provided to assist in this process.

Teacher Verbal Feedback Think Questions*

1. Am I more often telling the word than providing a clue?
2. What is the average self-correction rate of my students?
3. Do I assist poor readers with unknown words more often than good readers? If so, why?
4. Am I correcting miscues even when they do not alter the meaning of the text? If so, why?
5. Does one reader group tend to engage in more self-correction than other groups? If so, why?
6. Does one reader group have more miscues that go unaddressed than other groups?
7. What types of cues for oral reading errors do I provide and why?
8. What is *my* ultimate goal in reading instruction?
9. How do I handle interruptions from other students during oral reading? Do I practice what I preach?
10. How does my feedback influence the self-correction behavior of students?
11. Does my feedback differ across reader groups? If so, *how* and *why*?
12. Would students benefit more from a form of feedback different from that which I normally offer?
13. Am I allowing students time to self-correct (3–5 seconds)?
14. Am I further confusing students with my feedback?
15. Do I digress into minilessons in midsentence when students make a mistake? If so, why?
16. Do I analyze miscues to gain information about the reading strategies students employ?
17. Does the feedback I offer aid students in becoming independent, self-monitoring readers? If so, how?
18. Do I encourage students to ask themselves, "Did that make sense?" when they are reading both orally and silently? If not, why not?
19. Do students need the kind of feedback I am offering them?

* Adapted from "Teacher Interruptions During Oral Reading Instruction: Self-Monitoring as an Impetus for Change in Corrective Feedback" by M. Shake, 1986, *Remedial and Special Education, 7* (5), pp. 18–24.

Armed with an understanding of the problems, obstacles, and possibilities for helping students become fluent readers, we now turn our attention toward assessing students' reading fluency to inform and direct our selection of instructional strategies.

ASSESSING STUDENTS' READING FLUENCY

Assessing fluency has for many years focused exclusively upon how quickly students could read a given text. This is known as "reading rate." Reading teachers have historically used a *words per minute* (wpm) figure to indicate reading rate, even though an optimum rate has never been determined or validated. Although reading rate is one indicator of fluent oral/silent reading, it is only one. To adequately assess a student's ability to read fluently, one should consider at least four different areas: 1) automatic decoding of text, 2) reading rate or speed, 3) use of stress, pitch, and juncture (prosodic markers), and 4) mature phrasing or *chunking* of text.

Educators have in recent years begun to discuss how one might more *authentically* assess the ability to read fluently (Stayter & Allington, 1991). Most teachers feel that paper and pencil assessment tools appear to be inadequate, or at least incomplete, measures of fluency. Several approaches to assessing readers' fluency in more authentic, naturalistic, and holistic ways are described below. While none of these approaches is sufficient alone, they do offer a glimpse of the total fluency picture. Before beginning the discussion of each of these assessment strategies, however, we refer the reader to chapter 3, in which the processes for completing a running record are described. Running records provide access to much of the data necessary for each of these strategies.

AUDIOTAPING

Purpose

One of the simplest and most useful means of collecting fluency data for later analysis is through the use of *audiotaping*. The purpose of audiotaping is to gather reading fluency samples of special needs children over time in order to measure growth. In addition, these audiotapes function as miscue analysis documentation when conducting running records. Audiotapes may be kept and passed on from year to year through the student's elementary school experience. In one school where we have worked, the PTA provides 120-minute tapes for each child, beginning in the firstgrade year. Audiotapes are passed on through the grades until the children leave the elementary school. Parents are given these tapes when their child moves on to the middle school. Many parents consider these tapes to be as important as family photos and home videos of their child. Audiotapes such as these are vivid demonstrations of a child's progress over time, as well as demonstrating the efforts of many dedicated teachers who have helped the child learn to read.

Materials

The materials needed include one blank audiocassette tape per student (120-minute length strongly suggested); a portable audiocassette recorder with an internal microphone; and an audiocassette tape storage case.

Procedure

The text to be read for the audiotaping should be selected based on the nature and purpose of the information needed. For instance, information needed to document students' fluency progress over time will differ from information collected to compare one student's fluency to that of another. If a teacher wants to document a student's fluency progress over time, have the student select a favorite text to be practiced aloud or silently at least three times in preparation for audiotaping. Record the oral reading of the practiced, self-selected text. Taping several readings of self-selected, favorite texts over a sufficiently long period of time provides both teachers and parents with useful longitudinal information regarding a student's fluency progress.

On the other hand, there may be a need mandated by school districts or governmental agencies to compare a student's fluency performance with that of his peers in age or grade level. In this case, all students can be assigned the same text to be read, practice at least three times, and be recorded. Audiotaping the same sample text for all students allows for collection of comparative fluency data. In either case, audiotaping provides documentation of progress as well as data for more searching analyses of fluency to be made at a later date or at a time convenient to the teacher's schedule.

CURRICULUM-BASED ORAL READING FLUENCY NORMS FOR GRADES 2-5

One of the most common measures of oral reading fluency is reading rate or reading speed. In the past, reading rate was measured in terms of one of two existing scales—words per minute (WPM) and miscues or errors per minute (MPM). More recently, another measure has been developed to measure rate of fluency—words correct per minute (WCPM). A WCPM measure has been carefully researched and related to a set of Oral Reading Fluency Curriculum-Based Norms for grades 2–5 (Hasbrouck and Tindal, 1992). Data were collected to establish the oral reading fluency norms from 9,000 students between 1981 and 1990, in grades 2 through 5, in five midwestern and western states. Students attended a wide range of schools, including large urban and rural schools.

Purpose

The purposes for assessing oral reading fluency are varied. Some reasons include the following:

- screening students for special program eligibilty
- setting instructional goals and objectives
- assigning students to specific groups for instruction
- monitoring academic progress toward established goals
- special needs for assistance or instruction

Materials

A teacher selected passage of 200 to 300 words

Curriculum-based measurement procedures for assessing and scoring oral reading fluency

Cassette tape player/recorder with blank tape

Curriculum-based norms in oral reading fluency for grades 2–5 as shown in Figure 13.1

Procedures

The procedures for collecting oral reading fluency information are shown in Figure 13.2.

MULTIDIMENSIONAL FLUENCY SCALE

Purpose

Zutell and Rasinski (1991) have developed a *Multidimensional Fluency Scale* (MFS) which serves as a good informal assessment of fluency. Although no au-

Figure 13.1   Curriculum-Based Norms in Oral Reading Fluency for Grades 2–5 (Medians)

Grade	Percentile	Fall WCPM*	Winter WCPM	Spring WCPM
2	75	82	106	124
	50	53	78	94
	25	23	46	65
3	75	107	123	142
	50	79	93	114
	25	65	70	87
4	75	125	133	143
	50	99	112	118
	25	72	89	92
5	75	126	143	151
	50	105	118	128
	25	77	93	100

*Words correct per minute

Note: Based on Hasbrouck, J. E., & Tindal, G. (1992). "Curriculum-Based Oral Reading Fluency Norms for Students in Grades 2 Through 5." *Teaching Exceptional Children,* (Spring, 1995), 41–44.

Figure 13.2   Curriculum-Based Measurement Procedures for Assessing and Scoring Oral Reading Fluency

Say to the student: "When I say 'start' begin reading aloud at the top of this page. Read across the page (demonstrate by pointing). Try to read each word. If you come to a word you don't know, I'll tell it to you. Be sure to do your best reading. Are there any questions?

Say, "Start."

Following along on your copy of the story, mark the words that are read incorrectly. If a student stops or struggles with a word for 3 seconds, tell the student the word and mark it as incorrect. Place a vertical line after the last word read within 1 minute. Thank and praise the student.

The following guidelines determine which words are to be counted as correct:

1. **Words read correctly.** Words read correctly are those words that are pronounced correctly, given the reading context.
    a. The word "read" must be pronounced "reed" when presented in the context of "He will read the book," not as "red."
    b Repetitions are not counted as incorrect.
    c. Self-corrections within 3 seconds are counted as correctly read words.
2. **Words read incorrectly.** The following types of errors are counted: mispronunciations, substitutions, omissions. Futher, words not read within 3 seconds are counted as errors.
    a. Mispronunciations are words that are misread: dog for dig.
    b. Substitutions are words that are substituted for the stimulus word. This is often inferred by a one-to-one correspondence between word orders: dog for cat.
    c. Omissions are words skipped or not read. If a student skips an entire line, each words is counted as an error.
3. **3-second rule.** If a students is struggling to pronounce a word or hesitates for 3 seconds, the student is told the word, and it is counted as an error.

Note: From Shinn, M. R. (Ed.). (1989). *Curriculum-based measurement: Assessing special children* (pp. 239–240). New York: Guilford Press.

diorecording is necessary to use this instrument, it is recommended for accurate documentation. The purpose of the MFS is to provide a practical measurement of students' oral reading fluency that provides clear and valid information.

Materials

The materials needed included a student self-selected passage of 200–300 words, a Multidimensional Fluency Scale, and a cassette tape player/recorder with a blank tape.

Procedure

We recommend that students rehearse a familiar self-selected word passage (200–300 words) at least three times prior to using the Multidimensional Fluency Scale shown in Figure 13.3. It may be informative for teachers to also observe the difference in a student's fluency with a practiced, self-selected, familiar text and his reading of an unpracticed, teacher-selected, unfamiliar text chosen at the child's approximate grade level. The Multidimensional Fluency Scale shown in Figure 13.3 can be used to assess each students' reading fluency.

Fluency ratings can be taken during individual reading conferences or in group dramatizations including plays, Reader's Theater, and radio plays (Reutzel & Cooter, 1996). For radio plays, students can prepare a text for reading and record-

Figure 13.3   Multidimensional Fluency Scale

Use the following scales to rate reader fluency on the three dimensions of phrasing, smoothness, and pace.

A. Phrasing
  1. Monotonic, with little sense of phrase boundaries; frequent word-by-word reading
  2. Frequent two- and three-word phrases giving the impression of choppy reading; improper stress and intonation that fail to mark ends of sentences and clauses
  3. Mixture of run-ons, midsentence pauses for breath, and possibly some choppiness; reasonable stress/intonation
  4. Generally well-phrased, mostly in clause and sentence units, with adequate attention to expression

B. Smoothness
  1. Frequent extended pauses, hesitations, false starts, sound-outs, repetitions, and/or multiple attempts
  2. Several "rough spots" in text where extended pauses, hesitations, etc., are more frequent and disruptive
  3. Occasional breaks in smoothness caused by difficulties with specific words and/or structures
  4. Generally smooth reading with some breaks, but word and structure difficulties are resolved quickly, usually through self-correction

C. Pace (during sections of minimal disruption)
  1. Slow and laborious
  2. Moderately slow
  3. Uneven mixture of fast and slow reading
  4. Consistently conversational

Note: From "Training Teachers to Attend to Their Students' Oral Reading Fluency" by J. Zutell and T. Rasinski, 1991, *Theory into Practice, 30*(3), pp. 211–217.

ing on a cassette tape player, complete with sound effects, if they wish! After taping, the teacher can analyze the performance of individual students and provide helpful modeling and feedback for future improvement.

BALANCED READING PROGRAM INTERVENTIONS: STUDENTS WITH READING FLUENCY NEEDS

Indicators That Readers Have Learning Needs

- Slow and labored pacing during reading
- Poor flow or continuity indicated by frequent pauses, sounding out, and regressions
- Poor phrasing evidenced by choppy, word-by-word reading and improper stress and intonation (possibly indicating poor comprehension of the text)

Perhaps the most important thing to remember is that children with poor reading fluency must receive regular opportunities to read and reread for authentic and motivating reasons, such as to gather information, to present a dramatization, or simply to reread a favorite story. The strategies described below offer effective and varied means for teachers to help learners become more fluent readers in authentic and motivating ways!

ORAL RECITATION LESSON (ORL)

Purpose

Hoffman (1987) uses a lesson format that is drawn from the one-room schoolhouse period of American education. In essence, teachers modeled reading aloud, then students were assigned all or part of the text for practice and later asked to read aloud to the class during what was called "recitation." The Oral Recitation Lesson (ORL) shares many important theoretical and practical characteristics with the Shared Book Approach strategy described in chapter 10. According to Rasinski (1990a), the Shared Book Approach and the Oral Recitation Lesson are similar with respect to teacher modeling, repeated readings of text, independent reading, and the use of predictable and meaningful materials. Thus, the Shared Book Approach may be seen as a less formalized approach to developing fluency with at-risk readers (Nelson & Morris, 1986). However, for some readers, the Oral Recitation Lesson offers a structure and security often required by both teacher and learner.

Materials

Materials needed include student self-selected books appropriate for reading aloud.

Procedure

The Oral Recitation Lesson incorporates two basic components, with each made up of several subroutines, outlined as follows.

Components of the Oral Recitation Lesson

I. DIRECT INSTRUCTION

    A. Three Subroutines
       1. Comprehension
       2. Practice
       3. Performance

II. INDIRECT INSTRUCTION

    A. Two Subroutines
       1. Fluency practice
       2. Demonstrate expert reading

Direct instruction consists of three subroutines: a comprehension phase, a practice phase, and a performance phase. When beginning an Oral Recitation Lesson, the teacher reads a story aloud and leads the students through an analysis of the story's content by constructing a story grammar map and discussing the major elements of the story, such as setting, characters, goals, plans, events, and resolution. Students are asked to tell what they remember about these parts of the story and the teacher records their responses on the story grammar map. At the conclusion of this discussion, the story grammar map is used as an outline for students to write a story summary.

During the second subroutine, practice, the teacher works with students to improve their oral reading expression. The teacher models fluent reading aloud with parts of the text, then the students individually or chorally practice imitating the teacher's oral expressions. Choral readings of texts can be accomplished in a number of ways (see the discussion of Four-Way Oral Reading (Wood) later in this chapter.) Text segments modeled by the teacher during the practice phase may begin with only one or two sentences and gradually move toward modeling and practicing whole pages of text.

The third subroutine is the performance phase. Students select and perform a part of the text for others in the group, then listeners are encouraged to comment positively on the performance. We ask students to begin this activity by stating what they liked about the oral reading by their peer, then ask questions about parts of the reading that they liked less. Teacher modeling is very important with this latter activity. For instance, the teacher might model a question about a strange rendition of the Big Bad Wolf in "The Three Little Pigs" story by saying the following:

> I noticed that your voice had a nice and friendly tone when you read the Big Bad Wolf's part. I'm curious. Why did you choose to read his part that way, when so many other readers choose to use a mean-sounding voice for that character?

Many times the student has a perfectly logical reason for irregular intonation or other anomalies. Sometimes it is simply a matter of the student failing to spend enough time in practice. If so, this regular format helps students be aware that there is some accountability to these lessons.

The second major component of the Oral Recitation Lesson is an *indirect instruction* phase. During this part of the lesson, students practice a single story until they become expert readers. Hoffman (1987) defines an expert reader as one who reads with 98% accuracy and 75 words-per-minute fluency. For ten minutes each day, students practice reading a story or text segment in a soft or mumble-reading fashion. Teachers use this time to check students individually—making what we term "house calls"—for story mastery before moving on to another story. The direct instruction component creates a pool of stories from which the students can select a story for expert reading activities in the indirect instruction phase. In summary, ORL provides teachers with a workable strategy to break away from the traditional practice of round-robin oral reading.

CHUNKING TRAINING

Purpose

A critical step in improving students' reading fluency is to encourage them to read groups of words. An approach called *chunking* (Amble, 1967; Brozo, Schmelzer, & Spires, 1983) can be used to gradually expand students' fluency beyond word-by-word reading to reading clauses, phrases, and sentences.

Materials

Materials needed include a teacher-selected familiar reading passage, divided into phrases by making a slash (/) mark directly on the text. In the beginning the number of words-per-phrase group should be limited to 3 to 4 words. As students succeed with these smaller phrase groups, slash marks can be erased so that larger and larger phrase groups remain.

Procedure

Teachers also may wish to write the phrases on sentence strips and on chart paper for practice. Phrases are initially presented in the order in which they occur in the passage. In later practice sessions, phrase strips can be cut apart or reordered and flashed at random. This approach forces students to commit the words to memory, since they cannot rely on context clues. Consequently, words and phrases become part of the students' sight vocabularies and can be generalized to reading other texts and in other settings.

REPEATED READINGS

Purpose

With *repeated readings,* students simply read interesting passages orally over and over again. The basic purpose is to enhance students' reading fluency (Samuels, 1979; Dowhower, 1991). Although it might seem that reading a text again and again may lead to boredom, it actually has just the opposite effect.

Materials

In the beginning, texts selected for repeated readings should be short, predictable, and easy. Examples of poetry we recommend for repeated readings with at-risk readers include those authored by Shel Silverstein and Jack Prelutsky. Stories such as Bill Martin's *Brown Bear, Brown Bear* (1983), or Eric Carle's *The Very Hungry Caterpillar* 1987, are also wonderful places to start this activity. When students attain adequate speed and accuracy with easy texts, the length and difficulty of the stories and poems can gradually be increased.

Procedure

In this exercise each reading is timed and then recorded on a chart or graph. Students compete with themselves, trying to better their reading rate and to cut down on errors with each successive attempt. Also, with each attempt, students' comprehension and prosody, or vocal inflections, improve (Dowhower, 1987). Students having reading problems find it reinforcing to see visible evidence of their reading improvement. Figure 13.4 illustrates a graph for charting student progress in repeated readings.

Figure 13.4   Graph of Student's Fluency Progress

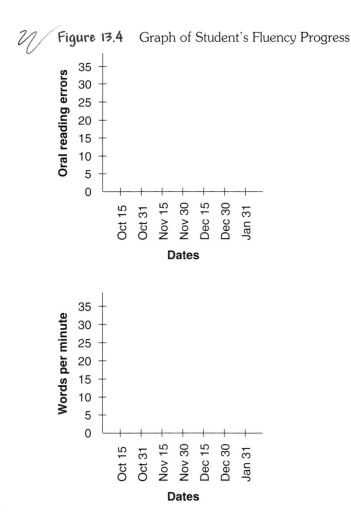

To increase reading rate, students must learn to recognize words without having to sound them out. As is shown in Figure 13.4, both the amount of time it takes to read the selection and the number of oral reading errors that occur during each trial can be graphed.

Repeated readings help students by expanding the total number of words they can recognize instantaneously and, as previously mentioned, help improve students' comprehension and oral elocution with each succeeding attempt. Students quickly experience improved confidence regarding reading aloud and positive attitudes toward the act of reading. Additionally, because high-frequency words (*the, and, but, was,* etc.) occur in literally all reading situations, the increase in automatic sight word knowledge developed through repeated readings transfers far beyond the practiced texts.

One way of supporting readers during repeated readings is to use a tape-recorded version of the story or poem. Students can read along with the tape to develop fluency similar to the model on the tape. Also, students can tape-record their oral reading performance as a source of immediate feedback. If two cassette tape player/recorders are available, let the student, using headphones, listen and read along with the taped version of the text. At the same time, have the second recorder recording the student's oral reading. To compare, the child can then either replay his version simultaneously with the teacher-recorded version, or simply listen only to his own rendition. Either way, the feedback can be both instant and effective.

Teachers can use the taped recording of repeated readings for further analysis of each at-risk readers' improvement in fluency and comprehension. Using a tape recorder also frees the teacher to work with other students, thereby conserving precious instructional time and leaving behind an audit trail of student readings for later assessment and documentation. On occasion, teachers should listen to the tape with the reader present, however, so that effective ways of reducing word recognition errors and increasing reading rate can be modeled by the teacher.

ASSISTED READING (DYAD, BUDDY, OR PAIRED)

Purpose

With *dyad* (also called *buddy,* or *paired*) *reading,* two students read the same text aloud in unison for mutual support (Greene, 1970; Eldredge & Quinn, 1988).

Materials

Initial dyad reading sessions should be structured so that the materials used are equally familiar and motivating for both students involved.

Procedure

Students can be paired according to their general reading level, but, more importantly, they should be paired according to their ability to work well with one another. A spirit of teamwork and cooperation must be present so that when one reader stumbles the other lends assistance. The dyad sessions can be tape-recorded and played back for the students and teachers to evaluate. Discussions or taped replays should center not just on word recognition accuracy, but also on reading rate, pausing, intonation, expressive oral interpretation, and comprehension of the text.

FOUR-WAY ORAL READINGS: CHORAL READING AND VARIATIONS

Purpose

In many classrooms, students having reading problems are asked to read aloud in a solo or round-robin fashion. However, research by Eldredge, Reutzel, and Hollingsworth (1996) has shown that round-robin oral reading is the least effective oral reading instruction that can be offered to young readers. Moreover, round-robin oral reading carries with it significant emotional and psychological risks for students.

Wood (1983) suggests an approach called four-way oral reading for reading a story orally in a group. In this approach, Wood points out that the oral reading of a text should be varied by using four different types of oral reading: 1) unison choral reading, 2) echoic or *imitative* reading, 3) paired reading, and 4) "mumble" reading. All of these approaches to oral reading, except mumble reading, are described elsewhere in this chapter. *Mumble reading*, or reading aloud quietly, is typically heard among young readers as they are initially told to read silently. These young readers tend to "mumble" as they attempt to read silently. Teachers should model this approach to oral reading before asking students to mumble read.

Materials

Easy-to-read texts are usually used, particularly because this activity involves two or more students.

Procedure

To use four-way oral reading, Wood (1983) suggests that the teacher introduce the story content and the varied methods to be used in reading it. The teacher should pause briefly during the oral reading of the story to help students reflect on the story developments thus far, then make predictions about the next part of the story to focus on and improve comprehension. During four-way oral reading, students are called upon randomly to read in groups of two or more so that no one will be put on the spot to read solo. All students participate repeatedly throughout the oral reading of the story, thus helping them to remain actively involved and to keep their place in the story. Also, students read together often, providing many minutes of reading aloud for pleasure and practice to support students having reading problems.

NEUROLOGICAL IMPRESS

Purpose

The *neurological impress method* (NIM) involves the student and the teacher in reading the same text aloud simultaneously (Heckleman, 1966, 1969). The use of multiple sensory systems associated with using NIM is thought to "impress" upon the student the fluid reading patterns of the teacher through direct modeling. It is assumed that exposing students to numerous examples of texts (read in a more sophisticated way than the at-risk students could achieve on their own) will enable them to learn the patterns of letter-sound correspondence in the language more naturally. This assumption stands to reason, when viewed in light of more recent advances in learning theory, especially those espoused by Vygotsky (1978).

Materials

Each NIM session is aimed at reading as much material as is possible in 10 minutes. The reading material selected for the first few sessions should be easy, predictable, and make sense to the reader. However, other more challenging materials can be used soon after.

Procedure

To use the NIM, the student sits slightly in front and to one side of the teacher as they hold the text. The teacher moves her finger beneath the words as they are spoken in near-unison fashion. Both the student and the teacher try to maintain a comfortably brisk, continuous rate of oral reading. The teacher's role is to keep the pace when the student starts to slow down. Pausing to analyze unknown words is not permitted. The teacher's voice is directed at the student's ear so that the words are seen, heard, and said simultaneously.

In the first few NIM sessions, students should become acquainted with the process by practicing on short, familiar texts. Since most students with reading problems have not read at an accelerated pace before, their first efforts often have a mumble-like quality. Most students with reading problems typically take some time to adjust to the NIM; however, within a few sessions, they start to feel at ease. Many students with reading problems say they enjoy the NIM because it allows them to read more challenging and interesting material like "good readers."

At first, the teacher's voice will dominate the oral reading, but in later sessions it should be reduced gradually. This will eventually allow the student to assume the vocal lead naturally. Usually three sessions per week are sufficient to obtain noticeable results. This routine should be followed for a minimum of 10 consecutive weeks (Henk, 1983).

The NIM can also be adapted for group use. The teacher tape-records 10 minutes of his or her own oral reading in advance. Individual students can read along with the tape while following the text independently, or the tape can be used in a listening center to permit the teacher to spend individual time with each student as others participate in reading with the tape. Despite the advantages of the prerecorded tape format, however, teachers' one-to-one interactions with individual students result in a better instructional experience.

READER'S THEATER/DRAMATIZATIONS

Purpose

Reader's Theater is a strategy in which students practice reading from a script, then share their oral reading with classmates and selected audiences (Sloyer, 1982). Unlike a play, students do not memorize lines or use elaborate stage sets to make their presentation. Emphasis is placed on presenting an interpretation of literature read in a dramatic style for an audience who imagines setting and actions.

Materials

Literature selected for Reader's Theater should be drawn from tales originating from the oral tradition, from poetry, or from quality picture books designed to be read aloud by children. Selections should be packed with action, have an element of suspense, and comprise an entire, meaningful story or episode. Also, texts selected for use in Reader's Theater should contain sufficient dialogue to make reading and preparing the text a challenge, as well as to involve several children as characters. A few examples of such texts include Martin and Archambault's *Knots on a Counting Rope* (1987), Viorst's *Alexander and the Terrible, Horrible, No Good, Very Bad Day* (1972), and Barbara Robinson's *The Best Christmas Pagent Ever* (1972).

Minimal props are often used in Reader's Theater, such as masks, hats, or simple costumes.

Procedure

If a story is selected for reading, students are assigned to read characters' parts. If poems are selected for a Reader's Theater, students may read alternating lines or groups of lines. Reader's Theater-in-the-Round, where the audience is in the center of the room, surrounded by the readers, is a fun and interesting variation for both the performers and the audience.

Students will often benefit from a discussion prior to reading a Reader's Theater script. This discussion helps students make connections between their own background experiences and the text to be read. Also, students having problems in reading usually benefit from listening to a previously recorded performance of the text as a model prior to the initial reading of the script.

Hennings (1974) described a simplified procedure for preparing Reader's Theater scripts for classroom performance. First, the text to be performed is read silently by the individual students. Second, the text is read again orally, sometimes using choral reading. After the second reading, children either choose their parts, or the teacher assigns parts to the children. We suggest that students select their three most desired parts, and write these choices on a slip of paper to submit to the teacher. Teachers should then do everything possible to assign the students one of their three choices. The third reading is also an oral reading, with students reading their parts with scripts in hand. There may be several rehearsal readings as students prepare for the final reading or performance in front of the class or a selected audience.

Reader's Theater offers students a unique opportunity to participate in reading along with other, perhaps more skilled readers. Participating in the mainstream classroom with better readers helps students having reading problems feel a part of their peer group, provides them with ready models of good reading, and demonstrates how good readers, through practice, become even better readers. Finally, working together with other readers fosters a sense of teamwork, support, and pride in personal and group accomplishment.

RADIO READING
Purpose

Radio reading (Searfoss, 1975) is a procedure for developing oral reading fluency in a group setting, a process that shields students with limited reading abilities from the sometimes harsh emotional consequences from peers.

Materials

In radio reading, each student is given a "script" to read aloud. Selections can be drawn from any print media, such as newspapers, magazines, or any print source that can be converted into a news story.

Procedure

A student acts as a news broadcaster and other students acts as listeners. Only the reader and the teacher have copies of the script. Because other students have no script to follow, minor word recognition errors will go unnoticed if the text is well presented. Students having reading problems have enjoyed Radio Reading from *Know Your World.* This publication is well-suited for use in radio reading activities because the content and level of difficulty make it possible for older readers with fluency problems to read with ease and enjoyment.

Before reading aloud to the group, students should rehearse the story silently to themselves or aloud to the teacher until they gain confidence. Emphasis is first placed on the meaning of the story so that the students can paraphrase any difficult portions of the text. Students are encouraged to keep the ideas flowing in the same way a broadcaster does.

IMITATIVE READING

Purpose

The primary aim of *imitative reading* is to improve word recognition accuracy, with a minor emphasis upon proper intonation and phrasing.

Materials

Materials for this type of intervention can be selected from several sources. Perhaps the best sources for reading aloud are predictable trade books. The following segment was taken from *This is the Place for Me* (Cole, 1986).

> Morty walked and walked. He came to a good house. "I like this house," he said. "Oh, oh," Morty said. "This is not the place for me." He dried himself off. And went looking for a house again. He found one . . . but it was to small. He found another . . . but it was too thin. He found another . . . but it was too scary! Poor Morty! He was all alone in the world. He had no place to live.

Texts such as these provide students with predictable language and events as well as repetitive language they can feel successful with from the start.

Procedure

In imitative reading, the teacher reads a segment of the text aloud while a student follows along silently (Huey, 1968). When finished, the student tries to echo or imitate what the teacher has read. In the early stages, very easy reading material should be used. More difficult reading material can be introduced gradually, as the length of the teacher-modeled oral reading segments increases.

To begin, the teacher should read only small segments of text. Most students can begin with a sentence, but sometimes it will be necessary to limit the segments read to phrases. When text is broken up in this way, the student should be required to echo whole sentences before the teacher continues reading.

Closed-Caption TV

Purpose

Several researchers (Neuman & Koskinen, 1992; Koskinen, Wilson, & Jensema, 1985) have found that closed-caption television is a particularly effective tool for motivating reluctant, at-risk, and language minority students in learning to read. In addition, it improves fluency and comprehension. Closed-caption television, which uses written subtitles, provides students with meaningful and motivating reading material.

Materials

Teachers should (Koskinen et.al., 1985) carefully select high-interest television programs, record and preview programs before making final selections, then introduce the program(s) to students with attention to vocabulary and prior knowledge factors.

Procedure

Three elements should be considered in a successful closed-caption lesson. First, watch a part of the captioned TV program together as a group (5–10 minutes). Stop the recorded tape and ask students to predict what will happen next in the program. Then, continue showing the program so that students can check their predictions. Second, watch a segment of the program that has examples of certain kinds of phonic patterns, word uses, or punctuation. For example, students can be alerted to the use of quotation marks and the fact that these marks signal dialogue. Students can then watch the remainder of the tape to identify the dialogue using their knowledge of quotation marks. Third, after watching a closed-caption TV program, students can practice reading aloud along with the captions. If necessary, both the auditory portion and the closed captioning can be played simultaneously to provide students with fluency problems support through their initial attempts to read. At some later point, students can be allowed to practice reading the captioning without the auditory portion of the program. Koskinen et al. (1985) add that they "do not recommend that the sound be turned off if this, in effect, turns off the children. The major advantage of captioned television is the multi-sensory stimulation of viewing the drama, hearing the sound, and seeing the captions." (p. 6)

Chapter Summary

In this chapter the hypotheses and principles of fluent reading have been described. Specific and selected assessment tools were presented for determining students' growth in fluency to inform instructional practice. Teachers were also offered several approaches for helping learners having reading difficulties become increasingly confident and fluent as readers. It is hoped that the assessment tools and strategies presented provide a starting point for developing more fluent readers.

REFERENCES

Allington, R. L. (1977). If they don't read much, how they ever gonna get good? *Journal of Reading, 21*, 57–61.

Allington, R. L. (1980a). Poor readers don't get to read much in reading groups. *Language Arts, 57*, 872–876.

Allington, R.L. (1980b). Teacher interruption behaviors during primary grade oral reading. *Journal of Educational Psychology, 72*, 371–377.

Allington, R. L. (1983). Fluency: The neglected reading goal. *The Reading Teacher, 36*, (6), 556–561.

Amarel, M., Bussis, A., & Chittenden, E. A. (1977). *An approach to the study of beginning reading: Longitudinal case studies.* Paper presented at the National Reading Conference, New Orleans, LA.

Amble, B. (1967). Reading by phrases. *California Journal of Education Research, 18*, 116–124.

Brozo, W., Schmelzer, R., & Spires, H. (1983). The beneficial effect of chunking on good readers' comprehension of expository prose. *Journal of Reading, 26*, 442–445.

Carle, E. (1981). *The very hungry caterpillar.* New York: HarperCollins.

Cole, J. (1986). *This is the place for me.* New York, NY: Scholastic, Inc.

Dowhower, S. (1987). Effects of repeated readings on second-grade transitional readers' fluency and comprehension. *Reading Research Quarterly, 22*, 389–406.

Dowhower, S. (1991). Speaking of prosody: Fluency's unattended bedfellow. *Theory into Practice, 30*(3), 158–164.

Durkin, D. (1966). *Children who read early: Two longitudinal studies.* New York, NY: Teachers College Press.

Durkin, D. (1974). A six-year study of children who learned to read in school at the age of four. *Reading Research Quarterly, 10*, 9–61.

Eldredge, J. L., & Quinn, D. W. (1988). Increasing reading performance of low-achieving second graders with dyad reading groups. *Journal of Educational Research, 82*, 40–46.

Eldredge, J. L., Reutzel, D. R., & Hollingsworth, P. M. (in press). Round room reading versus the shared book experience: Examining changes in oral reading practice. *Journal of Literacy Research.*

Gambrell, L. B., Wilson, R. M., & Gnatt, W. N. (1981). Classroom observations of task-attending behaviors of good and poor readers. *Journal of Educational Research, 74*, 400–404.

Greene, F. P. (1970). *Paired reading.* Unpublished manuscript, Syracuse University, New York.

Harris, T. L., & Hodges, R. E. (Eds.). (1981). *A dictionary of reading and related terms.* Newark, DE: International Reading Association.

Hasbrouck, J. E., & Tindal G. (1992). Curriculum-based oral reading fluency norms for students in grades 2 through 5, *Teaching Exceptional Children,* Spring 1995, 41–44.

Heckleman, R. G. (1966). Using the neurological impress remedial reading technique. *Academic Therapy, 1*, 235-239, 250.

Heckleman, R. G. (1969). A neurological impress method of remedial reading instruction. *Academic Therapy, 4*, 277, 282.

Henk, W. A. (1983). Adapting the NIM to improve comprehension. *Academic Therapy, 19*, 97–101.

Hennings, K. (1974). Drama reading, an on-going classroom activity at the elementary school level. *Elementary English, 51*, 48–51.

Hoffman, J. V. (1987). Rethinking the role of oral reading in basal instruction. *The Elementary School Journal, 87*(3), 367–374.

Huey, E. B. (1968). *The psychology and pedagogy of reading.* Cambridge, MA: MIT Press.

Koskinen, P., Wilson, R., & Jensema, C. (1985). Closed-captioned television: A new tool for reading instruction. *Reading World, 24*, 1–7.

Martin, B. (1983). *Brown bear, brown bear, what do you see?* New York: Henry Holt.

Martin, B., & Archambault, J. (1987). *Knots on a counting rope.* NY: H. Holt.

Nelson, L., & Morris, D. (1986). *Supported oral reading: A year-long intervention study in two inner-city primary grade classrooms.* Paper presented at the annual meeting of the National Reading Conference, Austin, Texas.

Neuman, S. B., & Koskinen, P. (1992). Captioned television as comprehensible input: Effects of incidental word learning from context for language minority students. *Reading Research Quarterly, 27*(1), 94–106.

Rasinski, T. (1989). Fluency for everyone: Incorporating fluency instruction in the classroom. *The Reading Teacher, 42*(9), 690–693.

Rasinski, T. (1990a). Effects of repeated reading and listening-while-reading on reading fluency. *The Journal of Educational Research, 83*(3), 147–150.

Rasinski, T. (1990b). Investigating measure of reading fluency. *Educational Research Quarterly, 14*(3), 37–44.

Reutzel, D. R., & Cooter, R. B. (1996). *Teaching children to read: From basals to books* (2nd ed.). New York: Merrill, an imprint of Prentice-Hall.

Robinson, B. (1972). *The Best Christmas Pageant Ever.* NY: Harper & Row.

Samuels, J. (1979). The method of repeated reading. *The Reading Teacher, 32*, 403-408.

Searfoss, L. W. (1975). Radio reading. *The Reading Teacher, 29*, 295–296.

Shake, M. (1986). Teacher interruptions during oral reading instruction: Self-monitoring as an impetus for change in corrective feedback. *Remedial and Special Education, 7*(5), 18–24.

Shinn, M. R. (Ed.). (1989) Curriculum-based measurement: *Assessing special children* pp. 239–240. New York: Guilford Press.

Sloyer, S. (1982). *Reader's theatre: Story dramatization in the classroom.* Urbana, Illinois: National Council of Teachers of English.

Stayter, F., & Allington, R. (1991). Fluency and the understanding of texts. *Theory into Practice, 30*(3), 143–148.

Viorst, J. (1972). *Alexander and the terrible, horrible, no good, very bad day.* New York: Atheneum.

Vygotsky, L. S. (1978). *Mind in society.* Cambridge, Massachusetts: Harvard University Press.

Wood, K. D. (1983). A variation on an old theme: 4-way oral reading. *The Reading Teacher, 37*(1), 38–41.

Zutell, J., & Rasinski, T. (1991). Training teachers to attend to their students' oral reading fluency. *Theory into Practice, 30*(3), 211–217.

Chapter 14

Reader Stance and Literature Response

Teachers in America's classrooms are rediscovering the use of children's literature as a primary vehicle for teaching literacy skills. This trend is also evident in current basal reading series that contain many reprinted excerpts of award-winning literature. One of the leading basal publishers, in fact, recently paid well over $50 million in royalties to children's book authors to cover the cost of reprinting their stories in that publisher's new reading series!

We feel that one of the most exciting changes in today's literacy instruction is a movement away from the traditional assumption that each text holds only one correct meaning or interpretation. For both the child and the teacher, this change transforms the act of reading and reading instruction from a pursuit to discover an author's (or, very often, the teacher's) single correct message to discovering meaning based, at least in part, on one's own life experiences.

An alternative approach, called *reader response*, provides for a much more active role for students (Bleich, 1978; Rosenblatt, 1978, 1989). Reader response advocates suggest that there are many possible meanings in a text, depending upon the reader's background and reaction to the text. Instruction guided by reader response seeks balance by considering the reader's background experiences, beliefs, and purposes for reading, as well as the author's style and intended meaning. The role of the teacher is to assist each child to develop a creative product—usually a written response in some form—that explains her understanding of the author's message.

Reader response activities seem to hold great promise for readers having learning problems as well as for mainstream learners. Increasing numbers of Title I and Special Education teachers are catching the spirit and excitement of using children's literature and response activities to spark learning among discouraged and often reluctant readers. Tunnell and Jacobs (1989) and Manning and Manning (1989) report excellent results from around the nation where students having reading problems are discovering anew the joy of reading and writing with real books rather than struggling to learn to read with the often sterile, controlled readers used in the past.

This chapter provides teachers with the information necessary to understand the shift in focus from text-centered instruction to a more balanced reading approach that brings quality texts and an active reader together. We begin with assessment tools that can help teachers determine where students are in their reading development and comprehension. This chapter also offers appropriate strategies for helping students to respond to written text in ways that greatly enhance their reading comprehension and to develop insights into different forms of writing and authoring.

BACKGROUND BRIEFING FOR TEACHERS: ASSESSING READER RESPONSE

Many teachers were reared with the tenets of *Critical Formalism* or *New Criticism* in their elementary, secondary, and post-secondary experiences with literature study. As undergraduate and graduate students, we were taught to love and admire the close and critical reading of poetry and prose. As we read, the text was considered an isolated object that we should objectively and dispassionately prepare to discuss and analyze. This process of literature study was almost like examining a glass prism and considering it from all possible points of view by carefully turning it about in space. By turning and handling it, the work's integrity would not be altered. Hence, literature was to be processed as an object separate from its social, political, or historical context. This was literature study without the influence of the reader or the writer. It was a rather sterile analysis of the text with attention directed toward genre and structure, as well as to such stylistic devices as mood, imagery, and metaphor. Christenbury (1992) captured the feeling of this approach when he wrote, "What for us was a celebration of the intricate art of literature for our students became a repugnant dissection of an already difficult text, robbing it of joy, making it a task, not a connection to life" (p. 34).

Out of an increasing sense of dissatisfaction with the *New Criticism* approach to literature study, Norman Holland (1975) and David Bleich (1978) proposed a more subjective position called *Subjective Criticism* that stated that the reader was most important. This position, however, became as untenable as the former position that emphasized the singular importance of the text.

Rosenblatt's (1978) *transactional theory* declared reading and literature study to be a carefully orchestrated relationship between reader and text. Reader response evolved, in part, out of the work of Rosenblatt (Kelly, 1990). A *transaction* suggests a special type of relationship between the reader and the text—an act that causes the reader to be motivated to construct a personal meaning for a particular text. Situational conditions, such as time, mood, pressures, reason, intents, and purposes for reading influence a reader's stance, or attitude, toward a piece of literature. Rosenblatt describes two stances—efferent and aesthetic—in discussing how readers may choose to focus their attention during reading.

Efferent Stance

When readers focus their attention on information to be remembered from reading a text, they are taking an *efferent stance*. For example, reading the driver's license manual in preparation for an upcoming driving examination exemplifies an efferent stance toward a text. Reading a novel for the purpose of writing a book report that summarizes the plot is another example of taking an efferent stance toward text. However, when readers assume an efferent stance toward a novel, the focus of their attention is upon memorizing or gleaning from the text to pass a test rather than upon enjoying and learning from the experience. Obviously, there is a need for another type of reader stance or motivation for reading a text—an aesthetic stance.

Aesthetic Stance

When adopting an *aesthetic stance,* the reader draws on past experiences, connects these experiences to the text, often savors the beauty of the literary art form, and becomes an integral participant in the unfolding events of the text. When reading John Sczeika's *The True Story of the Three Little Pigs* to students—even college students—they never remark how the text follows accepted narrative form or contains three major repetitive plot episodes! Instead, they connect the zany perspective of the wolf's account and their own past experiences with the original tale of the "The Three Little Pigs." Arising from the often bizarre twist of perspectives represented between the two stories, the humor of these perspectives often produces gales of laughter among students as they see the story through the eyes of the character "A. Wolf." Assuming an aesthetic stance toward a text leads to making personal connections and reporting feelings and images, as well as ideas about how the story may occur in our own lives.

The quality or validity of readers' responses is often a concern for teachers who have been schooled in the "single correct " interpretation of *New Criticism.* "How can we determine if a response to a text is valid?" is an oft-asked question. Karolides (1992) explains that the validity of a response depends on the degree to which an individual response

- includes the various features of the text and the nuances of language,
- includes aspects that do not reflect the text, and
- has led the reader to create a coherent reaction.

Discussion of texts as a class or shared responses in small groups lead students into Grand Conversations about literature. During these Grand Conversations, students will be exposed to a range of responses to a text. Such discussions can motivate students to extend, clarify, and understand their own reactions to the text read. Further, comparing their responses to those of peers can help students to recognize that there can be more than one valid interpretation of a text.

In the next part of this chapter, a listing of various informal tasks for assessing reader response are presented. These may be used to determine the quality of thought, preparation, diligence, and attitudes toward literature study and reader response.

ASSESSING READER STANCE AND LITERATURE RESPONSE

ASSESSING READING COMPREHENSION THROUGH QUESTIONING

Purpose

Teachers building balanced reading programs using trade books quickly find that they must construct minilessons and assessment strategies to account for reading skills to be taught. In Chapter 1 we discussed the "whole-to-parts-to-whole" process for teaching and assessing reading skills in a natural way. Angeletti (1991) developed a way to engage children in a blend of reading, writing, and talking about books that yielded the necessary skill-based accountability demanded by many schools, districts, states, and basal readers. Although conceived of as teaching strategy, Angeletti's approach to questioning is quite effective as an assessment procedure.

Materials

For this activity, you will need standard sized white letter paper, $11'' \times 14''$ colored construction paper, and a marker. If available, a computer with a word processing program and printer with large font or type size should be used for best results. Question cards should be produced similar to those shown in Figure 14.1.

Procedure

Begin by printing the question cards on white paper and mounting each question card on a colored construction paper backing. Next, pick a type of questioning you wish to emphasize. During shared reading or literature circle study, ask children questions of this chosen type for several days. After this, show the children the question card you have selected for emphasis. Model with a book how the question could be answered. Follow up with whole class practice with a shared book. Finally, practice in small groups and individually. Encourage students to select a question card to guide the construction of their responses in a literature log. Each of these responses to question cards can be judged against the type of "comprehension skill" represented by the question for documenting skill acquisition and instruction.

LITERATURE STUDY GROUP PREPARATION AND PARTICIPATION CHECKLIST

Purpose

Although many teachers recognize the value of literature study groups (also called literature study circles), they often feel a need to satisfy the political realities of documenting student progress and growth as a result of their teaching. One means for doing this is to develop a checklist outlining the expectations for those who participate in literature study groups. Such a checklist can be used to assess student readiness or preparation prior to participation in the literature study group as well as to yield qualitative information about each student's participation during the literature study group (Peterson & Eeds, 1990).

Materials

The *Literature Study Preparation and Participation Evaluation Record* shown in Figure 14.2 is the main item needed for this activity.

Procedure

One form should be duplicated for each student in the literature study group. We recommend that the "Preparation" section be completed prior to participation and reevaluated at the conclusion of the literature study session. The "Participation"

Figure 14.1   Question Cards

APPENDIX: Question Cards

Comparison and contrast card 1

Choose two characters from one story. Do the characters look alike? How are they alike? How are they different? What problems do the two characters have that are the same? How are the feelings of the characters different?

Comparison and contrast card 2

Choose two stories. How were the places where the stories took place alike or different? How were the stories the same? How were they different? How were the story endings different? Which story did you like better? Why? Which character did you like better? Why?

Opinions

What did you like about the main character? What did the character do that made you like him or her? What did you think about the ending? Was anything surprising to you in the story? What was it? Why were you surprised?

Inference

Look at the pictures and at the title. What do you know about the story before you begin to read it? Read the story. Think about the ending. If the story had continued, what might have happened? Why?

Drawing conclusions

Draw a picture of your favorite character. Tell as much as you can about what kind of person your character is. Tell things he or she did in the story. Is this a nice person? Why or why not? Would you like to have this person for a friend? Why or why not?

Characters

As you read a story you learn about the characters by what they say and do. Choose a character from your story. What kind of person is your character? Do you like him or her? Why? How would he or she act if you were with him or her?

Author's style

Every writer has his or her own way of writing called *style*. When we learn the author's style, we know what to expect from that writer. We often know whether books written by a particular author will be easy picture books or chapter books. We know what kind of characters are typical of the writer—animals that talk, or people like us. We might know whether there will be a happy ending. We know whether we would enjoy reading another book by the same author. Choose an author whose style you know and tell what you know about the author's style of writing. Give examples from books you have read by that author.

continued

Figure 14.1   Continued

Author's purpose

Sometimes authors write a story to teach you something. Sometimes they tell a story about something that happened to them. Sometimes they just want to entertain you. Or, they may have another reason for writing. Tell in one sentence why you think the author wrote the story you read. Then tell how you knew the author's reason for writing the story.

Type of literature

Tell what kind of book you are reading. Look for clues that let you know. If it is *fantasy* or *fiction*, for example, there may be animals that talk, or magic things may happen. If it is *realistic fiction*, there may be real people in the story, and the story could have happened, but the author made it up, perhaps using ideas from his or her own life. If you find rhyming words, short lines, and writing that makes every word count, you are reading *poetry*. Or, you may be reading facts from a book like an encyclopedia. If so, the book is *factual*. Think about what section of the library you would go to in order to find the book. Then put your book into one group and tell what clues let you know which type of book it is.

Note: Adapted from "Encouraging Students to Think About What They Read" by S. R. Angeletti, 1991, *The Reading Teacher, 45*(4), 288–296. Copyright 1991 by the International Reading Association.

section should then be completed at the end of the literature study to evaluate each participant. Other items may be added to Figure 14.2 to tailor its use to individual classroom needs.

STUDENT RESPONSE CHECKLIST
Purpose

Teachers want to know if children are making personal connections between their own lives and experiences and those recorded in the books they are reading. Some teachers may want to assess whether students are interpreting and making meaning, or are gaining insights in a story as they read. Peterson and Eeds (1990) have developed a *Response to Literature Checklist* that we have found particularly helpful in providing documentation of the way in which children respond to particular stories or books within that programmatic framework.

Materials

Copies of the Response to Literature Checklist in Figure 14.3 are needed for each student for this activity.

ℐⳑ **Figure 14.2**   Literature Study Preparation and Participation Evaluation Record

Record of Preparation for and Participation in Literature Study*

Name: _____   Date: _____

Author: _____   Title: _____

Preparation for Literature Study

Brought book to group	Yes _____	No _____
Contributed to developing a group reading plan	Yes _____	No _____
Worked according to group reading plan	Yes _____	No _____
Read the book	Yes _____	No _____
Took note of places to share (ones of interest, ones that were puzzling, etc.)	Yes _____	No _____
Did nightly assignments as they arose from the day's discussion	Yes _____	No _____

Participation in Literature Study

Overall participation in the dialogue	Weak _____	Good _____	Excellent _____
Overall quality of responses	Weak _____	Good _____	Excellent _____
Referred to text to support ideas and to clarify	Weak _____	Good _____	Excellent _____
Listened to others and modified responses where appropriate	Weak _____	Good _____	Excellent _____
_____ **	Weak _____	Good _____	Excellent _____
_____	Weak _____	Good _____	Excellent _____
_____	Weak _____	Good _____	Excellent _____

*We suggest using this form at the end of each literature study to evaluate each participant.

**The rest of the items are intended to tailor this evaluation to your individual students. Choose appropriate items to complete the form from those listed in the Response to Literature Checklist in Figure 14.3, or add those you think are most appropriate.

Note: From Peterson, Ralph L. (1990). *Grand Conversations: Literature Groups in Action.* Richmond Hill, Ontario: Scholastic-Tab Publications.

Procedure

A copy of the checklist should be made for each student. We recommend that the teacher not try to evaluate all students in every area of the checklist daily. Instead, select one or two students each day to observe (preferably without their knowledge). For example, you might decide to observe two students as they select and read books during Silent Sustained Reading (SSR) time while they are at their seats or in a reading nook. Then, for each of these students, you could complete Section I of the checklist: Enjoyment/Involvement. Another example of applying the checklist might include reading a student's reading log entry. You could determine whether the student was making sense of the reading or making personal connections. In this case, Sections II and III—Making Personal Connections and Interpretations/Making Meaning—would be used to assess the student's response to literature. Thus, the checklist should be used flexibly; teachers should not feel obligated to complete the checklist for every child during every observation. Instead, observations should be focused and selective.

Figure 14.3   Response to Literature Checklist

I. Enjoyment/Involvement

_____ Is aware of a variety of reading materials and can select those she/he enjoys reading

_____ Enjoys looking at pictures in picture story books

_____ Responds with emotion to text: laughs, cries, smiles

_____ Can get "lost" in a book

_____ Chooses to read during free time

_____ Wants to go on reading when time is up

_____ Shares reading experiences with classmates

_____ Has books on hand to read

_____ Chooses books in different genres

II. Making Personal Connections

_____ Seeks meaning in both pictures and the text in picture story books

_____ Can identify the works of authors that he/she enjoys

_____ Sees literature as a way of knowing about the world

_____ Draws on personal experiences in constructing meaning

_____ Draws on earlier reading experiences in making meaning from a text

III. Interpretation/Making Meaning

_____ Gets beyond "I like" in talking about story

_____ Makes comparisons between the works of individual authors and among the works of different authors

_____ Appreciates the value of pictures in picture story books and uses them to interpret story meaning

_____ Asks questions and seeks the help of others to clarify meaning

_____ Makes reasonable predictions about what will happen in a story

_____ Can disagree without disrupting the dialogue

_____ Can follow information important to getting to the meaning of the story

_____ Attends to multiple levels of meaning

_____ Is willing to think about and search out alternative points of view

_____ Values other perspectives as a means for increasing interpretative possibilities

_____ Turns to text to verify and clarify ideas

_____ Can modify interpretations in light of "new evidence"

_____ Can make implied relationships not stated in the text

_____ Can make statements about an author's intent drawn from the total work

_____ Is secure enough to put forward half-baked ideas to benefit from others' response

continued

Figure 14.3   Continued

IV. Insight into Story Elements

_____ Is growing in awareness of how elements function in story
_____ Can talk meaningfully about:

characters

setting

mood

incident

structure

symbol

time

tensions

_____ Draws on elements when interpreting text/constructing meaning with others
_____ Uses elements of literature in working to improve upon personal writing
_____ Is intrigued by how authors work
_____ Makes use of elements in making comparisons

Note: From Peterson, Ralph L. (1990). _Grand Conversations: Literature Groups in Action._ Richmond Hill, Ontario: Scholastic-Tab Publications.

STUDENT ATTITUDE SURVEY

Purpose

Developing positive attitudes toward reading and writing is the primary instructional goal for teachers of children. This is particularly true for teachers who work with readers having learning problems. Assessing the impact of using _real_ books on their student's reading and writing attitudes, however, can be challenging.

Over the years, several informal attitude measures have been developed and validated for classroom use. Heathington and Alexander (1978) have developed a primary and intermediate scale of reading attitude assessment. More recently, McKenna and Kear (1990) have developed and validated a new instrument that is simple and effective for measuring reading attitudes. They have incorporated into this instrument the Garfield cartoon character, but other characters, or figures ranging from smiling faces to frowning faces, may be substituted.

Materials

For each student, materials needed include one copy of the Reading Attitude Survey shown in Figure 14.4 and one copy of the Attitude Survey Scoring Sheet shown in Figure 14.5.

Figure 14.4   Elementary Reading Attitude Survey

School: _____   Grade: _____   Name: _____

1. How do you feel when you read a book on a rainy Saturday?

2. How do you feel when you read a book in school during free time?

3. How do you feel about reading for fun at home?

Note: GARFIELD © PAWS.

continued

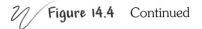 Figure 14.4   Continued

4. How do you feel about getting a book for a present?

5. How do you feel about spending free time reading?

6. How do you feel about starting a new book?

Note: GARFIELD © PAWS.

continued

✍ **Figure 14.4**   Continued

7. How do you feel about reading during summer vacation?

8. How do you feel about reading instead of playing?

9. How do you feel about going to a bookstore?

Note: GARFIELD © PAWS.

continued

 **Figure 14.4**   Continued

10. How do you feel about reading different kinds of books?

11. How do you feel when the teacher asks you questions about what you read?

12. How do you feel about doing reading workbook pages and worksheets?

Note: GARFIELD © PAWS.

continued

Figure 14.4 Continued

13. How do you feel about reading in school?

14. How do you feel about reading your schoolbooks?

15. How do you feel about learning from a book?

Note: GARFIELD © PAWS.

continued

 Figure 14.4   Continued

16. How do you feel when it's time for reading class?

17. How do you feel about the stories you read in reading class?

18. How do you feel when you read aloud in class?

Note: GARFIELD © PAWS.

continued

2/ **Figure 14.4   Continued**

19. How do you feel about using a dictionary?

20. How do you feel about taking a reading class?

Note: GARFIELD © PAWS.
From Elementary Reading Attitude Survey, McKenna, Michael C., & Kear, Dennis J. (1990, May). Measuring attitude toward reading: A new tool for teachers. *The Reading Teacher, 43*(9), 626-639. Copyright © 1990 by Michael C. McKenna and the International Reading Association. All rights reserved.

Procedure

Instructions for the instrument in Figure 14.4 are those described by McKenna and Kear (1990) in Figure 14.6. We suggest that you follow these instructions carefully so that the interpretive information found in Figure 14.7 can then be used.

DAILY READING RECORD

Purpose

Simple and easy-to-keep records of daily reading can give teachers an idea about how well students are progressing in developing positive reading habits. By using a version of the *Daily Reading Record* shown in Figure 14.8, students also develop

𝒲 **Figure 14.5**   Elementary Reading Attitude Survey Scoring Sheet

Student name: _____

Teacher: _____

Grade: _____   Administration date: _____

	Scoring guide
4 points	Happiest Garfield
3 points	Slightly smiling Garfield
2 points	Mildly upset Garfield
1 point	Very upset Garfield

Recreational reading

1. _____
2. _____
3. _____
4. _____
5. _____
6. _____
7. _____
8. _____
9. _____
10. _____

Raw score: _____

Academic reading

11. _____
12. _____
13. _____
14. _____
15. _____
16. _____
17. _____
18. _____
19. _____
20. _____

Raw score: _____

Full scale raw score (Recreational + Academic): _____

Percentile ranks   Recreational

Academic

Full scale

Note: From Elementary Reading Attitude Survey, McKenna, Michael C., & Kear, Dennis J. (1990, May). Measuring attitude toward reading: A new tool for teachers. *The Reading Teacher, 43*(9), 626-639. Copyright © 1990 by Michael C. McKenna and the International Reading Association. All rights reserved.

W Figure 14.6   Attitude Survey Directions

Directions for Use of Elementary Reading Attitude Survey

The *Elementary Reading Attitude Survey* provides a quick indication of student attitudes toward reading. It consists of 20 items and can be administered to an entire classroom in about 10 minutes. Each item presents a brief, simply worded statement about reading, followed by four pictures of Garfield. Each pose is designed to depict a different emotional state, ranging from very positive to very negative.

Administration

Begin by telling students that you wish to find out how they feel about reading. Emphasize that this is not a test and that there are no "right" answers. Encourage sincerity.

Distribute the survey forms and, if you wish to monitor the attitudes of specific students, ask them to write their names in the space at the top. Hold up a copy of the survey so that the students can see the first page. Point to the picture of Garfield at the far left of the first item. Ask the students to look at this same picture on their own survey forms. Discuss with them the mood Garfield seems to be in (very happy). Then move to the next picture and again discuss Garfield's mood (this time, a little happy). In the same way, move to the third and fourth pictures and talk about Garfield's moods—a little upset and very upset. It is helpful to point out the position of Garfield's mouth, especially in the middle two figures.

Explain that together you will read some statements about reading and that the students should think about how they feel about each statement. They should then circle the picture of Garfield that is closest to their own feelings. (Emphasize that the students should respond according to their own feelings, not as Garfield might respond!) Read each item aloud slowly and distinctly; then read it a second time while students are thinking. Be sure to read the item number and to remind students of page numbers when new pages are reached.

Scoring

To score the survey, count four points for each leftmost (happiest) Garfield circled, three for each slightly smiling Garfield, two for each mildly upset Garfield, and one point for each very upset (rightmost) Garfield. Three scores for each student can be obtained: the total for the first 10 items, the total for the second 10, and a composite total. The first half of the survey relates to attitude toward recreational reading; the second half relates to attitude toward academic aspects of reading.

Interpretation

You can interpret scores in two ways. One is to note informally where the score falls in regard to the four nodes of the scale. A total score of 50, for example, would fall about midway on the scale, between the slightly happy and slightly upset figures, therefore indicating a relatively indifferent overall attitude toward reading. The other approach is more formal. It involves converting the raw scores into percentile ranks by means of Figure 14.7. Be sure to use the norms for the right grade level and to note the column headings (*Rec* = recreational reading, *Aca* = academic reading, *Tot* = total raw score). If you wish to determine the average percentile rank for your class, average the raw scores first; then use the figure to locate the percentile rank corresponding to the raw score mean. Percentile ranks cannot be averaged directly.

Note: From Elementary Reading Attitude Survey, McKenna, Michael C., & Kear, Dennis J. (1990, May). Measuring attitude toward reading: A new tool for teachers. *The Reading Teacher, 43*(9), 626-639. Copyright © 1990 by Michael C. McKenna and the International Reading Association. All rights reserved.

W Figure 14.7 Interpretive Information for Survey

Midyear Percentile Ranks by Grade and Scale

Raw Scr	Grade 1 Rec Aca Tot	Grade 2 Rec Aca Tot	Grade 3 Rec Aca Tot	Grade 4 Rec Aca Tot	Grade 5 Rec Aca Tot	Grade 6 Rec Aca Tot
80	99	99	99	99	99	99
79	95	96	98	99	99	99
78	93	95	97	98	99	99
77	92	94	97	98	99	99
76	90	93	96	97	98	99
75	88	92	95	96	98	99
74	86	90	94	95	97	99
73	84	88	92	94	97	98
72	82	86	91	93	96	98
71	80	84	89	91	95	97
70	78	81	86	89	94	96
69	75	79	84	88	92	95
68	72	77	81	86	91	93
67	69	74	79	83	89	92
66	66	71	76	80	87	90
65	62	69	73	78	84	88
64	59	66	70	75	82	86
63	55	63	67	72	79	84
62	52	60	64	69	76	82
61	49	57	61	66	73	79
60	46	54	58	62	70	76
59	43	51	55	59	67	73
58	40	47	51	56	64	69
57	37	45	48	53	61	66
56	34	41	44	48	57	62
55	31	38	41	45	53	58
54	28	35	38	41	50	55
53	25	32	34	38	46	52
52	22	29	31	35	42	48
51	20	26	28	32	39	44
50	18	23	25	28	36	40
49	15	20	23	26	33	37
48	13	18	20	23	29	33
47	12	15	17	20	26	30
46	10	13	15	18	23	27
45	8	11	13	16	20	25
44	7	9	11	13	17	22

continued

Figure 14.7 Continued

Raw Scr	Grade 1 Rec	Aca	Tot	Grade 2 Rec	Aca	Tot	Grade 3 Rec	Aca	Tot	Grade 4 Rec	Aca	Tot	Grade 5 Rec	Aca	Tot	Grade 6 Rec	Aca	Tot
43			6			8			9			12			15			20
42			5			7			8			10			13			17
41			5			6			7			9			12			15
40	99	99	4	99	99	5	99	99	6	99	99	7	99	99	10	99	99	13
39	92	91	3	94	94	4	96	97	5	97	98	6	98	99	9	99	99	12
38	89	88	3	92	92	3	94	95	4	95	97	5	96	98	8	97	99	10
37	86	85	2	88	89	2	90	93	3	92	95	4	94	98	7	96	99	8
36	81	79	2	84	85	2	87	91	2	88	93	3	91	96	6	92	98	7
35	77	75	1	79	81	1	81	88	2	84	90	3	87	95	4	88	97	6
34	72	69	1	75	78	1	75	83	2	78	87	2	82	93	4	83	95	5
33	65	63	1	68	73	1	69	79	1	72	83	2	77	90	3	79	93	4
32	58	58	1	62	67	1	63	74	1	66	79	1	71	86	3	74	91	3
31	82	53	1	56	62	1	57	69	0	60	75	1	65	82	2	69	87	2
30	44	49	1	50	57	0	51	63	0	54	70	1	59	77	1	63	82	2
29	38	44	0	44	51	0	45	58	0	47	64	1	53	71	1	58	78	1
28	32	39	0	37	46	0	38	52	0	41	58	1	48	66	1	51	73	1
27	26	34	0	31	41	0	33	47	0	35	52	1	42	60	1	46	67	1
26	21	30	0	25	37	0	26	41	0	29	46	0	36	54	0	39	60	1
25	17	25	0	20	32	0	21	36	0	23	40	0	30	49	0	34	54	0
24	12	21	0	15	27	0	17	31	0	19	35	0	25	42	0	29	49	0
23	9	18	0	11	23	0	13	26	0	14	29	0	20	37	0	24	42	0
22	7	14	0	8	18	0	9	22	0	11	25	0	16	31	0	19	36	0
21	5	11	0	6	15	0	6	18	0	99	20	0	13	26	0	15	30	0
20	4	9	0	4	11	0	5	14	0	6	16	0	10	21	0	12	24	0
19	2	7		2	8		3	11		5	13		7	17		10	20	
18	2	5		2	6		2	8		3	9		6	13		8	15	
17	1	4		1	5		1	5		2	7		4	9		6	11	
16	1	3		1	3		1	4		2	5		3	6		4	8	
15	0	2		0	2		0	3		1	3		2	4		3	6	
14	0	2		0	1		0	1		1	2		1	2		1	3	
13	0	1		0	1		0	1		0	1		1	2		1	2	
12	0	1		0	0		0	0		0	1		0	1		0	1	
11	0	0		0	0		0	0		0	0		0	0		0	0	
10	0	0		0	0		0	0		0	0		0	0		0	0	

a greater sense of their own reading habits. Thus, these records provide documentation of how well students use their time for reading as well as inducing in students a sense of pride in what they are accomplishing.

A daily reading record should have a place to list the author(s) and title of the book as well as the date, time, and pages read. In addition, a brief written response may be encouraged, but is not usually required on the Daily Reading Record.

Materials

For each child, one copy of the *Daily Reading Record* form, found in Figure 14.8, is needed.

Procedure

A time at the end of each day's literature study period should be allocated for student record keeping. During this brief period of 2–4 minutes, students should log into their Daily Reading Records the information required and be encouraged to write a brief response if they desire. Daily Reading Record forms should be reviewed at least weekly by the teacher. We encourage teachers to avoid giving undue emphasis to the numbers of books read, recognizing instead the quality of the reading experience. Remember that "savoring" a good book takes time, just as fine food should be relished with appreciation.

BALANCED READING PROGRAM INTERVENTIONS: READER STANCE AND LITERATURE RESPONSE

Indicators That Readers Have Learning Needs

- Avoid reading books—particularly longer books
- Enjoy working on worksheets that require little reading, writing, or higher-order thinking
- Prefer to give yes or no answers to open-ended questions
- Express negative attitudes toward reading and writing
- Express a lack of confidence in ability to be successful in reading- or writing-related activities
- Lack ability to self-select books for individual reading

IMAGERY: MAKING MENTAL MOVIES OF TEXT

Purpose

When students make visual images about what they read, the mental "movies" provide an effective framework for organizing, remembering, and constructing meaning from text (Sadoski & Quast, 1990; Wilson & Gambrell, 1988). Unfortunately, some readers with learning problems do not spontaneously create mental movies as they read and thus miss out on the comprehension-monitoring boost that

Figure 14.8   Daily Reading Record

Student Reading Record Sheet

My Reading Record

Name: _____

Date	Pages read	Title	Comments

Figure 14.9   Imagery Hints

Hints on Imaging

1. Inform students that making pictures in their minds can help them understand what a story or passage is about. Specific directions, depending upon whether the text is narrative or expository, may be helpful. For example, "Make pictures in your mind of the interesting characters in this story." "Make pictures in your mind about the things that happened in this story." "Make a picture in your mind of our solar system." Using visual imagery in this manner encourages students to integrate information across the text as they engage in constructive processing.

2. Inform students that, when something is difficult to understand, it sometimes helps to try to make a picture in their minds. Using visual imagery can help students clarify meaning, and it encourages them to think about whether they are comprehending.

3. Encourage students to make visual images about stories or information they want to remember. Tell them that making pictures in their minds can help them remember. As a follow-up to story time or the silent reading of basal stories, have students think about the visual images they made and encourage them to use their images to help them retell the story to a partner (or, as homework, to retell the story to a parent or sibling). This activity will help students realize the value of using visual imagery to enhance memory.

mental movies can give them (Gambrell & Bales, 1986). Wilson and Gambrell (1988) indicate that specific instruction in how and when to apply *imagery* as a comprehension tool can be extremely helpful for students.

Materials

Activities and materials proposed by Wilson and Gambrell (1988) are summarized in Figure 14.9.

Procedure

Since research on visual imagery tells us that some students do not spontaneously use visual imagery, but can when directed to do so, teachers need to provide guidance and practice in the use of imagery. Wilson and Gambrell (1988) recommend the following considerations when selecting materials to be used to encourage visual imagery:

1. For modeling and teacher-guided practice activities, select brief passages of about paragraph length.

2. Choose passages that have strong potential for creating "mental movies" (i.e., those that typically contain rich descriptions of events and objects).

3. Point out that not all text material is easy to visualize—especially when the material is about unfamiliar and abstract concepts. Tell students that in those instances they should select another strategy that would be easier to use and more helpful (be prepared with suggestions that better fit some of the text types they are likely to encounter).

With minimal guidance and practice, students can learn and enjoy using visual imagery to enhance their reading experiences.

LITERATURE RESPONSE GROUPS (LITERATURE STUDY CIRCLES)

Purpose

The purpose of *literature response groups* (also known as *literature study circles*) is to emphasize the importance of reading and discussing children's literature or trade books (Eeds & Wells, 1989; Peterson & Eeds, 1990; Reutzel & Cooter, 1996; Samway, Whang, Cade, Gamil, Lubandina, & Phommanchanh, 1991; Short, Harste, & Burke, 1988). Samway and others (1991) reported that many students who participate in Literature Response Groups often go through dramatic changes in just one year:

> We noticed that in literature study circles the students naturally and spontaneously compared books and authors; initiated and sustained discussion topics as they arose; built their literary repertoires; and made associations between events and characters in books and their own lives. (p. 205).

Additionally, our own experiences with literature response groups/study circles have caused us to become great believers in this teaching and learning option.

Materials

You will need six to eight copies of four or five books that will interest students and duplicated choice ballots as shown in Figure 14.10. You will also need to prepare a book talk on each of the four or five books selected.

Figure 14.10   Choice Ballots

Literature Response Groups Choice Ballot

Name: _____

1st choice: _____

2nd choice: _____

3rd choice: _____

Procedure

To initiate Literature Response Groups, begin by selecting four or five books that will engender interest and discussion among students. Next, give a book talk on each of the four or five titles selected, enthusiastically presenting and describing each book to the students. Then, ask students to individually select their top three book choices they want to read. After the student ballots have been collected, make an assignment sheet for each book title. Give each student her first choice. If too many students want the same title, go to each student's second choice as you compile the assignments list. This system works well, since students always know that they get to read a book of their own choosing. After books are distributed the next day, give the students a large block of uninterrupted reading time in class to read. At the beginning of the year, students can read about 20 minutes without undue restlessness. However, later in the year children can often sustain free reading for up to one full hour.

As students complete several hours of independent reading, each Literature Response Group (comprising those studetns reading the same title, and thus interest-based) meets on a rotating basis for about 20 minutes with the teacher. Group members discuss and share their initial reactions to the book. We have found that meeting with one Literature Response Group per day—with a maximum of three days independent reading between meetings—works quite well.

Based on the group discussion, an assignment is given to the group to extend the discussion of the book into other interpretive media, i.e., writing, art, drama, etc. Each member of the Literature Response Group works on this assignment before returning to the group for a second meeting. This sequence of reading and working on an extension response assignment repeats until the entire book is completed. We recommend that the first extension assignment focus on personal responses and connections with the book. Subsequent assignments can focus on understanding literary elements, i.e., characterization, point of view, story elements, role of the narrator, etc. At the conclusion of the book, the literature study circle meets to determine a culminating project (Zarillo, 1989; Reutzel & Cooter, 1996). This project captures the group's interpretation and feelings about the entire book as demonstrated in a mural, story map, diorama, character wanted posters, etc.

RESPONSE JOURNALS AND LOGS

Purpose

Children grow as readers as they learn to use their knowledge, experiences, and feelings to construct a personal response text. *Response journals and logs* offer students "an active and concrete means of participating in the text" (Tashlik, 1987, p. 177). When personal responses are encouraged, students feel an innate need to share their ideas, feelings, and questions (Parsons, 1990; Stillman, 1987). Journal writing results in more complete and elaborate responses to literature than questions provoke and, most importantly, facilitates students' growth, confidence, and motivation to read (Wollman-Bonilla, 1991).

Materials

Collect reading materials 1) of high interest to students, 2) of high-quality literary merit, 3) within the reading abilities of the students, and 4) with text that helps integrate language arts within discipline-based content learning areas. Each student will also need a response journal. This can consist of almost any type of bound, lined, or unlined paper (e.g., loose-leaf paper, spiral notebook, composition notebook, stenographer's notebook, etc.).

Procedure

Using an overhead projector, begin by showing students several sample journal or log entries that reflect a range of possible responses. Text selections already familiar to students work best. Be sure to include honest feelings, questions, and reflections. Consider the following suggestions to guide responses based on Wollman-Bonilla (1991, p. 22):

1. What you like or disliked and why
2. What you wish had happened
3. What you wish the author had included
4. Your opinion of the characters
5. Your opinion of the illustrations, tables, and figures
6. What the text reminds you of
7. What you felt as you read
8. What you noticed about how you read
9. Questions you have after reading

Once students begin using journals or logs, teachers need to find time to respond to students' responses. This sends a clear message that journal responses are not simply a required exercise, but that someone cares about how the students feel about reading.

Perhaps the most important reason for replying to students' journal entries is to teach and support students. Finding time to do so is relatively easy. Do not feel that you must respond to each student every day, but simply respond on a rotating basis. As you do so, consider the following ideas:

- Share your own ideas and feelings about the book
- Provide additional information where needed
- Develop students' awareness of reading strategies and literary techniques
- Model elaborated responses
- Challenge students' thinking
- Offer alternative perspectives on the student's observations from a book

Journals and logs provide students with important evidence of their own growth in reading as well as substantial assessment data for teachers. Students can be brought to higher levels of thinking, greater strategic use of reading strategies, deeper understanding of literature, and improved skill in communicating their ideas through journal and log responses to literature. But the most important frequent outcome of journaling is an increase in the desire to read!

Art and Literature
Purpose

Drawing helps students understand that there are ways to respond to their reading, such as through music, art, drama, writing, and movement. Siegel (1983) claims that by translating and expressing what we know and feel from one communication system (written language, for example) into another (say, music, dance, or art), new knowledge and understanding are created. This process of "recasting" knowledge or feeling into another form of expression is called *transmediation*.

Materials

Artistic media of all varieties (e.g., paints, markers, brushes, easels, paper, pencils, chalk, crayons, cloth, etc.) are the materials needed for this activity.

Procedure

Figure 14.11 lists suggestions for art activities. Almost an infinite number of possibilities exist for using art to respond to literature.

Exploring Multiple Texts and Making Connections
Purpose

For students to become lifelong readers, they need to regularly enjoy rich and satisfying experiences with great books. It is sometimes difficult, however, to help students find books that offer positive experiences for every class member. Consequently, it is important to offer as many choices for students as possible (Poe, 1992), especially for comprehension instruction.

Reading comprehension instruction has often been viewed traditionally in terms of having individual students recount the story line or the main idea of the passage (Hartman, 1992). This is actually contrary to what better readers do, namely, comprehending text along a somewhat zigzag path. When reading is understood as a complex, layered process that cuts across the boundaries of single passages, stories, or texts, then using multiple texts to intensify readers' transactions takes on increasing importance. Hence, using multiple texts on a single topic or theme not only helps readers to develop and appreciate individual responses to books but also helps to develop their capacity to make intertextual links between different books.

Materials

Once a theme is chosen, you will need a selection of related texts to support that topic or theme. You will also need to develop a procedural minilesson on using multiple texts for literature study as discussed below in the procedures section.

Figure 14.11   Art Literature Response Ideas

Responding to Books Through Art

- Construct a mobile of your favorite characters from a book.
- Build a 3-D model of the setting from your favorite story.
- Draw a wanted poster for your favorite story character.
- Design a new book jacket for your favorite book.
- Construct an author mobile showing the titles and illustrations of your favorite author.
- Make flannel characters to support a retelling of your favorite story.
- Make a frieze to illustrate a book.
- Make an illustrated time line mural of events occurring in the book.
- Make a stained-glass window replica using tissue paper and cellophane.
- Make illustrated bookmarks.
- Make a TV Cranky of the book's plot with a box and rollers.
- Carve soap sculptures for a book's characters.
- Illustrate placemats from a favorite book.
- Make a mask for a character in a book.
- Construct a paper-bag puppet for a character in a book.
- Illustrate a mural-sized story map showing the setting and events of a book.

Procedure

To begin, invite students to write in their journals about the selected theme, e.g., *grandparents*. Students should express in their journals their feelings, thoughts, and associations concerning this concept. These prewriting entries can be used at the end of a literature study to compare their pre- and postreading thoughts and knowledge levels. Next, select three or four novels on the theme of grandparents, such as *Grandparents: A Special Kind of Love*; *Childtimes: A Three-Generation Memoir*; *Grandmother Came From Dworitz*; and *Grandpa, Me and the Wishing Star*. Introduce the three or four novels about grandparents by giving a brief book talk on each. Tell the children they will be reading these books to explore their own response.

During the weeks in which students are reading the novels, they should discuss them periodically in small literature discussion groups. Each group should comprise a mix of students who are reading the given book based on choice. In other words, their grouping should not be based on assumed ability levels. Students should decide as a group which days will be reading days and which will be discussion days. In these groups, students should share and expand upon their responses, developing understanding about why they and others in their group reacted as they did.

Teachers should sit in on these discussions regularly to evaluate students' participation in this important aspect of the unit. As students finish their books, they should write their response to the work as a whole. Whole-book responses give students an opportunity to synthesize their thoughts and feelings about the book, reflect on their experiences with it, and self-evaluate what they gained from reading it.

After writing whole-book responses, groups gather for a class discussion and presentation. Students in each group lead a panel discussion of each persons' responses to their group's book. When all groups have finished their presentations, students are invited to make comments that connect the commonalities among the three or four books read by members of the class. A comparison grid is often helpful for making these comparisons (Reutzel & Cooter, 1996). One example of a comparison grid is shown in Figure 14.12.

Finally, individual students usually engage in personal response projects intended to make stronger their connections to the text read. They often create a project that appropriately expresses their responses to an aspect of the book they read. Students share their projects with the class by explaining the relationship between their project, the book, and their feelings or thoughts about the book.

DRAMATIC INTERPRETATION OF LITERATURE

Purpose

McCaslin (1990) asserts that *creative drama* is an art, a socializing activity, and a way of learning. Drama as an art form to satisfy human needs and to foster the development and learning of children has been recognized by leading educators for many years (Rhodes & Dudley-Marling, 1988; Siks, 1983). As an oral and interpretive response to literature, Lynch-Brown and Tomlinson (1993) strongly recommend creative drama for use with children of all ages and abilities. McCaslin (1990)

Figure 14.12   Comparison Grid for the Grandfather Theme

	Grandparents: A Special Kind of Love	Childtimes: A Three-Generation Memoir	Grandmother Came from Dworitz	Grandpa, Me and the Wishing Star
Grandfather				
Significant other				
Problem				
Resolution				
Theme/Moral				

specifically recommends creative drama activities for students with learning problems. Creative drama is the act of informal playmaking comprised of several distinct techniques:

- Plays
- Movement and rhythms
- Pantomime
- Improvisation
- Puppetry and mask making
- Reader's and chamber theater

Creative drama offers teachers and children a wide array of possibilities for responding to literature through dramatic interpretation. McCaslin (1990) recommends that teachers bear in mind the following as they use creative drama for interpretive responses to literature:

1. Creative drama activities should be based on literature.
2. Dialogue is created by the actors: scripts are not prepared or memorized.
3. Improvisation is a critical feature of creative drama.
4. Acting is primarily through improvisation and movement: there is minimal use of props.
5. Creative drama is for the benefit of the performers, not for the approval of an audience.
6. No one dramatic interpretation of a story is correct. Several interpretations are to be encouraged.

Materials

Materials needed for dramatic interpretations include a good story, chapter, or literature book, and perhaps an assortment of props such as hats, glasses, puppets, clothes, etc. (optional)

Procedure

Creative drama is an enjoyable literature response alternative that makes use of children's imagination and oral language. Some educators have said, "Drama comes in the door of the school with every child" (Ward cited in Siks, 1983, p. 3). Literature-based drama may reenact a single scene from a chapter, a short picture book, or a brief story. It is best to begin with simple, short stories with two to six characters and a great deal of action. Folktales and fairy tales tend to fit this description well. When using creative drama to interpret literature responses, the following steps should be kept in mind:

1. Students listen to or read the story selected.
2. Students determine if this is a story they would like to act out. If so, they then read or listen to the story again, paying particular attention to the characters, action, and sequence of the story episode.

3. Students list the events on the board or on chart paper to review their sequence.

4. Students cast the play.

5. Actors use the list of sequenced events to plan actions, dialogue, and props suitable for the dramatization.

6. The cast of actors takes a few minutes to decide how the play will be presented and then rehearses it.

After the first performance, other students or groups can be invited to evaluate the success of the first performance. Actors in the performance can also self-evaluate their performance. Based on McCaslin (1990), we suggest the following questions to guide their evaluation:

Did the performance tell the story?

What did you like about the opening scene?

Did the characters show they were excited and interesting?

When we play it again, can you think of anything that would improve the performance?

Was anything important left out?

STUDENT-MADE COMIC BOOKS AS RESPONSE TO LITERATURE

Purpose

For many reluctant readers, *student-made comic books* provide much-needed relief from the monotonous rituals of basals readers, workbooks, and phonics instruction. Readers having difficulties with learning find the reading of comic books a delightful and meaningful departure from the norm of classroom reading materials and reading instruction. Not only students having reading problems, but people of all ages and abilities enjoy turning scenes, events, chapters, or books they have read into comic strips (Routman, 1991). Children love to study the ways in which the comic strip format frames the events of a book sequentially. They enjoy the color and format of each comic strip frame—especially the dialogue bubbles. For many teachers, comic strips represent a wonderful invitation to respond to literature as well as an equally wonderful invitation for other children to engage in reading a piece of literature.

Materials

You will need to collect the following for this activity: 8.5″ × 11″ sheets of unlined white paper; black and colored watercolor markers; a stencil for standardizing the size of comic strip frames; various artistic media such as paints, markers, and crayons for illustrations; and tools for bookbinding, such as a stapler, hole punch, rings, tape, coil, brass fasteners, etc.

Procedure

To begin a student-made comic book response project, children should be encouraged to first list in sequence the events of a story, chapter, or book. Then, the sequence should be reviewed with the text to check for accuracy. After reviewing the list of events for accuracy, the number of frames to be used in representing each of these major events in the story should be determined. Careful thought should go into how each frame can be used to tell the story in abbreviated form. The setting should be reread to help the artist capture its important aspects in the drawings. The dialogue can be paraphrased from the text or directly copied into the dialogue bubbles. Each frame is created in sequence to tell the story. Finally, the comic book is bound and shared with others to invite them to read the book or story. It is important to tell children that they can use their imagination from reading the story; that is, they should not feel obligated, if the story has illustrations, to attempt to reproduce them for their comic books. Comic books should be original and creative literature response enterprises.

LITERATURE RESPONSE SCRAPBOOKS

Purpose

Children love to collect things. They gather buttons, badges, prizes, pictures, objects, and all sorts of memorabilia to document the stories of their own lives. The natural propensity of children to collect things to tell their own stories can be turned into an exciting literature response enterprise. *Scrapbooks* represent a wonderful place for children to collect their individual and group responses to reading and sharing a literature book (Routman, 1991).

Materials

Assemble the following materials for this activity: 12″ × 18″ sheets of unlined white paper; black and colored watercolor markers; various artistic media, such as paints, markers, and crayons for illustrations; and various tools for bookbinding, such as a stapler, hole punch, rings, tape, coil, brass fasteners, etc.

Procedure

Students will enjoy putting together a scrapbook comprising artwork and written responses to important events, scenes, and characters from the literature books they are reading. Scrapbooks can be used to highlight settings, characters, or main events. Students' written responses, drawings, murals, maps, or other response enterprises can be collected in a group scrapbook to represent the group's responses to literature. These group scrapbooks can then be exhibited in the school library to interest other students in reading specific books. In fact, some students have found that reading each other's scrapbooks provides them with a good critical review of a book before they select it for their own reading.

LANGUAGE TO LITERACY CHARTS

Purpose

Roser, Hoffman, and Farest (1990) recommend the use of *language charts* to reflect children's thoughts and feelings about a book. These charts could be used to collect responses, to compare authors, illustrators, genre, or themes, and to examine story characters, settings, episodes, and resolutions. Language charts can be used daily and represent a variation on webs and comparison charts used effectively by others (Norton, 1991; Reutzel & Fawson, 1989).

Materials

Materials needed for this activity are broad-tip colored markers, a piece of white butcher paper 5–6 feet in length, and a lattice as shown in Figure 14.13.

Procedure

Language charts are constructed from large pieces of butcher paper ruled into a lattice or matrix with headings that help to focus children on relations among various books read in a unit or in various response groups. In Figure 14.13, the chart includes headings on title, characters, the goals or purposes of the characters, and how the author makes each of his books special or different. Children are invited to respond to each of Eric Carle's books separately under the first three headings. Under the final heading, children respond to the books by comparing the techniques the author used to make each book distinctive. One way to minimize the risk of language charts limiting the range of responses is to begin by simply recording students' initial, unorganized responses to literature in a *collection* language chart. Then, another more *focused* language chart with specific categories drawn from the collection language chart could be used to organize a chart as shown in Figure 14.13.

Figure 14.13   Example of a Language Chart for a Literacy Unit

Title	Character	Tell what happens in the story.	How does the author make each book different?
The Very Hungry Caterpillar	Caterpillar	The caterpillar is hungry and eats every day until he gets big and fat. Then he turns into a butterfly.	The pages have holes in them where the caterpillar has eaten through the pages. The caterpillar eats the pages to get the food on them. The pages start small and get bigger each day. So does the caterpillar.
The Very Busy Spider	Spider	The spider works everyday spinning her web until she has spun a beautiful design.	The pages have strands of the web on them. The strands feel rubbery. The web gets bigger each day. At the end the whole web can be seen and felt.
The Very Quiet Cricket	Cricket	The young cricket tries to say hello by rubbing his legs together. Nothing happens until one night he meets another cricket.	The cricket makes no noises until the end of the book. Then the last page opens up and the book makes a cricket noise.

ERIC CARLE

ORAL LANGUAGE: STORYTELLING AS RESPONSE

Purpose

Storytelling is first and foremost an art form (Sawyer, 1970). Cooter (1991) explains that storytelling—an ancient art form—is enjoying renewed attention nationally in language arts classrooms. Goodlad (1984), in his book, *A Place Called School*, punctuates the need for breaking the emotional neutrality of most American classrooms. Storytelling appears to offer a solution to this problem.

Although teachers may enjoy storytelling as an exciting teaching strategy, children can also find increased joy in responding to their reading through storytelling. We say this for at least two major reasons. First, children can learn more about the richness of our language through storytelling. And second, they can reach out to their environment and other persons through storytelling (Ross, 1980). Teaching students how to select and tell stories well is an important means of dramatically responding to literature and exploring new modes of self-expression.

Materials

Construct a poster showing the four steps to becoming a storyteller, as described in Figure 14.14.

Procedure

Tell children that a storytelling response to a story begins by selecting a story that suits their personality and preferences. The storyteller and the story must become emotionally linked to be believable. Therefore, children should not select storytelling as a reader response unless the story truly interests them. Next, encourage each child to prepare to tell the story by "picturing" the events, characters, setting, and episodes in the story in her mind's eye. She should read the story repeatedly until the story line is fully committed to memory . . . like a "mental movie." If a story has a specific sequence or linguistic dialect, children should learn the language of the story verbatim. Tell each child that practicing the storytelling alone in her bedroom or in front of a mirror allows for seeing herself as she is seen.

After rehearsing, some storytellers enjoy selecting props such as eyeglasses, hats, makeup, or puppets. Children storytellers can be invited to consider various

Figure 14.14   Storytelling Poster

Steps to Becoming a Storyteller

- Find a story that is just right for *you*.
- Prepare the story for telling.
- Use books, props, and voices.
- Get the audience involved.

simple props for telling their story. In addition, using different voices to tell a story is very effective. Varying the pitch of one's voice, adjusting the speed of speech, or using dialects or foreign accents establishes story characters as real and believable. However, subtlety is an important key, since extreme variations of one's voice can also detract from the story.

Finally, arrange a legitimate audience for children storytellers. Groups of classroom peers or younger children are the most readily available audiences for child storytellers. For some children, a performance at home with their families may be a sufficient audience. Encourage young storytellers to get their audiences involved in parts of the story. This can be accomplished by copying a repeated phrase in the text onto a large cue card for the audience members to read at various points in the storytelling. For example, in "The Gingerbread Man," the cue card might read: Run, run as fast as you can. You can't catch me, I'm the Gingerbread Man.

To bring a storytelling event to closure, teachers may wish to ask a child storyteller to construct a storytelling map modeled after a story grammar map (see chapter 10) in order to review the parts and plot of the story in a visual graphic form for display in the classroom.

CHAPTER SUMMARY

Responding to literature is a powerful interpretive tool that is preferred by teachers and children to answering questions about literature or participating in a typical discussion of literature. In this chapter, we not only present an alternative format for questioning students about their literature experiences, but we include assessment tools that probe student preparation and participation in literature response groups, how students respond to literature, what student attitudes are toward reading literature, and how students can be held accountable for their reading of literature by recording their reading experiences in a daily reading record. Once teachers know why and how students respond, and what they respond well to, they can strategically select one of the many literature response instructional strategies offered in this chapter.

For students who want or need to form mental pictures of what they read, several strategies for increasing understanding and application of imagery were presented. To help teachers organize for literature response instruction, a complete description of how to form and use literature study circles that participate in "grand conversations" was provided. Several interpretive literature response activities were suggested such as: writing in a log or journal; representing responses through visual art; making connections between and among similar and dissimilar reading selections or intertextual links; showing responses through dramatic performances; producing comic book summaries to represent a response to literature; and storytelling. Means for collecting and sharing literature responses ranged from suggested group literature response scrapbooks to group constructed language to literacy charts in which authors, genre, plot, etc., can be contrasted.

Literature response is a lively, active, and involving approach for sharing personal responses to stories and literature. Teachers find great professional and personal satisfaction in relating to students as participants in a literature response or study circle. Students enjoy a greater sense of personal voice when responses are heard and valued as compared to a question-answer-feedback cycle like those that have attended traditional discussions—something Durkin (1978) once called *comprehension interrogation.*

REFERENCES

Angeletti, S. R. (1991). Encouraging students to think about what they read. *The Reading Teacher, 45*(4), 288–296.

Bleich, D. (1978). *Subjective criticism.* Baltimore, MD: Johns Hopkins University Press.

Christenbury, L. (1992). The guy who wrote this poem seems to have the same feelings as you have: Reader response methodology. In N. J. Karolides (Ed.), *Reader response in the classroom: Evoking and interpreting meaning in literature.* New York: Longman.

Cooter, R. B. (1991). Storytelling in the language arts classroom. *Reading Research and Instruction, 30*(2), 71–76.

Eeds, M., & Wells, D. (1989). Grand conversations: An exploration of meaning construction in literature study groups. *Research in the Teaching of English, 23,* 4–29.

Gambrell, L., & Bales, R. J. (1986). Mental imagery and the comprehension-monitoring performance of fourth- and fifth-grade poor readers. *Reading Research Quarterly, 21*(4), 454–464.

Goodlad, J. I. (1984). *A place called school: Prospects for the future.* New York: McGraw-Hill.

Hartman, D. K. (1992). Eight readers reading: The intertextual links of able readers using multiple passages. *Reading Research Quarterly, 27*(2), 122–123.

Heathington, B. S., & Alexander, J. E. (1978). A child-based observation checklist to assess attitudes toward reading. *Reading Teacher 31*(7), 769–771.

Holland, N. N. (1975). *5 readers reading.* New Haven, CT: Yale University Press.

Karolides, N. J. (1992). *Reader response in the classroom: Evoking and interpreting meaning in literature.* New York: Longman.

Kelly, P. R. (1990). Guiding young students' response to literature. *The Reading Teacher, 43*(7), 464–471.

Lynch-Brown, C., & Tomlinson, C. M. (1993). *Essentials of children's literature.* Boston, MA: Allyn and Bacon.

Manning, G., & Manning, M. (1989). *Whole language: Beliefs and practices, K–8.* Washington, D.C.: National Education Association.

McCaslin, N. (1990). *Creative drama in the classroom.* New York: Longman.

McKenna, M. C., & Kear, D. J. (1990). Measuring attitude toward reading: A new tool for teachers. *The Reading Teacher, 43*(9), 626–639.

Norton, D. (1991). *Through the eyes of a child: An introduction to children's literature.* Columbus, OH: Charles E. Merrill Publishing.

Parsons, L. (1990). *Response Journals.* Portsmouth, NH: Heineman Educational Books.

Peterson, R., & Eeds, M. (1990). *Grand conversations: Literature groups in action.* New York: Scholastic.

Poe, E. A. (1992). Intensifying transactions through multiple text exploration. In N. J. Karolides (Ed.), *Reader response in the classroom: Evoking and interpreting meaning in literature.* New York: Longman.

Reutzel, D. R., & Cooter, R. B. (1996). *Teaching children to read: From basals to books* (2nd ed.). New York: Merrill, an imprint of Prentice-Hall.

Reutzel, D. R., & Fawson, P. C. (1989). Using a literature webbing strategy lesson with predictable books. *The Reading Teacher, 43*(3), 208–215.

Rhodes, L. K., & Dudley-Marling, C. (1988). *Readers and writers with a difference.* Portsmouth, NH: Heinemann Educational Books.

Rosenblatt, L. M. (1978). *The reader, the text, and the poem.* Carbondale, Illinois: Southern Illinois University Press.

Rosenblatt, L. M. (1989). Writing and reading: The transactional theory. In J. M. Mason (Ed.), *Reading and Writing Connections.* Boston, MA: Allyn and Bacon.

Roser, N. L., Hoffman, J. V., & Farest, C. (1990). Language, literature, and at-risk children. *The Reading Teacher, 43*(8), 554–561.

Ross, R. (1980). *Storyteller.* Columbus, OH: Charles E. Merrill Publishing Company.

Routman, R. (1991). *Invitations.* Portsmouth, NH: Heineman Educational Books.

Sadoski, M., & Quast, Z. (1990). Reader response and long-term recall for journalistic text: The roles of imagery, affect, and importance. *Reading Research Quarterly, 24*(4), 256–272.

Samway, K. D., Whange, G., Cade, C., Gamil, M., Lubandina, M. A., & Phmmanchanh, K. (1991). Reading the skeleton, the heart, and the brains of a book: Students' perspectives on literature study circles. *The Reading Teacher, 45*(3), 196–205.

Saywer, R. (1970). *The Way of the Storyteller.* New York: Penquin Books.

Short, K., Harste, J., & Burke, C. (1988). *Creating classrooms for authors.* Portsmouth, NH: Heineman Educational Books.

Siegel, M. (1983). *Reading as signification.* Unpublished doctoral dissertation, Indiana University.

Siks, G. B. (1983). *Drama with children.* New York: Harper and Row.

Stillman, P. (1987). Of myself, for myself. In T. Fulwiler (Ed.), *The journal book* (pp. 77–86). Portsmouth, NH: Heineman Educational Books.

Tashlik, P. (1987). I hear voices: The text, the journal and me. In T. Fulwiler (Ed.), *The journal book* (pp. 171–178). Portsmouth, NH: Heineman Educational Books.

Tunnell, M. O., & Jacobs, J. S. (1989). Using "real" books: Research findings on literature based reading instruction. *The Reading Teacher, 42,* 470–477.

Wilson, R. M., & Gambrell, L. B. (1988). *Reading Comprehension in the Elementary School.* Boston, MA: Allyn and Bacon.

Wollman-Bonilla, J. E. (1991). Reading journals: Invitations to participate in literature. *The Reading Teacher, 43*(2), 112–113.

Wollman-Bonilla, J. E. (1991). *Response journals.* New York: Scholastic Inc.

Zarillo, J. (1989). Teachers' interpretations of literature-based reading. *The Reading Teacher, 43*(1), 22–29.

Chapter 15

Developing Research and Reference Skills

As students develop as fluent readers they are challenged to apply their skills to learn more about the world in which they live. In chapter 11 we reviewed various ways students can apply their skills to read and better comprehend expository texts. In this chapter we describe ways students can be helped to acquire research and reference skills. These practical skills help students discover and draw upon various resources commonly found in library/media centers as they pursue knowledge in specific areas of interest.

BACKGROUND BRIEFING FOR TEACHERS

Readence, Bean, and Baldwin (1989) stated that the teaching of study strategies, which include research and reference skills, is crucial in helping students' independent learning. Research and reference skills include such diverse areas as notetaking, mapping known (and unknown) information areas, choosing sources for obtaining information (e.g., Internet search engines, reference materials, expert interviews, etc.), searching card catalogs electronically and manually, and interviewing content area teachers. Some of the key strategies offered in this chapter help students to choose areas to research, to organize new information, and to learn efficient ways to locate facts.

Much of what is contained in this chapter relates directly to *metacognition*—helping students to determine what they know or don't know about a topic. In addition, many of these activities help students understand *how* they know what they know. That is, students recognize which research and reference skills they have already partially internalized.

Another major component of this chapter is the chronicling of research logs and graphic organizers in the form of "maps" that can be used by students in carrying out their research. These tools help readers categorize known information, identify gaps in information, and self-select appropriate sources to fill those blank areas with pertinent facts. For example, a tool used to categorize is the research log on which students chart their common reading research habits.

We begin by suggesting ways that teachers can assess student knowledge of research and reference skills. In the latter part of the chapter we suggest strategies for research/reference skill improvement that can easily be modeled for students to improve their skills.

ASSESSING STUDENT KNOWLEDGE OF RESEARCH AND REFERENCE SKILLS

Investigations conducted by researchers to help teachers determine what research and reference skills students possess have been few. There are a few informal strategies, however, that can help teachers determine what students know about a topic of study or survey the kinds of materials that students may be using in their research. We have included in this section the strategies that have been most helpful in our classrooms. When used as teaching activities these strategies help students to recognize their own needs—an important motivational teaching practice.

RESEARCH LOGS

Purpose

An effective activity for determining the kinds of research methods and materials students are using is the *research log*. Research logs are a simple listing of materials used over time in the content classroom to complete research projects. By periodically reviewing research logs, teachers can survey patterns of reading/study behavior in their classrooms and plan instruction to help fill in gaps in students' knowledge about research resources.

Materials

Students will benefit from a structured research log form. A simple format for research logs is presented in Figure 15.1.

Procedure

First, develop a brief minilesson modeling how you would use a research log while completing a class assignment. Using a recent assignment as the context will save time in your minilesson and will lead students to contribute to the conversation. Once you have modeled how to record information on the log form, distribute copies of the research log to the students. If possible, introduce the research log just prior to beginning a new unit of study and provide a folder in which the logs may be kept. Check the logs at the midpoint of the unit of study to determine which research materials are being used, then offer research skills minilessons as needed. Review the logs again at the conclusion of the unit to determine student progress and for future lesson planning.

SELF-RATING SCALES

Purpose

It is often true that no one knows better how he is doing in reading than the reader himself. This is especially true when it comes to his ability to use research and reference materials in the library stacks. A teacher carrying out an assessment agenda

Figure 15.1   Research Log

Name: _____

Subject: _____ Period: _____ Homeroom: _____

Date	Assignment/ Topic	Materials Selected	Pages/ Programs Used	Notes

should never overlook the obvious—ask the student what he's good at doing! Although this may be best achieved in a one-on-one discussion setting, large class sizes frequently make this impractical. A good alternative to one-on-one interviews for older elementary children is a student *self-rating scale*. In applying this strategy, students complete a questionnaire that is custom-tailored to obtain specific information about the reader and his skills with research and reference tools—from the reader's point of view.

Materials

You will need to construct a self-rating scale that conforms to the research and reference skills you want each of your students to possess. Figure 15.2 shows an example of a self-rating scale.

Procedures

We prefer to use self-rating scales within the context of an actual unit of study about to commence or with a unit just completed. For example, let us assume that you are about to begin a new unit of study pertaining to "The Evolution of Surgery" in this country from 1900 to the present. After having a brief warm-up conversation

Figure 15.2   Self-Rating Scale

Self-Rating Scale: Researching the "Evolution of Surgery"

Name: _____   Date: _____

Directions: Answer the following questions as they pertain to how you will find out more about the ways surgery has improved in the United State in the last 100 years.

The first three things I will do to find out more about how surgery has improved in the United States in this century when I enter the library is:

   1.
   2.
   3.

Three things I know about entries (cards) in the card catalog in the library are:

   1.
   2.
   3.

Three sources of information I can use in this study of surgery are:

   1.
   2.
   3.

I can organize the information and data I find by . . . .

I feel I could use some help in understanding how to use library resources or research skills in these areas (check all that apply):

   _____ using the card catalog
   _____ taking notes
   _____ finding periodicals from a particular time period or topic
   _____ finding books that relate to our unit on surgery
   _____ using the Internet to find information
   _____ organizing information to write a report
   _____ interviewing experts
   _____ knowing where to begin my research
   _____ locating information quickly in a book

with the students about the field of medicine and surgery, distribute the self-rating scale you have developed. Once the students have completed their self-rating scales, collect and analyze the scales to determine in a cursory way the skills the students feel that they possess. (Note: This is only a survey of student perceptions. You will also need to collect further observations as the students begin to actually use library resources to complete assignments.)

PREREADING PLAN (PREP)

Purpose

This three-stage strategy by Langer (1981) helps teachers assess and activate the prior knowledge of students about a topic of study. This assessment and instruction activity may be used with a whole class or small groups. The first step uses a question to determine any associations students might have with a topic, concept, or term to be studied. The second step asks students to review and interpret their first impressions. The final step has students work with the teacher to identify existing gaps in their knowledge to help guide their research into the topic.

Materials

There are no materials required to do the PreP activity beyond the usual paper, pencils, and chalkboards normally found in classrooms. However, large pictures or other artifacts that relate to the topic of study may help jog students' memories in the first activity.

Procedure

As noted above, the first step is to ask students what they know about the topic to be studied. These *initial associations* provide insights into how much prior knowledge exists in the class and helps students to begin building concept-related associations about the topic (Cooter & Flynt, 1996). For example, in teaching a lesson about the Civil Rights movement of the 1960s, you might start off by asking your class, "What do you think of when you hear the words 'civil rights'?" Showing pictures from the 1950s and 1960s of lunch counter "sit-ins," the Little Rock, Arkansas, school desegregation incident, or of Rosa Parks and Dr. Martin Luther King Jr. could be quite helpful in stimulating initial discussion. After recording students' first associations, the next step is to have students think about or *reflect on their initial associations.* During this reflection stage your goal is to have students discuss and explain why the associations they had about the topic came to mind— What made you think of . . . ?" This interactive stage further taps prior knowledge, builds a common network of ideas about the topic, and facilitates a student-centered discussion.

The last stage of PreP is called *reformulation of knowledge.* Your goal is to have students recognize and define what they know about the topic before they begin research to learn more about it. We find that creating an outline or *concept web* about the topic helps many students see graphically what they already know, create categories for known information, and provoke questions about what must still be learned through the research process.

SEMANTIC MAPS

Purpose

Another useful strategy that can be used to activate students' prior knowledge of a topic and lead them to preview text material via student-centered discussion is the *semantic map.* Based on schema theory, semantic maps are essentially "road maps" of what is known by students with clusters of related information noted. Semantic maps can help students better understand metacognitively what is known and not known, as well as the research sources that can be employed to help find information. Because semantic maps depict known information in precisely the same way the brain stores information, they are inherently logical for students and can provide valuable insights for teachers.

Materials

You will need a large chart or tablet on an easel and colored markers to illustrate the semantic map. An alternative is to use an overhead projector, blank transparencies, and markers.

Procedure

The procedure starts with the teacher writing the topic on the chart or transparency. Similar to the PreP procedure discussed earlier, students are then asked to volunteer any information they associate with the identified topic. As the students offer them, the teacher lists their associations on the chart or transparency. Next, the teacher asks students to examine all headings, subheadings, and visuals in a textbook selection to be used as part of the introduction to gather more information. Students may do this work independently or with a partner. The new information is then added to the semantic map. At this time, students are asked to read the textbook selection carefully to provoke more discussion and to find more relevant information that can be added to the semantic map. A postreading discussion centers on the various questions that remain to be answered more completely and research sources that could be used in answering the questions. In Figure 15.3 we illustrate a typical semantic map that was created by students with teacher assistance regarding the Civil Rights movement topic mentioned earlier in the chapter. Note that a product that grew out of the semantic map's construction was a listing of research sources available for locating needed information.

BALANCED READING PROGRAM INTERVENTIONS: HELPING STUDENTS INCREASE KNOWLEDGE OF RESEARCH AND REFERENCE SKILLS

Indicators That Readers Have Learning Needs

- Poor organizational skills when approaching a learning task
- Consistent low performance on tests in the subject areas (i.e., social studies, the sciences, mathematics, etc.)
- Difficulty with tasks involving problem solving
- Inability to take strategic and effective notes during class
- Poor research skills (i.e., difficulty locating appropriate information in the library)
- Inability to retain information

W **Figure 15.3**   Semantic Map: Civil Rights Movement

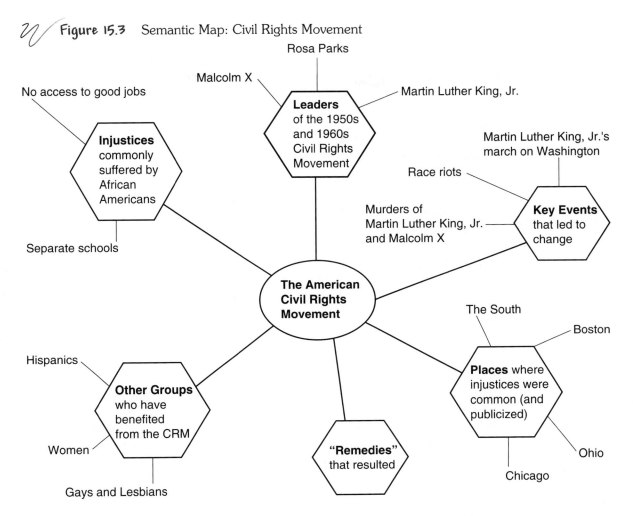

Questions to Answer

1. What are some of the greatest injustices suffered by African Americans that led to the Civil Rights Movement (CRM)?

2. Who were the Americans who seemed to have helped the CRM to be successful?

3. What were the key events that seemed to trigger the CRM?

4. Where were changes needed most in the United States?

5. What changes or remedies resulted?

Research Sources Available

History books, periodicals from that era, interviews with people who lived in the 1950s and 1960s, Internet searches, M.L. King Center in Atlanta, historians, card catalog entries, NAACP literature.

After a careful assessment of each student's current understanding of research and reference skills, teachers may find one or more of the following instructional strategies helpful. Perhaps the most important thing to keep in mind is that children who have a poorly developed sense of research and reference skills must be given numerous opportunities to practice and apply new knowledge (of course, this is true of all new skills). We begin this section with one of the most fundamental research tasks: taking notes.

RECOMMENDATIONS FOR TAKING NOTES

Purpose

There are many different systems for teaching students how to take notes as they listen (Cooter & Flynt, 1996). Among the notetaking systems that have been proposed are the Cornell System (Pauk, 1988) and the REST system (Morgan, Meeks, Schollaert, & Paul, 1986). The common threads of these systems are exemplified by recommendations about how notes should initially be recorded, the need for subsequent reorganization and expansion of the notes, and a strong recommendation for frequent review.

Materials

Students will need a notebook that can be used exclusively for learning notetaking.

Procedure

Before discussing each of the components of effective notetaking, we would first like to suggest a couple of general guidelines derived from the work of Cooter and Flynt (1996). First, students should be asked to obtain a single notebook specifically for use in learning notetaking skills. Dedicating a notebook for this purpose will help them keep the notes organized and will make it easier for you to collect and examine the notes. Second, if notetaking is important to you, then some type of credit should be given to students who do a good job of recording and organizing their notes. Finally, adapt the amount and style of lecturing to your students' ability level. If you have an advanced class, more sophisticated lectures might be warranted. On the other hand, if your class has little experience with notetaking and effective listening techniques, you might want to begin slowly and use a lot of visuals or perhaps a listening outline to assist students in determining and writing important information.

Two of the most popular notetaking systems are the *Cornell System* (Pauk, 1988) and *A Notetaking System for Learning* (Palmatier, 1973). These systems share several features that we recommend for use in training students in how to listen and take notes on lecture information.

First, students should divide their notebook paper into two columns. The left column should be about 2 or 3 inches wide, or one third of the paper width. The remaining two thirds of the page is used for recording the notes.

Second, students should write information in a modified outline form on the right side of the page. Students should indent subtopics and minor ideas using letters and numbers. They should be encouraged to use abbreviations to minimize time spent in writing down information. Heavily emphasized points should be marked with asterisks or stars.

Third, students should organize and expand their notes as soon as possible. Early in the school year, considerate teachers provide in-class time for this task. At this time the students literally rewrite their notes on similarly lined paper. The purpose is for the students to write all abbreviations, expand phrases, and make sure that the information is sequentially organized. This is obviously a form of practice.

Fourth, students fill in the left margin for aid in study and review. As they reread their notes, students identify topics, key terms, and questions that might assist them in remembering the lecture information recorded on the right side of the paper.

Fifth, students use their notes for study and review. Students can now cover up the right-hand side of the paper and use the memory triggers they have recorded on the left-hand side for review. As they move down the left-hand side of the page, students use the headings, key terms, and questions as a means of assessing their ability to remember and paraphrase what they have recorded.

SQ3R

All effective reading/study strategies are metacognitive in nature because they cause readers to establish purposes for study, to determine whether they have been successful in satisfying their purposes, and to adjust their tactics if they have failed or fallen short in achieving their purpose for studying. Reading/study strategies require the students to actively attend to text information; respond to the text in some way (taking notes, underlining, answering questions); spend more time on task; and review the material for long-term retention. If one examines a reading/study "how to" book, one often finds a plethora of reading/study strategies that are touted as either effective or tailor-made for specific subject matter areas. They are usually presented by an acronym that reflects the various steps of the strategy. The most time-honored of all these reading/study strategies is **SQ3R.** Originally developed by Francis Robinson (1946) as a technique to help soldiers study manuals during World War II (Stahl & Henk, 1986), SQ3R has been used widely in schools as a way of providing students with a specific, albeit intense, method for independent study. SQ3R has spawned many other similar-looking reading/study strategies; however, since most of the other reading/study strategies reflect much of what SQ3R recommends, we will confine this discussion to SQ3R. First, we would like to present the steps of SQ3R and then discuss the strategy's relative usefulness in content reading and study.

Survey: Begin a new unit of study by quickly reading all chapter headings, subheadings, margin notes, words printed in bold, pictures and their captions, and charts or diagrams. This will draw one's attention to some of the major topics to be learned.

Question: Based on your "survey," write several questions that pertain to the headings, sunbheadings, words in bold, and margin notes you discovered. This will alert you to some of the key information while reading.

(Note: We recommend that teachers model for students how to write questions on different levels of complexity, such as literal, inferential, and evaluative levels. Many students need a great deal of practice with higher-order thinking skills.)

Read: Read the chapter. As you do so, try to pay careful attention to information that answers the questions you created in the previous step. After reading, go back and answer each question in writing, being sure to note specific details from the chapter.

Recite: After you have answered all questions in detail, give yourself a quiz over those same questions and try to write your responses from memory. Any questions that gave you difficulty should be practiced by rereading the questions and answers aloud. Continue this practice until all questions and answers can be rewritten from memory.

Review: Once information has been learned and can be recited from memory, it should be reviewed daily so that it becomes permanent. The amount of time spent for review each day will depend on the complexity of the unit of study, but about twenty minutes per day is generally a good rule of thumb.

As you can see, SQ3R may require a great deal of effort on the part of the student and the teacher. Estimates suggest that a minimum of ten hours of teacher-lead instruction is required for low-achieving students to utilize SQ3R effectively (Orlando, 1980). In addition, the overall benefit of SQ3R on student achievement is not clear (Caverly & Orlando, 1991). We feel that teachers should stress only those components of SQ3R that can best serve students with a particular assignment.

Venn Diagram Hula Hoops

Purpose

Venn diagrams have been used for many years to help students understand similarities, differences, and common features of information gleaned from reading assignments. Venn diagrams are simply two overlapping circles used to graphically display three kinds of information. With *Venn Diagram Hula Hoops* (K. Cooter & Thomas, 1998), this concept is applied for students (elementary through high school) using the hula hoops first popularized in the 1950s.

Materials

You will need to purchase at least two hula hoops for each group of children (usually four students to a group) to be involved in this activity. For each group, sentence strips or tag board and watercolor markers are needed for use in writing information from the readings.

Procedure

With a simple passage, begin by modeling for the class how Venn diagrams are used. You can use a dry erase board, chart, chalkboard, or overhead projector for your modeling. For younger children—and perhaps for older ones, too—an easy-to-use comparison is the traditional telling of "The Three Little Pigs" contrasted to *The True Story of the Three Little Pigs by A. Wolf.* Another version of the story we enjoy using is "The Old Sow and the Three Shoats" found in Richard Chase's classic *Grandfather Tales* (1948). In Figure 15.4 we display how similarities, differences, and commonalties could be portrayed in the teacher's modeling exercise using Chase's version and the traditional story.

Once students seem to grasp the Venn diagram concept, repeat the modeling exercise in a large open space using the hula hoops. Simply ask the children to gather around in a circle where they can see the hula hoops laid across each other to form the familiar Venn diagram configuration. Be sure to print on sentence strips the appropriate name/title for each circle and place the labels above the corresponding circle or center section (i.e., "Traditional Three Pigs Story," "Old Sow and the Three Shoats," "Both Stories"). Using the very same descriptors that you suggested in the modeling activity and wrote on sentence strips or tag board strips (in this case, using the "Three Pigs" story descriptors), lay the sentence strips where appropriate within the diagram. Ask a volunteer if she can explain what each descriptor means in each circle or in the overlapping section.

Once students have demonstrated an understanding of how to use Venn diagram hula hoops, broaden the experience using nonfiction expository reading selections. Be sure to model first, then ask the students to do the task in small groups.

Figure 15.4 Venn Diagram Hula Hoops

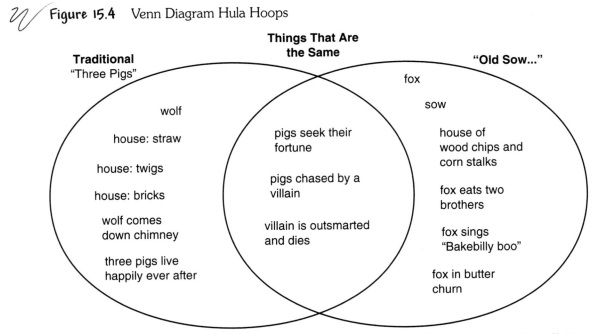

Note: Cooter, K. S., & Thomas M. (1998). *Venn diagram hula hoops.* Unpublished manuscript. Texas Christian University, Fort Worth, TX. Comparisons using the traditional telling of "The Three Little Pigs" and Richard Chase's (1948) "The Old Sow and the Three Shoats" from *Grandfather Tales* (Houghton Mifflin).

K-W-L-S Strategy Chart

Purpose

As described in chapter 9, the K-W-L strategy is effective in improving reading comprehension by causing students to activate, think about, and organize their prior knowledge as an aid to reading comprehension. Ogle (1986), the originator of K-W-L, asserts that this strategy is best suited for use with expository text. Sinatra (1997) has found success using K-W-L with informational texts when adding one additional step—asking students what they *still* want to know ("S") after the K-W-L routine has been completed. This addition to Ogle's original strategy helps create continuing interest in the topic under study, encourages a degree of metacognitive thinking (i.e., helping students realize what they know and do not yet know, and helps teachers assess student learning. We have adapted Signature's *K-W-L-S Strategy Chart* somewhat for use as a research tool.

Materials

Students will need a copy of the K-W-L-S Strategy Chart such as the one shown in Figure 15.5.

Procedure

As with a standard K-W-L activity, this version is intended as a metacognitive exercise to help guide students' learning. Begin by displaying an enlarged version of the K-W-L-S Strategy Chart at the front of the group, using either large tablet paper or transparencies and an overhead projector. Define and explain what each letter in the K-W-L-S Strategy Chart means and how an awareness of what one knows or does not know can help guide one efficiently through a research experience. This latter timesaving point can be motivational for most of us who hope to keep library search time to a minimum.

Next, use the enlarged chart to "walk through" the K-W-L-S procedure once using a combination of read-aloud and group participation. For example, let's say you have chosen a passage from a health textbook pertaining to heart disease to illustrate how the K-W-L-S Strategy Chart can be used as an aid in health research. Say to the students:

> "Before we try out the K-W-L-S Strategy Chart on our own, let's try it out once together. A topic we will be learning about next has to do with the human heart and ways to prevent heart disease. The first step in using a K-W-L-S Strategy Chart is to think about what we know about the topic. That is what the "K" represents on the chart. Let's list some of the things we already know about the heart. Any volunteers?"

Begin to list things that are known in the first column. Note that we have included at the bottom of that column a question that pertains to reference tools that helped students know what they already know about a subject. This helps students immediately think about tools they have used in some manner in the past, or—in other columns—tools they could use as they progress in their research.

Figure 15.5 K-W-L-S Strategy Chart

"K" What I "Know" . . .	"W" What I "Want" To Know . . .	"L" What I "Learned" . . .	"S" What I Am "Still" Needing To Know . . .
Reference tools that helped me know what I know:	**Reference tools** I will need to find out more:	**Reference tools** that helped me:	**Reference tools** I will need to find out more:

Name: _____   Date: _____
Topic: _____

The next step is to complete the "W" column by answering the question, "What information about the human heart and its diseases would I want to know (or need to know)?" Once the "W" column has been completed, use student participation up to this point as a springboard to discuss in some detail the library/media center tools that can be helpful for locating information. Next, using one of the library/media center tools, instruct your students to listen as you read aloud a passage you have selected pertaining to your question (in this case, a passage on heart disease might be chosen). Once you have completed the reading, go back to the K-W-L-S Strategy Chart and complete the section "L" describing the additional information you learned from listening to the passage.

At this point in a standard K-W-L activity the students would be finished. However, as Sinatra (1997) has observed, there are usually many more facts yet to be learned and questions left unanswered; hence, the addition of the stage "S" which essentially asks, "What do I *still* need to know about this subject?" Unanswered questions from the "W" stage of the activity, as well as any new questions emerging from the read-aloud activity, should be listed in this column. This final category sends some very important messages to students: 1) there are always some unanswered questions in almost every research project, 2) as you learn more information, that information often spawns new questions, 3) there are sources of information in the library/media center to help me find answers to my questions, and 4) my teacher will help me to learn how to use these resources effectively.

K-W-W-L

Purpose

Another variation of the K-W-L (Ogle, 1986) strategy is *K-W-W-L* (Bryan, 1997). Much like Sinatra's (1997) K-W-L-S Strategy Chart, this activity helps students to identify starting points for their research.

Materials

You will need to reproduce worksheets like the one shown in Figure 15.6 for each student, as well as an enlarged version with which you can model the activity.

Procedure

Follow the same process as described for the K-W-L-S Strategy Chart, only use the K-W-W-L figure instead. We have included a partially completed K-W-W-L chart in Figure 15.7 for use in your modeling exercise.

SELECTED MAPS FOR USE WITH INFORMATIONAL TEXT

Purpose

As noted earlier in the chapter, semantic maps and other graphic outlines can help teachers assess what students know or don't know about a topic. They can also be used as a research and study tool to help students chart important knowledge they

Figure 15.6   K-W-W-L Chart

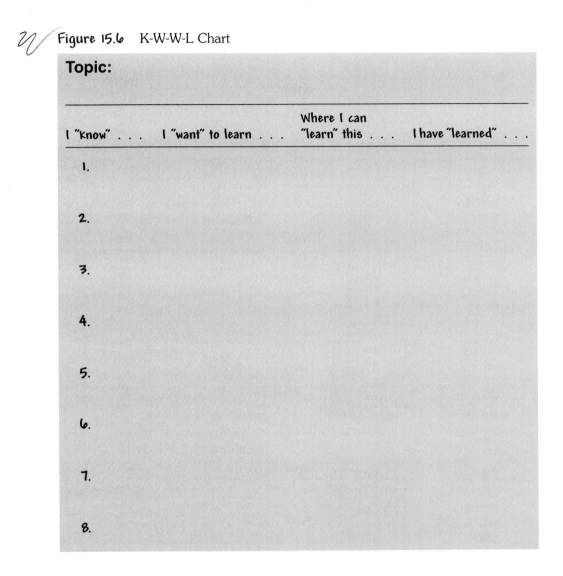

Topic:

_____

I "know" . . .	I "want" to learn . . .	Where I can "learn" this . . .	I have "learned" . . .

1.

2.

3.

4.

5.

6.

7.

8.

are acquiring, understand steps in a process or sequence, classify or categorize information, compare and contrast two or more features, determine causal patterns, and prepare and defend thesis statements concerning an area of study. In short, maps are a form of outlining and mental organization that help students determine which areas they must research.

Materials
Figures 15.8 through 15.13 display each map as described in the next section.

Figure 15.7   K-W-W-L Chart Example

Topic: "Oceans"

I Know . . .	I want to learn . . .	Where I can learn this . . .	I have learned . . .
1. Oceans have salt water.	What makes the ocean salty?	• encyclopedia • Internet search • ask a scientist	
2. Salt water burns your eyes.	Is salt water harmful to your eyes?	• ask a doctor • look for a book in the library on this subject	
3. There are many kinds of sharks.	Are all sharks "man eaters"?	• ask a marine biologist • check the Internet	
4. Oceans have waves and tides.	What causes the tides?	• look for a book in the library on oceans • ask a scientist at the university • call the TV station weather personnel	
5. Many kinds of fish live in the ocean.	What kinds of sea creatures live in the deep waters?	• look for a library book on fish • ask a scientist • check the encyclopedia • try an Internet search	
6. There are other forms of sea life found in the ocean.	What are some of the main kinds of sea life?	• same as #5	
7. Songs have been written about the sea.	How would I go about getting a list of songs about the sea?	• check with the music teacher • try a search on the Internet with <Amazon.com> for songs	
8.			

Notes:

Figure 15.8   Steps-in-a-Process Map

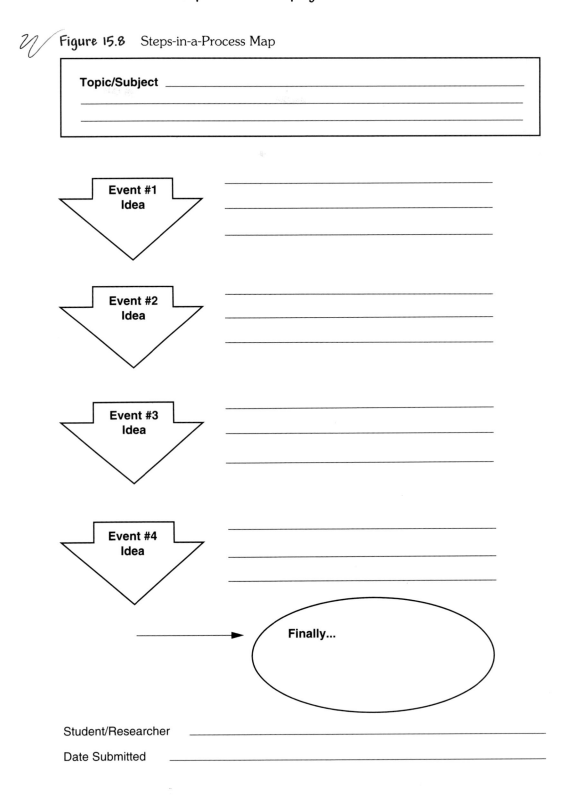

Figure 15.9   Comparison/Contrast Map

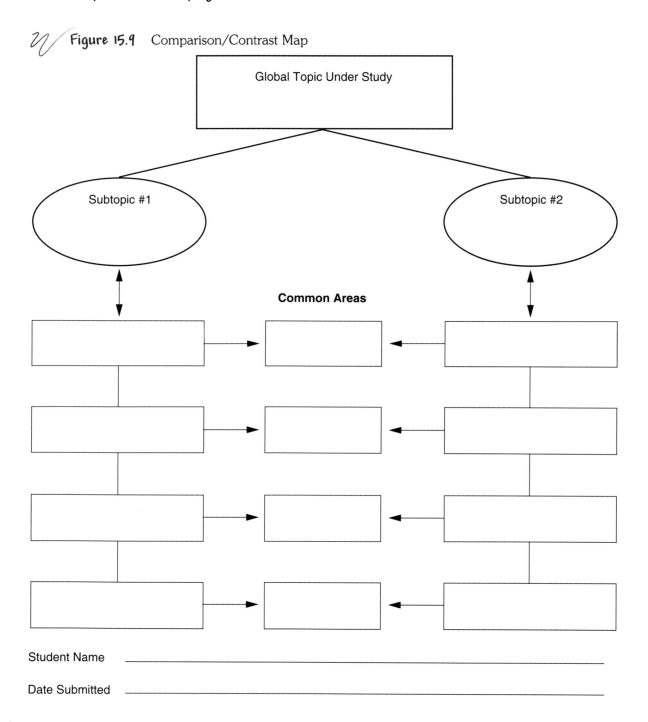

Student Name _____

Date Submitted _____

Figure 15.10   Same/Different Map

Topic or Main Idea _____

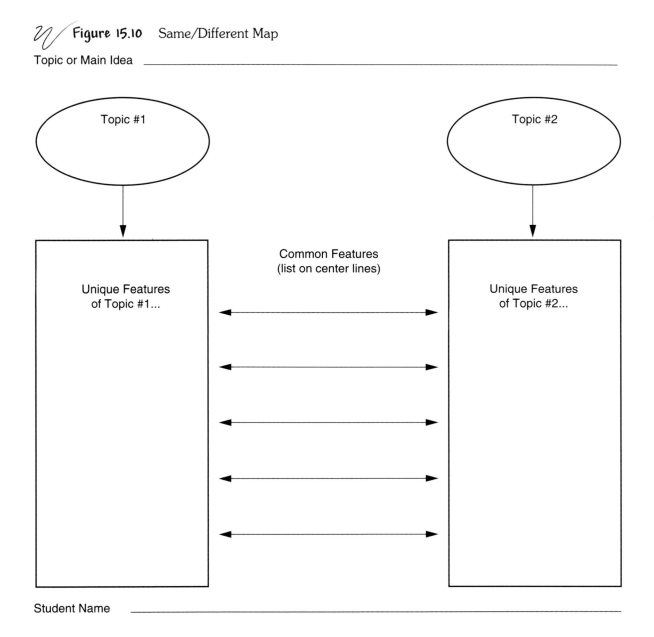

Topic #1

Topic #2

Unique Features
of Topic #1...

Common Features
(list on center lines)

Unique Features
of Topic #2...

Student Name   _____

Figure 15.11   Cause/Effect Map

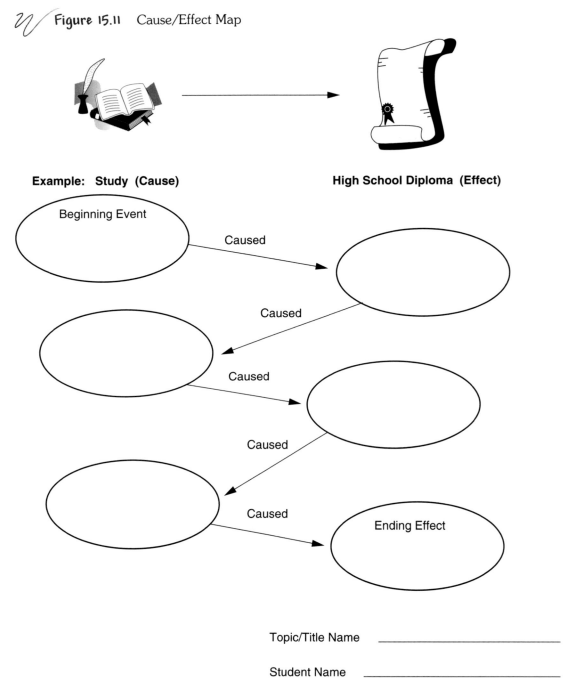

Example: Study (Cause)   **High School Diploma (Effect)**

Beginning Event

Caused

Caused

Caused

Caused

Caused

Ending Effect

Topic/Title Name   _____

Student Name   _____

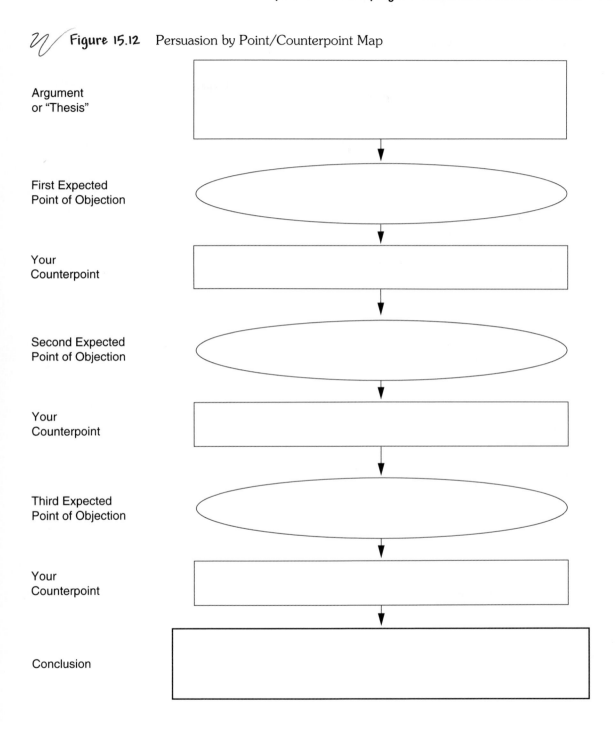

Figure 15.12   Persuasion by Point/Counterpoint Map

Argument or "Thesis"

First Expected Point of Objection

Your Counterpoint

Second Expected Point of Objection

Your Counterpoint

Third Expected Point of Objection

Your Counterpoint

Conclusion

Figure 15.13 Turning Point Map

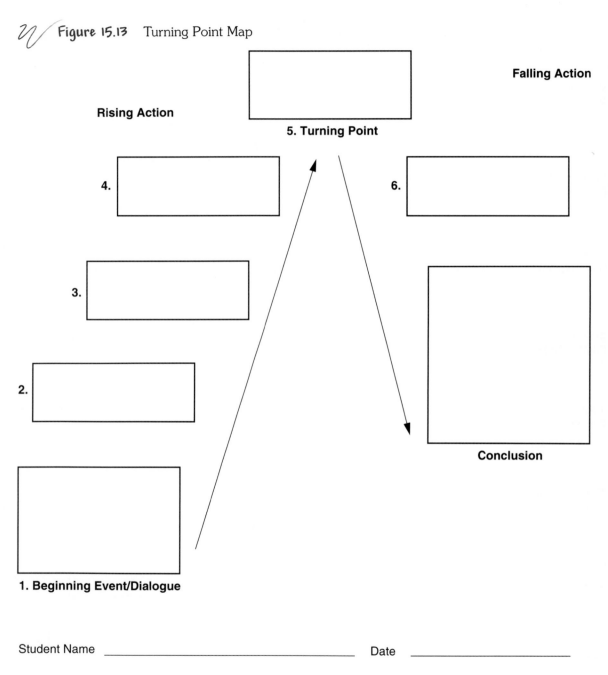

Falling Action

Rising Action

5. Turning Point

4.

6.

3.

2.

Conclusion

1. Beginning Event/Dialogue

Student Name _____ Date _____

Procedure

Sinatra, Gemake, Wielan, and Sinatra (1998) have identified several map forms and their usefulness with informational text. We offer below an abbreviated summary of their research targeting maps that we wish to emphasize.

Type of Map	Type of Text Structure	Type of Higher-Order Thinking
Steps-in-a-process	Time-related events with multiple episodes and/or a sequence of events, as with many science process steps or social studies events.	Students must be able to select and sequence events, describe processes in order. All are based on the student's ability to locate appropriate information sources.
Compare/Contrast *and* **Same/Different**	Comparison information structures found in many expository texts, particularly in the sciences, literature, social studies, health, and mathematics.	Often inferential or implied in texts, comparison requires students to identify qualities of sameness and differences. Thus, this activity provides a logical framework for identifying and using library/media resources.
Chain of Events	Causal patterns found in the text descriptions, most often the sciences, literature, and social studies.	Identification of causal events that trigger an (often predictable) outcome.
Persuasion by Point/Counterpoint	Derived typically from literature, social studies, and studies of the arts.	Identification of problems or issues, location of information to support a thesis/belief/judgment, charting opposing views, and formulating counterarguments in support of the thesis.
Turning Point Map	Useful primarily with literature and history texts.	Students are required to detect important events in sequence that contribute to a final outcome.

Note that students may be helped or "coached" by teachers to locate additional research materials or data bases to complete the map(s). In the end, it may be concluded that the construction of maps can indeed help students construct their own comprehension of the topic under study. Sinatra and colleagues (1998) urge teachers, as a next step, to challenge students to develop their own maps to represent new units of study, then present them to the class or group.

Chapter Summary

In this chapter we have reviewed a number of strategies for assessing and teaching research and reference skills. A common metacognitive element has been evident in that these strategies help students to better understand what they already know and what they need to know. In addition, many times students begin to consider sources for gaining information to answer unknown questions. Through effective modeling by the teacher, guided practice and mentoring, and much independent practice, students will gain critical research and reference skills that they will come to use as independent learners.

References

Bryan, J. (1998). K-W-W-L: Questioning the known. *The Reading Teacher, 51*(7), 1998.

Caverly, D. C., & Orlando, V. P. (1991). Textbook strategies. In R. F. Filippo & D. C. Caverly (Eds.), *Teaching reading and study strategies at the college level* (pp. 86–165). Newark, DE: International Reading Association.

Chase, R. (1948). *Grandfather Tales.* Boston: Houghton Mifflin.

Cooter, K. S., & Thomas, M. (1998). *Venn diagram hula hoops.* Unpublished manuscript, Texas Christian University, Fort Worth, TX.

Cooter, R. B., & Flynt, E. S. (1996). *Teaching reading in the content areas: Developing content literacy for all students.* Columbus, OH: Merrill/Prentice Hall.

Langer, J. (1981). From theory to practice: A prereading plan. *Journal of Reading, 25,* 152–156.

Morgan, R. F., Meeks, J., Schollaert, A., & Paul, J. (1986). *Critical reading/thinking skills for the college student.* Dubuque, IA: Kendall/Hunt.

Ogle, D. (1986). K-W-L: A teaching model that develops active reading of expository text. *The Reading Teacher, 39*(6), 564–570.

Orlando, V. P. (1986). Training students to use a modified version of SQ3R: An instructional strategy. *Reading World, 20,* 65–70.

Palmatier, R. A. (1973). A notetaking system for learning. *Journal of Reading, 17,* 36–39.

Pauk, W. (1988). *How to study in college.* Boston: Houghton Mifflin.

Readence, J. E., Bean, T. W., & Baldwin, R. S. (1989). *Content area reading: An integrated approach* (3rd ed.). Dubuque, IA: Kendall/Hunt.

Robinson, F. P. (1946). *Effective study.* New York: Harper Brothers.

Sinatra, R. (1997). *Inner-city games CAMP-US: Literacy training manual.* St. John's University.

Sinatra, R., Gemake, J., Wielan, O. P., & Sinatra, C. (1998). Teaching learners to think, read, and write more effectively. *The 1998 ASCD Annual Conference* (March 23, 1998). San Antonio, TX.

Stahl, N. A., & Henk, W. A. (1986). Tracing the roots of textbook study systems: An extended historical perspective. In J. A. Niles & R. V. Lalik (Eds.), *Solving problems in literacy: Learners, teachers,* *and researchers. Thirty-fifth yearbook of the National Reading Conference* (pp. 336–374). Rochester, NY: National Reading Conference.

Chapter 16

Assessing and Assisting Special Needs Readers: English as a Second Language

Increasing numbers of students in U.S. and Canadian school districts speak English as a second language. Limited language proficiency is one of several critical factors for some young learners who are at risk for failure in schools where English is the dominant language of learning and instruction. Until recently, few books on teaching and learning have attended to the English as a Second Language (ESL) risk factor (Fitzgerald, 1995; Gunderson, 1991). Many teachers find themselves in need of guidance to promote literacy success for ESL students (Boyle & Peregoy, 1990; Fitzgerald, 1993, 1994, 1995).

In this chapter, the current state of ESL instruction in reading and literacy instruction is discussed. The necessary preconditions for ESL students to succeed in literacy learning and how to structure classroom activities are also discussed.

Four assessment processes and tools for assessing proficiency, acquisition, and development of English as a second language for reading and writing are provided. Finally, a number of strategies currently recommended in the literature of language education are offered to help teachers provide successful learning experiences for ESL students.

BACKGROUND BRIEFING FOR TEACHERS: LEARNERS WITH SPECIAL NEEDS HAVING ENGLISH AS A SECOND LANGUAGE

There are many critical variables for helping ESL students become successful in reading and writing English (Au, 1993; Freeman & Freeman, 1992; McCauley & McCauley, 1992). Successful teaching tips include: 1) "scaffolding" instruction, 2) creating a low-anxiety environment for learning, 3) repeated readings, 4) language learning exercises that make sense, 5) opportunities for dramatic performance, 6) high expectations, and 7) language learning beginning in the first language. Each of these are elaborated upon briefly to help you understand how you can most effectively assist ESL students having reading problems primarily due to language competence or proficiency barriers.

SCAFFOLDING

Scaffolding refers to special ways that adults elaborate upon or expand children's early attempts to use oral or written language. Scaffolding facilitates effective communication at a level somewhat beyond a child's current level of linguistic capability (Applebee & Langer, 1983). For example, while reading a book a child may point and exclaim, "Bear, rrrrrr!" Her mother responds, "Yes, that's a bear. See his big claws and hear his roarrrr?" In this reply, the mother acknowledges the child's utterance and expands it to introduce new words and ideas (i.e., *claws*). Through natural conversation, the mother provides a scaffold or a next step to help the child's language grow. Boyle and Peregoy (1990) indicate that learning to read in a first and second language involves largely similar processes. However, at least two major differences have been identified for learning to read in a second language. First, comprehension may be slower because of a lack of proficiency in the second language. The second difference is that some students may lack background knowledge and experiences unique to the culture of the second language. These differences highlight the necessity to carefully scaffold instruction and experiences in second language learning. According to Boyle and Peregoy (1990, p. 196) scaffolded instruction has six characteristics:

1. Literacy scaffolds are applied to reading and writing activities aimed at functional, meaningful communication found in whole texts, such as stories, poems, reports, [and] recipes.
2. Literacy scaffolds make use of repeated language and discourse patterns that are therefore predictable.
3. Literacy scaffolds provide a model, offered by the teacher or by peers, for comprehending and producing particular written language patterns.
4. Literacy scaffolds support students in comprehending and producing written language at a level just slightly beyond their competence in the absence of the scaffold.
5. Literacy scaffolds are temporary and may be discontinued when the student is ready to work without them.
6. Literacy scaffolds use sentence and discussion or "discourse" patterns as language demonstrations.

Texts selected for use in an ESL learning situation must be whole, meaningful, and predictable. Also, ESL students must have competent English-speaking models to provide living models of English usage and to serve as resources for guiding the ESL students through the process of learning to read and write in English.

CREATING A LOW-ANXIETY LEARNING ENVIRONMENT

In addition to scaffolded instruction, Savignon (1983) indicates that for ESL students to acquire English successfully they must receive instruction in "an environment of trust and mutual confidence wherein learners may interact without fear or threat of failure" (p. 122). Students must feel free to take the risks associated with acquiring a second language, to make mistakes, and to try out their new language without fear. Creating a low-anxiety environment for learning, according to Terrell (1983), "must be the overriding concern in classroom activities if acquisition is to be achieved" (p. 273).

REPEATED READINGS

McCauley and McCauley (1992) cite another practice affecting success in acquiring a second language—*repeated practice*. Repeated readings of well-formed sentence patterns, stories, and essays are particularly useful for ESL students (Krashen, 1982). By hearing and participating in repeated readings of texts, students learn basic patterns of English phrasing (Hough, Nurss, & Enright, 1986; Schreiber, 1980) and learn to grasp intonation, rhythm, and aspects of spoken English.

LANGUAGE-LEARNING EXERCISES MUST MAKE SENSE!

Hernandez (1989) suggests that instruction for ESL students make use of demonstrations, gestures, manipulatives, diagrams, role-playing, facial expressions, and other techniques to create a context for learning language that makes sense. Second language learners usually learn another language best when, according to Krashen and Terrell (1983), they understand the message and when the new language is only a little beyond them. Thus, the best methods for teaching a second language provide sufficient context and support for understanding the gist of the message, but also just enough new information to "stretch" the learner. This relates to Clark and Clark's (1977) notion of a "Given-New" method of teaching language. They submit that language learners must be *given* enough information that they already know in order to benefit from the *new* information found in spoken or written language.

DRAMATIC PERFORMANCE

An opportunity to perform is key to improving and developing communicative competence in a second language. Drama is a standard recommended practice in ESL classrooms (Au, 1993; Freeman & Freeman, 1992; Hernandez, 1989). McCauley and McCauley (1992) recommend drama based on the work of Vygotsky (1978) saying, "Language learning is a social act; play is important for language learning; and speech and action are vital in learning. Vygotsky believed the best way for children to learn writing and reading is through play" (p. 528). Hence, drama allows second language learners the opportunity to try out the gestures, intonation patterns, and words of a new language.

HIGH EXPECTATIONS

It is important to accept each child without prejudice or preconception, particularly those who are having problems learning to read and write in English due to poor language proficiency and cultural barriers. Au (1993) describes two theories related to the failure of ESL students to achieve high levels of literacy: 1) Theory of Cultural Discontinuity, and 2) Theory of Structural Inequality. The *Theory of Cultural Discontinuity* centers on a mismatch between home and school cultures that results in potential misunderstandings between teachers and students in the classroom. This means that differences exist between the environment of the home and the world of the school that may lead to misunderstandings between students and teachers. The *Theory of Structural Inequality* suggests a mismatch between the culture of the home and the school related to the larger historical, political, economic, and social forces that have shaped relationships among ethnic groups in the United States. This theory suggests that teachers fall into familiar interaction patterns with linguistically different students. These patterns of structuring the classroom, grouping, assignments, and discussion can actually prevent students of diverse linguistic and cultural backgrounds from achieving high levels of literacy. All children are capable of learning when high expectations for their success are appropriately communicated.

An example of the effects of teacher expectations on one learner is reported by Olson (1988) in the California Tomorrow research report *Crossing the Schoolhouse Border.*

> A ninth-grade Mexican girl said, "It's very frustrating. I didn't feel good. I couldn't really adjust to life here. I felt really dumb. I would sit in class and not understand anything . . . . The teacher didn't expect me to do anything." (p. 64)

The expectations held and communicated to linguistically different students tend to function to enhance or limit second language learners' potential to become successful in a second language and culture.

LANGUAGE INSTRUCTION SHOULD BEGIN IN THE FIRST LANGUAGE WHEN POSSIBLE

Students need support from teachers to develop skills in their first language and culture in order to build concepts. This practice will ultimately facilitate the acquisition of English as a second language. Lucas, Henze and Donato (1990) conducted a comprehensive study of six high-school programs that had achieved high rates of academic success with ESL students. They found that the belief held in common by these schools was a "value placed on the students' languages and culture." Furthermore, Freeman and Freeman (1992) tell us that "if we want to build on the student's strengths, it is important to consider the language the student has been using for communication and for learning about the world before coming to school" (p. 193).

In some schools the number of different languages spoken by children may prohibit teaching all children in their native tongue. In some of these cases students have profited from instruction in English first without attention to the primary language (Barak & Swain, 1975; Gunderson, 1991; Tucker, Lambert, & D'Anglejan, 1973). However, when possible, it is advisable to use the student's first language facility as a springboard to assist in the learning of English.

In the next section of this chapter, a listing of various informal tasks for assessing ESL students' ability to use oral and written English is presented for teachers. These may help you to determine the knowledge levels, attitudes, experiences, and cultural backgrounds of students. Each task is aimed at assessing ESL students' comprehension and production abilities in using oral and written English.

Assessing Language Abilities of ESL and Limited English Proficiency (LEP) Students

Oral Language Assessment

Purpose

Gunderson (1991) asserts that teachers need to assess what students know about English in order to determine how instruction can be structured appropriately. To help with this process, Gunderson (1991) has developed the *Oral Language Assessment* (OLA) rubric to calculate which of four levels of English proficiency students have reached: 1) 0-Level English, 2) Very Limited English, 3) Limited English, and 4) Limited Fluency. Once teachers are able to discover the extent of English proficiency, they can provide ESL students with a program of literacy instruction that meets their needs.

Materials

Teachers will need a copy of the Oral Language Assessment (Gunderson, 1991) as shown in Figure 16.1.

Procedure

Students may be assessed by means of the OLA instrument at any time during the school day, but assessments are most appropriate where students are naturally drawn into verbal interaction with students and teachers. Student language proficiency can be observed in formal settings (e.g., the classroom) or informal settings (e.g., the lunchroom or playground). Students with 0-Level English proficiency cannot answer questions in English or speak in English about objects or events in their environment. For these students, placement in an appropriate instructional setting where Limited Proficiency (LP) in English can be achieved is critical. For language input to make sense as discussed earlier, 0-Level students must be placed in a language development program that will allow them to grow to at least a limited level of English proficiency. Without achieving the LP level of English proficiency orally, formal or informal instruction in reading and writing in English is considered inappropriate.

Students having Very Limited English (VLE) proficiency can speak only a few English words and respond to fairly simple questions. These children tend to avoid conversations and feel uncomfortable in language situations except those requiring only yes/no responses. These types of responses make VLE students fairly easy to identify. Gunderson (1991) indicates that VLE students "are very confused by reading activities *unless* they have a minimum of one to two years of language literacy instruction in their first language" (p. 25). Otherwise, these students, like the 0-Level students, need to be placed in a primary, or native, language-learning program for at least one to two years prior to the initiation of formal or informal reading and writing instruction in English.

Students with Limited English (LE) proficiency, in contrast, are able to respond to questions, will engage in conversations, and can produce an acceptable level of

Figure 16.1   Oral Language Assessment

0-Level English

a. Cannot answer even yes/no questions
b. Is unable to identify and name any objects
c. Understands no English
d. Often appears withdrawn and afraid

Very Limited English

a. Responds to simple questions with mostly yes/no or one-word responses
b. Speaks in 1-2 word phrases
c. Attempts no extended conversations
d. Seldom, if ever, initiates conversations

Limited English

a. Responds easily to simple questions
b. Produces simple sentences
c. Has difficulty elaborating when asked
d. Uses syntax/vocabulary adequately for personal, simple situations
e. Occasionally initiates conversations

Limited Fluency

a. Speaks with ease
b. Initiates conversations
c. May make phonological or grammatical errors, which can then become fossilized
d. Makes errors in more syntactically complex utterances
e. Freely and easily switches codes

English for communicative purposes. These students are ready for some reading and writing instruction regardless of their background in their native or primary language. Finally, students with Limited Fluency (LF) possess a good command of both expressive and receptive spoken English. These students tend to understand dialect differences in spoken language use. They understand the difference between approved forms of language; they speak standard forms of language in the classroom and dialect forms on the playground with their peers (Gunderson, 1983). Students with Limited Fluency are ready for reading and writing instruction regardless of their linguistic or cultural backgrounds.

THE CLOZE PROCEDURE

Purpose

The *cloze procedure* is "the use of a piece of writing in which certain words have been deleted and the pupil has to make maximum possible use of context clues available in predicting the missing words" (Bullock Report, D.E.S., 1975). Originally, Taylor (1953) suggested that the cloze procedure be used as a means of assessing the readability of text and, in turn, the reading ability of students. Hence, the cloze procedure is one of the longest standing and most recommended means of holistic assessment (Reutzel & Cooter, 1996) as well as a favorite assessment tool among ESL educators (Gunderson, 1991). Cloze tests are often teacher-made from the reading materials available for instruction. The object of a cloze test is for ESL students to supply missing words from a text by using their knowledge of English syntax and semantics. The cloze procedure has advantages over other types of tests because it puts students in direct contact with the materials they are to read.

Materials

Passages should be taken from the reading materials available to teachers for instructing ESL students. This recommendation is important for two reasons. First, the cloze test gives teachers information about how well ESL students can read materials they are going to be expected to read during instruction. Second, information determined from administration of a cloze test is most helpful when future instruction can be adjusted according to the real reading materials the student will eventually encounter in the classroom.

Procedure

Once a passage of 250 words is identified, a deletion plan should be selected. It is recommended that every fifth word in the passage be deleted, yielding a total of 50 deletions. It is important that the first and last sentence in the passage be left intact to supply the reader with necessary context. Consider the following incomplete example of a cloze test that uses an *every fifth-word* deletion pattern.

Many scientists believe that there are other forms of intelligent life somewhere in space. These forms may not _____ the way we do. _____ often show life forms _____ space with silly-looking _____. Movies often show them _____ frightening monsters. But have _____ ever wondered what those _____ life forms might think _____ us?

It has been shown that primary-aged (K–3) readers succeed better with an *every tenth-word* deletion pattern. For ESL students who have particular difficulty with cloze, an every-tenth-word deletion pattern may be considered as an alternative. Deletions should be replaced by uniform-sized blanks, typically of at least 15 letter spaces each. It is helpful if the passage is double- or triple-spaced for the actual test format. Students are given the test with no time limit and asked to fill in the deletions. If the object is to match a student's proficiency with a given text or reading series, it may be necessary to administer the cloze test using several different difficulty levels until the best possible match is found. The cloze test is scored by what is known as an *exact word replacement* method; only those responses that are exact word replacements for the word deleted from the original passage are scored as correct. The degree of match between text and reader is determined by using one of several sets of criteria. However, Gunderson (1991) recommends the following criteria designed expressly for ESL students:

Independent Level	Instructional Level	Frustration Level
70% correct	50–69% correct	49% or less correct

Teachers should be sensitive to the fact that most ESL students struggle with a cloze test and may exhibit frustration. In fact, the cloze procedure is not very useful for ESL students below the fourth grade (Gunderson, 1991). Every effort should be made to encourage completion of the test and to help ESL students understand that everyone struggles with the cloze test approach. Once a cloze test is scored, the results are classified into three levels: Independent, Instructional, and Frustration. The definitions of these terms are quite specific. Students who score at the Independent level are operating at a level at which no teacher intervention is necessary to be successful in reading a text of that difficulty. Students who score at the Instructional level are operating at a level at which the teacher will need to provide varying degrees of support for the student to be able to succeed in reading a selected text. Finally, a student who scores at the Frustration level will not succeed at reading a text selected at this difficulty level, no matter how much help is given by the teacher; it is simply too difficult for the student.

RUNNING RECORDS

Purpose

Running records have been used to assess reading abilities of linguistically and culturally diverse students in Australia and New Zealand for decades (Clay, 1985). Running records are an informal assessment procedure that can convey how well your students are progressing at various points in the school year. More importantly, running records help you understand the processes that your students use in reading and where you may be able to intervene with strategies to help them gain better understanding of their reading selections.

A running record is used to assess reading accuracy and also serves to allow students to monitor their own comprehension (called *metacognition*), reading fluency, and reading comprehension. Ideally, a running record is taken by inviting a student to read aloud a familiar text that has been practiced previously. The logic behind a running record is much the same as Graves's (1983) attitude about evaluating only finished writing products—teachers should evaluate their students' very best efforts.

Periodic running records can help teachers compile a comprehensive profile of the reading progress of ESL students. Similar to other approaches, such as informal reading inventories (IRI), running records can be interpreted to help teachers determine a good match between a student's reading ability and reading materials, as well as providing much-needed information to help teachers make other instructional decisions to assist ESL and LEP students in learning to read and write in English.

Materials

You will need the following materials when taking running records: a watch or stopwatch, a copy of the passage to be read, a pencil or pen, an audiotape for each student, and a cassette tape recorder with built-in microphone.

Procedure

Learning to take a running record is not difficult, but it requires about two hours of practice before you attempt to use the strategy for decision making in the classroom. The act of taking a running record is divided into three major components: 1) recording, 2) scoring, and 3) interpreting. Running records are taken without having to prepare a script. A simple photocopy of the text to be read will do. We suggest tape-recording the student's oral reading so that you may review the reading for accuracy as you prepare the running record. To record a running record, seat the child next to the examiner. Place the audiotape into the cassette recorder. Begin recording the session by inviting the child to read her story or passage aloud. After the child completes the reading, invite her to retell the story aloud. Directions for obtaining a quality retelling and for scoring an oral retelling can be found in chapter 10. When the retelling is complete, turn off the recorder and thank the reader. Once recorded, score the running record for the student. Make a paper copy of the passage read aloud. For example, if a passage was read aloud from the well-known story, *If You Give a Mouse a Cookie,* by Laura Joffe Numeroff (1985), you would make a copy of the pages read aloud by the student. Scoring the running record is accomplished by placing a check mark (✓) over each correctly pronounced word in the reading. Miscues (or errors) are noted by writing above the error the nature of the alteration or text deviation, as shown in Figure 16.2. Attempts (*c-coo-cookie*) and self-corrections (sc) do not count as errors, but are recorded nonetheless. Only uncorrected text deviations are counted as errors.

For assessment decisions, it is recommended that three running records be obtained for each child on various levels of text difficulty. Established criteria for oral reading evaluation based on words correctly read aloud is:

an easy (independent) text	95–100% accuracy
an instructional text	90–94% accuracy
a hard (frustration) text	80–89% accuracy

Errors, usually called *miscues,* are deviations from the printed text. Miscues are divided by the total number of words to determine an accuracy level. Next, self-

Figure 16.2   Running Record Example

✓ ✓ ✓ ✓   ✓   ✓ c-coo-cookie
If you give a mouse a cookie,

he is (sc)✓ ✓ ✓ ✓ ✓ ✓   ✓ ✓
he's going to ask for a glass of milk.

✓   ✓   ✓   ✓   ✓   ✓
When you give him the milk,

Student: I don't know that word.
Teacher: probably
✓   ✓ ✓ ✓ ✓
he'll probably ask you for a straw.

✓   ✓   ✓   ✓   ✓   ✓ n-nap-napkin
When he's finished, he'll ask for a napkin.

✓   ✓   ✓ ✓   ✓✓   ✓   ✓   ✓   ✓ ✓   ✓
Then he'll want to look in a mirror to make sure he doesn't

✓ ✓   ✓ mus-mustache
have a milk mustache.

✓   ✓   ✓   ✓   ✓   ✓
When he looks into the mirror,

✓   ✓   see   ✓   ✓   ✓   ✓✓
he might notice his hair needs a trim.

✓   ✓ prob-probably ✓ ✓ ✓   ✓ ✓ ——   ✓
So he'll probably ask for a pair of nail scissors.

✓   ✓   ✓   ✓   ✓   ✓✓
When he's finished giving himself a trim,

✓   ✓ ✓   ✓   ✓ clean   ✓
he'll want a broom to sweep up.

✓   ✓   cleaning
He'll start sweeping.

✓   ✓   ✓   ✓   ✓   ✓ clean (sc) ✓   ✓ ✓   ✓
He might get carried away and sweep every room in the house.

✓   ✓   ✓   ✓   ✓ cleaning ✓ ✓   ✓   ✓
He may even end up washing the floors as well.

Figure 16.2   Continued

Number of words in text __117__
Number of deviations from text __5__
Percentage of deviations to total number of words in text $5/117 = 4\%$ *
Number of self-corrections __2__
Proportion of self-corrections $2/7 = 29\%$
Accuracy rate __96%__
Time: __2 minutes, 18 seconds__
Fluency/Words per minute $117/2.3 = 51$ WPM
Major story ideas: ___7___ separate incidents or episodes
Retelling: __6 separate incidents recalled__
Order: __All incidents were in order__
Total possible elements: __7 episodes + 1 order = 8__
Student retelling score: __6 episodes + 1 order = 7__
Percentage of retelling comprehension: $7/8 = 88\%$

* By noting the percentage of miscues or oral reading errors and by studying the errors to determine patterns, you can know how reading development is progressing and where and when instruction can be profitably offered. Moreover, running records provide data that can be turned into grades if necessary to satisfy local or state mandates (although we do not recommend such a practice).

corrections are counted and divided by the number of errors to determine a self-correction rate. In the example shown in Figure 16.2, the reader corrected errors or miscues about 30% of the time. Finally, by using a watch or stopwatch, the reading can be timed and a fluency rating of words per minute (WPM), as shown in chapter 13, can be computed. Finally, oral retellings can be scored by examining the passage and the oral retelling for numbers of major ideas or story elements included in the retelling. These elements are then compared against the total number of story elements and/or major ideas in a passage by dividing the number included in the retelling by the total number of incidents or story elements in the passage or story. In addition, the order of the elements as told in the oral retelling should be included as one component to be scored correct or incorrect. In the example above, there were only 7 major elements. If a student retold, in order, 6 of 7 elements, the student would receive a total score of 7 out of 8 (7 story elements and 1 for order), or an 88% complete oral retelling. By way of interpretation, the child who read in the example reads and comprehends the book, *If You Give a Mouse a Cookie,* very well and would be considered to be reading this book at an independent reading level.

CULTURAL BACKGROUND AND PRIOR KNOWLEDGE RATING

Purpose

Many ESL and LEP students having reading and writing difficulties find that a lack of relevant background and cultural experiences is often to blame (Au, 1993). Without doubt, sensitive teachers are able to best assess problems in this potentially troubling arena for ESL students, but they often need specific tools to document their observations and intuitions. We have developed a somewhat formalized approach for assessing ESL and LEP students' experiential, knowledge, and culturally based experiences to help teachers know when individual or small groups of students have no, some, or elaborated background or cultural knowledge about a reading or writing topic. This approach uses semantic mapping (Johnson & Pearson, 1984) as a means for exploring students' knowledge and experience in concepts and events.

Materials

To make your semantic map(s), you will need several unlined sheets of paper or a chalkboard, appropriate writing media, and a text, theme, or subject that is to be read or written about. An example of a semantic map used to assess students' prior knowledge, background experiences, or cultural understandings is shown in Figure 16.3.

Procedure

To begin, the teacher selects a text or theme about which students will be learning, reading, or writing. An example may be the theme or topic of *Native Americans*. Next, reading materials about this topic or theme can be selected and potentially unfamiliar terms can be identified by the teacher and recorded in a topic concept list. Prior to reading these selections, the teacher gathers her students around and draws an oval containing the term *Native Americans* on the board. Next, she asks her students to call out their ideas about this topic or theme. Ideas are listed at the end of lines projecting outward from the central concept, Native Americans. The

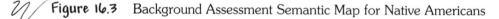

Figure 16.3   Background Assessment Semantic Map for Native Americans

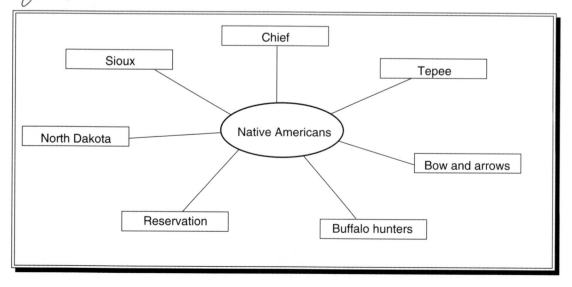

Figure 16.4   Langer's (1980) Analysis of Levels of Prior Knowledge

Much (3)	Some (2)	Little (1)
category labels	examples	personal associations
definitions	attributes	morphemes
analogies	defining characteristics	soundalikes
relationships		personal experiences

teacher can progress quickly through the list of terms by making a semantic map for each of the terms as necessary. Associations of the group are judged for adequacy of background and cultural knowledge based upon a scale developed by Langer (1980). Assessment criteria are shown in Figure 16.4.

When students exhibit little or no knowledge about a topic or theme, the teacher should take time to develop the necessary language and conceptual understanding. A variety of approaches, such as Social Contextual Diagrams (discussed in the next section), pictures, or artifacts are helpful means of teaching language, culture, and other concepts necessary to comprehend the text. On the other hand, when students have a great deal of knowledge about the subject, they obviously can go ahead and read about a topic without additional background preparation by the teacher. It is also helpful, on occasion, to select materials that represent each student's native language(s) and culture to validate her self-worth in the community of learners in a classroom. In these cases, the student can help her teachers and others learn about her culture by becoming the classroom teacher for a brief time.

BALANCED READING PROGRAM INTERVENTIONS: STUDENTS FOR WHOM ENGLISH IS A SECOND LANGUAGE

Indicators That Readers Have Learning Needs

- Informal and formal assessments suggest limited English proficiency (LEP)
- Limited background knowledge relative to reading materials commonly used in teaching-learning activities

PRINT IMMERSION

Purpose

For many years, teachers and students of foreign or second languages have known that the best context for learning a second language is in the context and culture wherein the language to be learned is used and is necessary to function in the society. This is equally true for ESL and LEP students in U.S. and Canadian schools (Gunderson, 1991). The purpose for immersing ESL students in English print-rich classrooms is to attempt to recreate, as much as possible, a context and culture wherein English is modeled, available, and necessary for students to learn and function. Teachers who immerse ESL students in English print-rich environments fill their classrooms with printed matter. Everything may be labeled—objects, locations, and processes are displayed in connection with the second language. Walls, ceilings, and floors are used as displays for printed directions, information, celebrations, and references in the second language. Learning a second language in social-situational contexts in which the second language abounds in use greatly enhances both opportunity and the actual rate of progress in second language acquisition and development. This is particularly true for students who are at risk due to their limited proficiency in English.

Materials

Taylor, Blum, and Logsdon (1986) have identified and tested several critical variables associated with designing a print-rich classroom environment. The characteristics of a *print-rich environment* identified by Taylor and colleagues (1986), as well as other variables, are presented in Figure 16.5. Teachers may wish to consult this listing as they plan their classroom environments and instructional activities.

Procedure

Print-rich classrooms immerse learners in an environment that serves as a ready reference for understanding written print. A good beginning point, Morrow (1989) suggests, is to label the classroom furniture, fixtures, and objects. We believe labeling objects or procedures in classrooms also ought to be functional (e.g., "Crayons in here," "Open here," and "Turn on here"). A *word wall* as described by Cunningham (1995) can be used to display sight words that ESL students want or need to learn to become proficient in oral and written English usage.

Figure 16.5 Characteristics of a Print-Rich Environment

Books and Stories:

A. Commercially published trade books
B. Commercially published big books
C. Commercially published reference books
D. Commercially published informational trade books
E. Individually authored child stories, i.e., shape books, minibooks, big books, accordion books, etc.
F. Group authored big books
G. Group authored chart stories
H. Group authored informational charts

Child Authored Messages:

A. Notes
B. Cards
C. Invitations
D. Letters
E. Announcements

Adult Authored Messages:

A. Notes
B. Cards
C. Invitations
D. Letters
E. Announcements

Reference, Informational, and Record-Keeping Lists:

A. Sign-in board for attendance
B. Color chart
C. Numbers chart
D. Alphabet chart
E. Logo language wall
F. Words we know list
G. Songs we know list
H. Our favorite books
I. Lunch menu

Directions:

A. Classroom rules
B. Use of centers
C. Activities directions
D. Recipes
E. Traffic, regulatory, and direction signs
F. Management schemes

continued

Figure 16.5   Continued

Scheduling:

A. Daily schedule
B. Calendar
C. Lunch time
D. Classroom helpers

Labeling:

A. Location of centers
B. Objects in the classroom
C. Containers for children's personal belongings
D. Mailboxes
E. Coat racks
F. Objects from home
G. Captioned drawings
H. Contents of cupboards

Writing:

A. Paper
B. Chalkboard
C. Blank chart paper
D. Blank big books
E. Pencils
F. Crayons
G. Markers
H. Three-hole punch
I. Binding materials
J. Stapler
K. Glue
L. Magnetic letters
M. Rubber letter stamps
N. Stencils

Supported or Self-Selected Reading:

A. Shared Reading Experience
B. Group Language Experience
C. Read-along tapes and books
D. Older children reading with younger
E. Senior citizen volunteers
F. Parents
G. Library Center, etc.

Note: From "The Development of Written Language Awareness: Environmental Aspects and Program Characteristics" by N. E. Taylor, I. H. Blum, and D. M. Logsdon, 1986, *Reading Research Quarterly, 21*(2), pp. 132–149. Copyright by the International Reading Association. All rights reserved.

In addition, a message board can be placed in a prominent location in the classroom for teachers and ESL students to write notes to one another. In an early childhood setting, a message board can be placed by the telephone in the play kitchen area to take down messages, leave messages, make lists for grocery shopping, and so forth.

On a daily basis, teachers often repeat specific phrases, requests, and directions. These common phrases and directions can be written in English on signs or direction cards. These cards should be large enough to hold up for students to read. A hole can be cut into the card for a handle. Some examples of direction cards are shown in the photo on page 384. Finally, a method for signaling learner's attention to the direction cards needs to be devised by the teacher. For example, ringing a hotel bell, whistling, or turning lights off and on can serve this purpose.

Songs, poems, jokes, riddles, dictation, and chants can be enlarged and printed on charts to further enrich the print environment. These charts can be placed around the room for learners to read alone or together with peers. Displays should be designed that provide learners with pertinent information about directions for center activities, sign-up boards for conferences, and classroom rules. Other displays about the room can provide color and number words that learners often need to consult during their writing.

WORD BANKS

Purpose

For over thirty years, the work of Sylvia Ashton-Warner (1963) has influenced language educators around the world. One of her major contributions was the use of *word banks* with LEP students in the junior (elementary) classes of New Zealand. Word banks formed the backbone of Ashton-Warner's Organic Reading Approach to teaching young children from diverse linguistic and cultural backgrounds to read and write English. Word banks—storage boxes of personally relevant and important "one-look," easy-to-learn words—were used to help young students learn how to read and write words of high emotional and personal appeal (see Figure 16.6). The word bank became the vehicle for tapping into a student's natural need to learn and experience oral and written language.

Figure 16.6 Example Word Bank

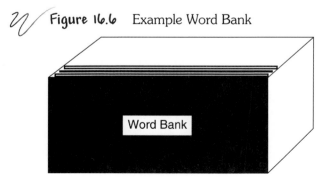

Word Bank

Materials

A box or file, such as a child's shoe box or a recipe file box, will be needed to house the word cards. Students also will need individual cards sized to fit the box selected.

Procedure

A word bank is simply a box or file in which a child collects cards bearing newly discovered or personally requested words to be practiced. Sylvia Ashton-Warner, in her popular book, *Teacher* (1963), describes key vocabulary words as "organic." That is, these are words that come from within the child and her own experiences. She states that key vocabulary words are like captions for important events in life that the child has experienced. Children come to the teacher at an appointed time or during a group experience and indicate which word(s) they would like to learn. For instance, the teacher may ask, "What word would you like to learn today?" The child may respond with a word of her choice, such as *police, ghost,* or *sing.* Sylvia Ashton-Warner found that the most common categories of key vocabulary words for children were *fear words* (*dog, bull, kill, police*), *sex* (as she called them) or "affection" words (*love, kiss, sing, darling*), *locomotion words* (*bus, car, truck, jet*), and a *miscellaneous* category that generally reflects cultural and other considerations (*socks, frog, beer*).

Ashton-Warner calls key vocabulary "one-look words," because one look is usually all that is required for permanent learning to take place. The reason that these words seem so easy for children to learn is that they usually carry strong emotional significance for the child. Once the child has shared with the teacher a word that she would like to learn, the teacher writes the word on an index card or a small piece of tag board using a dark marker. The student is then instructed to share the word with as many people as possible during the day. After the child has done so, the word is added to her word bank and practiced on other days alone and in conjunction with other students in the class. Each day, teachers help students to add new words to their word banks and to practice previously stored words.

LABELED PICTURES AND DIAGRAMS

Purpose

Pictures and diagrams, in which objects in the scene are labeled, are of great help to students learning a new language. The purpose of labeled pictures and diagrams is to allow students to experience language in settings other than the school classroom. Diagrams of the kitchen, bedroom, or bathroom at home can help students begin to learn and associate second-language terms with familiar or even somewhat unfamiliar objects in another setting. Other labeled pictures and diagrams of stores, libraries, mechanic shops, or hospitals can move students' potential for language learning well beyond the physical and social confines of the classroom.

Materials

Enlarged diagrams or photographs of culturally or socially accepted settings such as restaurants, hospitals, stores, homes, or churches are needed to create labeled pictures and diagrams. Objects and actions in each of these may need to be labeled in both the first and second languages. In Figure 16.7, a labeled diagram of a house is shown.

Procedure

Typically, a large piece of butcher paper or poster board can be used to make the labeled pictures and diagrams. Teachers with some artistic talent can freehand draw these, although many teachers simply choose to use an enlarged photocopy of a picture or diagram. Label the objects portrayed as shown in Figure 16.7. Enlarged labeled pictures and diagrams can be displayed in the classroom on the walls. Labeled pictures and diagrams that are not poster-sized can be stored in folders or binders as references for ESL and LEP learners.

ENVIRONMENTAL PRINT

Purpose

Using printed matter from the world outside the school enables second language learners to view their own lives, circumstances, and cultural contexts as places for learning and to apply their evolving knowledge of English as a second language.

Figure 16.7   Labeled Picture for Language Learning

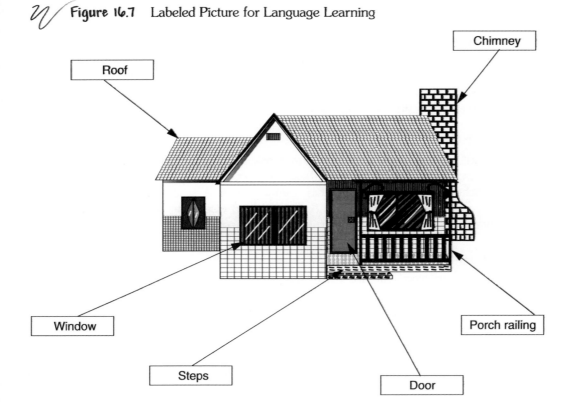

Signs, billboards, storefronts, bus schedules, and displays encountered in the everyday lives of ESL students can provide personally relevant bridges from learning English in the school classroom to learning and using English in the real world. The use of environmental print has proven worthwhile for developing oral and written language among younger learners of both first and second languages (Hiebert & Ham, 1981).

Materials

Environmental print includes signs, candy wrappers, bumper stickers, magazine advertisements, catalogue pictures, and containers for everyday products such as breakfast cereal.

Procedure

Students can collect environmental print they can read and store these items in scrapbooks, files, or envelopes. They can then use these easily recognizable print items to compose books or other written texts. Bulletin boards also can be covered with environmental print items. Some teachers organize environmental print items into alphabetical categories to practice alphabet knowledge. Environmental print items are an inexpensive means to provide wide access to print beyond the boundaries of school classrooms.

SENTENCE STRIPS

Purpose

Dictated sentences recorded on sentence strips can be used to further develop awareness of English sentence patterns (Gunderson, 1991; Heald-Taylor, 1991). Sentence strips are especially useful for teaching second language learners because the length of the text is limited and provides basic examples of the most rudimentary meaningful units in language.

Materials

You will need colored marking pens, masking tape for hanging the strips on the wall, and precut sentence strips (these can be purchased in a variety of colors from a teacher supply store). Another useful tool is a wall-mounted sentence strip hanger, as shown in Figure 16.8. Storing and displaying sentence strips can encourage incidental language learning in the classroom.

Procedure

When composing sentence strips, teachers may initially dictate the sentences, but students should be invited to dictate their own as soon as they indicate a willingness. Using words drawn from student word banks can become a rich resource for building sentences from known and familiar language. In addition, using words from a word bank allows students to manipulate words and sentences and provides a record of language development, as well. Sentence strips can be stored by punching a hole in the upper right-hand corner of each strip and hanging the strips on a cup hook, hanger, or wall-mounted pegs as shown in Figure 16.8. At some later

Figure 16. 8   Sentence Strip Wall Hanger

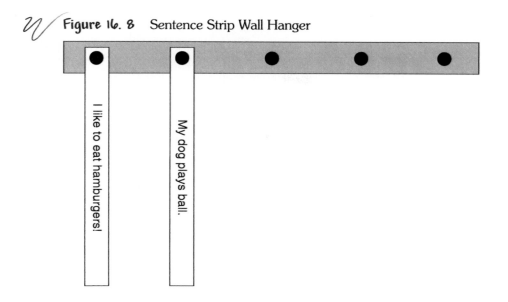

I like to eat hamburgers!

My dog plays ball.

point, sentence strips can be copied from stories and literature that the children are reading. Further, students can be invited to trace these sentence strips or to copy the sentences in a space provided directly below the original sentence on the strip.

An example of using sentence strips with ESL students is as follows: Begin by telling students that the class will practice reading in English. Then write the following sentence onto a sentence strip as students watch: "I like to eat hamburgers!" Now, say, while pointing to the sentence, "This says, 'I like to eat hamburgers!'" Next, point to the sentence strip and ask, "What does this say?" The student then responds by reading the text written on the sentence strip. Finally, encourage students to share their sentence strips with others by reading them aloud to one another.

Active Listening

Purpose

Reading researchers (Blum et al., 1995; Walters & Gunderson, 1985) have discovered reading achievement benefits for ESL students in listening to stories read aloud in their first and second languages. In some studies the stories were simply read aloud by volunteers, while in others they were prerecorded on cassette tapes. One of the many benefits cited was that students with Limited English Proficiency and an ability to read in the first language learned how terms from the first and second languages translate (Heald-Taylor, 1991).

Materials

Stories, poems, jokes, riddles, or other enticing texts to be read aloud, as always, are the starting point. Adult language models for the read-aloud experiences can be accomplished either through a volunteer program and/or by using prerecorded audiotapes.

Procedure

For some beginning students, wordless picture books are a good place to begin. Read the story or share the book in small, preplanned sections. Students could be asked later to dictate a story to match the pictures. The dictation could be typed on the computer by the teacher or a volunteer, then laser printed in a font that resembles type commonly found in a book. We recommend the fonts *Times, New York,* or *Helvetica.*) The print can then be recorded so that students can return to the book later and reading their own dictated language retelling the story from the pictures.

When using books selected for reading aloud, cease reading aloud at strategic points and ask students, "What do you think might happen next?" As a follow-up question, ask students to explain why they think a particular event will take place next in the story. Where a story employs a repeated pattern such as, "Little Pig, Little Pig, Let me _____!" it may be appropriate for the teacher to stop and invite the students to complete the pattern orally. In this way, students are drawn into careful and continuous active listening while hearing a text read aloud.

A slightly different version of *active listening* was employed in a study by Blum and others (1995) in which ESL students were provided audiotaped books to extend their classroom literacy instruction into the home context. Books were read at a pace that would allow beginning readers to follow along with audiotapes recorded by English-speaking adults. Three seconds were allowed for page turning after hearing a sound signaling the need to turn the page. Tape recorders equipped with electric cords were furnished by the school. Each night, ESL students were allowed to check out a backpack into which they would place the tape recorder, cord, book(s), and accompanying audiotape(s). Active listening procedures such as those outlined above were followed in listening to the audiotaped books at home. Blum and others (1995) found that all ESL learners received substantial benefit from active listening to audiotaped books at home.

PERSONAL DICTIONARIES

Purpose

For more proficient second language users and for older students, a *personal dictionary* can be developed to record spellings of words and/or word meanings in English. When younger students demonstrate limited fluency and proficiency in the second language, or when younger or older students begin to ask questions about how English words are spelled or about specific word meanings, they are ready to construct a personal dictionary (Gunderson, 1991). Personal dictionaries can be simple or elaborate in construction. They can be fixed in terms of numbers of pages, or flexible, allowing for more pages to be added with increased language acquisition. But one thing is certain: constructing personal dictionaries is well worth the effort!

Materials

To construct personal dictionaries, students will need a spiral-bound or loose-leaf notebook, various drawing media such as crayons, markers, and colored pencils, tabs for marking alphabetic divisions, and (possibly) laminating material for reinforcing the dictionary cover.

Procedure

In the beginning, students will need help setting up their dictionaries and learning how to make entries. Later, when students approach the teacher about how to spell a word or to find out what it means, the teacher can help students become more independent learners by encouraging the use of their personal dictionaries. Hints about determining how words begin and about listening to the order of the sounds in words can help students figure out where to record and how to spell words in their personal dictionaries. Or, when a student learns a new word, either from reading or from an outside context, that she wants to remember, she can write the new word in her dictionary and add a picture and a sentence explaining its meaning. Then, when a student asks how to spell a word or what a word means, a teacher can simply say "It's in your Personal Dictionary!" Making and using a personal dictionary helps students assume more control over their own learning and develops a real spirit of independence in accessing language for use in reading and writing.

STUDENT-MADE BIG BOOKS AND SHARING

Purpose

For younger students, writing or copying written English can be an important means of learning and of demonstrating learning of a second language. One means of involving students in writing English can be to ask students to create original big books, or to copy some of their favorite published books (Ernst & Richard, 1995). *Big books* are stories or literature that have been enlarged to be shared with a group of readers (Holdaway, 1979). These books are typically fairly simple, containing approximately three sentences per page, illustrations that support the text, and a text often using rhyme, rhythm, repetition, and a predictable or logical sequence of events (Lynch, 1986). Students who produce big books usually are invited to share these with a group of peers as a celebration of their growing independence and knowledge of English.

Materials

One way to construct big books is to use the following materials: 12″ × 18″ sheets of unlined white paper, 1 preprinted 12″ × 18″ sheet of lined paper for underlay, various artistic media such as paints, watercolor markers, and crayons for illustrations, and various tools for book binding (stapler, hole punch, rings, tape, coil, brass fasteners, etc.).

Procedure

ESL and LEP learners can produce big books independently or in concert with other peers. In fact, producing big books in cooperative learning teams is a very effective means of organizing ESL and LEP learners for language learning interaction. One of three types of big books can be produced by ESL learners. The first and easiest type of big book is called a *reproduction*. To construct a reproduction big book, encourage students to select a favorite book that has an easily understood pattern, such as the one found in the book *Brown Bear, Brown Bear* by Bill Martin (1983). The object of a reproduction is for the learner to copy or reproduce the book as near to the original version as possible (see Figure 16.9). The act of copying, editing, and studying the form, function, and message of the book and the print can help ESL students begin to sense success in managing the English language.

Another type of big book is known as an *innovation*. To make an innovation big book, students retain the general language patterns of the original big book, but change the topic or specific events of the story. For example, the text of the book *Brown Bear, Brown Bear* might be changed from an animal theme, to an insect theme, resulting in a book entitled *Brown Spider, Brown Spider*. A third type of big book for ESL students to produce is known as an *original* big book. Big books of this type result from original stories or tales as experienced in the lives of ESL or LEP students.

The process for creating any big book is fairly straightforward. Begin by selecting (or ask students to select) a book of high interest that contains predictable and patterned language. Next, if it is a new book for the students, invite them to study the illustrations carefully and discuss what they think the text might say. Read the book aloud to the children with excitement and enthusiasm, and invite them to join in at any point.

After reading, students can begin the production of an innovation or an original big book by producing the text for their story. Oftentimes, a draft or two will be

Figure 16.9   Example Big Book

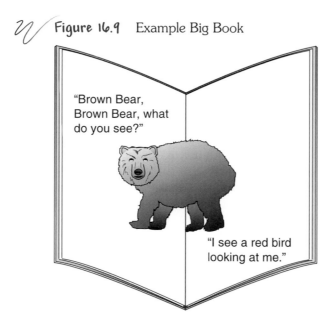

"Brown Bear, Brown Bear, what do you see?"

"I see a red bird looking at me."

constructed on traditional-sized paper to allow for conferencing, editing, and revisions. Once a final copy is readied for publication, the print can be transferred onto 12″ × 18″ pieces of unlined paper. Print should be distributed on the pages of the big book in such a way that space is left for the illustrations to augment the text. Once the print is located on each page, students can be guided in their selection of a medium for illustrating their book. You may wish to show ESL children picture books that exemplify the use of different media (i.e., crayon, collage, pastels, pen and ink, charcoal, and watercolor). Once the illustrations are complete, students should be directed to an area where they have access to binding materials and guidance for binding their big books. Various tools and media should be available for students to select just the right touch for binding their productions. Students should be helped to produce a book that contains essential book elements such as a title page bearing the names of illustrators and the publishing company, as well as a copyright page on which the date of publication or copyright appears. Attaching a library pocket and card in the front or back of each book adds a final touch of significance.

Once completed, big books can be used for read alouds by the students or the teacher in large group settings. Students can be organized into teams for reading big books or can read the big books unassisted. Taped versions of the big books also can be produced to be shared with younger or less proficient readers. Such an approach elevates the self-esteem of ESL or LEP readers.

LEARNING FROM CONTENT TEXTS

Purpose

For adolescent students, reading in content materials is an important means of learning new information and of acquiring a more sophisticated level of proficiency in a second language. Kang (1994) expresses concern that most ESL program curricula may be insufficient to help second language learners with the complexity and demands of content area classes. Even more concerning is the fact that most departmentalized subject matter or content area teachers are not well equipped to deal with ESL students in their classrooms. Very often, content area classrooms are a "sink or swim" experience for ESL students who fall further and further behind due to limited ability with English. Kang (1994) provides several important guidelines for helping mainstreamed ESL students in content area classes learn to read content materials with greater comprehension and success.

Materials

Materials needed include only a content area textbook being used in the curriculum (i.e., science, health, history, math, etc.).

Procedure

Three types of variables interact in a reading task to increase or decrease the difficulty of the reading act for ESL learners: linguistic, knowledge, and literacy.

Linguistic Variables   Limited knowledge of a second language will prevent learners from transferring their reading skills to the second language context or prevent them from making full use of semantic, syntactic, or other discourse clues in reading. Kang (1994) suggests the following activities to reduce the demands on students to learn academic content:

- Reduce the vocabulary load.
- Preteach key vocabulary concepts to be understood for reading the assigned passages.
- Use adjunct questions, highlighting text, notes or questions in the margins, graphic organizers, etc.
- Use postreading discussion groups to expose ESL learners to more complex language input.

Knowledge Variables   A second variable affecting an ESL student's ability to learn from reading content area texts is background knowledge. In some cases, a text may presuppose culture-specific background knowledge that is not part of an ESL student's experiences. Alternatively, some ESL readers may focus their reading too heavily upon the print, thus failing to activate their prior knowledge to assist in understanding content area text. In either of these scenarios, Kang (1994) suggests strategies for *before, during,* and *after reading* that may help ESL learners to succeed in reading content area texts.

Before Reading

- semantic mapping (see Chapter 8)
- structured overviews (see Chapters 9 and 11)
- discussion that highlights:

> contradictions
>
> opposing examples
>
> exceptions
>
> categorization
>
> comparisons
>
> related concepts in the native language

During Reading

- pattern guides (see Chapters 9 and 11)
- marginal glosses (see Chapter 15)

After Reading

- semantic feature analysis (see Chapter 8)
- small group discussion

Literacy Variables   In some cases, ESL students may have limited native language literacy skills. In still others, ESL students may have insufficient second language proficiency to use well-developed native language literacy skills. In either case, specific prereading, during reading, and postreading strategies can optimize ESL students' opportunities to read content texts that require processing information that is increasingly sophisticated, contains more concepts and abstract ideas, and employs more variable text patterns.

Before Reading

- Preview the text by showing students how to use headings, subheadings, boldfaced text, marginal glosses or notes, illustrations, or end-of-chapter questions.
- Help students set a purpose for reading by teaching self-questioning or student strategies.

During Reading

- Provide directions, signals, and questions to focus students' reading on an interaction with the text and their own knowledge.
- Suggest a study strategy and model its use with the text.
- Help students adjust their reading rate to the text difficulty.
- Help students develop skimming and scanning skills (see Chapter 15).
- Help students predict outcomes, make and confirm inferences, and solve problems.
- Help students use metacognitive monitoring skills (see Chapter 9).
- Remind students of when and how to use "fix up" or "repair" strategies when comprehension breaks down (see Chapter 9).

After Reading

- Help students get more experience with the organization of various text patterns in content area reading by writing text summaries or completing text pattern guides (see Chapters 9 and 11).

CHAPTER SUMMARY

In this chapter, seven research validated practices for assisting students with limited English proficiency were presented:

1. "Scaffolding" instruction
2. Creating a low-anxiety environment for learning
3. Repeated readings
4. Language learning exercises that make sense
5. Opportunities for dramatic performance

6. High expectations

7. Language learning beginning in the first language

Specific assessment ideas such as oral language assessment, cloze, running records, and cultural background and prior knowledge were offered to determine students' understanding and development of English language proficiency, as well as to determine the selection of instructional practices. Likewise, several approaches for helping learners acquire English language proficiency were discussed such as: immersion, word banks, labeled pictures and diagrams, environmental print, sentence strip, active listening, personal dictionaries, innovations and reproductions of big books, and content learning techniques. The use of these assessment approaches and teaching strategies will help learners internalize concepts and structure associated with the English language and prepare them for access to content knowledge in the school curriculum.

REFERENCES

Applebee, A. N., & Langer, J. A. (1983). Instructional scaffolding: Reading and writing as natural language activities. *Language Arts, 60,* 168–175.

Ashton-Warner, S. (1963). *Teacher.* New York: Simon & Schuster, Inc.

Au, K. H. (1993). *Literacy instruction in multicultural settings.* New York: Harcourt, Brace, and Jovanovich.

Barak, H. C., & Swain, M. (1975). Three-year evaluation of a large scale early grade French immersion program: The Ottawa study. *Language Learning, 25,* 1–30.

Blum, I. H., Koskinen, P. S., Tennat, N., Parker, E. M., Straub, M., and Curry, C. (1995). Using audiotaped books to extend classroom literacy instruction into the homes of second-language learners. *Journal of Reading Behavior, 27*(4), 535–563.

Boyle, O. F., & Peregoy, S. F. (1990). Literacy scaffolds: Strategies for first- and second-language readers and writers. *The Reading Teacher, 44,* 194–200.

Clark, H., & Clark, E. (1977). *Psychology and language: An introduction to psycholinguistics.* New York: Harcourt, Brace, & Jovanovich.

Clay, M. M. (1985). *The early detection of reading difficulties* (3rd ed.). Portsmouth, NH: Heinemann.

Cunningham, P. M., (1995). *Phonics they use: Words for reading and writing.* New York: HarperCollins.

Ernst, G., & Richard, K. J. (1995). Reading and writing pathways to conversation in the ESL classroom. *The Reading Teacher, 48*(4), 320–326.

Fitzgerald, J. (1993). Literacy and students who are learning English as a sceond language. *The Reading Teacher, 46*(8), 638–647.

Fitzgerald, J. (1994). Crossing boundaries: What do second-language-learning theories say to reading and writing teachers of English-as-a-second-language learners? *Reading Horizons, 34*(4), 339–355.

Fitzgerald, J. (1995). English-as-a-second-language reading instruction in the United States: A research review. *Journal of Reading Behavior, 27*(2), 115–152.

Freeman, Y. S., & Freeman, D. E. (1992). *Whole language for second language learners.* Portsmouth, NH: Heinemann Educational Books.

Graves, D. H. (1983). *Writing: Teachers and children at work*. Portsmouth, NH: Heinemann Educational Books.

Gunderson, L. (1983). ESL students: Don't throw them to the sharks. *Highway One, 6*, 33–44.

Gunderson, L. (1991). ESL literacy instruction: A guidebook to theory and practice. Englewood Cliffs, NJ: Prentice Hall Regents.

Heald-Taylor, G. (1991). *Whole language strategies for ESL students.* San Diego, CA: Dominie Press, Inc.

Hernandez, H. (1989). *Multicultural education: A teacher's guide to content and process*. London: Merrill.

Hiebert, E., & Ham, D. (1981). *Young children and environmental print.* Paper presented at the annual meeting of the National Reading Conference, Dallas, TX.

Holdaway, D. (1979). *The foundations of literacy.* New York: Ashton Scholastic.

Hough, R., Nurss, J. R., & Enright, D. S. (1986). Story reading with limited English speaking children in the regular classroom. *The Reading Teacher, 39,* 510–515.

Johnson, D. D., & Pearson, P. D. (1984). *Teaching reading vocabulary.* New York: Holt, Rinehart, & Winston.

Kang, H. W. (1994). Helping second language readers learn from content area text through collaboration and support. *The Journal of Reading, 37*(8), 646–652.

Krashen, S., & Terrell, T. (1983). *The natural approach: Language acquisition in the classroom.* Haywood, CA: Alemany Press.

Krashen, S. (1982). *Principles and practice in second language acquisition.* New York: Pergamon Press.

Langer, J. (1980). Relations between levels of prior knowledge and organization of recall. In M. L. Kamil and A. J. Moe (Eds.), *Perspectives on Reading Research and Instruction.* Washington, D.C.: 29th Yearbook of the National Reading Conference.

Lucas, T., Henze, R., & Donato, R. (1990). Promoting the success of Latina language-minority students: An exploratory study of six high schools. *Harvard Educational Review, 60,* 315–340.

Lynch, P. (1986). *Using big books and predictable books.* New York: Scholastic Inc.

Martin, B. (1983). *Brown bear, brown bear.* New York: Holt, Rinehart, & Winston.

McCauley, J. K., & McCauley, D. S. (1992). Using choral reading to promote language learning for ESL students. *The Reading Teacher, 45,* 526–533.

Morrow, L. M. (1989). *Literacy development in the early years: Helping children read and write.* Englewood Cliffs, NJ: Prentice Hall.

Numeroff, L. J. (1985). *If you give a mouse a cookie.* New York: Scholastic Inc.

Olson, L. (1988). *Crossing the schoolhouse border: Immigrant students and the California public schools.* San Francisco: California Tomorrow.

Reutzel, D. R., & Cooter, R. B. (1996). Teaching children to read: *From basals to books* (2nd ed.). Columbus, OH: Merrill/Prentice-Hall.

Savignon, S. J. (1983). *Communicative competence: Theory and classroom practice.* Reading, MA: Addison-Wesley.

Schreibner, P. A., (1980). On the acquisition of reading fluency. *Journal of Reading Behavior, 12,* 177–186.

Taylor, N. E., Blum, I. H., & Logsdon, D. M. (1986). The development of written language awareness: Environmental aspects and program characteristics. *Reading Research Quarterly, 21*(2), 132–149.

Taylor, W. L., (1953). Cloze procedure: A new tool for measuring readability. *Journalism Quarterly, 30,* 415–433.

Terrell, T. (1983). The natural approach to language teaching: An update. In J. W. Oller & P. A. Richard-Amato (Eds.), *Methods that work: A smorgasbord of ideas for language teach-*

ers (pp. 267–283). New York: Newbury House.

Thackray, D. (Editor) (1975). *Bullock report: A language for Life.* Durham, UK: UK Reading Association.

Tucker, G. R., Lambert, W. E., & D'Anglejan, A. (1973). Cognitive and attitudinal consequences of bilingual schooling: The St. Lambert project through grade five. *Journal of Educational Psychology, 65,* 141–149.

Vygotsky, L. S. (1978). *Mind in society.* Cambridge, Massachusetts: Harvard University Press.

Walters, K., & Gunderson, L. (1985). Effects of parent volunteers reading first language (L1) books to ESL students. *The Reading Teacher, 20,* 313–318.

Name Index

Subject Index